CONJUNCTIONS

Bi-Annual Volumes of New Writing

Edited by
Bradford Morrow

Contributing Editors
John Ashbery
Martine Bellen
Mei-mei Berssenbrugge
Mary Caponegro
Brian Evenson
William H. Gass
Peter Gizzi
Robert Kelly
Ann Lauterbach
Norman Manea
Rick Moody
Howard Norman
Joan Retallack
Joanna Scott
David Shields
Pctcr Straub
John Edgar Wideman

published by Bard College

EDITOR: Bradford Morrow
MANAGING EDITOR: Micaela Morrissette
SENIOR EDITORS: Robert Antoni, Peter Constantine, J. W. McCormack,
    Edie Meidav, Pat Sims, Alan Tinkler
COPY EDITOR: Pat Sims
ASSOCIATE EDITORS: Jedediah Berry, Jessica Loudis, Eric Olson
PUBLICITY: Mark R. Primoff, Darren O'Sullivan
EDITORIAL ASSISTANTS: Andrew Durbin, Kianoosh Hashemzadeh,
    Wendy Lotterman, Marie Myman, Nicole Nyhan, Cathy Schmitz,
    Lily Schroedel, Emma Smith-Stevens, Shawn Wen

State of the Arts

CONJUNCTIONS is published in the Spring and Fall of each
year by Bard College, Annandale-on-Hudson, NY 12504.
This issue is made possible in part with the generous funding of the National Endowment for the Arts, and with public funds from the New York State Council on the Arts, a
State Agency.

SUBSCRIPTIONS: Use our secure online ordering system at www.conjunctions.com,
or send subscription orders to CONJUNCTIONS, Bard College, Annandale-on-
Hudson, NY 12504. Single year (two volumes): $18.00 for individuals; $40.00 for institutions and overseas. Two years (four volumes): $32.00 for individuals; $80.00 for
institutions and overseas. Patron subscription (lifetime): $500.00. Overseas
subscribers please make payment by International Money Order. For information
about subscriptions, back issues, and advertising, contact us at (845) 758-7054 or
conjunctions@bard.edu.

Editorial communications should be sent to Bradford Morrow, *Conjunctions*,
21 East 10th Street, 3E, New York, NY 10003. Unsolicited manuscripts cannot be returned unless accompanied by a stamped, self-addressed envelope. Electronic and
simultaneous submissions will not be considered.

Conjunctions is listed and indexed in Humanities International Complete and
included in EBSCO*host*.

Visit the *Conjunctions* website at www.conjunctions.com and follow us on Facebook
and Twitter.

Cover design by Jerry Kelly, New York. Front cover painting: *The Abraham Pixler
Family*, American, ca. 1815. Watercolor, pen and iron gall ink, and gouache on off-white
laid paper. 10 x 8 in. (25.4 x 20.3 cm.). Gift of Edgar William and Bernice Chrysler
Garbisch, 1966 (66.242.3). Image copyright © The Metropolitan Museum of Art/Art
Resource, NY. Back cover painting by Joshua Pool (1787–?): *Family Record for Andrew
Bickford and Olive Clark*, Gloucester, MA, ca. 1820. Watercolor, pencil, and ink on
paper. 15 x 12 in. Collection American Folk Art Museum, New York. Gift of Ralph
Esmerian. 1998.17.6. Photo by John Parnell.

Available through D.A.P./Distributed Art Publishers, Inc., 155 Sixth Avenue, New
York, NY 10013. Telephone: (212) 627-1999. Fax: (212) 627-9484.

Printers: Edwards Brothers

Typesetter: Bill White, Typeworks

ISSN 0278-2324

ISBN 978-0-941964-73-9

Manufactured in the United States of America.

TABLE OF CONTENTS

KIN

Edited by Bradford Morrow

The Abraham Pixler Family, ca. 1815

EDITOR'S NOTE

WHAT IS MORE FRAUGHT than family? Even the most solipsistic among us can never wholly escape its pull. The monk, the hermit, the orphan, the runaway who renounces his parents and changes his name. The daughter estranged from her mother, the son who never knew his father. All of us, whether or not we love and embrace our families, are stamped DNA-deep by kinship. As a result, narratives of family form the bedrock of so much literature.

These fictions, essays, and poems address the familial bond from a variety of angles. A mother takes her boys sledding while contemplating the mysteries of the numerological universe. A daughter crosses over to the afterlife, where she encounters both her mother and herself. An adopted boy given to delinquency examines the naive love his suicidal mother has for his distant father. An uncle begins a process of mythic transmogrification by taking his favorite niece to a charity event, where he gives her the deed to all his earthly possessions. An urban father protects his young daughter from cranks and characters on the subway, even as he begins to realize he cannot shield her forever. A suburban mother who is losing her teenage daughter to a dangerous high school friend drugs the girl and herself in order to share a desperate moment of togetherness.

While it was tempting from time to time to expand our theme a little to include friendships—kindred spirits who can sometimes feel closer than flesh-and-blood relatives—in the end we hewed as close as we could to family itself, to kinfolk. Because family, however we define its boundaries, is so central to our lives, the extremes of human emotion are necessarily found in its precincts—from nurturing to violence, from loyalty to deceit, from murderous hatred to the kind of affection that crosses the border toward unshakable love.

—Bradford Morrow
October 2011
New York City

A Family Restaurant
Karen Russell

THIS MORNING, MY FATHER approached me waving the new menu from RAY'S ITALIAN FEATS, our rival across the street, and demanded that I type this up for you.

"Write the story. It's a menu, Leni, it's supposed to have the story."

"Which one?"

"Jesus, I don't know, the story, our story! The family story!"

I.

OUR STORY:

In 1929, my great-grandmother, Demetria Bakopoulos, boarded a boat from Kalymnos, Greece, with her first husband, Hektor Bakopoulos, and their four small children and followed a dotted line across the Atlantic, which I will try to draw for you on this revamped menu if Frank gives me the green light, and sailed into the coastal waters of southern Florida until they arrived at the island of: New Kalymnos. Hektor worked as a sponge fisherman until he had enough money saved to lease the storefront that became A FAMILY RESTAURANT and then, courteously, died. Permitting Demetria to make the business deal of a lifetime and remarry a cook from the merchant marines who could devein and butterfly shrimp like a Lilliputian surgeon. Demi's squirrel-faced eldest daughter, Eleni Bakopoulos, survived her mother and her stepfather and her three brothers and took over the business in 1952. For many years she was married to "an American investor," Richard "Rocky" Spry—our oldest patrons at A FAMILY RESTAURANT always speak about Rocky's investing in finger-quotation marks—and when Richard Spry left her, she reverted to her maiden name and let her sons know that their American surnames

8

had magically, elastically snapped back into the Old Country: Now they were Frank Bakopoulos, age seven, and Ed Bakopoulos, age four.

Frank is my father—you might catch a glimpse of him if you are sitting in the booths against the wall. That seventy-year-old man who keeps slapping his neck, in the apron that comes down to his calves? My dad. He's only making me write this to compete with that steaming load that eponymous Ray of RAY'S ITALIAN FEATS put on the back of *his* new menu, in which he lists all the cataclysms that his Sicilian ancestors survived en route to New Kalymnos—"Centuries of *la miseria*! Earthquakes, fire, typhus, hurricanes, shipwreck, famine, scurvy, mallpox." I think Ray forgot a letter there. All this they endured to deliver their "famous" pizza sauce to the Americas. That crappy sauce comes out of a box. Ray is a known defroster, a rat-faced liar who uses tomato paste and Kraft. We have no respect for Ray. I think he even enjoys that. Sometimes he eats with us on Sundays, when his restaurant is closed, and we heckle him; we've spent the last twenty years sharing our customers, volleying the families of New Kalymnos back and forth between our restaurants like the world's slowest game of tennis. Ray, a bachelor, has mimeographed a daguerreotype of someone else's enormous Italian family onto the front of his menu in beautiful sepia inks. You know I wouldn't take an oath that Ray is Italian? He does have that mustache, and he puts some spin on the ball when he pronounces words like *"arrabbiata,"* but I swear I would not be surprised if his obituary informs us that he was born in Milwaukee.

If you ate here between the years of 1971 and 1979, you remember this line from the old menu:
BE SURE TO SAVE ROOM FOR DESSERT: OUR "WORLD-FAMOUS" FROSTY TREAT, MAMA'S DEATHBED SHERBET!
If that's what you came for, I'm afraid you're out of luck. We haven't been able to serve that in decades. Not since my family forfeited our access to the secret ingredient.

Rocky Spry, my grandfather, chose our name, A FAMILY RESTAURANT. Hand painted the sign, olive-green letters on dandelion wood. (Prior to this the place was a Greek speakeasy: a blank door and an umbrella.) Rocky assured Eleni that American diners would respect their restaurant for its candor—"Look, why not call a spade a spade, right? We could put on airs, call ourselves a 'bistro.' But let's face the music here: We're a goddamn family restaurant. A squat-and-gobble. So why not say, one family to another: You can eat here. Bring the kids, put the baby in a booster seat, have an onion straw, here's a damn crayon and gin is on the way for old dad and mom."

Apparently, Rocky left the family one month after the new sign went up. It's what you walked under to get inside here. By now, I should have brought your water. My apologies if it's a busy night and it's taking a little while.

How did Mama explain my grandfather's disappearance to her boys? She didn't. She invented a new menu item, "Mama Bakopoulos's Goodnight Waffle," because Eddy, after his father disappeared from the restaurant and the house, began demanding breakfast at night. Every night, for nearly a year: breakfasts. Into adulthood, my uncle Ed would go on strange gluttonous sprees where he squirted strawberry syrup onto all foods, "like a dog pissing the house during a thunderstorm," was how my father explained it to me. This was decades before the self-help lexicographers defined my humongous, furious uncle Ed as an "emotional eater." But you know, I've been working in A FAMILY RESTAURANT for my entire lifetime and it seems to me that very few people are eating on "neutral."

Frank has an animal's nonchalance about his past. My father, on his father: "Leni. I really don't remember him. The guy could walk in here today and order a dog and I wouldn't recognize him."

"And what did Mama think about his leaving?"

"How the hell should I know?"

Ed and Frank were doomed by the restaurant to be Mama's Boys deep into adulthood: big-eared teenagers and then bearded men on the streets of New Kalymnos, but ageless in the warm restaurant lights. You and Mama Bakopoulos have already met—that's her shooting darts at you from the front of this menu. See? The lady in the cowl, with the face like a split baked potato? The small guy on her knee is my father, Frank, age eleven, man of the house by the time that picture was taken in 1961. The slightly cross-eyed kid whose furry homemade "sweater vest" appears to be a bunch of sewn-together bath mats? His brother, Eddy. And all of the decor in A FAMILY RESTAURANT belongs to her childhood: "Mama's Broken Victrola," "Mama's Bonnet That Looks Like a Detonating Pineapple," "Mama's Scary Wooden Toy from Oilikos."

Irene caught my father at a rare moment, when he was living away from home for the first time in his life, twenty-two and working for the electric company in Lefferts, New Jersey, on a contract job. Saving money, for a future that never quite came into focus. She fell in love with Frank before she'd heard word one about the family restaurant. She caught his eye at a no-name gas station, where he was standing in front of one of those big refrigerators—just to cool off, it seemed. This is my parents' "how we met" story. It was the single memory from their shared lifetime that could cause them both to light up. It's a lot more succinct than their second story, how they ceased to know one another.

"Oh my God!" Frank pretended to scream when he saw Irene, a fake scream so acoustically similar to the real deal that she screamed too, and dropped her car keys.

"No, dummy, I'm screaming because of how you *look*, see?" he'd explained in a slightly embarrassed new register. "You shouldn't be around the pumps, it's a fire hazard. You're, uh, you're dangerously hot."

"Huh?"

Later my father admitted to my mother that he'd flunked out of high school chemistry.

"You might react with the gas—and combust!"

"That doesn't even make sense."

Two months later, they were engaged.

"Be my wife?" He'd had blue chewing gum in his mouth when he asked her. Irene had never felt so happy in another human's company. When they kissed, they'd swapped the wad of gum back and forth with the goofiest solemnity until Frank swallowed the gum and had a coughing fit.

One night about a week later, she found her fiancé sitting with red eyes, Indian style, underneath the pay phone in her dormitory. His mother was very sick. Would Irene maybe take a leave of absence from the junior college, come with him to Florida? His brother had called him home to help take care of her.

"Yes," my mother said, quicker than a miner can strike a match, and unwittingly committing the next decade of her life to A FAMILY RESTAURANT. "Can we get married first, though?" In Irene's imagination the air of Florida was boiling, its waters thronged with dinosaurs. A part of her was afraid that if they didn't marry now, Frank's offer would dissolve in the shimmering Florida heat. They were flying back in time to Frank's childhood, a zone in which he hadn't

11

made her the offer, where she did not yet exist.

(They'd had a bit of a Who's On First routine when Frank tried to explain the restaurant to her: "Yes, but what's it called?" "A Family Restaurant . . ." "Frank! Stop teasing! OK: What is the name on the door of the freaking restaurant?" "That's the name, Irie, it's *A Family Restaurant*. . . ." "Oh my *God*, Frank.")

"I can't cook, you know," she told Frank on the bus ride to the airport. "My cooking is for shit." The ring was blue zirconium. On the flight down, Irene crooked her ring finger as if beckoning their future, shooting light all around the airplane cabin. *We are a married couple, in the sky.* Frank had paid for their tickets, God alone knew how.

A stewardess poured them a tomato-juice toast on the honeymoon Delta flight to Frank's home. *To us*, Irene waited for him to say.

"To Mama's health."

"To Mama." Irene twirled her celery through the bloodred cup. When the seat-belt sign lit up she straightened in her chair as if electrocuted. Who the hell was Mama? What did she really know about any of these people, the Bakopouloses or Bakopouli, with whom she'd just agreed to share her life? Now that the plane was in the air she could clearly see a stretch of questions, whole cities of questions that she should have asked before takeoff.

"Your mother knows about me?"

Frank shrugged. "Not exactly."

"You didn't tell her you got married?"

Sometimes when Frank argued with her it was like watching a bear jogging to keep its balance on a rolling barrel. There was something antic and hilarious in the timbre of his voice. Something dangerous too.

"Of course not! Mama just *had* a heart attack!" Frank stared at Irene incredulously, as if his new wife were the one with a weak heart. "We'll tell her in person. Easy does it. She'll like you."

It was hate at first sight. "Mama!" Frank had shouted up to his mother's window from the driveway when they got in late that night. "Come down! I'd like to introduce you to the new Mrs. Bakopoulos!" This was breaking the news gently? Irene wondered. She felt as if she were watching a wrecking ball smash into the side of the split-level house.

I don't know the details, but apparently this introduction went so disastrously that my mother crept upstairs, settling herself on the spaceship-themed coverlet on Frank's childhood bed while, downstairs, her new husband explained her presence in Mama's house to

12

Mama; Irene closed her eyes and counted to two hundred while she listened to a hailstorm of pots, followed by the sound of a groaning man hurling a discus.

"That?" shrugged Frank the following morning. "Yeah. Mama threw that there. I tried to stop her. It can't be good, you know, for her heart." There was a mop lying in the middle of the Bakopoulos lawn. Irene stepped delicately over it; the handle appeared to have struck and dented the Bakopouloses' mailbox. The mop looked like an effigy of Irene to Irene, with its pale hair askew on the grass. She shared this observation with Frank.

"That's nuts," said Frank. "That's a crazy way to think. Mama doesn't even know you yet. Now, hurry to the car, Irene. I'm the prep cook, you're the dishwasher. Mama's orders. She'll kill us if we're late."

DAY ONE AT A FAMILY RESTAURANT:

"Go help Mama clean," Frank said. "She'd like that."

"*I* clean!" Mama said, as if she were shouting out her own name, instead of merely volunteering to do the next verb on the chore wheel. Mama turned on the Porta Power vacuum and, without perhaps exactly intending to do so, chased Irene out of the restaurant like a bull charging a matador. Irene stood dazed in the sun, still holding a napkin. Days 2 through 182 were very much the same. In dreams Irene wiped the dishes and watched her own face shriveling, the young and vibrant layers of her life falling away like flower petals, all of the color and particularity draining out of her as she merged with the bleak, blank face of Mama.

No one lives forever. Irene gave herself this pep talk on Saturday nights, bunning sea dogs near the window with the big fan, straining to see the actual sea. Black waves tugged away from her, as if the world were on a wire, and the night would jump, retreat, jump again. Her eyes could only see so far into the twinkling mist that separated the island from the peninsula, but she had faith that it was there. Twenty minutes by boat. They could get back to it.

Frank bought Irene an old-fashioned green bicycle with a wide gray seat, an antique piece that I now own and ride around town. She tooled around the parking lot, waiting for his shift to end, her long legs whacking into the handlebars. Between her bruised knees and the green bicycle and the paint-blue island sky, Irene felt like a peacock trailing colors around the lot. She felt twelve, eleven, younger still, orbiting A FAMILY RESTAURANT on the bicycle and waiting for Frank to exit through the back doors and turn her into Mrs. Bakopoulos, his wife.

"Those are *hickeys*?" Mama accused her one day, peering out of the back door of A FAMILY RESTAURANT and pointing at Irene's knees.

"What? Mama, no—"

"They are *hick-eys*," she affirmed before Irene could explain her bruises, and tossed a bucket of steaming orange broth into the parking lot. The scene felt biblical, Irene later told Frank.

"If there had been a big rock next to the Toyota, your mother would have stoned me."

Frank made a face. "She's sick. Give her time."

The plan was that my parents would stay on the island for three or four weeks, just until Mama was back on her feet. But Mama was on her feet all the time, chasing down Frank and Irene. Belatedly, many months after their wedding day, she threw rice at Irene. "You make these ones? Is *sticky*," Mama charged, and Irene, whose face now resembled the cover illustration of *Beowulf*, covered by a golden chainmail of long-grain rice, could not acquit herself. Irene gave Mama half a year. More. Not once in all that time, according to Irene, did my grandmother volitionally meet her daughter-in-law's blue eyes, although sometimes Irene would look up from clearing a table to find Mama's eyes boring a hole into her shoulder, as if she were trying to amputate Irene's arm with an invisible mentally controlled laser. "Because my bra strap was showing, Leni. That's how she was."

Goddamn it. Frank said I had to get Our Story told in eight hundred words. So that it would fit on the back of the menu. I still have to tell you about the sherbet, with its radioactive glow; the secret ingredient. The days when Mama died and I was born.

Well, maybe I can staple pages.

Is it Happy Hour? Get the Shiver-Me-Timbers cocktail. It's on me, compliments of the house. Blame me for delaying your meal, and Frank will give you a generous pour and bring it out with a complimentary dish of mixed nuts. Growing up in A FAMILY RESTAURANT I made anything my toy—the forks, the foiled toothpicks. I was a lewd kid or something was wrong with my head and I thought these mixed nuts looked like naked sunbathers. Little nudist colonies of cashews. I used to line them up on the sunny windowsills while my parents fought about Frank's secret—"Shh, keep sleeping," I told them.

Did my mother pray for Frank's mom to die? Not in so many words. "Take her soul, Lord," she prayed vaguely, figuring that God was no dummy, he could read into that. Sometimes she intoned the prayers like a movie mobster—"Send Mama on a *long* vay-*cay*-shun."

Mama, meanwhile, appeared to be losing her mind. Her pain medications made her dotty. She wore a shower cap instead of her hairnet, brought a red bowling ball to work, terrified the Happy Hour crowd by bursting through the kitchen door with a bouquet of knives.

"You!" she told Irene in a low vibrato. "You look like an anteater pissing through its nose!"

What did that even mean?

"It's just an expression," said Frank wearily. "It's a shame that you don't speak Greek. In Greek, she is a comedian."

As Mama Bakopoulos weakened, my mother became bolder. "When are we leaving, Frank?" Right in front of Mama she would discuss her plans to raise her future children in California, to return to school.

"Frankie will never go with you there," she'd say with maddening confidence. "No. To that place, with you, never." She took her eldest son's hand and held it to her belly, and Frank inclined his head toward her; Irene shuddered. His posture was an eerie inversion of a father-to-be waiting for the kick. "Frankie will stay here with his mother."

"I'm not leaving you, Mama," Frank mumbled with a pained and apologetic smile. Weeks to live, was her doctors' latest assessment.

As Mama's health failed, so did the family business. Frank and Ed hired someone to do the cooking, a small, polite, slightly lethargic Portuguese woman named Domitila, who one night stole all the money in the till, two ten-pound sacks of crinkle-cut fries, the dainty ketchup spout, and a bottle of Johnny Walker Black.

Frank moved Mama to the cardiac ward; Irene learned that A FAMILY RESTAURANT was five months behind on rent. *We're closing down,* Irene thought, her heart speeding. Frank and Ed would be freed from the ten-block radius that hemmed the Bakopoulos men inside their childhood. She and Frank would start a family of their own.

Meanwhile, grief was doing strange things to Frank, who was after Irene for the first time in months with a new kind of intensity, mutely squeezing her and licking her next to the ice machine, cornering her against the freezers, corralling her between the stacked towers of baby booster chairs. His grip around her waist was almost suffocatingly tight. In the past, whenever they closed together, he'd lift her onto the bar, slide a hand up her skirt under the fulgurating pink and emerald lights of Mama's seashell sconces. But Irene would no longer fool around with Frank inside A FAMILY RESTAURANT. When Frank leaned in to kiss her, it was Mama's face that Irene saw leering at her.

"Outside," she said.

Gross. I'm so sorry about that—I know, you came here to eat—I too find other people's earnest sex lives extremely unappetizing. Particularly if the braid of legs in question belongs to one's parents. But, unavoidably, this too was part of the story of A FAMILY RESTAURANT.

II.

In the hospital, in her death throes, Frank's mother began to gurgle in odd syllabic patterns that he swore belonged to a foreign tongue. Pain-inflected utterances. Not just gibberish, but *language*—although nothing that sounded remotely close to Greek or English.

"You're right—it's the medication," Nurse Florentz said generously, giving my father the opportunity to allege something sane.

Moans rose from his mother's veiled bed, shimmering waves of sound that might mean anything. The curtain danced on its silver rings.

"Wait—hear that?"

"I'll see about the morphine levels," said Nurse Florentz.

But Frank knew his mother. He didn't agree with Nurse Florentz. He sat at the edge of her bed with a tape recorder, pausing only to gulp red gelatin cubes in the hospital cafeteria. Near the end of the tape he called his brother, Ed.

Ed said he couldn't hear much over the blenders—it was Happy Hour. "Happy Hour," said Frank, staring down at their mother's dark face. She was snoring lightly, exposing a tiny row of teeth that made him think for some reason of marshmallows dissolving in cocoa. How did anybody alive survive a parent's death? His mother, awake now, smiled weakly at Frank—an unrecognizably gentle smile—and in her final minutes she spoke real words to him, whispery but distinct, in Greek. Frank waited for a little while, then hit PAUSE on the tape.

Frank and Eddy held the funeral on the island but had Mama buried in Greece, in a Kalymnos plot, a few miles from her ancient home. Frank found a special translator in Kos who was able to help him with Mama's last instructions. It was a recipe that she had given him.

III.

The business was saved.

"You can cook now?" Irene asked him. "Since when?"

"I'm just following orders."

"*Whose?*"

Prior to Mama's death, A FAMILY RESTAURANT served the same innocuous American beach grub that you see listed inside this menu: Cokes and Sprites, cole slaw, hot dogs with mustard and a catarrh of green relish. "Looks like somebody sneezed on a weiner," Mama used to complain darkly. "What the Americans want to eat, though." She'd inherited the incredulity and Old World horror of her mother, Demi; like Demi, she read off the menu items as if she were reciting the terms of a humiliating war treaty: Hamburgers. Bacon Cheeseburgers. Clam Basket. Shrimp Basket. Chicken Fingers. (A macabre name that used to make me picture Foghorn Leghorn's amputated hands.) Prior to Mama's death, the only desserts on the menu were chocolate pie, apple pie, and the "Dieter's Delite Fruit Plate"—basically an unripe whole cantaloupe that Mama sometimes tossed disgustedly at skinny people like a basketball. Overnight, the menu changed to include: SPECIAL OF THE DAY #6: MAMA'S DEATHBED SHERBET.

"I'd like to order number six, the Special—'Ma's Deathbed Sherbet.'"

"Number six, please."

Some people were shy about ordering it.

"Fries and a Coke. And, ah . . . how's that number six?"

"Yes, I'd like the number six. Mama's, ah, Mama's . . . right, that's the one."

Frank served the sherbet so shockingly cold that it numbed the tongue. Whatever he was putting in it caused the dish to glow. The color was never quite the same—it was always pale orange, like a bowl of emulsifying sunshine, but sometimes a new batch would have these radishy-pink streaks, sometimes it could look almost minty. Adults who ordered the sherbet reported tasting the usual suspects— nutmeg, cloves, cinnamon, anise, raspberries, peach syrup, vanilla— and, invariably, Something Else. Their children only smiled; they looked like they were spooning up light.

I should clarify here that Mama's Deathbed Sherbet did not curse our customers or confer magical powers (at least, not to my knowledge). Nobody left their tables with X-ray vision or a beautiful new singing voice or an invulnerability to cancer. It was just a really good dessert.

Frank refused to tell anybody the "famous ingredient." How strange, I used to think, that a secret could achieve such notoriety— this hole that everybody on the island could see. Inside our house, Frank's secret was something round but empty, like the number zero—swallowed air. "It was her Will and Testament," he told my uncle. "She left it to me because I'm the oldest, Ed. Her executor." He'd shake his head almost theatrically, still trying to protect his kid brother. "Believe me, if you knew what I had to do to make the sherbet you wouldn't be jealous."

"Just *taste* it, Irene," my father was still begging her in those early days. "It's the best batch yet, honest to God."

Irene learned that she was pregnant on the same day that Mama died. At first, my mother refused to touch Mama Bakopoulos's dessert. One spring night, though, in her last trimester, when Frank was on another trip to Greece to procure the ingredient, Irene broke down and ate bowl after bowl of the orange sherbet; driven to it, I imagine, by the same spasms of hunger that can launch any pregnant woman into the streets in search of root beer and dill pickles, and by something even stranger. A rage that I can really only guess at here, cannibalistic, to consume her mother-in-law's last traces. Expunge Mama Bakopoulos from the kitchen.

Then I was born. Irene stared into the blanket that the nurses handed to her, jolted out of her wooziness. My mother, I'm told, began to wail with me. *No.* Even enervated from a forty-hour labor, Irene had to fight down a reflexive impulse to thrust me back at the nurse. She gritted her teeth, held on to me with all her strength. (And later the nurses would joke that the frightened new mother had clenched her jaw and splayed her palms across my back as though she were trying to keep her hands from flying off a hot stove top! A pretty girl with an ugly baby.) She looked again: There was my face, which was also the puckered, miniaturized face of Mama Bakopoulos. A little wailing red bud in the blue blanket.

Reincarnation, why rule it out?

"Frank?" my mother asked that first night. "Do you think the sherbet could . . . bring her back?"

Frank stared at her. "That's not funny, Irene."

Frank demanded that I be named for his mother; my mom viciously refused; many knock-down fights ensued; "Leni" was their compromise. That's me.

My first days were black ones for my mother. At times she was certain that I was an anchor, flung overboard by Mama from beyond the grave, intended to secure her permanent mooring at A FAMILY RESTAURANT. Some caul covered my face so that she couldn't see it—all she saw was Mama. Babies, what person alive is repelled by their smell, but Irene swore I smelled like Mama in her last days, vinegary and aged. Whenever she breast-fed me, she saw Mama's Deathbed Sherbet melting into spectacular colors in its glass dish. When she rocked me, she had to swallow back the singsong Greek melodies that Mama used to croon while sweeping out the kitchen. How had so much of Mama gotten absorbed into her bloodstream? Antibodies, didn't she have any of those against Eleni Bakopoulos? Those were the days when Irene grieved for her own mother more powerfully than she had since she was a teenager.

"Hush, little baby," she sang, and flipped the portrait of Mama that Frank had set on my nightstand. All night she sat by my crib, watching me sleep. Sometimes I wish I could dream those earliest dreams again, whatever I used to see in the time before I could recognize my own face. Yellow, red, and blue shapes swung on wires above me, a zoo mobile, while through the crib bars my mother's hand stroked my black hair. Mama Bakopoulos's curls were already coming in. Irene watched me like a mirror, waited for her blue eyes to open in my face, for her face to surface in my flesh. But I failed, I couldn't repeat any part of her. Frank says that our biological stalemate made him feel, for different reasons, as stunned and helpless as Irene did. He watched her watching me at the nursery's edge, both of them frozen.

Now my mother was in a sort of Chinese finger trap: She was never leaving Frank, and Frank was never leaving A FAMILY RESTAURANT. Several times a year, and never during the winter months, we all noted, my father flew to Kalymnos, Greece, for two weeks to retrieve more of the "secret ingredient." Whatever substance Frank was bringing back was compact enough to fit inside his beat-up blue duffel. He once let slide to Irene during an argument that he froze the ingredient, to preserve it, and that he only needed "a pinch" of it to make a batch of the sherbet.

By this time I was three or four years old and already on the clock, carrying a horseshoe tray of blue marine salt and quartered limes to the drunks, walking on tipsy feet myself. I remember feeling small as a cat as I moved between the trouser legs at the bar, peanuts bouncing off my head, bathed in the lush sour stench of our patrons' underarms. Once a big, gesticulating drunk brushed my earlobe with his lit cigarette and I howled so terribly—and salted the man, apparently—that Frank had to comp his hundred-dollar bar tab. In my earliest memories, my parents are always shouting to be heard over the happy din of other couples, other families. Their arguments peppered the air in the kitchen:

"Look at this!" Irene. "America is one of the fattest nations in the world. Maybe we should serve something else, Frank. Steamed zucchini! Carrots, raisins! Perhaps a slaw of some kind—"

"Sherbet is not a fried donut, honey, it's healthy! It's healthy for business, that's for sure." Frank shook his head. "You could thank me, you know. Do you think it's easy to make the stuff? Do you know how much money I've turned it into?"

"Change the menu," she hissed. "Serve something else. Anything else, Frank."

"Ed and Lisa are going to buy a home, did he tell you? Their mortgage payments start next month. And I've been thinking about private school for Leni. A new car to replace that shitbox LeBaron you drive." Frank paused. "I leave for Kalymnos tomorrow."

"And when are you coming home?"

"Soon."

Sherbet—to make it does not require the Rosetta Stone. Here is the ingredient list for ordinary sherbet:

- 7 ounces sugar
- 1½ tablespoons finely grated orange zest
- ¼ teaspoon salt
- 2 cups freshly squeezed orange juice

- 1 tablespoon freshly squeezed lemon juice
- 1 teaspoon vanilla extract
- 1½ cups very cold whole milk

As a child, I couldn't imagine where my father went for weeks at a stretch. Lisa was the first to broach the subject in the dining area. Lisa was Ed's girlfriend, my babysitter, and mom's sort of de facto sister-in-law, a lanky woman with wide-set, spacey eyes and incorrigible red curls who was so beautiful to me. She seemed like an alien as she floated beneath all of the framed Bakopoulos portraits that Mama had nailed to the dark walls. Lisa hostessed and waited on tables and bitched pleasantly about almost every aspect of the restaurant's operations.

"OK, Frank!" Lisa exploded one day, still trembling from the dinner rush. "Please just tell us: What are you keeping in that freezer? Are there perhaps some fucking bodies in the freezer? Are we all going to jail?"

"Yeah, is this some Soylent Green bullshit? Because *kids* eat that sherbet."

"I eat it," I said.

"Maybe it's an endangered animal. Like a rhino." Uncle Ed made himself hysterical. "Frank: Are you crushing up rhino balls or something? Is it a panda? I don't want to spend my days in a federal penitentiary because the secret ingredient is some eye-of-newt shit, only the newt is, you know, a goddamn panda."

Lisa and Irene stared at Ed.

Lisa took Ed's hand. "I was just teasing before—I'm sure Frank's just picking weird mushrooms somewhere. I don't think he's out in the bamboo strangling pandas." She frowned. "Or people. Can you picture your brother hurting *anybody*?"

Everybody looked at my mother. Who was staring at Frank. Gazes used to ricochet like bullets inside A FAMILY RESTAURANT.

"Where is Daddy going?" I asked that night.

"Away."

"But where?"

"Greece. He says."

"Why?"

"To make his mother happy."

This reason satisfied me. It seemed to satisfy almost everybody. To make a mother happy, she told me bitterly, was a perfectly satisfying

21

reason for doing anything. That Mama Bakopoulos had been dead for seven years seemed immaterial to the conversation. I told my mother that I thought Frank's reason was a plenty good one; at least, I understood it; every night, to please my mother, I was praying for a different face.

During the nine years we served Mama's Deathbed Sherbet, A FAMILY RESTAURANT never had to advertise: no church bulletins, no radio spots. We never had to change our underwhelming name. We were doing so well for that period that we'd been able to hire strangers to bus the tables, not kids from the high school (I'd begged my father) but a few slim, fickle men whom my father located with newspaper ads. They rarely stuck around our restaurant for long, I'm not sure why. During the interviews, my father seemed completely at a loss: "So do you steal?" he asked the applicants. "Do you work hard? You, ah, you like hot dogs?" I think he lacked the ability to judge the character of non-Bakopouloses.

Once Irene came downstairs to find Frank holding on to the phone with both hands, staring into the backyard—someone at Pepsi-Cola who vacationed on New Kalymnos and was a self-professed "number six addict" had just made him a high-six-figure offer for the recipe. "No, thank you," Frank said. He hung up with a sigh. The scale was wrong, Frank explained to my mother.

"We can't sell out. There's not enough of it to go around."

"Of what?"

"Of the secret ingredient. I can barely keep *us* supplied now!"

My dad wasn't interested in talking to reporters. He wouldn't even discuss it with a Tallahassee talk-show host, a TV laureate with a grin like a Halloween pumpkin whose message on our machine said he'd heard about the sherbet's "reputation for causing elation!"

"Come over, OK, we'll serve you a dish," Frank told the telephone. "My God, what part of 'secret ingredient' don't you people understand?"

We expanded; now we had two kitchens. Kitchen 1, anyone could walk into; Kitchen 2 was a galley-sized annex with a door to which only my father had the key. Through the porthole in the door to the public kitchen, I'd watch him assemble the sherbet's public ingredients: sugar, milk, and fruit. Zesting lemons, Frank smiled like a Buddha statue. I've never seen a grown man look happier performing any activity than my father did, zesting. Kitchen 2 had no windows.

Like everyone, I loved the glowing stuff. That first bright bite seemed to make your hunger huger, like a lit match dropped into a well. I liked to eat Mama's dessert in secret, under the tablecloth, with the bowl on my lap, the sweating glass sticking to my bare thighs. Going down, the sherbet burned. It slid along my throat until I clutched my ribs and rocked with the pleasure of it. I had nothing in my small world to which I could compare the flavor. Sometimes it seemed to contain whole orchards, and sometimes it was a single taste.

Happiness, it seemed, was one secret that our customers were eager to keep. You'd think the customers would demand to know Mama's ingredient, and perhaps they traded guesses in private, but I can't remember anyone asking me about it. We garnished number six with orange rinds and fat red strawberries, and if people commented at all that's what they chose to remark on—"Big strawberries, huh!" they'd say. Now I think that the families we served were wary of chasing the flavor off their tongues. Often the entire room of diners fell silent for an hour or more, a hundred spoons clinking musically on glass. "Fragrant," "piquant," "robust," "bittersweet"—none of that Zagat's argot came even close to describing its taste. As ever, Mama Bakopoulos had the last word.

"What a nice dessert," families said, and then left two hundred percent tips.

Once I overheard a wire-thin teenager covered in red and black wolf tattoos, a guy who did not look like he had a sweet tooth in his skull, whisper, "It's better than drugs."

Today I have some new theories about the popularity of our dessert at A FAMILY RESTAURANT. What we gave them was only disguised as food, I think. It seemed to nourish some hidden mouth, some universally parched place. Just writing about it here, I can feel that spot in me beginning to salivate. I don't know what to call it, but it's what I spent my early lifetime catering to at A FAMILY RESTAURANT.

Forgive me, I see we're approaching seventeen pages here. You must be starving. I'll finish up so you can order. Whatever you do, avoid the fish taco, Frank can't get that one right—it tastes like a sea kayak that sprang a leak. Are you maybe considering defecting to Ray's Italian Feats? Chucking our menu to read Ray's Family Story, a glib four hundred words printed underneath that grinning cartoon of a Roma tomato, with the arms and the legs? I don't blame you for that preference, but just remember—those laminated pictures of his *nonna* in her white twill mantelet, his handsome wife, the perfect children arrayed like a string of garlic bulbs around the rustic dock? It's complete bullshit, of course. Nobody has a family like that. And why is that tomato wearing Keds?

Nineteen seventy-five: A restaurant opened up across the street from us. Ray's Italian Feats.

"Italian Feats? What, he's turning Dago cartwheels over there?"

"I think it was supposed to be 'Feast.'"

This was confirmed by Ray: a misprint on the awning. "I plan to sue," he said genially. Back then his menu was just a list: garlic rolls and spaghetti marinara and several of the more convoluted pastas. It was devoid of any history or chummy cartoon tomatoes.

There was no open aggression between us, but sometimes we opened our back doors and let warring smells duel and tangle in the street between our restaurants. It was like the Sharks and the Jets, only olfactory.

One dusk I caught Ray staring into Kitchen 1, doing a pull-up onto our window ledge, his whole body tensed into the furious shrug of a cactus. I guess I should have called the police. "Scram, you trespassing defroster," is what I should have said. "You should be ashamed."

Instead, I led Ray around to the small back entrance to Kitchen 2. I watched him use his crowbar to jimmy the door. We stood breathing softly on the threshold, like some low-budget sci-fi movie—here we were, about to enter the spaceship, a dirty Chevy sedan inconveniently in the shot. I realized that I was holding Ray's hand—how had that happened?—my fingers gloved together with his sweaty stubs, pepperoncini wafting almost imperceptibly out of Ray's skin. Incredibly, Ray didn't curse at me or shake loose from my grip. I don't even think he was trying to steal our recipe necessarily—I think his hobbies just included petty crime. We entered the room. My father was standing with his back to the door, and I glimpsed something orange fluttering from his hands into a large mixing bowl.

I had never set foot in Kitchen 2. It was clean and orderly, a dollhouse version of Kitchen 1. Ray was already backing outside. Slowly, as if sensing our gazes falling on him like a net, my father stiffened and began to turn. "Is it you, Mama?" he said, softly but unmistakably.

We fled.

"How was work?" Irene asked Frank later that evening.

"Work was work," Frank smiled, the phrase he always used to double-knot his day. I studied his thick fingers with their blunt, clean nails, half expecting to see orange stains there. I never breathed a word about what I'd seen and heard that day to either of them. If my father was haunted, that was his problem. I was so tired of being mistaken by everyone for the ghost of Mama Bakopoulos.

One afternoon, Irene pulled my hair into a ponytail and put on sapphire earrings and walked us over to Ray's Italian Feats. Ray was wearing a bookie's visor indoors, stinking of hairspray and garlic, with a pompadour that never moved—I wondered if Aquanet could seep into your brain and paralyze the rest of you. The man was some kind of paradox, an original stereotype. Everything about him seemed inauthentic, but I couldn't tie this deception to any clear purpose. Where he was honest, it turned out, was when it came to his ingredients.

"What's in this?" she asked Ray. "And this?"

He narrowed his eyes. "You one of those that's allergic to wheat? Don't bring me any lawsuits." But he listed every ingredient for her.

"Ladies, you're gonna explode!" Ray said, bringing my mother her fourth dish, a densely layered fusilli. The tuna fusilli contained tuna, fusilli, black olives, tomato sauce, and oil. "Leni, look how delicious," she said, and punctured something that could only be a noodle. She smiled up at Ray. "Are you married?" Ray grinned back. "Who's asking?"

"So let me get this straight," Ray said, much deeper into the evening. "You're jealous of the ice cream?"

"It's sherbet."

"You're in some kind of fucked-up love triangle with your husband and a bunch of fruity creams?"

Which was better, I wondered, to frame it in Ray's terms or to say, "I'm in a love triangle with my dead mother-in-law?" What my mother said was, "I'm in a love triangle with a mystery." My ears perked up. I knew that Ray had seen my father sprinkle the orange substance into the bowl. Would he tell her? "A family secret."

"Does she know?" Ray said. "Your daughter?" And they both stared at me. Ray coughed. "I think she maybe does. She looks like she was probably born knowing the recipe. It's eerie, Irene. Kid's the spitting image—"

"I know *that*," I said, pulling at my face with my hands, and pushed away from the table.

As I grew older, Mama Bakopoulos began to surface out of my face like a galleon. My skin tone darkened from pink to olive; my eyes dulled to a somber green the exact shade of Swiss chard. Mama cracked her knuckles and so did I; Mama was mildly dyslexic, like me, always swapping numbers and vowels on the chalkboard menu; Mama had my crooked smile, my tree-trunk ankles. At school most of my friends dreamed of having a doppelgänger sister, but I'd missed her by a generation, my twin, my dead grandmother. Sometimes I fantasized that Mama Bakopoulos was still alive; she'd mother me better than this stranger with the flashing eyes, Irene.

"Your face is . . . ungrammatical!" Irene shouted at me once, and I knew what she meant. There was nothing horrifically wrong with it—basically, it was intelligible as a face—but it looked foreign, asymmetrical. "Un-American," she told me on another occasion. If I had known more of the story of A FAMILY RESTAURANT—if my mother had taken the time to inscribe our story on the menu, like I'm doing for you—I might have told her, "Mom, I'm not *her*." I am not the reincarnation of your mother-in-law, and I too wish I could get a do-over on my bone structure. Don't judge a book, Mom. I'm begging you. I'd stare at Mama's mulish face on the cover of our menus and have the oddest sensation, as if I were reading my obituary from the future.

This March will mark my forty-seventh spring as an employee of A FAMILY RESTAURANT. On Saturday nights I catch sight of my face in the wineglasses that I polish and I cannot believe that I'm still here.

When they were kids, imprisoned in the Bakopoulos kitchen while schools of other boys went glinting past the restaurant windows on bicycles, Frank and Ed had a favorite joke, a real eye roller about a head of romaine lettuce trapped in a fridge—

Knock! Knock!

Who's there?

Lettuce!

Lettuce who?

Let us out, it's freezing in here!

*

"Where are *you* going?" I asked my mother one night. Frank had left for Greece a week ago. She was tugging at the half-zipped lips of her bulging suitcase, trying to make it swallow the delicate bone of a white stiletto. I had never seen those shoes before. I had never seen my mom in makeup, red lipstick and blue eyeliner that looked clownishly superfluous on her beautiful face. When she turned to me, I saw how tired her eyes looked. Anybody could see how hungry she was, how deeply thirsty, and this seemed to be the rotten joke at the core of A FAMILY RESTAURANT—that its hostess and waitress and cook and barmaid, the woman who had spent a decade in its kitchen, could wind up famished.

"I haven't been sleeping, Leni," she told me simply. "I'm going to find your father. If he doesn't tell me this time—"

"Take me with you," I'd shouted. A test.

I knew then that she really was afraid of me. I've heard people complain, of their mothers, "Well, she looked at me as if I were a stranger!" But Irene looked me dead in the eye, as if she knew my exact dimensions, my past and my future, and was all the more terrified. Her fear was so convincing that I was persuaded too—I was a monster, a changeling daughter, Mama Bakopoulos risen from the dead. "It's a cloning," Frank laughingly acknowledged when patrons held up the cellophane-green menu with Mama Bakopoulos's portrait to my face. Don't judge a book. Don't judge a book. I wished I'd been born a boy. Had I looked like Frank or Ed, whose faces were only mildly traumatized by Mama, it might have been different for us. Decades later I am still trying to figure out what to say to my mother to let her know that I was locked in a prison too, staring out at her through the cage bars of my face bones.

To her credit, my mother didn't lie to me. She didn't say, "It's OK" or "See you soon" or "I'll be back."

"I've got to find out what it is, Leni."

I nodded, feeling that for once I was very close to my mother. I'd inherited her hunger. A cramp sent me lurching against the banister; suddenly I was dying to know the answer too. It did seem incredible, didn't it, that we'd been swallowing and digesting this ingredient for years without having the slightest clue what it was?

"Goodbye, Mom!" I called down. "Good luck!"

With my parents gone, Frank in search of the secret ingredient and Irene in search of Frank, I lived with Uncle Ed and Lisa. I had just turned eleven. That was the summer they were trying for a baby, a process Lisa related to me in cheerful, indelible detail ("and that is why your uncle Ed follows me into the shower!"); it made me wonder why I didn't have a brother or a sister. (Later Frank would tell me that Irene had refused to have another child, terrified that any future son or daughter would be "contaminated" with Mama.)

Lisa didn't believe that the orange sherbet was some kind of extra-genetic mechanism of heredity; she thought my mother was crazy. And I tried to believe Aunt Lisa; only I could feel my grandmother inside my body, see her curling through my black hair and hear her cracking out of my knuckles, a sound as awful as footsteps on ice. She was coming back to life. While my parents were gone, I cut my hair as short as a boy's and streaked it freakishly with lemon juice, read magazines about plastic-surgery options. One night, at Ed and Lisa's place, I scoured my face in the bathroom mirror with steel wool from the restaurant kitchen, trying to escape Mama's hex, until Lisa walked in on me and shrieked, applied peroxide to the pulpy mess I'd made of my skin.

Finally, emboldened by Ray's criminal ease with the crowbar, I broke into my father's secret larder. Kitchen 2 smelled like nothing at all: It was polished, the tiles almost blinding in the ticking light. I turned on the faucet, watched my hand blur under the jetting water. I stared at the quiet blades inside the blender and imagined putting my face inside it. I took the crowbar and began to hit the lock on the freezer, experimentally at first and then with all my might. When the lock fell away, I whistled—I honestly had not been expecting my anger to have any outcome whatsoever. The door opened with a little gasp. Inside was an enormous mixing bowl full of the orange sherbet, surrounded by tiers of bare and humming shelves. I hardly remember what I did next—I don't even think I stopped to get a spoon, my fingers sinking into the cream—but when I looked up, Uncle Ed was standing over me—it was six o'clock. Family sedans were honking at one another from the lot.

"Leni," was all he said, and from the curious, besotted, half-frightened way he was looking at me I guessed that he was watching his mother rise out of my odd green eyes. I stood up and let the empty bowl fall from my hands; it didn't break, and I remember staring down at my reflection in it with a stab of disappointment. It spun like a planet on the kitchen tiles.

"I'm so full, Uncle," I mumbled. I wiped at the liquid trickling out of my eyes and the corners of my lips. I didn't know this then, but

I'd just eaten the last-ever batch of our family recipe. For the next seven nights, I had dreams where I rinsed the suds from a thousand plates in the restaurant sink and saw Mama Bakopoulos regarding me somberly out of each one. That summer, only my father returned from Greece.

What astounds me now is that my father still defends my mother—more than that, he accepts the blame for her "sickness": her refusal to come back to New Kalymnos again, her inability to see me as separate from Mama. Even today he'll talk about Irene with the gentlest kind of sorrow, as if acknowledging that it was his cough that set her off, sent the germ of the infirmity somersaulting toward my mother.

"When did it start to go wrong, Dad?" I asked him recently.

"Oh," said Frank, thinking backward. Doing the etiology. "When I kissed her, I guess? That first time?" He shook his silver head. "Nah, I think we were still OK then. I think it must have been when I asked her to marry me."

He looked right at me, his gray eyes as steadily unsteady as the sea, and I imagined that my mother must have been about this same distance from him when he made the proposal. "When I asked her to become a part of the family. Maybe that was the cough that got her sick."

When Frank stopped making number six, customers begged him for an explanation, and no one was satisfied with his gruff response.

"There's none left."

"None of *what*?"

"The secret ingredient. I ran out of it."

"You can't find more? Grow some more!"

And Frank would avert his eyes, give his head an angry shake. Like everyone, I hounded him:

"What *was* it, Dad?"

"Leni," he said, touching my cheek gingerly. "I'm sorry. Really, it won't grow anymore. It got, ah"—he frowned, rummaging for the word he'd found in the dictionary to explain what had happened to it after Irene divorced him—"*extirpated*."

And I don't even think he was sorry, in a way—we stayed on at A FAMILY RESTAURANT but my father was always home now, and no longer a slave to the recipe, no longer the kitchen automaton of his dead mama. For years I burned with an anger that I found easiest to direct at my father, the paterfamilias who had cursed me with this face, the secret hoarder, who wouldn't even try to ease the beating pain in me by drawing me closer, telling me the whole recipe. For years the ingredient remained a permanent blank in Our Story. Gradually I came to accept that Frank was telling the truth on one count: Whatever glue had held the three of us together, the bloodred epoxy that makes a family, was gone.

And that's Our Story—I'm sure your order will be up soon, if I haven't brought it out already. I wish that I could bring you a sample of Mama's Deathbed Sherbet; forgive me for taking so much time describing a choice that isn't even on the menu. I suppose it's only fair, if you made it this far, to share the secret ingredient. Not too long ago, my father had a scary bout with pneumonia, in the same hospital where Mama died and I was born, and one night his gray eyes flew open on the hospital pillow and clapped on to my face; he began to give me, very slowly, in English, the entire recipe.

The flowers growing on her grave in Kalymnos, Greece, had been planted by my father—his mother's last wish. They were narcissus blooms, with brilliant orange coronas. Every few months he returned to harvest them. My mother's plane landed in Kos and she took the Kalymnos Star ferry to Pothia, arriving in the middle of the night, and asked everyone at the docks about my father's whereabouts until she was escorted by the single cab driver traveling the streets at that hour to the gates of the cemetery—the very spot, the driver confided, where he had only recently deposited her husband, Mr. Bakopoulos. All those years ago, Ed and Frank had paid a fantastic sum to have their mother interred here (for a dying woman, that Mama sure managed to croak out a lot of requests). Irene went crazy when she found Frank there, kneeling on the woman's grave and plucking up the blooms. The narcissus petals glowed a familiar orange, budding out of the soil that served as Mama's ceiling. Something unspeakable happened to them that night, something that is still humming, entirely unknown to me, behind the simple scroll of the recipe. Whatever words flew between them under the moon of Old Kalymnos must have been terrible, I think, and it's easy for me to imagine my mother pulling the flower beds up by their roots, like hair, clawing at the orange petals that she'd been forced to serve and swallow for more than a decade, and my father calling her crazy, crazy, trying to pin her arms behind her back. The following night she came back to the grave site, he told me, and salted the earth.

Falling

Sallie Tisdale

MY BROTHER, BRUCE, STILL calls me *Sis* and sometimes *baby sister*, but we don't see much of each other. For a long time we've been gradually drifting—if not apart, then into an accommodation of being apart.

We are both a bit skittish, abrupt, a little profane. Sometimes our conversations feel like the wrestling matches we used to have—fun, but a little painful. I call him, but he isn't good on the telephone. His voice rises and falls, the phone in his hand half forgotten as he throws a ball for his dog or tells my nephew to go do his homework. He comes back to me all at once, demanding, "What?" In the photos I've managed to snap over the years, he is almost always frowning at the camera or making a face.

When he has to come to the hated city and renew a few of his many licenses, he stays with me. He limps up the steps and throws open the heavy front door. "Sis!" he shouts, dropping his small suitcase and slapping my shoulder hard.

We open a bottle of wine and he props his tattered right knee on a pillow. Broad and strong and fighting his weight like everyone in our family, he fills a room.

"Totaled the Beemer on Christmas Eve." He is breezy. "James and me, we spun out on black ice going up the mountain. Thirty-five years I've been driving that road, never hit ice like that. But the Beemer did what it was supposed to—nobody hurt."

Now wait one damned minute here. That BMW was one of his most prized possessions. He totaled it? With James, my twelve-year-old nephew? On the *mountain*, in ice? Not to mention that he hasn't had steady work for a couple of years and had to let all the insurance lapse.

"My big regret, I just filled the gas tank. Now *that's* gone."

We drink for a while.

I ask him about the knee, about the next operation, put off with the insurance.

"I mostly drag my right leg around behind me," he says.

"Does it hurt when you ski?" I ask, watching him lounge on my couch like a king, head back on a pile of quilted pillows. He glances at me, like it was a stupid question. And of course it is; I can see the scars from across the room.

"It hurts right now, sitting here," he says.

For a long time, as most people do, I've nurtured a seed of doubt about my place in others' hearts. In all other hearts. Sometimes I find myself being careful around Bruce, afraid to upset him, because I can't take him for granted. His most abbreviated comments echo and sing to me; a single name or phrase evokes a world. But between siblings, there are no vows, no contracts. No promises. It is so goddamned dangerous to love somebody.

Bruce worked more than twenty-five years as a skier of one kind and another. The walls of his house are covered with pictures of him upside down in space, skis akimbo, flipping off lethal cornices over canyons of snow. Bruce can read snow—layer by layer, its crystal language. He knows when a cornice wants to fall, when a side of the mountain is turning to avalanche. He is trained to handle explosives; for years, it was his job to stand at the edge of a crevasse on skis and toss dynamite into a few hanging tons of ice. He is trained in emergency medicine and rope rescue and can fix a ski lift. He's won several gold medals in the Ski Patrol Olympics. For a while, his job title was mountain manager.

Summers were for construction jobs and river trips. He can run whitewater, so there are photos of him in the rapids too, in boats tossed like autumn leaves. He can handle Zodiacs and portage rafts along a cliff. He has a Coast Guard Master Marine license, so he can run bigger boats in open water. He loves fishing and rivers, but his life was about snow. Then the knee went, and the other knee and it was the end of all that. He still works a little on ski patrol, keeping his hand in, but the legs aren't up for more than that. Mostly he gets by as a part-time fishing guide in Alaska, scraping through the winters the way he used to scrape through summer.

We drink some more, and he tells me a few stories I've never heard before—harrowing accidents, close calls. Some are old stories, from our stupid kid years. Finally I have enough of listening. I pull up my pants leg and show him a little scar I'd gotten from being banged on some rocks in the surf. He answers with a long jagged line on his calf, and then we are both pulling up our shirtsleeves and yanking down our pants, bending over to point at the marks left behind.

*

I wake up in a room blurry with dawn. Strange light. The room is fogged and soft, and I know it is snowing. The whole world is falling in snow, the kind of snow that is without beginning—without end. I barely move, coy under the blankets with all the time in the world. And then I jump out into the cold room and fling up the blinds and holler for my brother.

Later Bruce and I make angels in the dry, sibilant snow. Our padded limbs swish in rhythm, whispering. The shattered sky falls like ash, covering me in tiny scraps of white. I can hear the tiny puffs of impact all around me. It covers me, it covers my brother an arm's length away, a new world covering the broken world, leaving us safe and clean and cold.

We grow up in a small town in a high, dry valley braced by mountains. He is two years older, but we look so much alike that we pass for twins, spend that much time together. Summer is clear and hot, and we live outside as much as in—soaring hours spent in fields and vacant lots, clambering over boulders and climbing into the great cups of maple trees. Winter is clear and cold. We do everything in the snow but ski—skiing is pricey beyond words. So we slide down the hills on battered silver discs and patched-up inner tubes, shooting recklessly through the trees. We build snow forts and snow caves and snow houses. We stuff snow down our little sister's shirt so she cries and goes home and can't tell Mom we're going into the culvert where we aren't allowed.

Our mother teaches fifth grade at the elementary school and our father teaches industrial arts at the high school. He fixes televisions and radios on the side, in a cluttered shop behind our house where the tools hang on pegboards in careful wax-pencil outlines. Dad is a volunteer fireman; all the able-bodied men in town are expected to volunteer. He drinks, more and more with each year, but he takes to driving the trucks, training other men. We grow up around policemen and firemen and ranchers—people who can fix things and build things, people who aren't afraid of weather or work. People who run into burning buildings without looking back.

At two, at four, at eight years of age, I stare at the Polaroid camera my mother holds. I look at her as though she is under a microscope. Bruce, beside me, a little taller, grins stiffly. He is the oldest, he is the only boy, so he is getting the lessons I can't have—how to use tools, build things, fix things. My father is an unsparing man, and he teaches with sudden slaps upside the head. Bruce is learning fast.

My grandparents own a small cabin on a big river, and sometimes we go up for days with boxes of groceries and books. We spend our days on the water, with little supervision. I like to swim across the wide, steady river to the sandy shelf under the cliff—swim with the un-flagging, graceless stroke of a strong child, the slow current tugging against me, pushing back. I can feel the cold pull of the deeper, darker water beneath. Sometimes Dad drives us a few miles up the river in the back of the pickup, and drops us off with our inner tubes to float back.

One day, when Bruce is almost twelve and I am just nine, we keep going past the cabin, around the blind curve of canyon wall where we are not allowed to go. We dip through a few shallow whorls and rocky turns, and then suddenly we're caught in a narrow slot of white water, real rapids. I still remember only froth and foam, the power of it, falling, and then a hazy view back up a small waterfall we had somehow ridden down. I sit huddled on the rock where Bruce has dropped me after pulling me up from the bottom of the pool by my hair, the way he'd been taught in his junior lifesaving course.

I've lost my shoes. We walk back on the road, its sharp gravel biting my feet. Water runs in trickles down my thighs. We walk through thirsty sunlight, the breathless air suddenly cool under the pines. We walk in silence down the dusty road, carrying our secrets together. Then: "Don't tell Mom," he says. And I nod. Telling Dad never occurs to either of us.

Telling the truth is a lot like telling lies, in the end. It is all just stories; like snow falling, they cover everything up. *Family*, for most of us, includes lifelong agreements about what is not said. Certainly the heart of my family is a maze of agreements, the main one being not to speak of things. At ten years, at twelve, at fourteen, I meet the camera with a mocking half smile, with scorn. Bruce gazes toward the horizon like Captain America. The fear of humiliation and the need for self-reliance is strong in us both, driving us differently. He wants to be perfect; he is taking lessons in it. I want the lessons too, but not the grades—not the snicking of the leather belt as our father pulls it off his waist and wraps it twice around his meaty hands.

I discover books and theater and politics and trouble, and he finds football and gymnastics. I can't fight fires or use a table saw so I do more dangerous things. I ride motorcycles with men I meet in the park. I talk back at the dinner table. Bruce wins his varsity letter and I start writing manifestos to my English teachers. *Truth* is what I insist on telling. I call it *speaking up*—words flying from my young mouth, flying up, filling the sky.

Right after graduation, Bruce leaves on a gymnastics scholarship to the Air Force Academy in Colorado Springs, eight thousand feet high in the Rockies. He shaves his head, learns to handle a rifle, marches for hours. He goes skiing for the first time. He never takes a lesson—just pushes off and flies.

While Bruce spit-polishes his shoes, his very short romance with the military already over, I am getting kicked out of English class. When I am sixteen I quit high school before they can fire me, and somehow talk myself into early admission at the college one state border and a world away from home. After a year, Bruce quits the academy and joins me. There is a little of Captain Kirk now, a nerd with cool depths. He lets his hair grow and falls in with a gang of ski bums who cut classes and head up the mountain whenever they can cadge enough gas money together. My father tears the Air Force Academy bumper sticker off his truck and won't speak to him.

When I leave college to test my ideas about truth and beauty in a commune, Bruce finds his way to the Rockies, and begins to study snow in earnest. Each morning, he wakes up to the cold, bright Colorado sky, and skis straight from his apartment steps to the slopes. He skis his last run to the door of the restaurant where he washes dishes and chops vegetables each evening. Late at night, he skis home, under sulfurous streetlights. In the cones of light snowflakes swirl, blinking in and out like shadows, extinguished when they touch the earth.

The writer Peter Stark describes how winter saved him: how, at a time when his life was out of control, he was able to use its canvas to "spread out the chaos that was once my life and assemble something that I hope approaches grace." We learn to walk by falling; we learn to relax into gravity until we dance with it. Skiing is just another way to fall, and dance. In the inhuman snows of the high mountains, there is not much more one can do; surrender is your only choice.

A few years ago, Bruce came to the city to receive an award for some outrageously complicated rescue involving ropes and winches and a whole night in the snow, and we went to a banquet room and ate bad chicken at big round tables with police and firemen and people who run toward what most people flee.

I'm comfortable underwater, in hospitals, in strange cities where I don't speak the language. But I can barely swing a hammer. I don't like being cold, and I'm scared of heights. People like my brother, my father, the men and women who speak this language of physical skill and risk sometimes seem like creatures from another time, made for battle and repair. Listening to their laconic, tech-laden slang, I can be stung by remorse, by that old, familiar wish—that I had become someone else. That I had done things differently all along.

There is something painfully obvious about it all, this overcompensation, this hoarding of skill. We've both done it; we've collected our gold stars, become experts in our fields, worked as professional helpers—that group a therapist might say has issues. Some lessons I never seem to learn. I sent a copy of each of my books to my father. He never mentioned them, and when I finally asked, he told me he didn't have time to read.

One day, Bruce takes me up to the top of his mountain. He leads me away from the lift and the runs, to a line of closure ropes at the top of the steepest bowl. He skis without poles, moves like a dancer. Directly below us is a glaciated cirque, a smooth plane dropping far away, an ocean of white.

"No way!" I say—almost shouting.

Bruce laughs, then gets a look at my face and stops smiling. "If you start to slide, turn your feet downhill," he says. "Dig your elbows in and keep your head down." Then he grins and throws his arms wide, taking in the slope, the trees, the whole damned mountain.

"Hey, Sis! You just have to ask yourself—what could *possibly* go wrong?"

Our mother is dead for many years when Dad dies, a few days before Christmas in the middle of a snowstorm. The day of his funeral is calm and clear, and many of the town's firemen come in dress uniform. One stands in each corner of the room during the service, holding bells, and at the end, they ring the signal for firemen returning to the station. Then the big red ladder truck leads the hearse to the cemetery.

We are left with four houses, two workshops, a garage, and the debris of many whiskey-laden years. Three of the houses are rentals in various states of repair, and the house where we were raised is reduced to narrow pathways through mazes of piled-up newspapers, books, clothes, laundry, and box after unlabeled box. Our sister lives in town and is the executor of the estate; she finds missing stock certificates, lost photographs, and a few hefty, long-expired checks in the detritus. But months later, Bruce and I decide it's really our turn, and make a date to tackle the garage, the final piece.

I drive alone down the interstate on a beautiful September day, listening to NPR for hours. I stop at gas stations and minimarts and everywhere there are people gathered around small televisions hanging from the ceiling, over the pepperoni sticks and Slurpee machines. No one says much. I reach Bruce's peaceful ranch house in a little town off the old highway, and we hug and sit silently in front of the television for a few more hours, watching the towers in their strange, slow, eternal fall, and we are both thinking about the firemen and neither of us says a word.

The next day we sort through boxes. The silence is broken only now and then—"Oh, look at this!" holding up a yearbook or a battered balsa-wood airplane. We find brass knuckles, a box of Super 8 porn flicks, a bottle of mercury, ancient calipers. "Remember this?" we say. We work all day.

Then we stand in the driveway between the house where we grew up and the little rental bungalow next door. It looks much the same, a tidy white house with a dark-green square of lawn. Behind Bruce, where we grew up, is a bed of thirsty old roses, a leaning fence, dead grass—the work of decades let go. And the crumbling chimney of our fireplace, the one he scrabbled up, screaming, when Dad chased him with the belt.

He tells me a story.

He was in his thirties, married, rearing three children, and living near the mountain where he was head of the ski patrol. He came down to town to help Dad paint the rental house. They prepped for a week and were ready to paint. Just as they opened the cans, the fire alarm went off. Dad dashed for his pickup and was gone without a word, the same way he had disappeared at the sound of the siren our entire lives. Bruce kept working.

"And, by God, I did it myself. I painted the whole damned house by myself that day. And I cleaned up too. It was done when he got home."

What are the words for how we stand here in the midst of things? On the top of the mountain, I had lifted my borrowed goggles, and the ocher world flipped into black and white: every shade of ash and pearl and dove, a floury, glaucous place with shadows dappled and milky. Snow without beginning, without end. The whole world was glistening and silky, like a fall of tinsel lay across the land. I felt, perhaps for the first time, his vast gladness of winter. What are the words for this kind of snow, snow that is always falling, has always been falling, snow that fills our hearts and turns us into angels?

"When he got home, he didn't say anything. He just walked around the whole house without saying anything. He looked at every bit of it and the paint cans and the brushes. And finally he said, 'Good job.' And that was it."

Standing on this broken asphalt in a driveway I know rut by rut, I look at him. He stands up straight, holds his head back. Captain America.

"It was the first time he ever told me I did a good job."

We are all riding down our lives, a few hidden rapids around the bend. Hang on tight. Sometimes we walk back home again, together.

Rapid Transit
Rick Moody

GUY COMES ON THE TRAIN, Sunday morning. I have slept about one hour, and here I am again with some psychotic mother*#%$er going to give me the whole Jesus-believing-in-me thing, the if-only-I-will-be-reborn thing, no patience, not another ounce, and he's going to confront every passenger, like, for example, my sleeping daughter, *#%$!, I'm going to have to deal with him; she's been up all night, screaming, she's the stuck pig, and I feel sympathy, sure, what person wouldn't wake up screaming if perchance she came to understand the great *#%$!ing buffet of human cruelties laid out ahead, bracing for the worst, therefore, remedial lessons in reading the New Testament, conspiracy theories, Tea Party rhetoric, after which my daughter will awake, *#%$!, and he has the wild, unsteady gaze indicating that he can keep the psychotic symptoms in remission only for so long, he won't be able to resist chucking my daughter under the chin with his infected hands, but instead of saying anything about the New Testament, the Flight Out of Egypt, the parting of the Red Sea, what he actually says is, You put that on your sandwich? That nasty stuff? Do you have any idea what is in that? and I guess he's talking about the consistency of this product he has foresworn, and I suppose if I had to think about the liquid mechanics of this product, its polysyllabic chemical additives, its preservatives and stabilizers, I would not eat it either, and he goes on about how it ruins each and every meal preparation it adorns, it ruins America, like if you put this product in a sandwich it's ashes in your mouth, or if you put this product in a salad, it's like that salad is all clotted together, like what's in a baby's diaper, you know I'm really worried that this is it, intemperate ranting about lunch foods, and the psychotic *#%$!er is coming straight for me and my kid, it's the diaper reference, he sees her, she's a sympathetic audience, a diaper consumer, how many steps to the emergency brake, what kind of guy talks about this type of thing on a Sunday morning, lunch foods, condiments, the illuminati; and there's some kind of racial profiling implied too, though he's polite enough to avoid saying it, which is that it's a white folks thing, you can tell that he's thinking it, me and the other ofays on the number two all implicated in this thing, like we probably work in some kind of support business, you know, whether it's the promotion or the public relations sector, consulting for some conglomerate, all mayo all the time, and the rant nears its conclusion, maybe inevitably, and he whips out the jar of the stuff, from some pocket in his manky overcoat, *#%$!, it's really an old jar, and a small jar, probably unearthed from a time capsule of foods that white folks approve of, he goes, Certain kinda things can be forgiven, know what I'm talking about, places where we got to be able to meet up together, but, man, shit got to go, then, with a big electrifying smile, the panhandler starts in with "You Send Me," by Sam Cooke, and though he's kind of iffy in terms of intonation, he has good timing, good phrasing, knows all the verses, his rendering is serviceable enough that it does wake my nineteen-month-old bundle of joy, and she laughs, and yet— on the way to the next car—he leaves his tiny jar behind and . . .

Guy comes on the train, Sunday, and I have been singing my daughter to sleep at the end of the aisle, and the words I have been singing are the words *Sendero Luminoso, Sendero Luminoso,* excellent words, when the wheels abrade the tracks in the turns, announcer comes on the PA with all the subtlety of an Armalite fusillade, you got to sing whatever words you got to sing, if it's the phrase *Stalinist Purge, Stalinist Purge, Stalinist Purge,* that's what you sing, or you sing *Great Leap Forward, Great Leap Forward,* and if Mao's Little Red Book were the only thing that kept my daughter resting I would recite the whole of it to my daughter from memory, besides, you can't really quarrel with rhetorical flourishes like You young people, full of vigor and vitality, are in the bloom of life, like the sun at eight or nine in the morning; so, guy steps across the threshold, because he always *does* come on the *#%$!ing train on Sunday morning; and then if I didn't know better, I'd say that the panhandler is the chairman of Goldman Sachs, no *#%$!, I know his *#%$!ing name, the chairman of Goldman Sachs, but I'm not going to say his name, because you can't read the *#%$!ing paper without knowing his name, I mean it's just not all that likely that the chairman of Goldman Sachs would be on this train, the number two, because he can afford a *#%$!ing car service, even with his reduced bonus, with which he could house the entire street-dwelling population of the cities of the nation for a year or something, he wouldn't be on the *#%$!ing train because he's got a private jet and a limousine, probably a fleet of limousines, Lloyd Blankfein wouldn't be on the plane, nor would Hank Paulson be on the train, nor would Robert Rubin be on the *#%$!ing train, Timothy Geithner would not be on the train. None of those guys from the world of finance would be on the train, with torn clothes, discharge from the eyes, but this *#%$!er is bald, white, male, and thus he has a Goldman Sachs demeanor, which means no human feelings, and I'm telling all of this to my daughter, who is meanwhile slowly drooling on my sweatshirt, and it turns out this guy, despite appearances, happens to be the Communist panhandler, meaning the guy who argues that it's the collapse of the market economy that has brought him to this place of misfortune, he's trying to get his *#%$!ing disability check, right, and he's trying to get a room through some kind of path-back-to-ownership government initiative, just needs a little to tide him over, and it's really important that everyone on the train (ten others, some slumped in two-seaters, hoods pulled down) realize that it's the system that creates these injustices, it's the system that doesn't account for persons of dignity who once were able to work and who through macroeconomic shock waves have been lifted out of the economy and deposited elsewhere like silt in the globalized delta, with *nothing*; the system, the guy says (*Sendero Luminoso, Sendero Luminoso*), is especially calibrated to favor heartlessness over compassion, and that's why this guy has to be out here on the trains, because the system is against him. Not a winning formula, rhetorically speaking, and none of the persons in the two-seaters is awaking, and whatever it is that I'm singing to my daughter, words about some rather dangerous rebel group from Latin America who kidnapped, slaughtered, and drug trafficked in order to mount a menacing alternative to a local authoritarian government, is doing the trick in terms of insuring that my daughter doesn't wake, and the Communist panhandler therefore quickly realizes that this is not a reliable place for targeted giving, this car among cars linked together on a Sunday morning, especially when the Communist message, for everyone except my daughter, has a soporific effect, comrades, I gotta . . .

Guy comes on the train, Sunday, a.m., and this is the guy, first such, who recognizes that this performance is life or death, and what life or death means to this particular hustler is that he understands that he is a figment in the sleepy reverie of my daughter, it's a wonder

41

that no one has *#%$!ing figured this out before, none of the pan-
handlers has figured it out, though there's always some needy party,
especially on a Sunday, doing his cons, but not one of those *#%$!ers
has figured out that if he wakes my daughter in the middle of his spiel
then he is liable to vanish, disappear, dematerialize—as thoroughly,
as completely, as the image on the television set when switched off;
when we see someone in a dream, I tell my daughter, oh profligate
sleeper, we find it difficult later to describe that person, unless the
person stands in for a party we already know, like, I had a dream and
my deceased sister was alive again and there she was, bottled blonde,
drinking, laughing, spreading good cheer; otherwise the figures of our
dream life look one minute like this and then one minute like that,
and I wish I could tell my daughter analogically more about what
dreams are like, but the thing about dreams is that you sort of can't
say, for example, there are unicorns and they are pink, or there is your
mother, but your mother is a Sri Lankan washerwoman with gigan-
tic breasts, or there are cave people who are routing telephone traffic
with some kind of primitive switchboard made of bones, or it's the day
of the college examination and you are obligated to answer the essay
question by shaking your penis at those around you; these images
may all be true to the lexical vocabulary of dreams, and yet they may
not suggest the deep feeling that comes with the oneiric, which seems
to be deeper than almost anything we experience, no matter the nonsense of the dream, and this guy is no exception, he's wearing a vinyl
tracksuit, some old work shoes, and he is either an American Indian
or a Mexican guy; Chicano guys always *#%$!ing slay me, their
melancholy always a mockery of every other kind of privation, they
come to this place for a break, and they get *#%$!ed every which
way, my daughter must know this, and I guess this must be true for
my daughter too, because I'm watching her dream this guy, and this
guy knows that his request for funds has to be lodged at top speed
because he only has so long before my daughter awakes, and then
he will dematerialize, and he *#%$!ing needs to do the work, clear
the profits, get off the train before all of that, and yet, unfortunately,
we have entered into one of those long subway tunnels—under the
river—and so the guy is stuck with us for a solid three minutes, and
his tale of woe, delivered mostly in Spanish (a moment of triumph
for the multiculturalism of my city), is a monologue of keenest desperation, because the guy knows that he could be wiped out at any
moment; a tour de force, frankly, this episode, and I attempt to rock
my daughter because I do not want her to awake and disappear the

guy, she is heedless of her responsibility, as dreamer, it's just another dream to her, or perhaps a nightmare, and though lives hang in the balance, his monologue in Spanish could be *#%$!ing funny to her, the disenfranchisement of it, because everything is either funny or terrifying— these are the infantile settings—and, alas, at the last moment, just as we near the stop, the stop where the Mexican figment could slip out of the door, with his few meager dimes, the train goes into one of those curves, metal strikes metal, there's ear splitting, and all at once my daughter . . .

Why shouldn't there be a dwarf, after all, because it's every other *#%$!ing kind of unfortunate, and if you are up *#%$!ing early on a Sunday, no good reason, your confederates, those sprawled out on the molded plastic seats, the limbless, the pockmarked, and every kind of raving mother*#%$!er, naturally include a dwarf. And the dwarf has that kind of lurching bowlegged quality that dwarves have as they come marching along, and—a certain dwarf cuteness. Wait. That's not a dwarf at all. That is my daughter! As babies eventually will, my daughter seems to have learned to walk! To toddle! And her toddling is not qualitatively different from the unsteady gait of the subway drunk, or the subway dwarf, and there is no certainty—as train unfettered by heavy tunnel traffic gallops along—that she will be able to complete her march end to end, no flickering candle in a stiff breeze could be any less reliable than my daughter making her way through the train, carrying that hat. Whose hat? It could only be my hat, because whose *#%$!ing hat could she have had besides mine, and by hat, here, I mean a hat that an adult would wear, a gray fedora, scuffed up, whose band ought to have been replaced; somehow, despite her poor motor skills, she clutches the fedora, overturned, with its *#%$!ing emptiness upward, and she goes from side to side, with her baby blues, mumbles some nonsense, mostly consisting of the word *lodi*, at least that has been how I have phonetically rendered it, lodi lodi lodi, lodi lodi lodi lodi, waiting, gazing, staring, while whichever passenger before her, in an increasing state of total *#%$!ing capitulation, antes up, which is to say drops some *#%$!ing coin in the *#%$!ing hat, and then even more, lodi, lodi, lodi, lodi, lodi, lodi, or, if you want to be more phonetically exact, lo-DEE, lo-DEE, lo-DEE, lo-DEE, there's nothing studied about her articulations, or else, contrarily, never has there been a panhandler more adept than my daughter, who has the one reliable quality that will induce a subway rider to part with funds, cuteness, I mean, *#%$!, my daughter is *#%$!ing cute, cuter than a dwarf, and if, for example, you attempted to make a diagram of cuteness that had at its apex a German polar bear cub, and at the other extreme a strand of virus, my daughter, I must *#%$!ing inform you, would be just ahead of Knut, and that is why as she works the aisle with such relentless *#%$!ing effectiveness, changing her spiel slightly, and the new spiel sounds something like bappy, bappy, bappy, bappy, bappy, bappy, bappy, bappy, bappy, and I'm going to confess right here that I have subjected her terminologies to historical and philological scrutiny, but I can't say precisely what she means, don't really know, and neither do any of the people on this train, some of whom are thinking, *#%$!, they don't want to have to work on a Sunday morning, but actually it's the fact that the day feels so empty of inspiration, so wrung out, that has them paralyzed, thirsty for guidance, as if they are in a holiday choir but have never learned the piece being sung, such that they will give some tiny dwarf, no dwarf at all, some of the money that they owe elsewhere, because who in this moment does not owe the money elsewhere, and the dwarf gathers up the funds, but where does she take the funds? And at what point do I reveal that I am genetically related to her? At what point must I accept responsibility for her natural ability for this profession at which she is already so successful though she cannot yet speak, save for the words lo-Dee and bappy? Do I get a cut?

And so it happens that I come to be the panhandler myself, because all will serve; all will make this dramatic, stylized request, and indeed, you're *#%$!ing right, I do say something just like this, Never think it won't happen to you, such a downer, and I really should purge it from the script, except there's no script, there are only certain routines that I fall back on, because they are written into my five-year plan, My daughter and me, we got nowhere to go, and sometimes I say, We're really sorry to interrupt your reading, though most everyone is tranquilized by video games; it's not that I want to be irritating, it's that I am exhausted, Never meant to come to this, we were just minding our own business, and I'm holding her hands in that really uncomfortable way you have to hold a *#%$!ing toddler, so that she can toddle without falling over, and actually I do this even though she could probably do it herself now, but she looks more pitiable like this; doesn't matter what I say, it matters that I am married, once had a good job, and like to smoke Latin American plant residues, you would not expect me to be wearing the homely knockoff sneakers from a charitable agency, and so I am carrying my daughter, and using my daughter and my misfortune to chisel you: Everything that you have was given to you by chance, and this accounts for all of it, sofa, and television, stuff in the cabinet, the fancy crockware that you fetch down from the high shelf for company, and if you happen to have a car, if you are lucky enough to have a car, this car was given to you by chance not because you deserve it, and the same goes for every bit of real estate in your real-estate portfolio, just the mere idea of real-estate ownership is indefensible, you have done nothing to deserve ownership of a real-estate portfolio, and since that is the case you should think about giving some of what you have to myself and my daughter. We're going to proceed through this car so slowly that it'll seem we shall never leave, and we'll be glad to take some of your disbursements, which we think of not as a redistribution, but rather as an atonement for the fact that you deserve nothing that you own. Jewelry is especially welcome here, so if some of you women have rings that you are trying not to sport here on the train, this might be a good time for you to hand over some of these jewels, because in any event you are living with the fear the jewelry will somehow be separated from you because you recognize that you do not deserve the jewelry, and we can help with that; now would be a good time to hand it over; and what about all of you persons with gold teeth, you have been spending all this money on your teeth, trying to have a smile that reflects how you feel about yourself, that you are golden, but now you have an opportunity to indicate—by allowing us to extract your golden teeth and to melt down these veneers and monetize them—that you are willing to give abundantly to the starveling children of distant lands, and while it is true that we are not the starveling children of distant lands, it would be wise for you to hand over some of your accursed ingatherings; I'm also thinking about your credit and debit cards, a great many of you will have more than one credit or debit card, issued by a recently bailed-out financial services corporation, just because you are worried about running one credit card up to its limit, and so you keep other cards in reserve, for emergencies, and, well, here we are, we are an emergency, and you ought not refuse our emergency, and so we would be happy to borrow your credit cards from you for a limited time, and we have some of those fancy devices they have in Europe, where you can debit the funds on the run, and so we'd be happy to borrow the card from you for a brief

45

moment and to make a deduction on behalf of ourselves. And what about the rest of you? We offer other financial transactions. For example, we can store your loose change, since change is heavy and can really pile up, especially pennies; we can take this change from you, and because it is a choking hazard for my daughter she is carrying this attractive commemorative jar, a jar that invokes this day on which we came around on the trains to help you with your remorse, and into this commemorative jar my daughter would be happy to ingather all such change as is weighing down your trousers or purse. We'd be happy to give you a full accounting of all the expenses on which my daughter spends your change; we are also particularly happy to take the larger denominations, some of those dollar coins that people mistake for quarters, impractical and best given away, or foreign currencies, and if you have already disbursed your change, and if you have no jewelry, and your teeth are all repaired with porcelain or some other fill that is unredeemable, we are nonetheless certain that you have stock certificates, or you have a pension plan, and while you cannot cash out your pension plan until you are of retirement age, you can name the two of us, my daughter and me, as beneficiaries of your pension plan, and we'd be happy to help you call the relevant parties, and we will help alert them to the paperwork, and, in fact, we also do have a 900 number already engaged, and, for each call that you place, fifty cents will be deposited in our account in the Cayman Islands, and if that's easier for you, that would be a fine way to contribute, and so when you think of all the ways, web-based, telephonic, and through simple old-fashioned hand-to-hand transfer, that enable you to provide us the necessary funds, I think you have to pause to consider all the good that you will be doing. You could give to your public library, or to the museum, or perhaps to some charity devoted to eliminating disease among children; these charities are admirable, but they are not charities that have anything to do with us, and in any case with us you undoubtedly get more bang for your philanthropic buck, with us you can really make an immediate difference, and if you think that I will stop talking eventually, you have . . .

Guy comes on the train, as if from the storied past of panhandling, silencing the car entire, laying waste to superficial interpretation of the ubiquitous professionals called panhandlers, laying waste to metaphor, to all who would claim an understanding of the issues, to all who would imagine that they could separate the charlatans from the needy, silencing those who claim that this is fraudulence and hoodwinkery, silence, in the car, punctuated by the restful and subsonic frequencies of train motion, all is hushed, arrested, he is from the storied past, from some origin of beseechment when only the grossest of disfigurement would do the trick, and my daughter is asleep, and I am grateful for her slumbering, because I know that while I grew up on this sight, the sight of the guy on the skateboard, I would spare her, at least for now, I don't want her to see the horror of the guy on the skateboard, and to have to wrestle with the horror, while trying to engage with him as though he were an individual, instead of a guy who had no lower half of his body and who thus comes through the subway cars fused to his skateboard, beseeching, and who summons in his inexplicable biology only thoughts of the extralarge epidemic of sorrow that is urban living; I'm not ready yet for her to see, to feel, the sanding away of innocence that comes from bearing witness thus, of course, he is collecting from those at the other end of the car first, and there is scarcely a heart hard enough to refuse, and I am thinking not of how he could still be circulating, since he was a figment of my own past, my unprofessional days, my woolgathering days, how the *#%$! he can function, with no *#%$!-ing lower torso even. Does he have a portion of a liver, or a liver and pancreas, does he have at least one kidney? Can he do without bladder and rectum, transverse colon, lower organs? Can he be attached to various yellowy collection bags, with their viscous syrups, so that he can easily go without excremental orifices? How is he then closed off? With what lacing and interlacing of interventions? And was he always like this, or was he made thus by explosion or accident? And how did he learn to accomplish so much with just his arms? Walk between cars, jam the skateboard under his arm between cars, somehow opening the doors, squeezing through, so that he may travel down the length of the next car too, separating the fortunate from their gains? What are the absolutely essential parts of a body for a person to feel whole, for a person to feel that he is a person? How much can you cut away from a body before a person is not? And how much money is a lost limb worth, and does this price go up when more limbs are lost? Is it necessarily the case that the guy on the skateboard has someone to look after him, or does he live alone, as he looks like he must do, because it is so hard to imagine him as a social animal, though he works in a professional space that is all about social interactions, in this case, the turning over of monies to him by persons in the subways of our city? Does he know everything about the subways? Is he one of those guys who could tell you about all the discontinued lines and about all the route changes? I grow more uncomfortable as he makes his way down the car, this is *under-statement*, and partly it is understatement because the guy on the skateboard says nothing. The guy on the skateboard waits, draws himself to a halt in front of various riders, and this is the simple dialect of the encounter, he waits for the fumbling with the billfold, but that is not it at all, because he is waiting for something else, for his royal flush of disabilities to dawn in the eyes of the other, yes, I am a prisoner of my own *#%$ing recollection of the guy on the skateboard, and of my desire to protect my daughter from the sight of him, and so I am thinking about how I might get the *#%$ out of the way of the guy on the skateboard, I am enumerating the options, and yet this set of options is not long because I am in the last car. There is no next place to go, in running oppositely away from the guy on the skateboard, I could go around the guy on the skateboard, clutching my daughter to me, but then I would need to recognize him as I pass, as he works his way to a pair of ladies evidently on their way to church, with their bonnets, their Sunday best, and these ladies calmly put aside Gideon-sized paperbacks, reach into pocketbooks, and how can they do so calmly, I don't know, but they do, and then there is a guy wearing some kind of uniform, maybe for a muffler-repair franchise, and he has a roll of small bills, and he peels off some bills, and do I detect a certain amount of fear and trembling at the beholding of the guy on the skateboard? No, the muffler-repair expert gives nothing away, except the bills, and then in silence the guy on the skateboard approaches that family of four, the father, who seems to watch placidly as his wife wrestles with the two kids, one in a stroller, one without, and on it goes, the family of four, until the guy on the skateboard arrives, and stands before them, *ecce homo, ecce homo*, behold, and the reaction of the father is *#%$ what the *#%$ do you want you just want some kind of *#%$ing money, can't you see that my family wants to be left in *#%$ing peace, but then the father, on the point of blowing up, takes in the guy on the skateboard, comes to understand this vessel of misfortune, body no longer a body, and yet still a *person*, this person is fused to some temporary technological solution, so that he might still command a certain amount of cash money, and this is what I am whispering to my daughter, as the guy on the skateboard draws closer, because he is completing the transaction with the Hispanic family now, and there is a guy just down the bench from me, a white guy wired up to the hilt, stuff stuck in his ears, wires coming out, something in his hand that beeps and vibrates, he has running clothes on, some kind of device strapped onto his arm meant to track systoles and diastoles, he has space-age running shoes and shorts, and he has a number on his chest, which means that he is about to compete, and he is like the guy on the skateboard, a body attached to devices, and I am whispering to my daughter, as the guy with the running clothes reaches into a special pocket in the tongue of his $300 running shoes and exhumes another dollar or two that he places into the gloved hand of the skateboard guy, who again says nothing, and now there is nothing separating us, myself and the guy on the skateboard, moment of moments, his silence is historical, and what I think is that there are things that cannot be imagined, but only remembered, and then there are things that cannot be remembered, but only reconstructed, and then there are things that cannot be reconstructed, only dreamed, and then that there are things that cannot be dreamed, because they represent what *is*, and the guy on the skateboard, whether living or dead, is what is, and every other living thing out there, on the *#%$ing trains and in the world, thinks that it is what is, but in truth there is nothing like the guy on the skateboard standing on the subway asking for money, and as he stands before me, I reach into my pocket, and what I say is Don't wake her. And then I look into his eyes.

Two Poems
Rae Armantrout

PROBLEM AREAS

Descended
from the peacock's
blind eyes

and the chimp's
acute suspicions,

we invented astrology

to give purpose
to the stars.

*

We've been raptured

to our fathers' shoulders
where we've hidden

the past in the future;
the future in the past.

*

Now time is continuous.

We must renounce
each breath.

Rae Armantrout

SUGGESTION

Your brain feels swollen,
as if it's floating
on a string, no, on two,
each held in the balled fist
of an eye.

The feeling produces this image:
two crying children—
brother and sister?—
clutching strings
in an old city of brick, stone.

What does this image explain?

*

"In the beginning"

In the end,

these are—

there are—

only suggestions:

"Clockwise" or "counter"—

though there are no clocks.

"Horizontal" or "vertical"—

though there is no horizon.

*

Being aware of anything outside yourself
means you aren't sleeping

so you have pushed things away.
Now you are alone with pain.

Pain is as large as you are
and is not obedient.

If you *became* pain, perhaps,
then you could rest.

But it is not possible
to merge with pain.

32 Lemmas

Karen Hays

1

2

THE DAY MY SON'S first pet dies, the three of us drive by a gas station where a boot-shod man on a ladder is swapping out propaganda on the station's illumined sign. Perching a conservative few steps below the ladder's apex puts the guy at a good level to look down on the moraines that separate his from the neighboring businesses. Below him, palatial mounds of snow inch their way fingerlike over the pavement. These are the pale lobes of winter's extrudable stomach. Every year they latch on to sites least trafficked and, after a taste or two, begin growing plucky. Pretty soon they are gulping up ground faster than man or machine can contend with, digesting it in crusty, white noise increments, wholly and tonguelessly swallowing it.

This, my son tells me, is the exact way that echinoderms do it. Guts on the outside.

As predators go, winter may rival an urchin in spines and dim wits but still the season gains on us, narrowing to precarious what remains of the city's navigable spaces. Blowers, plows, and broken-backed shovelers do their parts to keep the hulking organ at bay, but its enzymes need skimming nightly. Blades lay bare the scar tissue that in no time is again mucked over. Dirty chunky scree calves from wheel wells. Fresh snow is turned to chemical slush and pocked with salt sometimes turquoise. Frozen-in footprints boast glares proud and burnished. Ankle-deep ruts bare bits of gasping blacktop.

I'm overdoing it, yes, but look. If blue was a veneer you could pucker from the sky with a tool like this letter hanger's, that texture alone would come close to the delicacy of human skin here. A supple layer, a too-thin skin. Guts are on the inside, but not deep enough, but only just barely.

And yet here we are by the dauntless half million, scuttling like hermit crabs between climate-controlled shells, trawling a reef that's dead white but vaunts citywide wireless. Here am I in my cold car watching this gas station guy with flickering interest, my thoughts intercalated with a wordless panic over what to do about the dead pet.

How tenuous the man looks atop his ladder in his brittle coveralls husk. How not altogether up for the job—his one hand clinging to the aluminum frame while the other leverages the long, hook-ended pole. One by one, he snags the letters from a cardboard box on the ground below, then lifts them wobbling high up over his head—they are red like sunlight through eyelids and the traffic light that keeps us idling—and slides them into the panel's rules.

They teach you the lines of prose poems ought to stack like a billboard's—laminated for strength, boxed to stuff and carry. Lines—left-right justified, otherwise they'd be friable—run parallel

and nonintersecting. A fractallike
rhyme comes together: the rungs on the
ladder and the ridges on the rungs and (if
they're at all like mine or my two sons')
the treads of this man's two boots. What
patterns we claim against this hostile
terrain. What harmonics we make
among the textural rubble.

The letter hanger is nearly finished
when the light turns, but, charmingly,
something is missing, because this is
how the sign reads when our tires gain
purchase through the felty layers of
rubber-spun snow and finally we begin to
roll:

REM VE ROAD SALT NOW

3

Two out of three isn't bad. The mind
concatenates meaning from familiar words
whose vowels have gone missing.
Absences often go unperceived even. In
the backseat my son with the cloud breath
and permanent circles under his eyes has
no idea that the *shongololo* croaked while
beside her terrarium he lay sleeping, that I
found her this morning in the sphagnum
among disembarking commensal mites
and uneaten mushroom gills.

Shon go lo lo. That flagellated word.
That slippery corrugation. It is a black-
and-white bar code, a tail undulating
against its own blunt head. It is
onomatopoeic, but not for the song the
pair of them made most nights. Always
she was climbing up and sliding back; the
glacial crack and gnash of my son's cusps
randomly punctuated her bristly testing of
the glass.

On a normal morning, the *shongololo* would have returned to her
diurnal hiding position, curled in the

hollow of that damp, disintegrating log. On a normal morning, he rises and doesn't bother looking because he knows they keep opposite hours—the map-making boy and his Paleozoic night sentinel.

(A lemma is something to be taken for granted.)

Two is unique in that it is the only even prime number. And therefore often (and cheaply) called *the oddest*.

4

5

Strangely, none of us grows more neurons when we acquire new knowledge. When we learn to count and to read, the parts of our cerebral cortexes that shelter our car-tographic tools—our senses of color, shape, and x-y-z whereabouts—cede brain space to make way for concepts of letters and larger numbers.

Small numbers, however, are firmly rooted in the province of the senses. Quantities of three or less we know by numeric epiphany. They arise in our minds by stealth, simultaneously and all-of-a-*subitus*, with the same incontestable immediacy that color does. We needn't parse a pair or a trio to know its count. Instead, we sense its twoness or threeness as fast as and in the same way that we know a familiar face—with no need to scrutinize its terrain of eyes, nose, and mouth first. This process of knowing the count without counting—subitization, it is called—is inborn and appears to be present in animals ranging from pigeons to bonobos.

For humans, one, two, and three are the *a*, *m*, and *d* that add up to the names of our parents' faces (the sounds we pronounce first and by instinct, which help us sync our breaths and mouths and voices, whose sums turn into summonses, what segues to a lifetime of language); it is on their foundation that numeration builds.

(In psycholinguistics, *lemma* refers to the syntactic intermediate that lives between a word conceived and a word pronounced.)

Two and three are the only consecutive prime numbers.

6

7

By *three*, I mean *me and two sons*. By *of*, I mean *divisible*. By *us*, I mean like a prime number: *only by our own count and the irreproachable number* (one).

One is multiplicative identity. It is the only number that is also a mirror.

Stretching up tall in the driver's seat accords me a view of my preschool-aged son in the right half of my rearview. I see his features in reverse, but they are too symmetric for me to tell it. His downcast eyes are a swimming, dubitable color. His chapped lips roll in on themselves then burst forth in big spitty explosions; there's an action-figure battle playing out in the down-puffed amphitheater of his lap. From his mouth flow wispy little threads of narration; breath clouds are unwritten comic-strip bubbles. Thoughts ballooning.

Sitting back and looking up and left, I see my boy of dark circles and (unbeknownst to him) recently dead pet. He's scrawling in the frozen breath that's crystallized on the inside of his window. His name he writes backwards. His schoolwork he writes backwards, too. What looking glass divides him from a world full of folks who, like him, read jabberwocky? Is it tempered like the car window or mercurial like Alice's?

I make a palindrome when I look at

57

myself in the mirror. Circles aside, my eyes and my older son's are a near-perfect match, but not in ways that bear on how or what we see through them. There is a push-pull here. An outer and an inner limit to how close we can get.

(A stutter. Staccato. . . . Lemma held in limbo. A lemma is a fraction. What I mean to say is . . .)

Prime numbers separated by the count of two are called *twins*.

8

9

10

11

Starting at the number three, two is the least possible difference between prime numbers. As numbers grow larger, consecutive primes distance themselves farther and farther away from one another. The push gets more propulsive.

No matter how big they get, however, primes still occasionally snap back to a duo, one composite in between. (*Put him back in his cage!* said my first son of his then baby brother, pointing to the bars of the crib.) The Twin Prime Conjecture (and I find it comforting) proposes that the pull part of the prime dynamic keeps up with the push part forever and ever. Not just as far as we can see, but for as long as there are numbers.

12

13

Counting equals Exhaustive Searching plus Mindless Word Recitation.

14

15

16

17

Of course, a lemma is also a heading.

REM VE ROAD SALT NOW is a

suspension bridge with rotted-out decking. Something to peek through. Some scary shit under.

I read somewhere that when our minds wander, we blink more than when we're focused. Our eyes gate how much comes in from the outside. Lids slide down like the lash-legged *shongololo*.

Like wipers set on intermittent. On the other side of the windshield, cold gusts bully the exhaust of the cars in front of us, twirling up little tornadic puffs then batting them completely out of existence. Behind me, ice shavings shingle and curl around the tip of my older son's gloved pointer finger. He studies each one like it's a question orphaned from its answer.

It's not the ray of the mind, whose infinity stretches along dark unstaked axes, but the cool numeric scale that will soothe him. Ascending and descending that. Smaller hearts pulse faster and therefore not as long as those that are larger. Elephants outlive hummingbirds by fifty years or more. I'll bet the *shongololo*'s heart beat the length of his footprint by four or so inches. I'll bet it was thin enough to cradle in one of his palm creases. (The heart line is, at least on my two hands, the deepest.)

On what scale do you balance the weight of a heart breaking? With what radar, its speed? I arm myself with statistics, but only what I can anoint with my hand oil is truly conceivable to me. The skin on my fingertips was folded and bucked like mountain ranges in utero, but my eyes cannot hold mountains—in spite of book knowledge and rare calamitous evidence—as anything other than sedentary, eternal, slumberous, inert. Fingerprints are incidental signatures evolved not for gripping (as it was long believed), but for reading the waves generated by skimming the finer textures.

On the opposite end of the spectrum:

When I worry a stone, I do not feel its electrons buzz and thrum in the exquisite geometry of their lattices. Those conversations are inaudible against the charge that sings inside my skin. Rock-smashed fingers shuttle pain the speed of cheetahs and Mack trucks along micrometer-wide axons, and at least for a while that feeling is all that *matters*: highway speed now: seventy miles per hour.

(Lemmas are to language formation what derivatives are to calculus: instantaneous rates of change, fluxions, or, as one of calculus's early detractors famously put it: *the ghosts of departed quantities.*[1])

18

19

Only the tactile sense, to which the fleshy digits belong, is more handed than our sense of numerosity. In a study last spring, researchers were able to guess the exact numbers that participants were thinking of by measuring the changing vector of their gazes. Turns out, people look upward and to the right when the number they're thinking of is greater than the number they thought of last, down and left when it is less. The study's investigators were able to predict precise numbers because the degree of a person's focal shift correlates to the magnitude of his or her imaginary addition or subtraction. An easy set of multiplication/division equations.

One through Three may eschew the instincts for searching, spotlighting, and naming that, like a trio of Sherpas, assist us on our dextral ascents into higher and higher numbers, but Four and Up resort to our spatial senses. Quantity gets yoked to direction. The number is higher or it is lower.

The treads and risers of our mental number lines are so well worn, we don't feel our eyes when they effortlessly climb and descend them. We look without seeing where we are going. Kind of like how, when I am intent on a passage's meaning, my lips shape the words even though I'm silently reading.

Reading is like climbing stairs, but sideways: Our eyes make saccadic jumps of one to twenty characters and then briefly fixate. A study conducted by University of Southampton psychologists revealed that in only about half of these fixations do both eyes focus on the same letter. Nearly forty percent of the time, the right eye focuses two characters to the right of the letter the left eye is trained on. The remaining ten percent of the time, they cross so that the right eye looks two letters to the left of the character the left eye is looking at. What minds of their own our peepers have.

What cloistered memories; what nightly adventures. When we recount for someone out loud the order in which something happened to us, our eyes go back in time by retracing their gazes (up and left in the mirror, this boy of dead pet); in slumber they rove over our dreams as if real landscapes stretched before us.

20
21
22
23

Snow may be crunchy like exoskeletons underfoot. At its coldest, snow is Styrofoam squeaky. Warm, it is slappingly wet.

Ice can be thin and brittle like crazed Plexiglas. More often it is thick and beige, soapstone creamy. On the same square of city sidewalk, ice may present itself as a boulder of smoky quartz (semiprecious) and also a just-hocked loogie.

City snow is splattered with soft drinks, dribbled with dog piss, sprayed with wiper fluid. It is a failure of objectivity to find color here grotesque.

Thoroughfares tend to be littered with

Karen Hays

unpaired articles of clothing. Boots, mittens, baby socks, and sneakers. Most commonly stiff gloves point the way of their stray owners. How startling it was to see the disembodied hand between lanes of opposing traffic the other day, poking as it was—heavenward.

Where skin is in need of such careful girding (some part nevertheless always prickling, stinging, going numb, ominously burning), the act of undressing, of unpeeling all the way down to one's own warmth, can be overwhelmingly sensuous. Disrobing is like going to the beach in reverse; the heat you seek comes not from the sun burning eight light-minutes away, but from some real-time kindling just beneath the skin. A good windburn will accentuate this inside-out basking feeling.

I am dressed in eighteen square feet of infrequently navigated and salt-covered skin. Tending to every square inch (2,619, according to one website's algorithm) not only prevents them all from being frostbitten, but also anchors me in euclidean space, grounds me against the dreaded ghosty feeling. That is when I look in the mirror and, try as I might, fail to see more than one feature at a time—only a familiar but Brobdingnagian eye (farsighted left, nearsighted right) looking horrifically back, sometimes just my little mouth gone speechless.

(Since there are three types of cones in our eyes, any perceived color can be mapped as a single point in three-dimensional euclidean space. When illumination experts contoured the spectrum of color available to our species, they found it to be not triangular, but tongue shaped. They named this lick The Gamut. White lives at the volumetric center of the rounded mound, about a third of the way out from the root. Chartreuse and turquoise occupy the sides where we were wrongly taught we tasted salt, just in back and on either side of sweetness.)

24

25
26
27
28
29

Euclid's's fifth axiom of geometry states that given a line and a point not on it, it is possible to draw exactly one line through the point such that the new line is parallel to the preexisting line.

30
31

If I am a point and REM VE ROAD SALT NOW is the line already existing, then the one and only parallel line through me must read: I AM G NE ALREADY (because a line that's traversable is a time line by nature).

32
33
34
35
36
37

Recently I took Stanislas Dehaene's book *The Number Sense* out from the library. In it, the author describes a study in which he discovered the following:

When given a pair of numbers and asked to quickly indicate which of the two is larger, people perform differently depending on which hand they are responding with. People compare large numbers more accurately if answering with their right hands and small numbers more accurately if using their left hands. Unless, that is, their hands are crossed. Then the effect is reversed so that the left hand (on the right side of the body) deals more deftly with large numbers, and the right hand (on the left side) does a better job with smaller numbers.

Our mental number lines are tied not to our hands but to the vectors of our peripheral vision. Morbidly, I imagine our mental number lines sticking like invisible spears through opposite sides of our heads. Through the temples, to be exact. Arrows point right (because, like, how counterintuitive are negative numbers?). The elliptical head represents the origin, or zero. If there were some magic mirror that could show this, I would write on my chest's reflection in red lipstick: *I'm with infinity.*

38

39

40

41

An inaccurate count results when the eye is impetuous or dazzled; numbers spoken by rote can't keep up because they are automatons—manacled, soulless.

42

43

Infinity, in all its galling Ouroboros glory, sucks. It was around 300 BC when Euclid demonstrated via proof by contradiction (*reductio ad absurdum*) that, as there exist endlessly many numbers, there exist endlessly many prime numbers. Less than a century later, Archimedes toiled over *The Sand Reckoner* with the goal of tallying the quantity of spheroidal grains that could fit into the whole entire universe, rather than confront the obvious discomfiting answer. To be sure, infinity offers a dark and wintry vista. Mathematicians suit up in number before attempting the expedition. Searching not for life, but for its exalted and tidied-up proxy: pattern.

44

45

46

47

If: Dreaming is counting minus recitation.
And (according to the cofounder of calculus): *Music is the pleasure the human mind experiences from counting without being aware it is counting.*[2]
Which is to say: *Music is a secret and unconscious mathematical problem of the soul.*[3]
Then: Dreaming is the score of problem solving.

48

49

50

51

52
53

On a not abnormal morning, the profiles of mountain ranges have assembled themselves on the dream distilleries of my children's pillows. Boy divided by sleep equals dreams, remainder: halite. I imagine the kids are athletes from secret worlds when I see those zigzagging watermarks—heavy weights lighten up in order to compete in the dream division of children (when, goodness knows, they should be resting).

Sweat is the price and prize of teeth-clenching adventures. Water molecules lift off on the wings of nightmares, but the body's salt stays behind. In the morning, the mineral evidence crosscuts the comic relief motifs of my babies' pillows.

Here at last is a physical proxy for their nocturnal descents, a range for an intrepid parent to rappel, count down, measure against. How many, would you say, parts per thousand pure animal fear or human anguish is this crust?

Do the subconscious scuffles revive the ancient ionic species? Does their heat drive the salt like periodic cicadas up to an air-skimmed surface? For what do the elements hunger when they beadily swell and roll from the pores of that young skin? Little sodium. Little chloride. It isn't food that urges them. Not sex. Do they home toward the Archean sea from which life first culled them? Are they pissed about the four billion years of intervening incarnations and extinctions? Do they miss that old brine like a boy does his mother when left alone to best his own cliff-side demons?

Is this why I love the craggy outlines when I find them—the atoms clinging to one another in a fragrant, chalky embrace? Because so little escapes the weave of a dreamer's pillow?

REM VE ROAD
SALT NOW

54
55
56
57

58
59

Primes, it is often said, are the atoms of mathematics. They are the carbon, hydrogen, oxygen, ad infinitum (here the metaphor falls apart—there are currently only 118 known chemical elements) of math's fertile planet. The rest of the numbers, the numbers in between the primes (composites, they are called), are the organic compounds—the sugars, proteins, peptides, etc. that combining primes makes.

The Fundamental Theorem of Arithmetic states that each and every positive number greater than one can be produced by multiplying a unique set of prime numbers. (One is untouchable.) Like snowflakes or DNA, no two are the same.

But how to complete the syllogism? If primes are atoms, from what stellar plasma did Two and Three, the first elemental numbers, condense? (One is like the entity whose fingers snapped the prime numbers into being; it is divisible by itself only—a reflection looking at its reflection looking at its reflection. . . .)

And by whose rules do the primes play?

Recent research is interdisciplinary; quantum physicists have discovered that the push-pull of prime numbers applies to the energy levels of atomic nuclei. But in order for that rhyme to be audible, the primes had to be translated into the mathematical language of music. The physics of a plucked string begins a lovely story that takes place in a hummocky terrain of imaginary numbers. (The story culminates in what is decidedly the biggest unsolved math problem ever. It ends with a one-million-dollar bounty from the Clay Mathematics Institute.)

60

61

The Flaming Lips' "Yoshimi Battles the Pink Robots, Part 1" is playing on our local public radio station. The volume has to be way up in order for me to hear over the barely effectual blast of the eyeball-desiccating defroster. I don't really mind if I can't hear, so long as I can at least feel it. Sometimes when I am alone and the speakers aren't cutting it, I drum my sternum pretty hard to the music.

Touch and sound make a decent swap only at blistering

decibels. Even though I could easily reach behind me and grab a small or even smaller booted ankle, I wouldn't have a clue without looking if one of their owners was speaking to me. When I was the size my kids are currently, I loved riding unheard in the backseat, but I worry that they feel bereft behind that taxi-like sonic barrier.

For me, radio stations were colorful buoys a-bob a hostile sea of gray static. Alone in the backseat of my mother's Pinto, I clung on and listened, pleased at the chance to hum along without anyone noticing.

The thing about songs is that some are prehensile. Like them or not, they grip you back. Some are harder to shake than others. (Many times I was called to pry the *shongololo's* feet from an encircled wrist or tickled pit.)

Synesthetes are people for whom imagined and actual sensations are indivisible. Dehaene writes that many more synesthetes ascribe colors than sound to numbers. Most who see numbers as colored report that either zero and one, or eight and nine, manifest as black and white respectively.

For my money, zero is white. As white as the absence of subtractive color (the light-absorbing kind), the spars that interlock the burred snow, and the light sum of every wavelength (shining through the quantity the figure stands for, beacon bright).

Zero is all as well as naught. Ellipse and the opposite of ellipsis. Zero is a placeholder, our youngest digit, the crowning (says Dehaene) development in the evolution of written numbers. Zero is a link in the charm bracelet that concatenates quantity from a set of digits that has one or more nil orders.

Zero is the good cop to One's straight and narrow, the huggier half of the two Boolean operators.

(When I was a kindergartner, a trio from MIT made public an algorithm that is now the key to encrypting credit card information for online transactions. The success of this method hinges on the unique properties of prime numbers: the relative ease of generating humongous primes, and the extreme difficulty of factoring humongous nonprimes into their prime constituents. It's like pulling a shade of gray from the sidewalk and exactly matching it with a drop-by-drop blend of primary colors.)

At our urban, curbside rate of exchange, O is as good as zero is as good as nothing. There is a tautological arrangement. Still, I know where the gas station's missing glyph got off to—I can see it in my rearview as I steer us toward the nearest best sledding hill: an errant half clings purplish to each of my son's lower lids. Here are two parts of a hole bruised and cracked open, parenthetical arcs paired with the nictitating creases of his lovely oiled upper lids. (These shutters rank second among the human body's thinnest skins; the union of the first thinnests made this—his skin.) They are twin palms cupped around his way of seeing things, hematomas from looking so hard through tallying binoculars. *Don't I have a unique way of life, wouldn't you say, Mom, don't I have a different way of looking at the world through my eyes, aren't I one of a kind?* (He sits suddenly upright in his bed.)

New bone is lain down in microscopic laminations night after arduous night. Little crystals are ground from the deciduous speleothems that line his mouth. Sleep has a gravity we all fall into, but what equal and opposite thing returns us? Whose breath cools the brow and blows the dusty blankets from these sculptures before they rise up, forgetting?

(A lemma is the meaning of a word on its way to becoming sound coded.)

62

63

64

65

66

67

A character who's assigned him- or herself the moniker *Endlessoblivion* has contributed a cool graphic to the Wikipedia page on prime numbers. Though a rectangle that reads from left to right and top to bottom, the plot is neither billboard nor prose poem. Instead this box is packed with pixels, each representing an odd number (two naturally discounted, since it is *the oddest*). The primes are black dots. Composites white. The first dot represents the number one; the final represents the product of the first eight prime numbers minus one.

What's remarkable in this image is the way the pixels

align in soft vertical laminations; light and dark bands alternate with varying thicknesses; a mirror could be placed down the middle as the image seems not uniform yet bilaterally symmetric; taken all together, the stripes look like tire tracks; here road snow is gray and weirdly starchy. At first blush, this pattern by far trumps the accidental coolness of a car-wash solicitation, or any beauty to be wrung from a meditation on what can or can't be divided from us (blink blink blink). But *Endlessoblivion* hasn't decrypted a magical code, only figured out where to crop the chaos. A little harmony sings through and the mind scrabbles to make equivalences.

68

69

70

71

Some argue that, since numbers themselves are a human contrivance, admiration of the primes is just a form of lovesickness for our own elegant if tautological scheme of convenience; add to the infinitude of numbers a crafty array of operations and you have infinitely many ways to make equivalences. Like language in some ways. (*Nightmares are the steampunk machinery whose bang and hum waken what's primordial in us. Nightmares are the winged things on whose backs we are borne into hostile terrains. Watering is the nightmare I had the other night in which I forgot then remembered too late everyone who my forgetting rendered winged and missing, the animals dead already.*) Many others, of course, think that there is some transcendental truth waiting to be revealed in that mysterious suite of smug numbers, each divisible only by itself and the mirrorlike number.

What so fiendishly tickles about the primes is their apparent lack of pattern, the way they seem to crop as weeds among the counting numbers—at random. *The Music of the Primes* author, Marcus du Sautoy, describes the distribution of primes as a "formless ebb and flow" that has confounded mathematicians for over two thousand years.[4] It is tempting to believe that if we could squint infinitely far into the numerical vista or peer at some portion of it through the proper looking glass, an entrancing pattern would emerge from the chilly, star-flecked chaos. Many mathematicians are banking on this, have bet the sum of their lives' work (proof after proof) on this.

Anything less would be, as one of du Sautoy's interviewees put it, evidence of a "malicious god."

On the colloquial use of *random*:

In his essay "The Laughter of Copernicus," Jim Holt claims numbers and laughter are the two most ancestral cultural wonders of the world. By year million, he writes, when the primes have been stripped of their mystery, number and humor will have undergone a wholesale reversal. Our descendants will look upon mathematics (whose MO is redundancy) as parochial and ephemeral, largely irrelevant; while humor (which relies on surprise and incongruity) will be viewed as inexhaustible, timeless, and universal.

These days the word "random" is used to praise as irreverent or disparage as dumb what catches us unaware. My older son has taken to saying it too much for my taste lately (growing up, he is). Depending on its implication, "random" segues to mirthful or smug giggles. Maybe, in year million, when the unknown has been dispatched by pointillistic plots and unassailable patterns, our humanoid descendents (if they exist) will wax nostalgic for the good old days of the prime number riddle. Maybe our heat-adapted progeny will be jonesing for a few pleasant surprises.

In his look into the future, Holt takes a glance back over his shoulder to describe the going theory on humor; evolutionary biologists believe laughter arose in our primate ancestors as a way to communicate a threat passed, to dispel the attending panic. A contagious way of saying, "False alarm," or "At your ease, Monkey," "Go on back to bed now."

Last night I dreamt of a winter so warm that more than just the nutty teenagers went about in their shirtsleeves. Snowier winters are one of the counterintuitive results of global warming (more heat means more water in the atmosphere). In our city, winter is less than halfway over and already we've received several inches more than our annual average (fifty-six or so total). Dehaene says we need to see something in order for it to make real *sense*. That's why none of us really gets numbers once they dip below zero.

Zero is white like snow to me, accumulating by subtraction, heaping up to the heftiest, muffling nothing. But One. One is an arc, a trajectory, the ink that lines it, a slice through a plane. It is identity and what stretches between the unknowable ends of a journey. One is first and final, the font for eschatologists counting down to the very last, hachure by hachure, vertical by slant: *shongololo* black.

In the terrarium, the creature was bent at her head end, hooked like what pulls the joker off his stage—death a forced exit, legs the last to go. Legs. Now she is dead, we can finally count them.

72

73

Random (r): prime..

Random prime (r'): a *treading* bird is a male bird fucking..............

74

75

76

77

78

79

Dear son,

What can be counted is finite.

Because you can't tally something doesn't mean it goes on forever.

Please look up to read the skywriting. I hired this airplane. I got a dirigible to fly a banner. I hope you don't mind, but it cost extra to have the letters face backwards. I skimped a little and I'm sorry. Look up into that place that some call heaven.

DAED SI TEP ROUY DNA UOY EVOL I

80

81

82

83

Modus tollendo tollens, the way that denies by denying.

No knowledge of death, therefore no sadness.

Like the letter hanger, my son is on a fulcrum.

But my kid won't feel torque until he's a few hours further out on this lever of knowing. That's when he'll reel back to the day he brought the creature home with him, a gift for his sixth birthday. He'll recall how her body skidded and clanked inside the washed-out tub from the scoop-your-own olive bar, her fear leaking muskily through the duly perforated lid. He'll remember how he felt nervous riding alone with her in his lap in the backseat of the car. And what he determined right away to name her. He'll remember waiting for her to unfurl in the center of the circular alphabet rug the day he shared her with his kindergarten class and how—when after a long, long wait she finally did—the teacher backed up and the children all screamed. He'll remember how slowly she began making her way toward the outside of their elbow-by-knee abecedarian ring. How some kids exclaimed over the detached legs or strands of poop they imagined in the pieces of sphagnum that floofed from her undercarriage as she went. The nervous laughter that attended.

I'll remember how automatic were the movements that guided inky hands to cover loose-toothed mouths. Like the *shongololo* might make herself at home in one of those craggy caves. Like she might sprout segmented legs along the rims of one of those pink carpets (their fear-tacky tongues). Like legs could animate the whole grody store of nasty things they ever wanted to say after learning how not to. Like she might rout their sinuses with that scared acrid smell, shit her perfectly spheroidal pellets in their throats and their ears.

Modus. That is the name he gave her. The measure and the manner.

How does one measure the slow death of something hostage and not heartily enough loved? The good, on-gripping kind of pet. Prehensile and prong footed. No pink-tongued turtle. No tongue-less fish.

The creature's exoskeleton, her test (as in *shell*, or refractory crucible, that burning nocturnal light) will a longer time than her insides keep.

On the day the *shongololo* dies, I slam the car's hatch down, leaving the heat inside to invisibly dwindle. Then our sleds clatter plastic over the curb.

84
85
86
87
88
89

How could we have been so wrong about something as dear and empirically available to us as our own tongues? Why, more than three hundred years after the invention of modern calculus and the earliest observance of retinal rods and cones, were we still favoring the four-taste map of the tongue? The theory that sour, salty, bitter, and sweet are detected by distinct, nonoverlapping provinces of buds was debunked when I was one. Still I grew up believing that ice cream was most delicious if held like an elusive word (a lemma prolonged) on the tip of my tongue (green on The Gamut). Of course we taste all flavors on all surfaces at once.

Imagine the brain is a billboard full to the edges with back-lit characters. Changing its message requires dropping and adding some letters. Maybe becoming literate and number savvy means new imperatives replace old, but surely some of the same letters are used. That we allocate left-right space to our mental number lines is good testimony to the indivisibility of acquired knowledge and the senses. Dehaene suggests that people with grapheme versions of synesthesia, those for whom numbers and letters appear colored or as fixed locations in space, may have their preschool neurons and their kindergarten neurons uniquely intertwined; the tools they learned for the touted trio of Rs have become hybridized with the tools they use to navigate—their feel for color, space, and shape.

90
91
92
93
94
95
96
97

Every winter kids from the adjacent middle school sculpt little moguls into one side of the sledding hill. A germ of a ripple is all it takes for the wave to begin taking shape. Even the yellow lines that divide the streets this time of year develop a sinusoidal slink. What textural harmonics even our potholes make. The inanimate propagate in sound waves.

98
99
100
101

In this way are some bright children infected with the cicada song of prime numbers.

Take the young Carl Friedrich, year 1792. Instead of sleeping, the myopic boy is up tabulating numbers in his secret diary. His father forbids using the lamp oil at this hour, so Carl burns the candle he fashioned from a reamed-out turnip, wad of cotton, and fat lovingly donated from his mother's larder. Although the odor is accidental and

73

dinnery, he smells in it the embers of his wooden spinning wheel—the one he used to coax linen from flax up until his father conceded the boy was a genius, assumed (wrongly) that early death would be the cost to his son of mathematical brilliance, and torched the dizzying disc. There is a harmony in the chaos that, before Gauss, everyone else missed.

Scientists believe that thirteen- and seventeen-year cicadas cycle with such strange periodicity because rising from the ground after sucking tree roots for a prime count of years makes it statistically less likely that their emergence will coincide with that of a coevolving predator fungus. Periodic cicadas exploit the indivisibility of primes as a survival strategy.

Gauss's predecessors were like fungal hackers trying to divine equations that would predict when, like a lawless insect, a random prime would surface. Gauss looked instead at how populations change over time; he studied how the primes were metered along the number line.

Plotting the counting numbers on the x axis and the corresponding count of prime numbers on the y gives what is known as the Staircase of the Primes. Climbing up and to the right, treads grow wider and wider (except in the case of the previously described twin primes). Risers always go up by the count of one prime number.

The teenaged Gauss figured out that you can estimate the tally of primes up to a given number (N) by dividing N by its natural logarithm. When graphed, this equation makes a sledding hill of the prime's staircase. The curve is easily skimmed—the ride far-flinging but too fast to hit its target. Gauss's formula overestimates the number of primes, especially at the smaller numbers.

102

103

The first three odd primes are the three primary colors—indivisible blue (3), red (5), and yellow (7).

Blue is the number of us in the car most days as well as my age when my big sister went off to kindergarten and came back bogarting the skills to read. Blue is the letter *a* for the long *a* sound in my own name and the quality of my eyes that I was given to believe somehow defined me (back when *Karen* was the biggest word I could read).

Thirteen and thirty-one and 103 and 131 are all brighter or dingier shades of periwinkle.

Twenty-five (5^2) is crimson.

Composite numbers are secondary colors.

Six is orange, but I don't think much about it except when it combines with the other colors.

Four is green for the long *e* it shares with my sister's good Irish name, the name's two different *e* pronunciations (2^2=4), the shade of her eyes, the way you envy a sibling, the date of her birth, the fourteenth.

Fourteen is avocado flesh and the lit-from-within lakes where we swam late in summer.

Forty-five is a pimento-stuffed olive.

Eight is maroon.

Eighteen is *shongololo*, her iodide secretions, the bitter back of the tongue.

Nine is purple.

Sixty-three is the city snow at night: the orange of a sodium street lamp sidling up to the blue shadow it cast.

Sixty-seven is the inside of a mango.

Sixty-nine is a bird-of-paradise flower—orange the plumes, purple the beak.

One is black. Zero, white. Gray, eleven.

Two is indeed *the oddest*.

For the dyad of kindred spirits, or the writer with her trusted reader: Two is translucence.

Colors are imaginary friends who hold our eyes, not hands.

We name them (they are *colors*), exchange feelings with them (you are sad and I am *blue*), and believe in them so needily we forget that color is our own contrivance.

The sole property, the force and form of color—its wavelength—is always in flux. At the hind end of sight, our brains perform an instantaneous algorithm, adjusting the reflectance our eyes perceive for ambient luminosity, and tricking us into falsely assuming color constancy. Without this calculation, the palettes of our world would swim. Colors would waver like they do in the eyes of cameras.

It would be fun if, just for a while, color was the kind of belief you could spurn. More likely, though, this vision would descend like a guilty conscience on you (a pet can die from neglect, if she is unfed or her heater comes unplugged or her terrarium gets too dry or the opposite— moldy), like looking panic stricken in the mirror and seeing not your own face, but a schizoid dot-to-dot of features. Simultanagnosia is the medical word for missing the forest for the trees, for having to labor to count to three.

I'm no synesthete; numbers don't actually look colored to me when I see them on a page. I'm just associative (a quality that caps my ability to do math). More, I'm a cartographer with a secondhand sense of space (learned, not inborn) and a physiological addiction to texture. My optometrist tells me that I have no binocular depth perception (pursuant to a kindergarten fever). My eyes run relays instead of working in tandem. While those with stereovision use subconscious trigonometry to triangulate distances, we stereoblind rely on size, converging lines, and texture. One eye searches exhaustively while the other counts the steps.

Whatever. All I know is that I hanker for new ground, my feet are tireless, I'll climb high to perch on a panoramic vista even if what I see (the big deal) is less a sucking expanse and more a paint-by-numbers canvas. The maps I make . . .

(A lemma is the canonical version of a word. Straight up, dictionary style. No conjugation. [THE] [MAP] [I] [MAKE] [BE])

104

105

106

107

. . . are mosaics of blind spots with shamefully fudged boundaries, nothing spared, however, on the colored squares of their legends.

The autumn I turned four and matriculated at Wee Wisdom preschool, Kenneth Appel and Wolfgang Haken published their definitive proof of the Four-Color Theorem. For the full duration of a century and a quarter prior to that, stain-fingered mathematicians toiled over models they hoped would either validate or debunk the proposal that four shades are all that are necessary to color a map such that no two provinces that share a boundary also share a color.

Appel and Haken's proof raised hackles in the mathematical community because of its apparent sidestepping inelegance. The Four-Color Theorem is not hand checkable; the pair made then-innovative use of a computer to churn through their mind-numbing heaps of maps and, in so doing, lifted the curtain on experimental mathematics, a discipline that seeks to codify and reveal patterns that are too far beyond the cognitive vista of technology-free humans to see. Still, there are those who don't truck with the interpretive dance of machines. They argue that a proof is not a proof unless it can be verified, top to bottom, by a human being. Plenty continue to stalk the Four-Color Theorem within the quaint, candle-lit rubric of algebra. In the end, both methods seem just fine to me.

Here I offer an equation in which letters replace sounds whose combinations convey ideas more graspable than an infinitude of shapes and numbers: There is something tender (if not warm) in how we build staircases from formulas and then notch our way limbo style beneath the curve of our own enlightenment, ascending, we hope, toward some overarching revelation or searing truth, toward proof. Treads are the lemmas the risers agree on. We inch our way up by steps of consensus, not leaps of faith. The fallacious notion of equivalence is the greenest, the first and most necessary one we ever take.

Starting out in one of the lower grades I tried an experiment to help make the kidscape of a new school year more navigable to me. I began by listing the names of my classmates on the left-hand margin of a sheet of graph paper. Every afternoon when I got home from the bus, I took out my crayons and went down the roster row by row, choosing some color or scheme of colors that I felt best evoked my interaction with that kid for the day, and then shading in a subjective number of blocks to the right of his or her name. The x axis represented both a time line and, as in a bar chart, my logarithmic depth of feeling.

At some unknowable point, I grew more concerned with the 2-D mosaic I was creating than the throughgoing relationships I had intended to contour. A case of ontology recapitulating phylogeny: The cartographer in me ceded to the mathematician. Looking at my plot, I saw cumulonimbi threatening a skyline of weirdly windowed scrapers. In the end, it was the way my graph had begun resembling a poorly played game of Tetris—the white rectangles for my apathy or some kid's absence, the black squares glaring like fire damage on the days when some punk called me a name or kicked me in the shins—that led me to abandon my quotidian coloring. It was too hard to know where to begin filling in squares once a hole had been rent. Too ugly how my sap and sentiment had led me away from the economy of the Four-Color Theorem (which, needless to say, I didn't know about then). What I had wanted was a board game to play, a turn to take, to win.

Back in the 1800s, while topologists were exhausting themselves with the Four-Color Theorem, psychologists were charting the following law by ounce and by Paris line and by lumen: The increments by which we register sensation are exponential, not linear. Wrote nineteenth-century psychologist E. H. Weber of the senses: "When noting a difference between things that have been compared, we do not perceive the difference between the things, but the ratio of the difference to their magnitude."[5] Weber's Law can be modeled mathematically with a fulcrum and a balance beam. It explains why turning up the radio a notch is more noticeable when the volume starts out low than when "Yoshimi Battles the Pink Robots, Part 1" is blaring to begin with. Why adding one to a small number affects a greater sense of change than does adding a tick to a point already vanished in the distance. Why Gauss's logarithmic equation overestimates the count of primes most where numbers are smallest.

"You have no idea how much poetry there is," wrote Gauss, "in a table of logarithms."[6] For him, a prehensile song singing. For us all, a surprisingly primal song singing. The going theory is that the mental number line on which we plot quantity (the spear projecting from both sides of our heads) starts out logarithmic. As youngsters, we accord lots of space to small, graspable numbers, spreading them wide apart. Moving rightward into bigger quantities, however, the numbers get compressed; we squeeze the digits closer and closer together. Dehaene says that clumping the big ones allows us to be frugal with the actual space they take in our brains. (Not only do we map amounts in the substanceless realm of our mental number lines, but we also carry a constellation of numbers in the neuronal labyrinth of our brains; number-specific neurons fire whenever we hear that count of beats, see that count of footprints. Read that number. Hear it pronounced. An x-y-z coordinate there. E-mail and street address, both.) In Americans, the crinkles in our logarithmic lines begin to flatten between ages three and eight. In exchange for a broadened concept of what-is-big, they get ironed. Like classmates navigating the hallway under their teacher's watchful eye, the notches arrange themselves with equidistance in a single-file line.

And then there are imaginary numbers, numbers i and $-i$. These are the square roots of negative real numbers. (Multiply i and $-i$, and you get -1.) Imaginary numbers had been on the radar of mathematicians for almost two millennia before Gauss got the idea to give them their own line perpendicular to the real number line.

If the mental/real number line projects sideways through the temples, the imaginary number line pokes fore and aft through forehead and crown. Your number sense resides toward the top of your head in your brain's parietal sulcus. Close by is the sheaf of body maps that allow you to do things like scratch an itch in total darkness. Here also is your intuition for reading—without text, only body language—the intent of others when they're reaching for something. The imaginary number line skewers you there. Positive imaginary numbers stretch like the future in front. Negative imaginary numbers dwindle like the past behind.

It wasn't until Gauss's pupil Bernhard Riemann came along that pictorial descriptions of real or imaginary mathematics were accepted. Equations were all. As Descartes put it: "Sense perceptions are sense deceptions."[7] Undaunted, Riemann stepped through the looking glass (as du Sautoy puts it) of imaginary numbers into a highly textured terrain, accidentally stumbling there upon the secret harmony of prime numbers.

(Lemmas are what a mathematical proof is made of.)

108

109

The winter after I turned thirty-one the skin on my belly split into silvery zigzagged seams (stairways to fundus), and the Four-Color Theorem was definitively proven a second time, this time by a Microsoft employee and his interactive theorem assistant software, Coq (resulting in an addendum to the software that was poetically named Ssreflect, for Small Scale Reflection). Now my youngest son is learning the symbols that mean add, take away, and equal to. His teacher says he is a whiz with numbers, but he doesn't want to talk about that. Instead he complains that a boy he calls The Interrupter repeatedly tests the colors of his crayons against their wrappers by making chicken scratches on his (and not The Interrupter's) papers.

Ways in which an essay is unlike the paper it is colored on:

Like a map with anchored corners, euclidean space is flat. It applies to small-scale geometry and the world prior to Aristotle.

In the nineteenth century, Riemann rewrote Euclid's axioms to describe the geometry of spherical surfaces. On Earth, the shortest distance between two points is a great circle, not a straight line. The fifth axiom of elliptical geometry states that, given a line and a point not on it, there is either more than one line through a point that is parallel to the preexisting line, or no lines at all.

This essay takes place on the half dome of the human brain. Given the labyrinth of wrinkles there, it seems more likely that there are infinitely many parallel lines than none at all. This Brobdingnagian eye has mouth, will (see it or not) speak.

110
111
112
113

What matters is not the order in which the eye selects items to be counted, but the order in which the number words are spoken. The two processes go on in tandem, but the mouth's is inflexible while the eye's may be random.

114
115
116
117
118
119
120
121
122

123
124
125
126
127

What the child learning to count discovers is how, as if by magic, the final word spoken is also the amount in his collection.

Time takes a revelation and makes it sensible.

This moment like Venus pokes a bright finger through the dark dome of what I recall of my early life: riding alone in the backseat of my mother's car with no one talking; the music on; my mom in her depressed, nearly divorced stage, driving; beside her, my sister with her dowser's-wand sensibility divining for something quenchable below the surface of our mom's skin. The day that stands out, that glows with the combined light of all my early memories, we were on our way to the grocery. When the car turned off into the parking lot a little faster than normal, I slid on the seat, or rather it slid under me, and I felt the effect of my momentous body wanting—like all things aloft—to stay its course. I felt it refusing the car's veer, the steering wheel's arc, my mother's will. And I thought something like *This is what it is to be alive.* More, it hardened in me. What had swum and darted like the retinal kite tails one chases when staring up into a sky so overwhelmingly full of nothing, all of a sudden assembled itself into something I could see head-on. It swelled and cured into a terrible awareness the same approximate shape and heft of me. It felt hollow like missing lunch and lonely like too much time spent sky gazing. It made me feel both bold and milquetoasty. It was like: *I am some dumb thoughts stuck in a body and so are my sister and mother and even the woman in the Piggly Wiggly with the beehive hairdo whom none of us can yet see, but whom we can all three, if and whenever we want to, picture sitting and tallying with rubber thimbles on the neat numerals of her paper-coughing register. Even though the invisible molecules of our hand sweat will salt the same coins, the same shrink-wrapped head of lettuce, the same brown paper-cut bag, itemized receipt, we will none of us truly intersect one another. The cashier doesn't feel us coming any more than she will feel the loss of us when we are gone. We are privileged with prescience and worthlessness, all of us at the same time ignorant and unique and hostage to our cells and in these pleasant ways both immiscible and identical to one another.* Like that, only wordless. It was an understanding of the ego, not the heart or the noggin, though certainly its ripples fanned those other margins. I am divisible from the world, but the world is indivisible from me. The self is total and cannot be cleaved. We are a colony of monads forging connections. Perhaps then began my obsession with linkage. Perhaps then was born my obsession with translating and color coding things. I used to imagine the pencil tip that scribbled in the shadows of the Piggly Wiggly woman's pincushiony scalp whenever she scratched her itch. No mother or anthropologist would ever bend to read that asemic writing, but I dearly longed to. The cash register expectorated blue numbers whose glyphs spelled things like *The Real World* and *When You're Older* and *Just Us Three* and *Your Missing Father*. There was the question of who was responsible for the parting. Nodding meant you accepted what was hard because what was best was also sensible. Nodding is also dancing. We wave our hands and point our fingers, clearing the fog that otherwise prevents us from seeing past our own breath on the windows. Inside, thoughts careen around or scrabble or else just bump halfhearted against the container. Like the animals my sister and I found in our garden and tried to make into our pets. Unexpressed and inexpressible. For me there was my body staying its course as the car turned a little too quickly down the dropped drive and into the supermarket parking lot—lifting off in private and then falling back. While I was airborne, the world was tared to scale the new weight of me. A bushel with her basket subtracted. I had been summed for the first time with the algorithm of the ego, a self plus self-awareness, me and the *evanescent increment*, the *ghost of departed quantities*.[8] It felt not like these words at all, but like a One, followed by a Zero, then a One again. A foot lifted and set back down a single pace ahead.

128

129

130

131

Here is the peculiar crunch-squeak under boot. Here is that coldest craggy feeling in the nose—stalactites guarding the cavernous entries to the sinuses. Here is a chance to suss the different conductivities of what's sheltered by the skin—fat, muscle, and cartilage hold on to warmth more or less greedily. Nose ass thighs toes ears sing the cold at different frequencies. To the eyes, the cold is all brightness; it brings tears to bead with greater viscosity. Here is the rarefied air—even the atoms are cinched down on themselves, leaving more space in between, giving the birds to wing weirdly though the day is nearly windless.

Here is the mineral world I love. For each oxygen, two little hydrogens—the trio shuttlecock shaped. An infinity of these frozen kaleidoscopic under gorgon's cold gaze. A honeycomb of hexagons perpetrated fractallike into flakes. An ecstasy of these. Ten million million million molecules of water per crystal. On our way down, the powder will dust our faces like it was sanding sugar and we were unfrosted cakes. At the bottom we'll blink it off our coated lashes, watch how fast the little stars sink into the heat of each other's cheeks and—blink—dilute the salt of our skin. Artificial tears, not tears of artifice. On the climb back up our socks will crouch in the damp place that is missed on all our footprints; snow will somehow sift in, wet our ankles. How deep is this? A single flake is ten quintillion.

How do you measure the slow death of something hostage and not heartily enough loved? Something whose presence was assumed more often than seen. Three hundred twenty lined-up flecks of ground pepper? One seventh of a smoot? In what units do you convey the meandering length and slink of so many articulated black checkers? A string of game pieces conveyed on a rippling broom of countless pricking feet. The brightest red underneath (five, the highest hand of hearts or diamonds, what's handed you overheated or straight-up freezing—the royal flush). Her red shone like accordion folds when, like a black river, she twisted.

Modus. The measure and the manner. The animal was the first to colonize land, the earliest terrestrial oxygen breather. There were rows of pinprick spiracles in her hull I was careful to avoid when misting, lest I suffocate her. She was a living fossil, dirt maker, detritus feeder. Given *shongololo*s have been around since the Silurian, and following a simple calculation (that follows the Copernican, or Mediocrity Principle, which states there are no unique observers—what's been around a long while will last a long while longer), her kind is ninety-five percent likely to enjoy somewhere between ten million and seventeen billion more years on our planet. Contrast this with the same algorithm's output for *h. sapiens*: between five thousand years and 7.8 million (7.8 million is also the number of digits in the largest prime number so far calculated by computer).

She had a pair of compound eyes and two beaded antennae that slowly and dully tested. We eagerly awaited a molting (a new *king-me*, quattro of legs, and set of eye divots for every exoskeleton!), but she must have been an adult when we brought her home in the olive tub, because she never did. Legs. The kids in his class wanted to know if there were really a thousand. Had she shed that skin, we would have had a chance while she was still alive to count them. Two, four, six, ten . . . twenty . . . one hundred and logarithmically many. Because when she was alive, they were always waving.

A vibrating violin string produces an oscillation. Like a snowflake whose hexagonal symmetry is perpetrated from its first hydrogen bonds to the six-pinnacled thing that melts on your face, the violin's sound is a composite of different-sized sine waves. What you hold in your ears is the combination of the fundamental frequency plus its countless smaller overtones. Smaller waves ride larger waves ride larger waves . . . which ride the fundamental. When the waves are integer multiples of each other, the sound is exquisitely pleasing. Added together graphically, the sine waves amount to a set of zigzagging staircases. A series of escalators ascending to nothing. In math terms, this is the harmonic series, the sum of which is infinity.

From a human perspective, how does infinity differ from ten quintillion or the Silurian? Surely I am ten quintillion of something; the germ of my wavy DNA began taking shape long before the Silurian, my body is part of what sums to infinity. But these are scales I can only strain to visit in my imagination. Reimann, though. Reimann fed real and imaginary numbers into an equation derived from the harmonic series. What he got back was a topographically mapped song; its east-west axis was both the real number line and loudness; its north-south axis was both the imaginary number line and pitch. What Reimann crossed into was a landscape of sound.

How long, how far, how fast? Before us shape and space cede to reflectance. There are no objects from which to triangulate distance. Only the blind of white and our three shadows thrown down small and the same color blue. It might be halite or the bleached skeletons of wave-sieved sea creatures beneath us. Earth's future fossils, a no-man's land: Sleds will skim it, but our feet sink in. It might be White Sands where black beetles tap gypsum crystals; beetle feet reckon like postapocalyptic Archimedeses; their landslide footprints fill up the arthropod hourglasses. A college-aged version of me log-rolled with her geology- and math-geek homeys down these sunset-colored dunes—bitter-tasting shrooms in all of our sensory-piqued systems. Or no, look. Blind lemurs climb trees one handed in order to sit and lick the *shongololo*'s striped narcotic coil. On the ground, jonesing lemurs turn stones over to find one more terror-stricken *shongololo*.

In the terrarium, Modus's chassis was uncharacteristically straight, only bent at her head end for a change. She was hooked like the tool that hangs the gas station's letters—death a blank slate, legs the last to go. Maybe she died treading. No muffled desperate crying out for life, thank God. On the hill's descent, our buoyant stomachs lag behind the rest of us. Arms, legs, hands, feet—ripple top to bottom. Legs—now she is dead we can finally count them. Now we scream out laughter. The way we come down. *At your ease, Monkey.* A flurry of cut snow settling.

Tracks and trails and the principle of crosscutting relationships: That which cuts through is more recent. Here lines are proxies for countless sled frolics.

Reimann steps through his looking glass and lands at his graph's origin. He stands facing north. Panning left to right, he sees a high unnavigable plateau vertiginously ascending, then a finger poking infinitely high from the low ground just before him, and then an undular terrain smoothing like a pleated skirt to a flat plain in the east. He sets out to explore the ridges and valleys. They are east-west trending. Climbing and descending, he discovers something novel about them. Between peaks are isolated low points corresponding to sea level.

He calls these "the zeros."

As far as Reimann can see, the zeros line up along real number ½. He understands that these divots are not artifacts; in fact, they order the land forms that surround them. In terms of sonics, these are musical notes. The farther north he goes, the faster they oscillate, the higher they are in pitch. But the zeros fall on a *line*. That means that every note is playing at precisely the same volume. The zeros are harmonics. In a stroke of genius, Reimann realizes that, as notes are to music what primes are to numbers, the zeros correspond to the primes. He knows that a point off the dotted line of zeros (far as he treads, he doesn't find one) would be like one instrument playing too quietly or too loudly in the symphony of numbers. A zero off the line would turn the harmonic hum of his landscape into a white-noise cacophony and, on the opposite side of the looking glass, the primes would fall into a predictable pattern. Harmony on one side is dissonance on the other.

Reimann proposes that all zeros fall on the magic ley line, but does not himself calculate more than three or so. To date, the first ten trillion zeros have been found, as predicted, on "the critical line," R=½: none too close together, none too far apart. But no count of zeros will prove the Reimann Hypothesis. Infinite anything cannot be counted. Neither can infinite nothing. A tautological trick is needed to collect the one-million-dollar bounty. An all-new chain of metaphors.

Reimann's solution adds the overtones to Gauss's sledding hill that are necessary to turn it into the true Staircase of the Primes. If a mathematical proof is a mountain climb, du Sautoy says the Reimann Hypothesis is body-strewn Everest. (Check out his book to learn the count of mathematicians who committed suicide after failing to take its summit.)

One hundred thirty-one is a palindrome (M-O-M) that is also a prime number. At 131 there is a prime number riser. One hundred thirty-two is a good guess for the number of leg pairs on a ten-or-so-inch *shongololo*.

There will be the question of whose fault it is she's dead and whether I believe in souls and if so, how-heartedly and for whose benefit do I, and anyway what does it look like, what does it weigh, where does it lurk below the skin, and how does it exit, and anyway where would it go. Where did hers go and how about you prove it. *We're scientists*, he said to me, *what we believe in are questions and answers.*

I know it is time to call it when I'm tugging the youngest up the hill while he lies sky gazing in the sled, his limbs limp and face crazy red. In herky-jerky steps my oldest and I mar upward, march, mark the untrod snow, thrust our toes in over and over again. Fingers are numb from pulling the weighted strings in our gloves and clumsy crustacean mittens. *Boys, there's something I want to talk to you about before we get home. Boys, there's something. Boys, there's. Boys.* Face muscles lose their feeling. Back home we'll undo our fake exoskeletons, thighs pricking, and die our pet millipede's death in reverse. Legs the first to go. NOW SALT ROAD REM VE.

132

WORKS CONSULTED

Association for Psychological Science, "Out of Mind, Out of Sight: Blinking Eyes Indicate Mind Wandering," *Science Daily*, April 30, 2010, http://www.sciencedaily.com/releases/2010/04/100429153959.htm (accessed January 29, 2011).

British Association for the Advancement of Science. "Reading Process Is Surprisingly Different than Previously Thought, Technology Shows," *Science Daily*, Sept 11, 2007, http://www.sciencedaily.com/releases/2007/09/070910092543.htm (accessed January 29, 2011).

E. H. Weber, *The Sense of Touch* (New York: Academic Press for Experimental Psychology Society, 1978).

George Berkeley, *The Analyst; or, A discourse addressed to an infidel mathematician: Wherein it is examined whether the object, principles, and inferences of the modern analysis are more distinctly conceived, or more evidently deduced, than religious mysteries and points of faith* (London, 1754).

Gottfried Liebniz in Marcus du Sautoy, *The Music of the Primes: Searching to Solve the Greatest Mystery in Mathematics* (New York: Harper Collins, 2003), 77–78.

Guy Waldo Dunnington, *Carl Friedrich Gauss, Titan of Science; a Study of His Life and Work* (New York: Exposition Press, 1955).

Jim Holt, "The Laughter of Copernicus," in *Year Million: Science at the Far Edge of Knowledge*, ed. Damien Broderick (New York: Atlas and Company, 2008).

Marcus du Sautoy, *The Music of the Primes: Searching to Solve the Greatest Mystery in Mathematics* (New York: Harper Collins, 2003).

Marcus du Sautoy, *The Music of the Primes*, bonus DVD (Silver Spring, MD: Athena, 2009).

Stanislas Dehaene, *Number Sense: How the Mind Creates Mathematics* (New York: Oxford University Press, 1997).

University of Melbourne. "Poker Face Busted? Our Eye Position Betrays the Numbers We Have in Mind, New Study," *Science Daily*, March 24, 2010, http://www.sciencedaily.com/releases/2010/03/100323110109.htm (accessed January 29, 2011).

[1]George Berkeley, 59.
[2]Gottfried Liebniz in du Sautoy, 77–78.
[3]Gottfried Liebniz, source unknown.
[4]Marcus du Sautoy, 310.
[5]E. H. Weber, 131.
[6]Carl Gauss in du Sautoy, 51.
[7]René Descartes in du Sautoy, 70.
[8]George Berkeley, 59.

Scott & Ben
Robert Clark

I FIRST READ *The Great Gatsby* when I was a sophomore in high school in English class, the only course at St. Paul Academy that interested me. The school advertised itself as a country day school, which, located in the center of our city, it scarcely seemed to me to be, but more chiefly it claimed to be a college preparatory school, which it certainly was. Its sole mission was to ship its graduates off to the Ivy League or at least eastern colleges. As early as the fourth grade I was warned that if I didn't start studying harder then and there, I wouldn't get accepted eight years later at "a good school" and this, I was given to understand, would be a kind of ultimate and irrevocable failure.

My father, Thomas Clark, had attended St. Paul Academy and so had my grandfather, Benjamin Griggs, and so, I vaguely knew, had F. Scott Fitzgerald. The school made little of this fact when it made anything of it at all. It was dimly known that Fitzgerald had stayed until 1912, his own sophomore year, when he went east to be "prepped" at a boarding school. St. Paul Academy at that time lacked the luster to guarantee admission at, say, Princeton, where Fitzgerald

later matriculated. (My grandfather, a grade below him, followed the same path east and finished up at Yale.)

It was known that while at St. Paul Academy, Fitzgerald had contributed some journeyman fiction and drama pieces to the school paper, called *Now and Then*. I can't recall any of these ever having been displayed, read, or their existence in any way noted. In fact, the only mention of Fitzgerald I can remember being made at our school was the quotation from a 1910 issue of *Now and Then* that said, "If anybody can poison Scotty or stop his mouth in some way, the school at large and myself will be obliged." The remark was at Fitzgerald's expense, implying that the school had wanted to bring "Scotty" down a peg and that now in 1967, by repeating it, it still did. That, and the silence otherwise accorded his one-time presence there, suggested that as far as St. Paul Academy was concerned, Fitzgerald was a failure, even if he had gotten into Princeton.

It seemed, then, that the book we read in English class might have been written by someone else entirely, with no relation to this largely unnoted alumnus of our school. Rather, it fell into the larger realm of literature, of Shakespeare and Yeats, and of Hemingway's *The Old Man and the Sea* and Hersey's *Hiroshima*, which we also read that year. I can't say that these others didn't make an impression, but I think Fitzgerald ultimately touched us more deeply, or at least me, and I passed my time at St. Paul Academy in a state of aching boredom and resentment.

Maybe the teacher understood that *Gatsby* was a young person's book, if only in the way it so embodied an adolescent vision of the life the young might hope to have after high school and college: that yearning for wealth, success, and glamour alloyed to a stunningly innocent faith in the goodness of beauty and of the beauty and goodness of the opposite sex. And for me and my schoolmates its power was doubled by also being a story of midwesterners trying their luck in the East, the log of a voyage out from and back to St. Paul, even if in our reading of *Gatsby* we evaded the question of whether returning home was a kind of defeat.

In 1990, although I'd managed to stay away from St. Paul for the better part of twenty years, I came back for a little while. It was the last time I saw my grandfather and I asked him about Fitzgerald. I'd gathered from my mother that he'd actually known him slightly. My grandfather's mind had grown clouded in recent years or at least he'd become a little abstracted, and I was looking for a subject that might engage him.

He and my grandmother were sitting in their bedroom in their St. Paul apartment, she tucked into her twin bed watching a daytime game show on the television, he sitting on a chair next to her. My grandfather had always seemed a reticent, unforthcoming, and even forbidding figure, and I supposed—not without reason—that he saw me as an aimless, self-involved young man of no commendable prospects. He was wearing a bathrobe—of flannel, in a shade of oxblood, or so I want to say. I asked him something like, "Tell me about F. Scott Fitzgerald" and, after a moment, he exhaled and looked up at me. Then he looked back down, as though at his hands resting in his lap, and began to shake his head from side to side in broad arcs. I thought at first this indicated a kind of wistfulness, of recollecting a time that was very long ago when they had all been young and foolish but innocent. I am sure it contained that, but he continued to shake his head, perhaps just a moment longer, and then the gesture took on the character of a deep and widening regret, grief, or even anger. He stopped and looked up at me again and I am sure he said, "What a waste." But I do not really know if he had even opened his mouth, or if I had merely read it in the shaking of his head.

I could see he had nothing more to say about it, and I changed the subject to baseball or, more pointlessly, to whether he would get up to his house on Lake Superior that summer. We both knew, of course, that he would not. He was dead within a year.

Some months later, I reread *The Great Gatsby*, and also read *This Side of Paradise*, *The Beautiful and the Damned*, and *Tender Is the Night* for the first time. This was not my idea, but my wife's. She loved these books, she thought I would love them too, and perhaps she felt they contained something I needed. So I read them. Shortly after that I wrote my own first novel. Then I began to try to answer the question I had put to my grandfather or, perhaps more exactly, to read the forlorn motion he had made in response.

F. Scott Fitzgerald died on December 21, 1940. I don't know if much was made of it in St. Paul or at my grandfather's home. It was Christmastime. My mother was putting in her college application to Vassar, where Fitzgerald's daughter, Scottie, had matriculated a year earlier. Certainly no one was surprised, even if he was scarcely forty-four years old: His death, sooner rather than later, was inevitable. It was not the culmination or apotheosis of anything. In *Tender Is the Night*, he'd written,

> Dick Diver doesn't want to be just one of these clever boys.
> He must be destroyed a little, he must be less intact. And if
> life won't do it for him, it's no substitute to go out and get
> himself a disease or a broken heart or an inferiority complex.

Dick is an alcoholic but he's also a kind of Romantic saint, a martyr. He has to annihilate himself to achieve his great work. Fitzgerald had to do the same thing. The writer doesn't shape his material: It shapes him. He submits to it and is subsumed within it, even unto death.

While composing *Tender Is the Night*, Scott was also reading Oswald Spengler's *The Decline of the West*, which argued that civilizations and their history are not progressive but entropic; they flourish and then fizzle and die out. And since his midtwenties when he was writing *Gatsby*, Fitzgerald had been a connoisseur of old love. He had an uncanny sense of the sentimentality people developed about their historical selves, especially the young self and the pangs of memory that sustain and enlarge it. It's a highly refined sort of self-consciousness, a fashioning of legends about one's own life, as if to say, just then, for that moment, one's life *signified*.

I can't say that my grandfather ever read *Tender Is the Night* or even *The Great Gatsby*. I know his library did contain *This Side of Paradise*, which was written in St. Paul after Fitzgerald's discharge from the military, and *The Beautiful and the Damned*, which was published during Scott's last stay there in 1922.

I discovered this and a little more the summer after my grandfather died. I went to help clear out his house on Lake Superior. Its contents

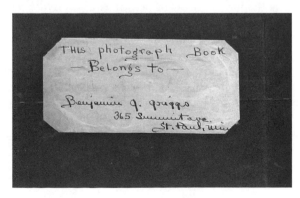

were not of much interest to his other relatives and I came away with a carload of photographs and slides, scrapbooks, and bric-a-brac.

Over the next several years I delved. I studied my grandfather's relics, not so much to understand him as to keep his presence within reach, to prevent it from sinking irretrievably into the past. It seemed to me that somehow the point of my own life was tied to the persistence of his, that without it I would become unmoored. At the same time I was reading Fitzgerald and then one and then another biography of him. I needed Scott too, as a talisman, if not as a mentor or model. You wouldn't want to emulate his life, and as for his art, I had no illusions about my talent. But it seemed to me very important that someone from the same world as mine, right down to the same school and the same neighborhood, could be a writer, and a writer of genius.

Then, in a Fitzgerald biography, I came across my grandfather's name, Ben Griggs. He and Scott Fitzgerald had played together, known each other as boys. They'd gone to dancing classes together, roughhoused in the vacant lot next to the Griggs family home on Summit Avenue, played detective, Indians, and explorers in the alleys and lanes behind it, and admired and played kissing games with the same girls. My grandfather had never mentioned any of this.

Of course, he never spoke of even reading Fitzgerald. And perhaps he didn't need to. He'd lived in the same collegiate milieu Fitzgerald described in *This Side of Paradise* and he was acquainted with the orgiastic consumption of bootleg liquor recorded in *The Beautiful and the Damned*. He was, like most of his generation or at least the swatch of it to which he belonged, an accomplished drinker. That too had been part of the upper-middle-class collegiate portfolio of the "Yale man" he became. So when he won a squash championship, a characteristic display of his athleticism, the trophy he received was an engraved silver cocktail shaker. This was at the apex of Prohibition, when merely to fill the shaker was a violation of federal law. It was among the things I took away from his house and I have it now in my own kitchen. It's dented and the silver plate is mottled with brownish-orange patches like liver spots that no amount of polish will remove. It's seen much use, sloughed off several skins, and now it's retired, under my care, eighty-five years on.

After seeing my grandfather's name in the Fitzgerald biography, I asked my mother more about their connection, and the first thing that came to her mind was related to drinking. She said that when Scott returned with Zelda to live in St. Paul for a year in 1921 and '22, they'd gone for a bobsled ride with my grandfather and grandmother. Zelda was so drunk she'd fallen off the sled, not once but several times, and had pulled others off with her. My grandmother, a formidable debutante from Philadelphia and just then affianced to my grandfather, was not amused by this, and there was not much further contact—so my mother said—between the Fitzgeralds and the Griggses.

To me, this story had the whiff of the apocryphal about it, of well-known facts about the protagonists—in this case, their drinking—embroidered onto an archetypal Minnesota winter scene. But there in the December 1921 entry in Scott's ledger—his month-by-month record of his life—is the phrase "bob rides." That this likely relates to humiliations or untoward incidents during these rides is almost certain, for Scott's ledger tended to highlight not his successes or fond memories but his failures: the embarrassments, broken friendships, and evictions that increasingly characterized his life in those years and which in 1924 and '26 attained such a quantity that Scott was moved to compose a separate "Snub List" of people who had dropped him or given him the cold shoulder.

So it's not unsurprising that my grandparents might have been among this number, however amenable they were to fun and boozing. The rest of St. Paul had done pretty much the same, and so the Fitzgeralds soon left for the East, for New York, Long Island, and Europe, to the denouement of their lives. My grandfather never saw either of them again. The one photograph he possessed of Scott shows him holding forth, gesticulating toward an audience oblivious to him. He seems, as he would put it himself, "a bit tight."

For all that, something came out of that year in St. Paul, or at least was laid to rest. It had been Scott's second homecoming in as many years. The first time, in 1919, he'd come back a relative failure, having left Princeton without graduating, served in the military without seeing action, and suffered the rejection of his first novel. My grandfather, I later learned, set him up with a job at the Griggs wholesale grocery business, but at the last minute Scott turned it down. Instead he shuttered himself in his parents' home and revised his novel once more. It was published a year later as *This Side of Paradise*. And with that, the next time he returned to St. Paul, in 1921, he was a success, even a celebrity, for all the good that did him.

I used to walk by the house where Scott finished that first novel every morning on my way to school. There was a vicious dog in the next block and my paternal grandparents lived just down and across the street in one of the ugliest homes to grace Summit Avenue. Directly across from the Fitzgerald house, from the room where Scott wrote the book that launched his career, there was a vacant lot, and it was here that I got drunk for the first time, on peppermint schnapps, aged sixteen. I am pretty sure that I passed out briefly in the snow that night, and I suppose I might have frozen to death. These things have happened in St. Paul, even to boys like me.

Initially, Scott made a positive impression on his second homecoming and did not overplay the triumphant author. He organized amateur dramatics and produced a satirical newspaper for the University Club in which he, my grandfather, and all their cohort were featured. In one issue, a Griggs relation is described as having been delegated to lead the cotillion but "unfortunately arrived in no condition to lead anything." In another, my grandfather is pictured in a

EVERY PICTURE TELLS A STORY

Miss Betty Griggs, at the left, is so enamored of her Gordon Sports Jacket she just can't help hugging it. Mr. B. G. Griggs is demonstrating how a G. S. J. accentuates the slender boyish figure so fashionable these days. It's not so easy to psychoanalyze Mr. George Smith, our state professional champion—perhaps he's thinking that, armored with a Gordon Jacket he *can't* lose, or now that he has one, that losing or winning is of small importance—who knows! At the right Mrs. Walter Kennedy has just made a 666 yard drive straight down the fairway, due entirely—*almost entirely*—to the fact she is confident she looks her smartest in that Gordon Sports Coat. That golfer hiding behind the tree in the background is so ashamed—his papa wouldn't buy him a G. S. J.—It's a *grand* picture.

mock fashion layout wearing plus fours, slender, leaning insouciantly against a golf club, a cigarette between his fingers, his hair parted down the middle, just like Scott's.

But then followed the sleigh rides, and then he and Zelda moved for the summer to the White Bear Yacht Club in Dellwood. During Scott's childhood, the St. Paul elite kept their summer "cottages" (in truth, quite substantial houses) here, but in 1921, with the advent of the automobile, Dellwood was becoming an upper-crust suburb. By the time I was a boy that transformation was complete. As a teenager, I was invited to a St. Paul Academy party at a large house on the lake. It was that night that I first experienced the inchoate yet clear sensation of being somewhere I didn't belong. There was wealth, of course, and a kind of effortless confidence that seemed to go with it. At the turn of the century my great-grandparents themselves had had a "cottage" here, but in the intervening sixty years the fortunes of my family had subsided to the upper tiers of the middle class.

The kids from Dellwood were nice enough: They condescended to me in the antique, gracious sense of the word. But something in the atmosphere—the breeze off the lake, the quickening stars at dusk—made me talk too much or clam up at inopportune times or say the wrong things. There was a girl, pretty and easily amused, born of and for this place, and she drew me toward her. But before I spoke, before she even looked back at me, I saw and knew that she was meant for other things and persons than me, consecrated to a vocation beyond

93

anything I might attain. Had I the talent, I might have written, "Her body hovered delicately on the last edge of childhood, she was almost eighteen, nearly complete, but the dew was still on her." She might have been out of reach, but I could have made an image of her with such words.

At Dellwood, Scott and Zelda's drinking and rowdiness became more than St. Paul could bear. After repeated complaints and warnings, he and Zelda were told to leave the club. They moved to the Commodore Hotel for six weeks and then they left St. Paul for New York. Scott never went back, although he kept up a correspondence with Elizabeth Ames Jackson, his closest female childhood friend there, a role she also played with my grandfather. They had been in France together at the same time during World War I, she a nurse's aide, Ben an ambulance driver. I was brought up calling her "Aunt Betty."

So Scott had lost St. Paul, perhaps as he needed to or intended to, but what he took away was *The Great Gatsby*, or at least the vital germ of it. It's generally assumed *Gatsby* was based on Scott and Zelda's residences in Westport, Connecticut, before their move to St. Paul, and in Great Neck, Long Island, immediately afterward,

from events and personalities then current in the world of New York bootleggers and stock speculators. But those elements were less the core of the novel than its superstructure. He took its heart—its preoccupations and raison d'être—away with him from White Bear Lake. During his last few weeks in St. Paul, Scott wrote a short story called "Winter Dreams." It's about a working-class boy named Dexter who grows up among the swells who summer at a resort called Black Bear Lake. He works as a caddy and at age fourteen, he encounters a spoiled and pretty rich girl on the cusp of adolescence.

Dexter gives her no further thought and scrimps and saves to attend an eastern college. After graduation he returns to open a successful chain of steam laundries and, at age twenty-three, finds himself back on the golf course where he once caddied, playing a round with the wealthy men whose clubs he used to carry. They don't remember him in that role, but as he walks the course, he has "the sense of being a trespasser" and "found himself glancing at the four caddies who trailed them, trying to catch a gleam or gesture that would remind him of himself, that would lessen the gap that lay between his present and his past."

What he does rediscover is the girl, still lovely and spoiled, now a bored, coquettish twenty-year-old. Over the next two years they have a cat-and-mouse courtship. Finally, just as Dexter is on the verge of marrying another girl, she offers herself. Dexter breaks his engagement, and is, of course, then dropped by the girl. She's not, and never has been, meant for him.

Seven years later, a client brings him news of the beautiful girl: She's living in Detroit, married to a man who drinks too much and abuses her. And, the client adds, she's no longer beautiful.

> Something had been taken from him . . . gingham on the golf-links and the dry sun and the gold color of her neck's soft down. . . . Why, these things were no longer in the world! They had existed and existed no longer. Even the grief he could have borne was left behind in the country of illusion, of youth, of the richness of life, where his winter dreams had flourished.

It's all here, the parts that mattered, the cruel and tender logic of *Gatsby*: "So we beat on, boats against the current, borne back ceaselessly into the past"; the fact that time and youth are not a progress but a regress from adulthood back toward childhood, from the East back to the Midwest, from hope to regret. It's all he needed for the rest of his life and the rest of his work.

*

I spent ten years, as much time as Scott spent writing *Tender Is the Night*, excavating the pasts of my grandfather and of F. Scott Fitzgerald. I don't think it was ever a morbid obsession, but it hovered over everything I did.

I became a Roman Catholic, the religion of Scott's youth, although I am as sure as I can be that that had nothing to do with it. I often wondered why there is so little trace of his religion in his work; why, as far as I could see, the "Catholic element" he had once promised Max Perkins would factor in *Gatsby* was nowhere in evidence in the finished book. After my conversion, I wrote a family memoir called *My Grandfather's House*, and perhaps, as far as the past went, I should have stopped there. I couldn't: I went full bore at Fitzgerald and his circle. I wrote a book proposal for a group biography of Fitzgerald, Ernest Hemingway, and John Dos Passos that two dozen New York publishers could not see any point in. It was both old hat and, I suspect, grandiose. But I couldn't let the research go to waste, and in fact I did more research, as though I couldn't stop myself. After a further year I wrote a ninety-five-page essay on Fitzgerald's life during the composition of *Tender Is the Night*. What I'd created was both too long to be published as an essay and too short to be a book. I sent it out to journals and publishers. The rejections were apologetic and kind—the essay was "beautifully written" and obviously reflected a great deal of labor—but it seemed as though I were being congratulated for accumulating a particularly fine collection of stamps or baseball cards.

I put that project aside long enough to write a novel about writers and artists living in Europe, about the dangers of pursuing beauty and art too intently. It too was rejected by a score of major publishers, among them Scott's old house, Scribner's. Around that time I became depressed and bitter. I drank too much and my marriage and friendships began to fray. I took medication and tried to give up writing.

Things began to go a little better—they often do despite Spengler's sureties. I got a grant to write a nonfiction book and I began to write essays. And I took out my boxes of Scott Fitzgerald and Ben Griggs memorabilia once more: the family scrapbooks, letters, and photos, but also the Xeroxes I'd taken away from hours of digging in the Fitzgerald archive at Princeton. And at the very end of it, by way of a rare book dealer, I finally read Scott's student contributions to St. Paul Academy's *Now and Then*.

Excluding some short poems and drama, these amounted to four pieces, and the fact that they had later gone utterly unremarked upon at St. Paul Academy spoke, for me, in their favor. My own experience there suggested that the school was willfully indifferent to art, imagination, or any kind of nonconformity. Scott's *Now and Then* juvenilia might be—must be, I couldn't help but think—possessed of his genius; might, in fact, contain its seed, its secret.

But reading them, despite my hopes, I had to confess that even as specimens of precocity most of the pieces were at best tiresome exercises. One was a clumsy mystery and another a football tale, "Reade, Substitute Half," in which a heretofore mediocrity on the team saves the day.

There was something more in the last story, "A Debt of Honor." On its face, it wasn't much more than "Reade, Substitute Half" transposed to the Civil War. Private John Sanderson of the Confederate Army is court-martialed for falling asleep on sentry duty, an offense serious enough to warrant the firing squad. But General Robert E. Lee himself intervenes, commuting Sanderson's sentence "on account of your extreme youth." Six weeks later, at Chancellorsville, he single-handedly charges a Union infantry emplacement and sends its defenders fleeing. Later that day searchers find "the body of him who had once been John Sanderson, Third Virginia. He had paid his debt."

I liked those closing phrases, the melancholy irony of "him who had once been John Sanderson," the final tolling of "Third Virginia," and the fact of Sanderson's sacrificing himself for what would be, after all, the losing side. I suppose, however, that, when all is said and done, it's pat in the manner of most high-minded tributes to duty and sacrifice, that it substitutes sentiment for genuine tragedy.

But Scott was thirteen years old when he wrote this. He was, I felt, entitled to view death as an ennobling abstraction. At the same time, I couldn't help but feel he was already beginning to explore the notion of attaining glory through some variety of suicide, of rendering death beautiful by taking it into your own hands, by giving yourself a past—a legend that signifies—rather than a future. Even then Scott was on his way to making himself a failure artist, working in the medium of grief.

So finally, I thought, I'd found him, or the first sign of what he was going to become. I suppose he could have ended up like my grandfather. He might have objected that his family was already on the downward slope while the Griggses were still living on Summit Avenue. But the Griggses were also in their descent. They just didn't know it. And now I'm here as the residue of Spengler's law of decline. The difference was one of degree, temperament, and illusion. Even as a boy, Scott was looking back into the past while my grandfather imagined the prospects before him.

Other than that, they were alike in so many ways: They both had a romantic and sentimental view of women, family, and friendship, and became uxorious husbands, diligent genealogists, and keepers of scrapbooks and correspondence. They made notes about everything that transpired in their lives and, in my grandfather's case, took thousands of photographs. College was probably the great watershed of their histories, and perhaps the one great difference between them was that my grandfather became a "Yale man" and remained one. Hanging near the well-stocked bar in his basement den was a picture of him holding a football, grinning, around the time of his seventieth birthday, with the caption "Yale '16: Still Carrying the Ball." Scott, by contrast, never graduated from his college and so, even if only to him, his credentials as a "Princeton man" were suspect and incomplete. And maybe on that account, he remained fixed in the past, stuck fast in his junior year. He had gotten into "a good school" but didn't finish the job. The laws of St. Paul Academy might be every bit as iron as those of Marx, Hegel, and Spengler.

That's not to say that my grandfather did not contemplate and even revel in his own past. But his vision was nostalgic rather than tragic. He could examine the past and laugh or shrug or even weep, but then, like a scrapbook, he could close it and put it away.

I suppose that may mean that he never comprehended it as Scott had and that his perspective might be called superficial or sentimental. Surely the World War I of Scott's imagination was more terrible than the real war my grandfather experienced, even with its screaming wounded and severed limbs. He was satisfied with a certain banality in that regard. He did not try to make art of the past or of himself. But perhaps he knew that to go there deeply, entirely, perfectly—deliberately—you have to die. And that, I think, is why he shook his head so heavily that day I asked him about him and Scott. It was not just that by dying at age forty-four Scott had died before his time, but that he had been dead already for a long while.

I'm fourteen years older than Fitzgerald was at his death. That is not particularly old, but at the same time death is no longer a theoretical possibility for me but an incipient fact: I have, at age fifty-eight, more of a past than I do a future.

We're told it's not a good thing to think too much about this, to "dwell" on death. But it is among the dead that we do dwell. They built the better part of the world we inhabit—its history, culture, points of pride, and grudges—and our existence is entirely contingent on theirs: We were conceived through their eros and their hope. Their flesh became our flesh; the tinder of their spirit ignited ours. Their monuments are all around us, our own selves among them.

It's all too easy—at least it has been for me—to see the world as a graveyard, to miss the vital truth that while we share the world with the dead, we too have some business here. We live in debt—like the thirteen-year-old Scott's John Sanderson—to the dead, but we repay it by keeping ourselves alive, by tending their habitations, which are our homes too.

Art is contingent on imagination, and if you have an especially active imagination, as Scott Fitzgerald certainly did, you see the past more deeply and intently than other people. You may see ghosts, and eventually see them more than you see the living, and you may begin to see yourself among them. Their world—your need to be in it, to sustain and be sustained by it—is more real than the actual world: The past becomes present.

I was trying to keep these things—absence and presence—in balance, to honor and love the past, Scott and Ben, while continuing to live among the living. And I began to feel that going too deep into memory and art—at least for me—*was* morbid, the one leading to a directionless grief and the other to a hollow aestheticism, a preoccupation with specters and surfaces.

But I needed to look into two more things. The first was Scott's "Thoughtbook," a kind of diary he kept in 1910 and early 1911, just after he'd published "A Debt of Honor" in *Now and Then*. His spelling is poor (a lifetime affliction) and his handwriting is crabbed and clumsy in the manner of a fourteen-year-old, stagy with flamboyant serifs and capitals. It looks like my handwriting at that age, like any boy's, I suppose, and the events it describes are banal. The entries are mostly about the other kids Scott knows, about who he likes and who likes him, about who is most popular, and especially about the girls Scott has crushes on and whether they like him back. There was Violet Stockton:

> . . . She had some sort of book called flirting by sighns and Jack and I got it away from Violet and showed it too all the boys. Violet got very mad and went into the house. I got very mad and therfor *I* went home . . . *I just hate Violet.*

Scott transferred his affections to Margaret Armstrong, but that too ended in tragedy at my grandfather's house:

> One Saturday night about two weeks later my finish came. We were over at Ben Grigg's, four boys, Reub, Ben, Ted & I, and four girls Margaret, Marie, Elizabeth & Dorothy & that evening Margaret got an awful crush on Reuben which at the time I write this is still active.

That is the end of the "Thoughtbook." And for a time thereafter, Scott later recorded in his *Ledger*, he "became desperately holy."

That seems to have been the last time religion mattered to him. He went to Mass a few times at Princeton and when he died he was denied a Catholic burial on account of not having taken Communion for such a long time. But my path and his had crossed in a church: Back in St. Paul one Christmas Eve after college, Scott, having gotten more than a little tight at a dinner party, "felt religion descend upon me. . . . A warm current seemed to run through my body. My sins were washed away and I felt, as my host drained a drop or so from the ultimate bottle, that my life was beginning all over again."

He went to the Episcopal church a block behind his parents' house on Summit Avenue, St. John the Evangelist. He began looking for a friend in the brimming pews with whom he might sit and, searching the congregation, weaved up the aisle toward the pulpit. There he met the eyes of the rector, said, "Don't mind me, go on with the sermon," and turned around and headed back down the aisle and out the door.

St. John's was my grandparents' church, the church where they and my mother and father were married, where the Griggses had a family pew, second row on the left, directly behind the spot where Scott stood during his drunken outburst. At the same age Scott was when he began his "Thoughtbook," I too became "desperately holy." I was baptized, confirmed, and served as an altar boy in that same church, under the gaze of the white stone angel whose hands held the font. Scott must have stumbled past her as he approached the pulpit that Christmas Eve. I spent hundreds of hours in that church, and I still think of sitting in my grandfather's pew, on Christmas Eve, a soft, persistent snow falling outside like the tolling of a bell. I wrote a scene, set precisely there, in my first novel, of a patrician family daydreaming at midnight Mass as the life they think is theirs by right, unbeknownst to them, is crumbling away.

Scott seems to have felt he had desecrated a holy place that Christmas Eve. He memorialized that night in a piece called "The Most Disgraceful Thing I Ever Did" written a year after he'd left St. Paul for keeps. For me, St. John's was only holy in the way it had been for him, as a repository of memory and yearning, the warm burrow of an imagined past. It had nothing much to do with mercy or God: The altar candles are guttering and will leave a terrible darkness.

*

I still wanted to look at one last thing connected to Scott and Ben: my grandfather's boyhood photo album. It's exactly contemporaneous with Scott's "Thoughtbook," and there they all are, in their knicker-bockers and caps and pinafores and hair bows, at Summit Avenue and Dellwood: Reuben, Ben, and Ted, and Margaret, Marie, Eliza-beth, and Dorothy. It's only Scott who's not present, for whatever reason. Was he simply not around when my grandfather was taking pictures or did my grandfather exclude him, perhaps out of some kind of contempt—there might have been that too in the shaking of his head seventy-five years later—or a preconscious sense that Scott was, yes, a failure?

I've never been able to escape either Scott or Ben: When I render the account of my own life up to now, I see I've attained neither my grandfather's well-earned contentment nor Scott's hard-earned genius, neither their angels nor their demons.

Better to imagine that I simply took a different course, my own path, the one I needed to follow to find myself. We were very big on finding ourselves when I was the age Scott was at Princeton, and I suppose it came, as our parents had said all along, to no more than following our immediate desires and inclinations. I was going to be a painter, then a filmmaker, then an academic and public intellectual, and, finally, a writer. Coming from St. Paul, Minnesota, from the milieu of Summit Avenue and St. Paul Academy, with a tender and elegiac conception of love, of winters long ago and all the dying falls, and of childhood and youth, I knew against whom I must take the measure of myself. And as things stand, I have failed. Scott and Zelda knew what it took: It takes everything.

My grandfather knew all this about me from my childhood and adolescence. That day a dozen years ago, shrouded in his oxblood robe, shaking his head, he foresaw the rest. As for Scott, his story was no more than an alternate life to my grandfather's own—tragedy instead of comedy—which a neighborhood boy he had once known had chosen.

Perhaps it took no great wisdom or experience to understand this about me. Maybe that girl at Dellwood had known, had telegraphed to me, by the slightest rotation of her tanned shoulder cupped in her candy-heart-pink shift, that, yes, as Scott had written in *Tender Is the Night*, "all the old things are true," that my fears were facts. Scott himself wrote that "my finish came" one night in the Griggses' parlor in 1911. It was just a pretty girl, but it was always a pretty girl with Scott. So it really was all over then, and the rest of his life was mere phantasm, a ghost writing his memoir, over and over again. People in St. Paul, my grandfather among them, were losing track of him. It seems to me now, as I prepare to put both him and Ben aside—to save myself as best I can, to find some mercy—that at age fourteen Scott was already Dick Diver, a walking, breathing absence. Scott had written of Dick's disappearance and uncertain where-abouts at the very end of *Tender Is the Night*:

> Dick opened an office in Buffalo, but evidently without suc-cess . . . a few months later . . . he was in a little town named Batavia, New York, practising general medicine, and later . . . he was in Lockport, doing the same thing . . . his latest note was post-marked from Hornell, New York, which is some distance from Geneva and a very small town; in any case he is almost certainly in that section of the country, in one town or another.

I too am a wanderer, less in the manner of Dick Diver than of Fitzgerald himself, or, rather, a kind of aesthetic tourist who takes his inspiration from Fitzgerald and his ilk. I have been to every address in Paris that Fitzgerald (and Hemingway too) occupied dur-ing the 1920s and I tracked down the villa on the Côte d'Azur upon which Dick Diver's was modeled. I've gone to England, Germany, Austria, and Italy on the track of other writers and artists. Sometimes, standing across the street from one or another house or apartment, I feel conspicuous. I wonder if I've been observed by the current occu-pants of the property and seem suspicious, if I'll be confronted and asked the nature of my business, something I doubt I could explain.

That has never happened. In truth, I think I must be a spectral presence in these places, scarcely visible. And at none of these visitations—but perhaps it is more honest to call them hauntings—have I ever seen anyone leaving or entering or the slightest motion through a window or so much as a trace of smoke or vapor from a chimney or vent. There is, for me, no one home. There was, of course, once upon a time, of that I am sure.

Swim for the Little One First
Noy Holland

HOW NICE YOU COULD come to visit. See our home, how we live, how the leaves sweep down. The fields green still.

We turned our clocks back. I brought squash in, tossed a sheet across the withering vines. We're to expect a frost once the wind quits, wind from the north, flurries. A chance.

We'll move the rabbits in in the morning, light the stove. Chicory in your coffee, honey how you like. On the radio the news.

Dark falls and the wind comes up and leaves flock out of the trees. I tug the windows shut and yet, inside, doors keep sailing open. Leaves shore up in the kitchen. The floorboards buckle and heave. These old houses. Every wall leans toward the south, toward you, your modest hills, your clemencies of weather.

It can't be easy. It is a distance. Our stairs are steep and narrow. You will never make it up them; you would never make it down. We would have to keep you, as eccentrics keep their reptiles, captive in a tub.

We have the dog you gave us. We have reasonable jobs in town. Sick pool, personal time. Time to travel. I took a lover from the tropical regions once who washed my feet in the sand. Children loved him. He owned a shirt he never wore. He danced, with keening grace, with my Isabel, who has lived so far to be five.

Your room is freshly painted. Your bed is your bed you slept in in Kentucky when you were a boy. The sheets are the sheets Mother monogrammed when she took your name when you married.

If you need anything, if you are up in the night. There is the wing-back chair to sleep in. Whiskey in the pantry. Pecan cake in the breadbox—your father's favorite, the cake your mother made you.

Our house is yours, naturally.

You need only ask.

I am awake in the night in the yellow room at the top of the narrow stairs. Tap your cane on the stairs—I'm sure to hear it.

*

We keep our boy with us in our bed. Our boy looks like your boy, like my brother. We gave him your name you gave my brother, the name your mother gave you. He is the third Frederick, a grandson at last. Papa, we named him for you.

My lover's name was Artemio.

Quieres tomar mi leche? he used to ask.

He danced beautifully, in keeping with the custom of his people. Isabel bent her back across his arm and dragged her hair through the sand.

My brother was Frederick the second.

He skied out of an avalanche that caught you—we've told the story a thousand times. Your ski swung around and put a gash in your leg and by this wound Freddy tracked you. He skied you out of that chute on his back. You were knocked out; you waked in the hospital. Remembered nothing. You remember nothing of it now. It can't have happened, you insist, even now. He was weak, your boy, he wasn't like you. The second Frederick.

We should have named our boy Jack. Jack the first, Jack the only. Manuel, we should have named him, Carlito. *Gordito*—little fat boy.

You should have said, *Freddy, thank you.* Instead you said, *It can't have been you.*

In sleep, my brother, my boy at my breast, makes his visits too. He is not himself but I know it is him. He is not the boy who set the house ablaze, not the boy who sawed the heads off snakes and skewered mice with a pitchfork. Freddy stands at the door until morning, waiting to be seen. He sees nothing. He has no eyes, no mouth, no reason he can speak of to be here.

The trees thrash in the wind. Apples shake loose and drop to the ground—a sound loud enough to wake me.

Pachew, you said, and aimed your cane at my girl.

Your cane is wound about with electric tape. The shaft is splintered— you fault the dog. The dog was digging at your peas, *how many times?* You broke your cane across its back.

Pachew.

You will have peas at Christmas and pecans and cabbage in your garden still growing.

Here, snow will heap past the window sash. The bears hunker down and the rabbits, and the frogs endure the season frozen solid. Ice pries slate from the rooftop. When snow slides off the roof, and ice, all at once, the house thunders, and quakes on its rubble footing. The dog gnaws at the door, and Isabel cries out.

My girl sleepwalks, so you know. Isabel talks in her sleep. We mustn't wake her—only follow at her heels quietly until she makes her way back to bed.

Isabel is likely to walk to the church next door and swing from the rope in the belfry. The bells startle her—but she can't wake. She is afraid and calls out for me—but she can't see me, she can't hear. I have to hold her to keep her from looking for me as though I am nowhere near.

I am near, Papa, not to worry. Only tap on the stairs should you need me.

You have sight in one eye. One leg is shorter. Your joints swell and wear away and you are older of a sudden, eighty soon, tomorrow we'll mark your birthday.

Your boy killed himself on your birthday.

At dinner your wife fell from her chair, asleep. A long way to come and you are tired. You don't sleep well. You ache in the night. Your friends are dying. You wake with your hand thrown over your face not knowing it is you.

It's your hand, Papa. You can't feel it. Your hand lies across your eyes. You can't move it. It won't come to you what it is.

You may hear birds in the chimney in your room. They often catch there. Their feet scratch the flue. No harm.

You'll hear the wind scrub the hill we live on.

You'll hear me. I sleep lightly, I am up in the night. I am in the room above you, awake when the baby wakes hungry, carrying him across the floor.

His first curl is on the shelf and his umbilical knot in your room where you are sleeping. I buried his afterbirth in the garden deeper than the dog likes to dig.

I keep Freddy's old teeth the tooth fairy left. I keep the lamp Mother made from your ski boot that Freddy dumped the blood you lost out of when he brought you down off the mountain. You bled wildly. By the blood from the wound, Freddy found you, by the stains on the snow, the blood pooling in your boot. That was lucky.

That lamp made Mother feel lucky. Mother drilled a hole through the bottom of your boot and ran a shaft up through it and filled the boot with cement she threaded wire through.

Funny, what you keep, what keeps at you.

I keep a feather I found in Freddy's pocket.

I keep an acorn I kicked the morning Isabel was born, out walking on the dirt road, my water streaming over my knees.

I keep a satin bow from the attic of the house where we lived when Freddy was alive.

You paid a bounty on birds when Freddy was alive, on pigeons and the obnoxious grackle; a nickel for every rabbit trapped, a dollar for the brazen weasel who ran across your shoe.

He killed to please you. Freddy got rich trying to please you. He drowned mice by the dozen in a bucket and a mother raccoon in a wheelbarrow and the last sorry runt of a puppy your bird dog dropped in the barn. The pup wouldn't amount to much—you had him kill it. Freddy blasted the daubed nests of swallows with their splotchy eggs inside.

You taught him what to kill, what to run off, to save.

What Freddy killed he put to rest with great ceremony, with flute song, in a common grave, quietly, secretly weeping. Spare the song-birds, you taught him, for their pleasing song—the plain and faith-ful phoebe, the thrush and homely wren. Spare the heron, shoot the goose, kill the cuckoo bird that hides its eggs for other birds to raise.

We ran skunks off. We brought a fox home to save and you shot it.

He needed toughening, you always said so. Freddy needed a keener eye.

My brother was pretty; he was beaten in school. He had been born too soon. His lungs were weak. I tried to be your boy—so Freddy wouldn't have to be your boy. Wouldn't get to, I think I should say.

*

Freddy shot a house cat once, out hunting with you, the first and last time you took him with you.

"He's a hazard," you told Mother.

And gave her the geese it was her job to pluck and the pheasant and the dove. Birds are stacked top to bottom in your freezer—pinkish, yellow, their feet still on, more birds than you will eat in a lifetime. Mother plucked the birds on the bottom of the stack and stacked on these are the fresher kill, the birds your next wife plucked for you, bright mallards and drakes, their heads loose on their necks, their feathers carried off by the wind.

My lover called me *la flaca*, the skinny one.

I liked the smell of him, and his mighty arms. I like a little how easily he will accomplish nothing.

He had a scooter we rode around on on sand roads, through tiny towns. He rode me out to see a tribe of monkeys. One stole my necklace. One unlaced my shoes. Those monkeys were the greedy kings of that town, the *pendejos*, the thugs. They chased dogs off. They stole wallets—stole mine—snatched anything loose.

"Why did you bring me here?" I asked him.

"To teach you to live, *mi flaca*, with nothing."

He lived in a lean-to of lashed-together palm fronds. The floor was sand. He had a bucket and a bed. He had a rag he dried my feet with. All night, I could hear the sea.

All night, certain nights, I knew he would kill me. He had strength he wasn't using.

He would scalp me, pretend to be me—my mind blasted clean, ecstatic, swinging my yellow hair.

Here is how Freddy went about it: He made a blow dart with straight pins and bamboo and climbed, wheezing, into the hayloft. By dinner, he was hivey, dripping, blotched. He couldn't eat for sneezing. You've forgotten this. It wasn't so, you say. But, Papa, it was.

For hours Freddy lay in the hayloft waiting for the pigeons you hated, waiting for the kill. I liked to watch him. My brother was patient. I saw a snake go over his neck once. He was good at keeping still.

Freddy gave me his old dog you hated—his stuffed dog, old Snoopy dog. He gave it up to me for your birthday.

He didn't need it: He wasn't a kid anymore. He loved it foolishly. You were sure to take it from him; he took it from himself. The dog's big head drooped and swiveled: The stuffing had gone out of its neck.

It smelled awful, my husband insisted, but to me it smelled like Freddy and the bed that Freddy slept in in the house where Freddy died. And so I kept it.

I keep the satin bow I meant to give you.

I keep the shell Artemio gave me.

He gave me little; I asked little. He wanted money and I gave it to him. I gave him a shirt and shoes.

He has two shirts now and one ragged bucket—to wash sand from the feet of his women he brings to his lean-to to bed.

Nothing stops you. You hunt and fish and travel.

You are buried by an avalanche and your dead boy digs you out.

You keep moving, marry again, keep your hair, your pornography, it can't be easy but here you are. Come to visit. Come to see at last your grandbaby, a little man to carry on. He is Freddy but not like Freddy—this one loud and plump and strong. Not a quitter.

Don't be a quitter.

"Where's my mister?" you say.

"Where's my water?"

Sit tight: Here it comes.

Here comes your boy to save you, digging in from above. You won't even need to thank him—only lie there. It is all you can do.

Bleed, and maybe he'll find you. Breathe. Except the heat from your breath melts the snow against your face. The snow freezes to ice. It makes a mask of ice. That's what kills you.

Except it doesn't. You live to be eighty. You could live to be a hundred and eighty, your grandchildren buried, your new wife dead, sitting in a wingback chair.

Carry on, is your counsel. *Don't be a quitter.*

You stashed food for a year in the basement of our house, taught us to divine for water, to forage for windfall apples under the ice and snow. You taught us the stars to go by and which snakes were safe to catch and how to gut and skin. How to read wind and cloud for weather. How to make an arrow true.

We needed toughening; you meant to toughen us.

We lit fires with flint how you taught us. Learned our roots and berries. We'd snare rabbits, shoot geese. We'd know mushrooms, cache food. Train a pigeon to carry messages to Mother.

Mother, we live in a tree house now the phoebes are happy in. We have water. We know a cave very near and kill rabbits. There is plenty here to do.

Chipmunks eat at the walls of our house. A bear rubs its back against the clapboards: That's how it sounds. But that is only the arborvitae, Papa, pressed against the house by the wind. Not to worry.

Of course you worry. You stop breathing in your sleep. You find your hand across your face. Your wife has to wake to wake you, so spent she falls out of her chair.

You wake gasping. Your mouth is grainy and dry. Your feet are such a long way from you, bleeding into the snow: not yours.

They are too old to be yours. You can't feel them.

Papa, sleep.

Let yourself rest. We'll have a party for you tomorrow, a nice meal. I'll spend the day in the kitchen.

Isabel wants to hang streamers for you and have a water slide and balloons. She wants cupcakes and rainbow sprinkles. All her bunnies can come.

We'll take a walk when you wake. I'll show you the fort my Isabel built with apples and yellow leaves. Our apples were sweet and wormy this year; all but the last have dropped from the trees. They lie in the grass, two tiny bites taken from them. Into two soft apples, Isabel pushed two sticks to stake her rabbit by. I'll have to show you. He wears a collar like a cat. She gets him tied up, the apples at his sides, to watch her, *you have to watch me*, jumping rope in the sun on the church steps, singing jumping songs, singing *rabbit*.

111

*

Freddy brought you a bird at a party once. He was blotchy and proud. "Here I got one, Papa."

"You dummy," you called him, it's true.

You held the bird by the neck to show the others, the silver pin still in its breast. Everybody had a good laugh at my brother: He'd killed a mourning dove, not a pigeon.

Freddy whacked that bird against the side of the barn until its insides were coming out.

Freddy killed every bird he could get to after that, didn't matter, every beetle and snake and rodent, and brought them to me as a cat does, and with him a stick to hit him with. Freddy wanted all the wrong things, I knew. I hit him. I did what he asked me. I hit him until we both felt better.

I helped him light a fire with his socks. Because he had lost his coat. This was later. You had had to buy him a new coat and he had lost it and we were afraid of what you would do.

So we lit a fire in Freddy's closet. We would say the coat burned in the fire. It wasn't Freddy's fault. His coat was hanging right there where it was supposed to hang. There was a fire, we'd say. We were in the barn, we'd say. We didn't know the first thing about it.

Here is how Freddy went about it: He fed the ladder through the open window.

It never mattered to Freddy how hard a thing was once he had the idea.

He used the apple-picking ladder, tapered at the top for going up among the trees and wider as you went down. He'd climbed a ladder with the ladder on his back—it would never have made the turn on the stairs.

I went up there to look for a bow for you for the gift I'd gotten for your birthday. I wanted a yellow bow. I wanted paper with purple dots. I have no idea what I meant to give you only how I meant to wrap it.

There were paintings tacked to the rafters of that house that Freddy and I had painted: volcanoes the lava spat out of, a black-and-white smiling cow. He painted lightning, pyroclastic flow.

The sun blazed in the attic windows. Flies knocked against the glass, stupid in the cold that was coming. The cold made a fringe of ice on the pond and the last apples swung in the wind in the trees and rotted in the bent-over grass.

He had no shoes on. I thought: He's lost them.

His feet were red from the cold from coming through the grass to feed the apple-picking ladder through the window. He didn't care how hard. Freddy was stubborn. He had a feather in his hat. He lashed the ladder to his back to use his hands to climb—no way could he have made it up those stairs.

The geese were moving. The bears were drunk on apples.

The sun made buttery squares at that hour against the chimney where the ladder had fallen. Freddy kicked the ladder out when the time came. It had rained and his feet were muddy and the sun threw his shadow against the brick.

I stood under him. His foot crossed under his other foot like the feet of Christ in pictures. He sort of turned in the wind. I thought to hit him. I was wearing my pleated skirt.

I sat a long while at the window up there with Freddy at my back and looked out. A few apples hung in the trees still where the branches were too weak to climb. The trees were young still. We had to go to our knees to mow under them. That became my job, a boy's job. The sky heaped up behind me. The storms came in from the west in that house over the fruitful hills.

Hear that?

My husband laughs in his sleep. He wakes himself up laughing.

Otherwise you can forget he is here.

Once a cowbird flapped out of the chimney in your room. Its wing was broken. A cowboy bird, Freddy called it.

It's funny what you remember, funny what you forget.

Once a bear came and ate the bees—left the honey, ate the bees. Pulled the bird feeders down, drunk on windfall apples.

I get out of bed with the baby and carry him across the room. He nearly glows, looking up at me, his face so plump and pale.

My husband has left his shoes in the middle of the room. It has been raining and his shoes are muddy.

He's still laughing. The owl starts up in the orchard. The leather splits and the toes turn up. He doesn't sound like any man I know.

Count your blessings, Mother always said: He doesn't wake himself up screaming; he is a happy drunk; he dreams funny dreams; you can forget he is even here.

That owl. We have barn owls, horned owls, eagles. Owl is a funny word.

That's a barn owl, calling across the field. I leave our ladder stood up in the tree the owl likes and, nights I can't sleep, climb toward him. He holds himself very still.

If he has flown, I won't know, you can't hear them. I could knock right into him. Sometimes my knees give out. It is unnerving: to be seen so clearly by something you can scarcely see.

Pachew, pachew, pachew, you said, and aimed your cane at my children.

Freddy was barefoot; his feet were muddy. One foot went over the other as if to stand in the air on himself.

After my brother died, a redtail attacked you. You were riding your spotted mare, who threw you. The hawk went after your eyes.

You had a redtail stuffed and the head of a moose. A turkey, a small bear. You had hooves of elk made into ashtrays with a skinny fringe of hide. You had a pair of geese hollowed out and stuffed, lifting off, friends for life. A gift to yourself on your birthday.

Your boy killed himself on your birthday. That is punishment enough for many lifetimes. For this, you don't need me.

I'll make a fresh cake. Corn pudding, how you like, and collards. I'll soak a ham. Maybe I'll polish your shoes like I used to.

We'll sing a pleasing song—your wife and I, and Isabel. That's the trick: Sing a pleasing song. Dress yourself up pretty.

Let me know what you hope for for your birthday, Papa, something small, a watch, a wallet. Soap on a rope—the old standby. A gleaming golden cane.

Only ask for it.
If there is anything you want—someone will get it for you.
My daughter will. Your wife will, or I will. Somebody always has.

Interrupted Elegy
Octavio Paz

—Translated from Spanish by Eliot Weinberger

Today I remember the dead in my house.
We'll never forget the first death,
though he died in a flash, so suddenly
he never reached his bed or the holy oil.
I hear his cane hesitating on a step of the staircase,
the body gaining strength with a sigh,
the door that opens, the corpse that enters.

From a door to dying there's little space
and hardly enough time to sit down,
raise your head, look at the clock,
and realize: it's eight fifteen.

Today I remember the dead in my house.
The woman who died night after night
and her dying was a long good-bye,
a train that never left.
The greed of her mouth,
hanging on the thread of a sigh,
her eyes never closing, making signs,
wandering from the lamp to my eyes,

a fixed gaze that embraces another gaze,
far off, that suffocates in the embrace
and in the end escapes and watches from the riverbank
how the soul sinks and loses its body
and finds no eyes to grab hold of. . . .
Was that gaze inviting me to die?
Perhaps we die only because no one
wants to die with us, no one
wants to look us in the eye.

Today I remember the dead in my house.
The one who left for a few hours
and no one knew into what silence he had gone.
After dinner, each night,
the colorless pause that leads to emptiness
or the endless sentence half hanging
from the spider's thread of silence
opens a corridor for him to return:
We hear his footsteps, he climbs, he stops. . . .
And someone among us gets up
and closes the door shut.
But he, on the other side, insists.
He lies in wait in every recess and hollow,
he wanders among yawns, at the edge of things.
Though we shut the door, he insists.

Today I remember the dead in my house.
Faces forgotten in my mind, faces
without eyes, staring eyes, emptied out:
Am I searching in them for my secret,
the god of blood my blood moves,
the god of ice, the god who devours me?
His silence is the mirror of my life,
in my life his death is prolonged,
I am the final error of his errors.

Today I remember the dead in my house.
The scattered thoughts, the scattered
act, the names strewn
(lacunae, empty zones, holes
where stubborn memory rummages)
the dispersion of encounters,
the ego with its abstract wink, always shared
with another ego that is the same, the rages,
desire and its masks, the buried
snake, the slow erosions,
the hope, the fear, the act
and its opposite: within me they persist,
they beg to eat the bread, the fruit, the body,
to drink the water that was denied to them.

But there is no water now, everything is dry,
the bread is tasteless, the fruit bitter,
love domesticated, masticated,
in cages with invisible bars,
the onanist ape and the trained bitch,
what you devour devours you,
your victim is also your executioner.
Heap of dead days, crumpled newspapers,
and nights stripped of bark,
and in the dawn of the swollen eyelids,
the gesture with which we undo
the running knot, the necktie,
and now the lights have gone out in the streets
—*greet the sun, spider, be not rancorous*—
and more dead than living go off to bed.

The world is a circular desert,
heaven is closed and hell empty.

[1948]

Mother Box
Sarah Blackman

THE PEOPLE SHE KNEW, she had met under difficult circumstances. She wasn't the sort of girl who made friends—rather, she had contacts in the art world. She was a jazz pianist and a poet, a singer/songwriter, had taken up painting with acrylics and was practicing kinesthetic spiritualism. Also, she was taking a kind of medication that made her hair fall out along her part so that her part was becoming wider and whiter, the hair that remained on her head looking darker and coarser by contrast. Her mother called and wanted to know why her hair was falling out. "Why don't you *do* something about it?" her mother asked. "What kind of a person are you that this is all right?"

Of course, she was the sort of person who had a lot of secrets. Her secrets were how she understood it was herself and not, say, a peanut or a broken-bottomed chair. Listen, she was sort of a reprehensible figure. We knew it was cruel, but she did not like us either and would sing wherever she went in piping notes like she was saying, "What WEEP? What WEEP?" over and over again. When we asked her what she was singing, she told us she was exercising her voice for an upcoming performance and then expressed one of her secrets, which were stale and sodden, private examinations into the nature of the body suspended in a state of decay. Oh, oh! Our lives were so much worse now that she was in them. She had a dream about an onion, the she that was an onion. It was a secret she told us and that night we too had vegetative dreams, the fetid earth heaving above us, our best-loved selves dissolving in the slip of gray rot.

Her mother called. She danced for us at a party, partially on a table-top, partially on a stage she created by using stacks of the host's books for a backdrop. She invited us to notice the way she used only the muscles in her thighs to express the narrative. It was a story about a swan, a lucky oatcake, a boat, and an evening sky. The apotheosis was conducted through a series of facial exercises that were guaranteed to keep her looking ten years younger than her chronological age. "My cellular age is only seventeen," she told us. Her mother called. She was invited to play the harp, a new accomplishment, at the wedding of a friend of one of our friends. The bride was enthusiastic. She was marrying on a golf course, beside a lake, in the country, at the end of a road lined with beeches. There was going to be a breakfast buffet. We were invited. We called our mothers. "This is not just some other tale of woe," we told our mothers, "this is non-quotidian, unparalleled, unable to be surmounted by ordinary measure." Our mothers are sometimes ferocious women, but all alive. Our mothers, at some point, guided our trembling fathers inside them and said it was OK, whatever they did next would be all right.

We thought this would be a sort of new beginning. We all moved to this town with some species of hope and had also started over a number of times before. At a party, we took the wrong door out of the bathroom and ended up in her bedroom. She had a tapestry tacked to her ceiling that was red and black and gold and filled with hundreds of tiny mirrors like the hundreds of eyes of a watchful peacock. It was horrible to see ourselves in the peacock eyes of her bedroom. We had ingested something. Someone knew what it was. The rest of the house was lit with blue and green lights like the loudest place there is under the ocean, but her room was dark and still as if the air couldn't move without a tremendous effort of will. One of her secrets was that she had almost been raped. It was when she was in college, a school on the coast that was nevertheless very far from the ocean. She wrote a one-act play about it and performed it wearing a giant papier-mâché onion with holes cut in the bottom for her legs. There was also a hole for her mouth, so she could speak, and during the play she would walk and speak, lost inside the enormous onion, which had sat too long in its pantry, was sprouting a viridian-green shoot that bobbed tremulously from its crest. "From my window I could smell the sea, salt spray, whale bone, smell the boom Boom BOOM of the waves broken against the shore, all this wreckage, all this birth," was one of the lines she shouted from inside the onion. We were in the audience, of course. We could not make ourselves just stay home. Every one of us had taken his hand and put it here, put it here. "Let's just get this over with," we had said, and then nothing else for a long time. Her mother called. "I made up the part about the ocean," she told us. "They were re-tarring the parking lot, so all I could really smell was asphalt. But everything else is true," she told us. "Everything else is witness."

Her mother called. She was performing body modifications, had split her tongue so it could lick and flit like a snake's tongue testing the air in the room. Her mother said, "Have you talked to the doctor yet? Have you put on some weight? Have you gotten a chromosomal scan? Have you examined your stool against a chart showing optimum consistency and shape?" Our mothers once came into our rooms at night and sat at the foot of the bed. We were reminded again how much bigger we were than our mothers by the only very small creak of the mattress beneath their weight. Our mothers wanted to know if we'd made any decisions, if we knew how fast the time was passing, if we thought we could wait forever. Did we think we could wait forever? We were supposed to have the ability to start all over. Just one more time. Some of us had painted all the walls of the house green as an onion shoot. Some of us put his hand here and said, "Tell that to your wife." Her mother called. At the wedding, she wore a dress made out of stinging nettles. She was so red with it her skin began to crack and weep a thin pink plasma. Of course, the bride was upset. From her room we had taken three little bottles of pills: blue pills, green pills, black pills with glossy coating. We mixed them together with some other things we had on our own. "Oops," we told our mothers.

The bride and groom had rented some boats shaped like swans for the wedding party to arrive in. It was supposed to be a stately performance, at sunrise, across a lake gently heaving with large-mouth bass and catfish and some kinds of game trout imported from more wintery climes. The groom was a great outdoorsman. He was a young buck. She played a kind of polka beat she said she had learned from a Transylvanian aroma therapist she met while touring the European circuit. Then she moved into an atonal dirge. Her skin wept so much from the nettles she left a thick pink slick on the chair when she took a break for lemonade and a turn at the breakfast buffet. Her mother called. We were all such good friends. We hated each other. We took turns spinning at the end of the dock, breaking our teeth when we fell onto the rocky shore. Put your hand here. Put your hand here. None of the boats capsized, but the ladies were still discomfited. It had taken a long time to make it from one place to another. The day was steaming up from the lake bed. When the day reached the tops of the beeches it turned white, just like that. Her mother called. We had no shoes on. We had never had any shoes at all. Someone gave us a drink as pink as a berry, as sharp as a nettle. Nevertheless, at the end of the morning, they were legally obliged.

She set up a scaffold in front of the library. For a while she hung there from a pair of gold hooks she inserted below her shoulder blades. She had bled herself pale, breasts flat against her ribs, hair

121

receded almost to the tips of her ears where it flared like the shawl of an inky bird, the sort of bird that builds bowers. An architect bird we almost believed, at that moment, would take flight. Her mother called. One of her secrets was that she actually had been raped. She told us one night while we drank a juice made of nettles and dandelion leaves. We had turned over a new leaf, were cleansing ourselves by means of starvation and herbal unguents we rubbed on the soles of our feet so that everywhere we walked we left traces of our toxins. Our mothers thought we were taking things too far. "Who are you trying to prove this to?" our mothers asked. Meanwhile, some of us had gotten married. Our husbands had long torsos, blue veins, delicate hands and feet. We told them about the time we lay on her bed under the tapestry, what we saw, what we took. "He was a stranger," she said. "I left the door unlocked." She made a fetish doll with his features and carried it in her pocket everywhere she went. Her mother called. "What do you think this is doing to your father?" her mother wanted to know.

She was interested in the opposing impulses of Thanatos and Eros, Edo-era pornographic scrolls, tribal dance, basket weaving, the intricate structures of the inner ear, past-life revitalization, crystal theology, scribing through the entrails of freshly slaughtered beeves. Our husbands liked to turn us on our sides. They knew how to direct things so we did not have to see them, could only feel the hand on our hip, on our breast. Our husbands inside of us pushed past us and into a place that was suddenly white, just like that. We were like babies, wet and small. Our husbands wanted to know what we were thinking, why we were thinking, what we were doing, if we'd held on to any of those pills? "When it was over I asked him to marry me," she said. The doll had a wide mouth, always wet, always open. She touched the doll's face. Her mother called.

Listen, we knew it was cruel, but we had to have something. Our lives were not what we had been led to expect. There were things that had happened and kept happening over and over, like a hundred small mirrors in a dark room. She was interested in self-flagellation; she was documenting cases of scoliosis among teenage prostitutes; she had injected an ink in her eyes that turned the whites permanently black. Her mother called. For a terrible season we all dreamed we had given birth to an onion. We held it to our breasts, rubbing it back and forth on our breasts. Finally, we cut it up and made it into a soup. "This is the only chance you'll have," our mothers said. "I didn't believe it either, but it's true."

She told us so many things we couldn't keep track of what we didn't know about her. Our husbands might like us to have a baby. Our husbands think we should be mothers. Using an ancient Maori technique, she tattooed an exhaustive portrait of a man's back onto her front. The man's legs were spread over her legs, his back over her breasts, the back of his head with its thick brown hair inked over her face. The man was slimmer and taller than she and where his legs parted, the pear droop of his sac obscured her pudenda. Her mother called. We said, "It's like she was raised by cardboard boxes. It's like she emits a ravenous void." Our mothers matured into beautiful women. They paint their nails a coral color, let their hair gray. When she talks her words come from the base of the man's brain, where his breathing is regulated, where his body remembers only itself. Oh, oh! From her room we took pills and a sense of darkness, a stack of letters she had addressed but never mailed. We wrote a letter to her mother. Our husbands put their fingers in our mouths and our ears. We asked them to. "Put your hand here," we said, but they were not always ours to command. Sometimes our husbands had the tusks of a boar or a single swan's wing. Sometimes their tongues were made of jade, their hands of thorns, their cocks trembling bundles of lilies still tightly furled.

Of course, we were right and hardly knew it. At the party, she danced for us. She left the doll in an empty space on the bookshelf as an audience. There were many delicious snack foods served. We were eating for two, had to go to the bathroom almost all the time. On her back she had tattooed a man's front. When she is coming, he goes with wide eyes, a simple expression. We clung to our husband's shirtfronts. We were delirious, dizzy. There was a knock at the door. She showed us how the narrative was contained by the gesture of her upper lip; she unrolled a scroll from her mouth; she pulled out the last of her hair and scattered it like feathers. Some of it fell into our water glasses where it floated, feathers on a river, caught in an eddy, going nowhere. We answered the door and it was her mother. There was a strange feeling inside us all the time. Inside us was a white day, but we could not go there, could not remember it. We had a sense we were standing at the end of something like a dock, something else spread out flat and fathomless before us. Our husbands honked and flapped their wings.

Her mother was a cardboard box. On her mother's side was stamped This End Up and Fragile in red block letters. On her mother's open flap someone had written her address with a black felt-tip pen. We didn't know what we expected her to do. All the lights in the house were blue and green. Nothing had changed; the music was too loud. Right at that moment our mothers were calling our homes, trying to get ahold of us. We hadn't thought it through. She came. The man went. Her mother was on the porch. It was raining and her mother was getting wet. There was a sound like droning, a sound like wings beating against the water. "Mother Box," she said. "Mother Box," she said. "Mother Box," she said. Her mother didn't say anything. Absentmindedly, we continued eating the snacks. After all we had been through, after all we had done. "Put your hand here," we told our husbands, but they had gone out through the back door. She went to her mother and crawled inside her. She turned around three times like a dog. It was a terrible place to be, to remember. "What WEEP," she sang. We don't know when she fell asleep, or when we all did. In the morning, when the sun reached the tops of the beeches, we were surprised to discover that nothing had changed.

The Clouds, The Apples, Their Lives

Ann Beattie

WILLIE MARSH, FOURTEEN, wished only to visit Blanch Liddicoat. The Liddicoat family, of Derry, New Hampshire, lived three hours' walk, or more than an hour's horse ride, from Willie's house, though, and his father, Rupert, needed his help in the barn. He needed it every day of the week, including Sundays, especially now that he'd learned of Willie's interest in Blanch. First his son was doing pointless things, such as making watercolors of the new-mown hay that nobody in his right mind would have looked at and even known they were looking at hay, and if they might have, what would have been the point of *that*? Now that it was September, and the apples were starting to fall, Rupert would have to call on him not only for barn chores, but apple picking. There was no longer any Mrs. Marsh, though her half sister, Deborah, had come to help out during Mrs. Marsh's illness and had stayed because her suitor, Mr. DeWitt Lyall, had written her a letter saying that he would not be her suitor any longer and that he was going to marry his third cousin from Boston. She had wadded up the letter and submerged it in a vase of sunflowers mixed with Queen Anne's lace, pushing down hard into the slightly yellowed water—or at least as deeply as she could without toppling the vase, as she loudly proclaimed all men to be scoundrels, Mr. Marsh not excepted. He stood only five feet away, silent, forcing boiled apples through a sieve.

Willie, reading a pamphlet that had been left by a traveling salesman, suspected Sister Deborah might have plunged her hand into the fireplace after reading the letter, if the fire had been laid and had been as conveniently close as the vase. He began to fear her hand.

A week later, however, Deborah was again Willie's ally; she had begun rouging her cheeks again and smiling when Willie's friend Hopward came to play the fiddle, and occasionally she took some leftovers out to the barn cat who—being male—had also not been in her good graces.

"Mr. Marsh thinks he's so smart, that he saw it coming with De-Witt," she said to Willie. "Well, he wouldn't see anything less than a tornado coming, and that too late to do anything about it. Your mother might be alive today if he'd had any sense and tried to get her some medicine when she first needed it. I'm not going to let my situation color all my perceptions of gentlemen, because I'm sure there are still some out there, leaving aside your father, who may be many things, but who has never been a true gentleman, and leaving aside you, though you still have the chance to be, with Blanch Liddicoat, who is an attractive and kind young woman with a great gift for embroidery."

"If we talked this way in the future, how do you think it would sound?" Willie asked. "I mean, do you think there will still be gentlemen in the future?"

"The future? You're your father's own son. Every Monday he is thinking about Tuesday, and every Tuesday, Wednesday, and so on through the week. He's fretting over the few apples that have fallen and gotten bruised because they weren't picked, when the apple tree's not yet begun growing its bounty."

"But I don't mean about my father. I mean, do you think there might come a time when a girl such as Blanch might get a horse and come for a visit, instead of sending word that if I want to visit, I must write her mother and make an arrangement?"

"You would like that, for some reason?"

"Yes, because what could Father say if Blanch rode up on a horse? He would not tell her to turn around and go home. He would ask you to make her an iced tea, wouldn't he? And we could talk and take a stroll."

"Oh, so I am to be the tea maker and I am to drop whatever I'm doing to come along on this 'stroll'? That is your idea of having things be more flexible, with my time spent offering refreshments and being a chaperone?"

"You have already done so much for us, Sister. I don't mean to take more of your time."

"Nor did DeWitt Lyall, either, after presenting me with all his bouquets and letters written with his lovely amber ink."

"He was not worthy of you."

"He was not."

"Maybe in the future you will find someone more appreciative of music, as you are, who is pleased to live in the country instead of yearning after Boston's city life."

"I doubt he would have yearned for it so much if Cousin Isabelle did not live there."

"He was not worthy of you."

"Thank you. Now may we move on to feeding the animals, instead of my waiting for you to finish painting?"

"Only a minute more, because you have only one chance when watercoloring. If you make a mistake, it can't really be put right."

"Who would see this mistake, since you are watercoloring a stack of hay?"

"No, it is much more than that. It is the sky behind it, and the field."

Sister Deborah put aside her knitting and walked to her nephew's chair in front of the window. She saw that the composition contained more than just the haystack, though Willie had started with that. He was filling in the sky now, leaving an area that formed a white cloud even without paint. She thought that that was how life was, sometimes: You included what was most important, but other aspects—other areas—took care of themselves. They didn't not exist just because you hadn't addressed them. That was a double negative. Her teacher, Miss Stevenson, had told her to avoid double negatives by speaking an affirmative: *They do exist, even if you haven't addressed them.*

Addressed put her in mind of the terrible letter again, just when she had begun to put it out of her mind. She put her hand on Willie's shoulder. She said, "Willie, why don't I write my own note to Blanch and ask her to come give advice on my handiwork? If you will make the tea yourself, I will do you that favor, and your father will be forced to be a gentleman, which is good practice for him."

"Would you do that?" Willie said, though it was not really a question because she had volunteered that she would.

How exactly did you make iced tea so that it wasn't cloudy? His mother had had a method for that, but he could not remember what she had said about it.

He dipped his brush in China White paint and filled in the puff of cloud quickly, excited, the composition done.

"Oh! That wasn't necessary!" cried Sister.

"What wasn't?" he said. Something that someone was doing outside? But there was no one there. He saw only the haystack, now both where it stood and on his watercolor pad. It was to be a gift to Blanch, but now, overcome by confusion and gratitude, he thought to say that the picture was a gift for her, for Sister. Who was already looking down at it, frowning. It was for Sister, who had just blurted out another of her confusing remarks.

Blanch Liddicoat went outside to tend the flowers. That morning she had helped her sister, Neila, make an apple pie—really, two apple pies, though one was considerably smaller than the other—and after she weeded the garden and picked a few choice flowers to put in the little blue vase that had come all the way from France, she would write a letter to Miss Deborah Moulton not only to thank her for the compliment about the sampler she had recently completed, but to say that she did not feel able to give any helpful information about how one might stitch better, as she was "all thumbs." Their mother had always told her that. Neila was talented in all things: singing, baking, and needlework, and had a talent, as well, for memorizing poems and reciting them with great feeling. Blanch looked to her older sister for guidance in all things, including the exact wording of the letter she would be writing.

The gladiolas were slim stemmed and proud, coral colored with a bit of white like a ruffle deep inside. She lowered her cutting knife and turned to the phlox, of which there were so many that she cut two almost without thinking, a pink and a white. Her mother found the flowers "common" but Blanch thought them the equal of any other. The iris would not bloom again until next spring, though she could look at the spot in the garden and know where they would appear again, come late May or early June. It seemed an eternity away. Her father and his helper were haying the fields. Poor Neila had had to work at his side when she was younger, though she had developed such a dreadful sensitivity to the stuff, she stayed inside with the window closed when the haying days came and baked bread or pies or contributed in some other way. Blanch had never hayed. She did not concentrate easily, often had the bad luck to be stung by bees, and was "a dreamer," according to their mother, not likely to marry unless she met another dreamer. Like her older daughter, Mother was able to memorize—though she favored biblical passages and would, after great prompting, recite them one-on-one, but never to a group. Modesty was a virtue, as was purity, and Mother had considered this in bestowing Blanch's name. Neila had been named for her maternal grandmother. Neila had also been given Grandma's golden locket, which dangled a heart embedded with the tiniest speck of sapphire, which flashed like finches' wings when their undersides caught the sun. It had been her father's idea that Blanch be given the small French vase that had been brought by Cousin Chester, who had sailed away and married a lady from Marseilles—Blanch too would then have a "souvenir" from a family member. Really, though everyone enjoyed the vase, it was *hers*, and had made her garden so much more important.

She was kneeling on a garden cushion, her two cut flowers put in a bucket with water in it at her side, when Neila came out of the house and said, "I have decided to go help in the field, because I believe I have outgrown my sensitivity to hay. I have opened the kitchen window and breathed deeply, and though I can smell the hay, it does not make me at all dizzy, and I do not want to be like you and dawdle all day, when others are working."

Dawdling! She had weeded until her garden gloves were brown, all the fingers . . . and didn't everyone exclaim that she arranged even a simple flower or two perfectly in the admirable little vase, didn't her efforts benefit every member of the family? Sometimes Neila could be just terrible in the things she would say. She had asked to borrow Neila's necklace once, and Neila had grabbed the dangling heart in her hand as if her sister had reached for it, and said it was not hers to lend—not hers!—and that Mother had seen that the heart was meant to dangle near Neila's own, it was not something that could be passed around. If Neila had meant to be wicked, she could hardly have said anything worse. Blanch had tried to forgive Neila for saying such a thing, thinking she must have another of her headaches, or that she, Blanch, did not understand how important it must be to Neila to be connected as she was to their grandmother, but it was not always easy to look the other way. It made her think that she would not ask her sister's advice, after all, about how to reply to Willie Marsh's aunt. It might make Neila say something spiteful if she found out yet another compliment had been bestowed on Blanch.

She went inside and cut the stems a second time, carefully pouring a trickle of water into the vase, putting first the white, then the pink phlox in it. The effect was as beautiful as rouge on a lady's cheek: The vase suddenly brightened. She carried it to the table in the parlor and centered it on the white doily, stepping back to admire the perfection. And because she was not an idle person, regardless of Neila's unkind remark, she set to writing the letter right away, taking the fountain pen from the little tray that was its home, unscrewing the cap and placing it back on the tray so it would not roll away. Before she knew it, she had written sincere words of thanks and had also said that while she would not presume to give advice, nevertheless it would be a pleasure to view what she knew to be Aunt Deborah's own excellent work, and adding that the idea of having an iced tea would make it a perfect afternoon. She wondered whether to send greetings to Willie, but decided that it would be too forward, unless she decided to send her regards to everyone, which she did not think necessary. She thought that Aunt Deborah had merely been making it clear that the visit was to include some talk about needlework, but that Willie and his father would also be there to socialize. Hoping that their friend might stop by, and that there might be some music, seemed unlikely, though even if she did not write it, she did hope that would happen. Willie had said to her that when the fiddle was played, she had tapped her foot so delicately, he had admired her keeping the beat so subtly but surely.

Blanch was thinking that if there was reason to visit many times, Willie Marsh might fall in love with her. If he did, she would try to fall in love with him. She would like to marry and stay close to her parents, and—she indulged a not very nice thought of her own— what would her sister have to say then, when she asked to borrow the locket for her wedding, as something borrowed *and* something blue? The entire plan seemed perfect, at least in terms of getting her way with her sister, whom, she had to admit, she was bearing a grudge toward, just when the terrible thing happened.

It meant there would be no visit to the Marsh house, no step closer to walking down the aisle, no thought of her, Blanch, at all, until it became clear (as it later would) that poor Neila would recover. There was shouting in the field. She dropped the pen, slightly spattering the letter she would not even send, it would turn out. It was her father, carrying Neila, her skirts blown up so that you could see every bit of one leg, her black shoes like the hooves of some dead animal. Oh, it was a terrible sight, her father rushing toward the house with Neila looking like laundry twisted on the clothesline in a sudden storm, her hair every which way, her head bent back so that you could not even see her face, just the swirl of hair, like water eddying around a drain. Two things had just happened: Neila had stepped on a beehive in the ground, rousing the worst and most dangerous of bees, and as she shrieked and turned, she fell headfirst into a pile of hay, which cut her poor face and set her sneezing until she could not get her breath and collapsed and sprawled there, all of it happening in just seconds. The helper ran behind them, swarmed by bees himself, his scythe no protection. The bees made a visible little tornado that moved quickly forward until it seemed to rise right out of Father's head as he kept running and screaming, running across the field.

Her necklace was lost, but no one noticed for the two days she was hardly able to moan, no one noticed though she threw her head from side to side, until finally Blanch did notice and though the light was fading fast, went into the field with the oil lamp and searched and searched until she found it. She did find it! The chain was broken but that could be repaired in town. She found the necklace that meant everything to Neila, as Neila meant everything to her. She would get credit for finding it, for whispering right in her sister's ear that she had, weaving the chain through Neila's limp fingers as she slept so fitfully. It brought her back to consciousness sooner, Blanch thought (though she thought it silently, aware that saying so would express the Sin of Pride).

Poor Neila was sick for so long, and Mother worried that her face above her eyebrow might scar, and dabbed a special plant extract on it every night, sitting for long periods of time, stroking her poor daughter's sweaty brow above the cut.

What happened to the idea of marriage to Willie Marsh? Blanch forgot all about it, and later married a man named Joseph Ryson, who had a twin brother who married in a double wedding with his brother

131

the same day, taking as his bride a widow with a little son, and all of them then set off together for Cleveland, Ohio. Neila remained on the farm, though she walked the grounds—those times she did—as if the earth might shift below her any second. And she wore men's work boots, never again her black buckled shoes. She never married either, but her necklace was repaired and her pies were sold for the highest price at the church bake sale, with a ledger kept secretly of what everyone would pay, and at the end of the day, the winner of the pie was announced.

Willie Marsh won the pie in October 1900. And it's said he sat down and ate it at a picnic table on the grounds of the church, talking about what a talented family the Liddicoat family was, with the ladies able to memorize and to recite lines like actors on a stage, and Neila the best baker of all the bakers in town, and her sister, Blanch, off on a big adventure in Ohio, where he'd heard there were catfish in the river you could scoop up in a net while you were standing on the banks, and where the sky was so blue that the clouds seemed like visitors: Just when you least expected it, you'd look up and someone from the past would be standing at your door, knocking. You'd make out their features even though they were older and squint them into a recognizable face, you'd know who they were even though their arrival was so unexpected, even though they were just blowing through town.

Blanch, Blanch, Blanch, he thought, as he ate his pie. His friend Bill, who'd come with him, dug in with his own fork, having no such thoughts, and having contributed fifteen cents toward winning Neila's pie, both of them having offered everything they had.

Charlie Moon's Last Performance
Clark Knowles

EVEN NOW, TWENTY YEARS since *Moon over Manhattan* was canceled, people see me and shout, Hey, *Char*-lie! Or, Charlie Moon, what'd you get into this time? Or, I bet you're planning something big, aren't you, Charlie Moon? I'm used to being recognized and don't mind being called Charlie instead of my given name. If I hear someone shouting Erik or Charlie, I'll turn my head, smile, wave, sign an autograph—either name, whichever you want—pose for a picture, chat with you while we wait for the light to change, answer your questions while we eat our sandwiches at the counter at Newberry's, promise to call your nephew on his birthday because he's a huge fan and watches the reruns and pretty much has every episode memorized, lend you a few bucks for a taxi, address inconsistencies you've noticed in the show, or explain that I've not kept up with Denise Garrity or Fred Thurman or Barbara Stevens or Nat Goldman, who played my mother, father, sister, and brother, respectively, or explain that no, I'm not destitute as per the rumors, nor a junkie in recovery living at a halfway house, nor was I killed in Sadr City working for a private security firm employed by the CIA to fight insurgents bent on destroying the infrastructure of a rebuilt Iraq, nor did I develop a fetish of any sort, but particularly not for photographs of young boys in private-school uniforms akin to the ones my character wore on the show, and no, I kept no memorabilia from the set aside from the family photo that sat on the sideboard in the dining room and always seemed a warm and realistic prop on the otherwise cool and echoing soundstage, and yes, the story you heard about my real family is true, and yes, it was due to our tragedy that the show was canceled, at least in part, because the photos and videos taken at the beach the day my father—the real man, Arthur Blaine, whom I remember now only in snippets, his oven-mitt-sized hands, for instance, or his shaggy hair and perpetual stubble—was caught in a riptide and dragged out to sea showed a distraught son and wife, each standing near the waterline, scanning the glass-flat sea, occasionally pointing, raising an arm at the slightest prospect of a body, a hand, a head, each of us stoic for

133

a few minutes, each of us growing more distressed, lifeguards paddling back and forth on surfboards, helicopters thumping their way overhead and toward the horizon, growing smaller and smaller until they were so distant that it seemed inconceivable that my father could have been pulled so far so fast and both of us certain for a long time—two hours at least—that we'd simply not looked hard enough, or not in the right places, and my mother refusing to leave the beach as the sun went down. We'd come to Hawaii to film the season six finale—it was a big deal at the time, the show was at the top of its game, a top-ten Nielsen stalwart. On this final day before we were to return stateside to rest, regroup, and prepare for season seven, we convened on the beach, a huge caravan of actors and technicians and directors and assistants. The rest of the cast and crew gradually disappeared from the photos until it was just my mother and me crying, standing, sitting, watching, waiting, the sun lower and lower in the sky, our bodies less and less whole, more and more shadow, silhouettes blending against the dark blur of water, ephemeral, lost. When those pictures surfaced in every major newspaper and the videos played on every major news outlet the next day and in the weeks and months that followed—there were dozens of paparazzi with telephoto and zoom lenses and black bags and thousands of photographs to sell, and camera crews that videoed every second, for the sake of completeness—the producers of *Moon over Manhattan* became acutely aware of the impossibility of continuing production of the show. Who could look at the tear-streaked face of Erik Blaine and see, ever again, the lovable scamp Charlie Moon?

What I'm not trying to say is that I blame the producers or have any negative feelings for them at all. I don't. They've been nothing but supportive. Jerry Eiger has continued to send Christmas cards and the occasional script my way. My wife, Beth, handles my correspondence—especially during the inevitable influx on the anniversary of my father's death, or following a showing of one of the numerous "Where Are They Now" specials, or the upcoming release of the *Complete Moon over Manhattan DVD Box Set* (also available as a digital download on Amazon and at iTunes) with actor and director commentaries, four "making of" documentaries, the official footage from the beach of my final moments in front of the camera, cheeks lacquered by tears, and most spectacularly, the never-before-seen two-part season-six finale. Beth has been gearing up for a wave of interest in my life and says that I'm probably more famous now than ever and if I wanted to, I could easily resume a career in television or films. The television scripts have been interesting, particularly one entitled *Extinction*, in which I would play the blind leader of a group of hunted alien pilgrims searching the galaxy for a safe haven. The films have been mostly low grade, but Beth argues that most child actors get offered no scripts and that perhaps I should be less picky, less judgmental about what is good and what is not good. She says that I should be grateful to be remembered and more willing to play a wide range of characters in different sorts of projects before I'm completely forgotten and wind up hoping to be cast in some reality show like *Celebrity Dorm* or *SoberQuest* or *Talent Now!*, which is exactly what happened to Barb Stevens (*Celebrity Get Fit!*) and Nat Goldman (*Across the Globe: Celebrity Edition*), although appearing on those two shows didn't harm either of their careers. In fact, it might have been their willingness to reveal their flaws—weight gain, anger issues—that ignited the renewed interest in *Moon over Manhattan*, which in turn led to the development and release of the box set. When we gathered to record the commentary for the set, both Barb and Nat looked healthy: Barb svelte in her newly sculpted body; Nat tanned and calm (one of the challenges in *ATG* led him to a Buddhist monastery and though he eventually lost to Traci McDowell, the star of the early eighties dramedy about two lovable orphans, *Lost and Found*, Nat credits the show with turning his life around and allowing him to see the broad path toward enlightenment), and they were genuinely happy to see me, nearly crying as we hugged. We hadn't reunited since leaving Hawaii nearly twenty years ago, when my mother and I retreated from the spotlight. Beth wondered whether their emotional response was designed for the cameras, which filmed the reunion as a part of the planned *Moon over Manhattan* television special, or a spontaneous reaction to seeing me, their old colleague and TV brother. After all, she'd said, neither Denise Garrity nor Fred Thurman had such extreme reactions. Of course, my TV parents had moved on quickly to other work. Denise starred in the acclaimed drama *Queens*, in which she played a working-class matriarch in the titular borough; Fred returned to Broadway, where he got his start, and made a splash with his Tony-nominated portrayal of Alexander Hamilton in the hit musical *Revolution!* They most likely had less invested in our short time together on screen. Beth is happy that people remember *Moon over Manhattan*, but she's never put any real pressure on me to return to acting. She does occasionally remind me that if one doesn't use God's freely given gifts, it's like spitting in God's face, but she understands how tough it must be for me to return to the work that led my family to Hawaii and into everything else. Some nights, while we are sitting together after dinner, watching television, she'll point out roles she says I could do in my sleep. Do you know this director? she'll say. Or, didn't I see a letter from this producer? Have you called him? I bet he could open some doors. Beth is beautiful, a lean and fervent blonde of the type that populate the networks' prime-time lineups. She's athletic and sensuous and organized and I love her very much, but she is a horrible actor and she cannot hide from me the fact that she desperately wants to be more famous than she is, that she wants access to bigger stars and fancier parties than the ones we are invited to. She wants us to be richer and perhaps live in a swankier neighborhood. She leaves me notes that are meant to boost my self-esteem, but she cannot hide, not completely, her resentment of my complacency. We have plenty of money. The residuals, coupled with my well-invested salary from the show's original run and boosted by my father's life insurance policy, leave us without financial worry. Beth is a personal trainer and I work at my charities. On weekends, we travel to Cape Cod, where we have a home in Osterville. Materially, we have more than so many people. So very much more.

My mother is a grief counselor and nondenominational chaplain at Northstar Hospice Services, a guiding light for those entering the final stages of this life and the loved ones bereaved by the passage between worlds. It was, she tells many people, those transformative few hours on the beach with me that put her on this path. Before the currents of the Pacific captured my father—who was a marvelous swimmer, by the way, capable of treading water for an unfathomably long time, and of swimming lap after lap in the pool—she'd been in denial of mortality. Her life, she says, was fear based and built upon ignoring the unknown. Even the love she'd felt for her husband and son was based on the illusion that death was not inevitable. Standing on the beach, she realized she'd spent her life afraid of the dark, as if she'd been running from room to room in a mansion turning on lights, keeping the place bright as a football stadium, but the lights wouldn't stay lit, darkness was always at her heels, and she'd sprint through the halls again and again, furiously retracing her steps, flipping the same switches in an effort to ward off the encroaching fear.

It got to the point—again, these are my mother's words, part of her comforting process—that she was more concerned with keeping the lights on than fearful of what might be waiting in the dark. Her industrious lamp lighting had become the "job" of living. And certainly it was awful, of course, to know that her husband had been swept away. All of the questions that accompany such an event came to her on the beach, such as: Why her husband and no one else? Why did he have to stay in the water so long? Who was he trying to impress anyway? What was she supposed to do now? The questions coursed through her as she scanned the ocean, which in the videos looks remarkably calm, but roils and heaves and foams in our memories as if the gods were singularly angry with me and her. In the videos, we stand near the waterline. The waves break in neat curls a few yards away and roll toward us in lazy lines. I was scared too, but whether because of my age or perhaps my own fearful composition did not have the epiphanies central to my mother's instantaneous acceptance and embrace of death as the entrance to another stage.

I've seen my mother comfort the loved ones of the dead and dying and while it is true that she is very earnest and often relies on the well-lit mansion analogy to the point of being corny, it is also evident that she truly believes the tale of her spiritual evolution. The people at Northstar need her sort of kindergarten approach to understanding dying because no one ever really speaks of it. My mother has aged nicely and at fifty-four could easily pass for late thirties and perhaps her physical vitality adds to her ability to comfort. She seems the sort of person who has certainly come to grips with some great tragedy, the type of person who has the inner spiritual strength that exudes a physical beauty. And true to her word, she no longer partakes in many of the denial-based activities she once had so much faith in: She no longer wears makeup or watches television; she is earthy in her endeavors, growing and eating much of her own food; she sits an hour's meditation twice daily; she attends prayer groups and survivor groups and bereavement groups and provides solace to the dying, touching their withered, papery hands, reading to them from a tattered collection of the world's greatest poetry, or from donated copies of *Reader's Digest*, or sometimes not saying anything at all, just being with the person when no one else will, waiting while the lights are dimmed one by one, until the house is dark and the body empty and cold. She helps prepare the bodies, clean them and drape them in sheets, as gentle with them in death as she was with them in life. She'll even talk to them, knowing as she does that their spirits often hover in the room, afraid to completely sever the ties to the physical. And then she'll comfort the family, bring them into the room, stay if they need her, and quietly exit if they don't. Her loving attentions do not go unnoticed. The families she works with do not forget her. They keep in touch and many have become friends, inspired by her story and her actions to become hospice volunteers themselves. She is a beloved figure throughout the community, in nearly all the local churches and temples, as she stands bravely and acceptingly in the doorway between the two worlds. So why do I cringe when I see her? Why does the sight of her name on my caller ID fill me with dread? I don't want to give the impression that I don't love my mother because it's simply not true. I love her deeply and am grateful for the sacrifices she made for me—the sacrifice of pulling me away from the acting life being the most important—but that does not change the fact that like Beth, my mother is a horrible actor. She is certainly talented enough for those she ministers to, and Beth, keen in so many other ways, admires my mother the way one bad actor will admire the work of another bad actor, because it makes their own acting deficiencies less pronounced, but the coat my mother dons as she prepares for her days of fearlessness and open acceptance of death has many loose strings and pulling them only unravels the fabric. Like most bad actors, she's continually breaking and regaining character. The line is not unbroken between who she is and whom she portrays. She is always two people: actor and character. Beth too shares this duality, as do most people. The good actors, it goes without saying, disappear.

Let me pause to reveal my motivation: My father has been swept away and my mother and I and most of the cast and crew of *Moon over Manhattan* and dozens of paparazzi and hundreds of tourists are gathered at the beach waiting for something. I'm just about to turn eleven. Certainly, what I remember of that day is reliable, though tinted in fallibility. We came down to the beach a bit later than usual. We'd just wrapped the final days of shooting and everyone attended the wrap party and the adults were hungover or just plain tired, emptied of any and all reserves after our two-week working vacation. My father was a fit man, as I've said, lean, very tan, and he'd not shaven in days. He too once had acting ambitions, but he wasn't as coolly exotic as James Dean or as dangerous as a young Paul Newman, or as un-Hollywood rugged as Charles Bronson. He was just a simple man with a face that lives nowhere but in a handful of pictures and my memory, stubbled on that day, features symmetrical but not distinguished. Given a different uniform or outfit, he could have been any extra on the beach—the guy who rented the chairs or the cop who patrolled the sands with a long, loping stride—anyone. In fact, my father's only success in acting came as an extra. He was in dozens of crowd scenes and if you knew where to look, he'd be there, under a hat, ear just visible. Once, in a scene filmed in a movie theater, my father's face appeared in the frame as he was pretending to laugh. For a split second he hovered there in the darkened movie palace, his face blending in with the crowd, his smile so wide and his laugh so genuine that you wondered why he couldn't have gone further in his career. My mother, on the other hand, was quite beautiful and vain. Though hungover, she'd made herself up nicely and wore a tiny bikini—tiny for the times, mind you, nothing compared to the skin on display at the average public beach these days. I was at an odd age—I knew about girls and about breasts and I'd sneaked peeks at the *Playboys* hidden underneath my father's workbench, not quite understanding the poses or the women who looked oily and angry, and unable to explain why I kept returning to the workbench or why I was so disappointed to find a well-thumbed older issue, or why I was ecstatic to find new issues, new women to ogle in the earliest stages of my sexual dawn—so I knew my mother had the same parts as these models, but I couldn't yet put together the sameness of their sexuality. I was also not yet old enough to be embarrassed by a mother wearing a bikini, not old enough to send her away, to banish her from my presence, as I would do within a year's time. Half a dozen beautiful women accompanied her, though I would not have seen them as beautiful then. Many of them were mothers, young and brimming with adulation for their infants and toddlers and attentive without being cloying to those of us a bit older. For the bulk of the afternoon, the men lay quietly on their towels and sipped water or drank cocktails from plastic cups brought by a succession of waiters wearing white slacks and flowered shirts. The women played with their children, or, like my mother, took walks up and down the beach to avoid sitting with their husbands or children. What the cameras never showed and what no one but me knows was that the night before, my father and mother had been in an awful argument. They hadn't shouted at each other—there were no raised voices—but from my

room in our suite, I could easily hear the invective-laced tirade un-
leashed sotto voce by my father, who had discovered my mother's
dalliance with my costar Barb Stevens's father, a strange, brooding
man who I remember only as a shadow at the back of the studio
as we filmed, or hunched beside Barb as they walked to the car after
we taped. My father accused my mother of things that I did not
understand, used words that I did not yet know, and for many years
afterward, shielded as I was by mother's spiritual evolution, those
words—whore and slut—and those accusations—of adultery and for-
nication—were my secret, my own hoarded treasure. I do not know
which was worse, that they were applied to my mother, or that she
did not deny them. My resistance toward learning the exact defini-
tions of those words was perhaps my attempt at denying them for
her, since she remained silent on the night in question. They didn't
know I was listening. I doubt either of them thought for one moment
that their son, normally a sound, nearly catatonic sleeper, would
have heard the hushed yet insistent broadsides. Worst of all was the
long silence that followed, although to imply an actual silence is but
a half-truth. There were the urgent and violent disturbances of my
father's rage—all masked by the absence of words. What would cause
me, a young and naive ten-year-old, to rise from my bed and creep to
the French doors and peel back the curtain to view what I could not
hear? I did not fully understand what I saw, only that my father was
hurting my mother. She lay on her stomach on the bed, her skirt
bunched at her hips. My father was fully clothed, but his pants were
undone. His belt and its silver buckle jerked back and forth like a
downed electric line as he thrust into my mother. How long did it
last? How long did I watch? Why did I not come to her rescue? How
did I return to my bed and fall into a deep sleep? These are questions
I cannot answer. Several years later, when I read and understood the
definition of rape, I plucked the word from its context to secure in
the same lockbox in which I stored the other secret words. I would
say them at night, roll them off my tongue.

After a few hours of lying alone, my father rose from his beach towel
and looked up and down the beach. Not finding my mother, he
strode down the sands and into the water. I sat, soaked and pruney,
having spent the better part of the afternoon hopping on and off a
skimboard, gliding over the sand. I had come back to find my father
staring blankly toward the ocean, not acknowledging me in any way.

In fact, it seems now that he rose from the towel just as I returned, perhaps to avoid a conversation about what I had seen or heard. We hadn't spoken at all that morning and he'd given me no indication that he suspected me of eavesdropping. Perhaps he was simply occupied by his own roiling thoughts, and I, still attached to the child's belief that his parents' lives are but mere extensions of his own, joined him in mutual self-absorption. To this day, I have no insight into what certainly must've been the severe emotional ramifications of accusing one's wife of infidelity and unleashing a tide of rage. Was my father a violent and virulent character? To my knowledge, there had never before been any hint of those qualities, no indication that could become a man induced to rape by some unsealed tomb of jealousy. For all I knew, the jealousy had been unfounded, my mother's fidelity untainted. As I replay the event as an adult, I see my mother as she is now—the calm, restrained, careful patterns of speech. I can see her adjusting her glasses and piecing together her thoughts as a writer might, so that she might make herself clear the first time, and cannot help but imagine this same woman slowly gathering her defense, building some case, an argument with which to refute the story only to have her attempt at reasoned assessment and rebuttal cut short by my father's hands pushing her to the bed and raising her skirts and doing his damnedest to belittle, in his own way, their vows of love and cherishment. Then, of course, she would have had little recourse. Once begun, he did not stop until his orgasm released the stew of fetid anger. She kept her face buried in the blankets, her body limp, as if she weren't there. Perhaps even then she foresaw the looming ugliness of the following day. This indignity would become but a scrim through which she filtered the consumptive unhappiness that led to her renewal. Of course, the calm, comforting mother I place into this memory did not exist then, nor did my own critical observatory skills. What I saw, though burned with sufficient force into memory, has undoubtedly undergone many revisions and alterations. My mother was younger, used to attention, more easily angered, prone to flirtatious banter and to fishing for compliments from men, even strange men, or men I did not know, such as the clerk in the store where we bought my shoes, whom she often touched lightly on the shoulder when she believed I had wandered from the aisle, or in the barbershop where I received my haircuts, where she laughed more freely and spoke in a hoarse, throaty drawl as she sat with the men on the plump vinyl couch near the front window, or with Jerry Eiger himself, with whom she often sat during filming and whom I once observed with his hand beneath my mother's shirt in the green-room. I realized only later that it was this sexual luminosity that undid my father and led directly to his silence on the beach, to his measured walk to the water as I looked on, to his quick immersion into the ocean, a leaping dive toward deeper water, and to his fierce strokes away from land. I watched him swim farther and farther, not tempted to worry, glad in fact that he was away, at least for a while, and that I did not have to look at him or remember the grimace on his face, the face so like everyman, so run of the mill. At some point, he was swept under. I do not remember seeing him one instant and not seeing him the next. It came to me slowly that I could not find him and it took some time for me to stop searching the horizon and look to see if anyone else was worried. My friends and coworkers were all around me, busy with their serious day of relaxation. A number of younger children built sand castles close to the water. Jerry Eiger and the other producers were sipping drinks and laughing under a large floral canopy. A slew of hotel guests populated the sand with their shiny, colorful accoutrements: canvas beach chairs, plastic buckets, coolers, and pastel umbrellas. I swallowed my early panic and set my head on a swivel until I saw my mother coming up the long stretch of beach that led to a jetty a mile distant. I ran from the towel, not caring where I stepped or in whose face I kicked sand. Someone shouted, Hey watch it, Mr. TV Star, but I paid no attention. It was my greatest role, or the first moments of the role I've been playing ever since. By the time I reached my mother, I'd worked myself into a feverish state and could barely speak. Distraught, I told her that the ocean had swallowed my father and that he was lost. She studied me. I could see she was searching for fissures in my character, places where the mask was insufficient, but she could find none. Her own mask was not so infallible. The despair that enveloped her was sporadic; she occasionally had to hold her head in her hands to hide her face while she regrouped, extracted the shaking, weeping incoherent mess for the cameras, calling up the reserves of emotional fortitude required to keep us on the beach long after it was clear he was gone forever, while the cameras preserved the loving image of our hopefulness, of our courage as we scanned the horizon until it was indistinct, a gray line dividing two gray fields. Eventually a few stars flickered above our heads, or perhaps Venus or Mars, and we took that as our cue to leave. It occurred to me later that this final act of my father's was perhaps designed to be a great exit, that the assumed riptide was in fact nonexistent and that he had simply swum until he could swim no more, a penance for attacking his wife. But his facade was too good and his motivation unclear. The scene now lives as tragedy, not suicide. My mother's character, shaky at first, became convincing enough for the public. They never saw that glimmer of satisfaction that I occasionally witnessed in the mirror, that half smile that belied her grief and unveiled the actor. I don't blame her for playing the role. It's easier to be the bereaved wife than the survivor of spousal rape. Part of me loves her more adamantly for preserving the illusion, for transforming the scars into a life of service. What disappoints me most uniformly is the sloppy craft, the fact that I can see too clearly the division of character. She knows, I believe, that I can see the duality of the performance, though we have never spoken of such things. She knows that from an acting standpoint, I outshine her best efforts. Even in our most casual moments, at my most relaxed, when I am as far from stage as it is possible for an actor to be, I challenge anyone to see the slightest chink in the design, or the briefest lapse of character. I dare you, in fact, to uncover anything, anything at all that will lead you back to the blank slate onto which I am projected. Without hesitation, I assure you that you will never succeed. Beth, my adoring but simple wife, is incapable of this, as she is sufficiently taxed simply maintaining her role. My mother plays many roles and has little time to study me in mine. The producers of *Moon over Manhattan*, my old costars, my acquaintances—all of them convinced I'm still the poor boy who lost his father at sea, who lost his family, his livelihood, his future. What a pity, they say, that his mother pulled him from the limelight, that she didn't allow him the opportunity to accept the outpouring of love from his coworkers and fans from around the world. What a shame that his acting career was cut so short. To them I say: Nonsense. We all know the fate of child actors. We know what they become. Soon, the DVD of *Moon over Manhattan* will hit the shelves along with the never-before-aired final episode of season six. The royalties of this set alone will ensure that I never have to audition for another part, ever again. And why would I want to? I already have the role of a lifetime.

Shhhhhh, Arthur's Studying
Peter Orner

ARTHUR WAS A QUIET BOY who grew into a quiet man. When he and Walt Kaplan were boys it was always, *Shhhhhh, Arthur's studying.* There's got to be at least one yeshiva butcher in every family and a yeshiva butcher's got to have quiet. *Go play outside, Walt, your brother's studying.*

And so Walt went to work in their father's furniture store and Arthur went to college, first to Brown and then to Columbia for his PhD in classics. Arthur's face was pale. He always looked as though he'd been dusted with flour. This added to his gravitas, and Walt, like the rest of the family, was proud that Arthur looked the part of a scholar ghost.

His first book appeared in 1968. For a man who lived such a quiet life (he'd married a wan, squirrelly-looking girl and they lived in Brooklyn without children), the book nearly caused a scandal. The title was innocuous enough: *Catiline and His Role in the Roman Revolution.* Yet the book was a surprisingly graphic and spirited defense of Catiline. The man made trouble two thousand years ago and here he is making more havoc via the pen of meek little Arthur Kaplan who came out of the womb speaking Hebrew and Latin. . . .

Villainous fiend, murderer, robber, corrupter of youth and donkeys, venal proprietor, traitor! Plutarch topped it off with the accusation that Catiline had deflowered his own daughter. And all this in the prologue!

What? The family gasped. What? What? Don't get us wrong. An author is an author is an author and our Arthur is an author. His name's right there on a book. But incest? Donkeys? Maybe he should have been out in the street playing stickball with Walt.

"Maybe nobody will read it."

"Ah, yes. Of course, that's it. Nobody will read it."

"But we'll put it on the shelf."

"Yes, absolutely, the shelf."

*

144

ROMAN UPHEAVAL TOPIC OF A BOOK BY DR. KAPLAN
Can Catiline be cleared?
The reputation of the Roman conspirator assigned to infamy
in the polemics of Cicero has been reclaimed. . . .

—Fall River Herald News

September 25, 1968

Arthur's triumphant appearance in Fall River. He gave a short speech at his alma mater, BMC Durfee High School, noting that the destruction of Catiline's reputation was the result of the same sort of mudslinging that characterizes the politics of today. "And you think the Romans were violent? Maybe we ought to look at ourselves in this year, 1968. . . . It is not a man who is heard but his critics. Because critics always shout louder and use more colorful language. Elections bring out the poet in politicians, don't they? Take, for instance, the consular elections of 64 BC when Cicero called Piso (father of Caesar's last wife, Calpurnia), among other things, brute, plague, butcher, linkboy of Catiline, lump of carrion, drunken fool, inhuman lunatic, feces, epicurean pig, assassin, temple robber, plunderer of Macedonia, infuriated pirate egged on by desire for booty and rapine. . . . And yet, it must be said that, compared to Catiline, Piso was a lunch counter."

This was followed by a strangely long pause. Arthur leaned over the podium, gaped at his audience, and waited. He repeated it. "Piso was a lunch counter." His sad, pasty face, his eyes imploring. (Cousin Ida nudged Cousin Frieda and whispered, *Must he make those awful lists?*) It was Walt who finally, mercifully, laughed. Ah, a lunch counter! Piso was a lunch counter! My brother the scholar was never known for his sense of humor. You sell furniture, you gotta have a sense of humor. Are you finished with this speech, Arthur?

And yet one night, about a month or so later, it was Walt who, after dinner, went and took the book off the shelf in the living room where Sarah had safely stored it for posterity. He carried it upstairs to his study in the flat of his hand like a waiter carrying drinks. Then he locked the door and went to Rome. Night was thinning into morning by the time Catiline uttered the last of his famous last words: *But if fortune frowns on your bravery, take care not to die unavenged. Do not be captured and slaughtered like cattle, but fighting like heroes leave the enemy a bloody and tearful victory.*

Walt hears trumpets. If fortune frowns . . . Viva Catiline! Viva the traitor!

145

Furthermore, as my brother argues, no self-respecting republic should be without a little healthy rebellion. It keeps everybody honest and with a blowhard like Cicero believing every word that rolled off his golden tongue no matter how ridiculous—somebody had to draw a line across the forum with his sword. *Even, yes, if it costs your life.* Walt slides off his chair and onto the carpet. He stares at the ceiling. His study is a box that envelopes him, protects him. There are days he mourns this room, wonders how it will go on without him when he's gone. Yet right now the distance between himself on the floor and the ceiling is intolerable.

I'm lying in a grave in my own house. To think there are people who believe that when it's all over the angels sing and we float up higher and higher. . . . They don't doubt. They believe. Before I put on my other sock, I've doubted the entire day.

After the Battle of Pistoria, they brought Catiline's severed head back to Rome in a basket.

This has to mean something.

Once, in this very room, a jay rammed into the window. Then he backed up and flew into it again. Again. Again. Again, until he finally dropped into the dirt by the side of the house. And they say only man is heroic enough to pursue lost causes.

This morning, my people sleep. My own brother, the scholar, has faith enough—believes in enough—to devote his life to raising an ancient debaucher from the dead; he sleeps in leafy Brooklyn. My wife and daughter sleep across the hall. The dawn sun claws upward. I sink into carpet. How can I arise to protect my people if I don't even own a sword?

How can you shout farewell if you never go anywhere?

Lamentation
Rachel Tzvia Back

—For my father, on his dying

1.

In worded a world
how broken
from beginning:

sunburst and blossoms all
subterfuges
of creation ruses

of beauty—
fragrant thicket no less
complicit:

we exist
in a shattered vessel
shards at our bare feet—

Someone's mother cries out
Stand still or
you'll get hurt—and

you try hard in the slivered
moment
not to move.

2.

Day asks: What does it matter
putting this anticipated
loss

on the page our
un-readiness
for imagined emptiness

of after—
why
direct half-

worded sorrow to tell
his tale or
your own

inked in another—it's
just another
loss what

does it matter
it has always been
already

shattered—
Day asks
then asks again.

3.

Because what
can be said?
In the end

the spoken stands
with bare spindly arms
around

its unspoken
brother what
fear

fastens
with tight knots to
your ravaged throat so

what you do
speak is always
poor and pale

shadows
of what
you do not.

4.

You are dying.

But you do not say so
we do not say—
together

in steadfast
not-saying
alone the winds

orbit and echo
inner chambers where we
linger in

your researching
options thick
folders of studies

long letters to the scattered
family reports
of shifting numbers

platelets and neutrophiles
knotted
defiance of

your fall

5.

But *our* alphabet
aleph-bet
          aleph

prepares itself
for radical
          unraveling:

aleph at
          abyss edge
          acerbic sky above and
          air or ache all
          abeyant but un
          abating

bet because
                    ballast or balm
                    bond to
                    before behind be
                              always

aleph
          again un
          availed avale our
          Av awhile then
          away and
                    absent

Aba

6.

Six feet tall broad and bearded
traveling a world
(in a hospital bed)

professor and scientist
(huddled under
the covers)

in coat and tie commanding
(postchemo hair white wisps
wistfully

soft) an auditorium
of students.
When I'd describe you

it would always be:
He's a large man, he *fills*
the room   (wound

at your neck
gaping)   oh
small child

of poverty—
always
your wide-chested gestures

of generosity.

7.

Thus loss
installs itself among us   looses
an arrow—

Bow bent
we are set
as mark for the arrow

into unblemished skies
scars each hour our
forever altered

father
failing
falling

toward
harrowed
        Oh hollow

the heart's a
hollow, a hole in which, a window in
which, a cloud—

earth.

8.

Cut loose　(not
yet)　we are
at

a loss
we are
in

a loss
and
lost in

lost to
what
we are

bound to
bound by
now slowly

losing
in days
and numbered

hours

9. *Dream-inquiry 1*

There were mourners in the orchard
    under the almond blossoms
        wrapped in black
prayer shawls
    their feet bare in the dirt
        heads bowed
before day's last
    gold thread & hue and
        I knew
when night would
    lie down at last among
        nestled leaves in
the steep
    and stolen instant, then
        the gathered mourners
together
    would lift their black shawls
        to suddenly tassled winds
and take
flight—

Death's shadow
is always white.

10.

Hope is a whirl
> *of dead leaves*
>> *a reflection*
of their gold
>> *rustling in the wind*—is

imagined inlet water-
moored buoy miracled
railing

at cliff's unforgiving edge—
in the hospital bed
the fever broken

your eyes open
blood replenished
mysterious

elements restored
you recite their names
one by one:

lymphocytes
monocytes
albumin creatinine—

creation's secrets
(modeh ani)
spoken as prayer.

11.

Each morning you bind yourself
to yourself
with tefillin: black straps

set
as a seal
upon thine heart

around your
upper arm, faith
at your forehead—

two quiet black boxes
guard parchment
within will

tell a tale after   *Well*
of living waters
sweet streams from Lebanon.

If you bind the straps
tight enough
might

they hold you
to this world
awhile longer?

12.

In the prayer hall the Orphan
rises alone
to praise

the Name: *raised*
lauded extolled
exalted

adored and
blessed—not a word
on Death.

So will my brothers
in prayer
shawls stand

in the quorum
quiet
prayer halls as

early morning light
receding
bares their grief—

you see
they are become
fatherless.

13.

And where will we
my sisters and I
stand—how

will we grieve (she
sat alone
badad)

wanting to be
a sownding of sisters lamentation
of swans.

To your eldest daughter you
confide
you are dreaming now

how your mother hovers
above you fevered
child

she covers
in comforters
their feathered weight

forgotten
winged
embrace.

14.

Wayward daughter who imagines
the after before
even as you

wrestle disease
refuse surrender.
This wayward

writing
on imagined
mourning morning prayers

while you wake
and I wake
in fear—

what crimes
to the spirit
do I commit—

then I return
unrepentant
to the unrepenting

page.

15.

By the door by the snow by the night
falling
in whitelaced

grace and ribboned
light floating
in the hushed air, there

you once saw me
suddenly
no longer a child—

it was all in my hair
falling, burnt spring
on my shoulders.

This was long ago—in slow
motion you pulled it all back
tucking it out of sight

then covered
my head with the hood
at the threshold *So*

you'll stay warm, you said
waiting to watch me
walk away

into white night.

16.

White robed at the feast
full moon and you
insisting

we listen
again follow
again

as into hidden
caverns
in the face

of a rocky hill secret
library
waiting—

musky low-stone ceiling
moss-covered and root-
latticed walls

clinging to each curve
lipped shelf pulling
toward earth every

fallen word
caught in your palm, psalms
at your lips:

17.

Now chanted
(in wine-stained
robe) as dusty

opening talismanic
offerings
and codes:

The Days of Awe (your favorite)
Stalks from the Gleaning
Sefer Mitsvot Gadol (The Great Book of Commandments)

The Book of Questions
The Book of Creation
The Book of Remembering & Forgetting

The Work of the Makhinites (four brothers, the oldest was Nathan)
The Book of the Perfumer (12th-century Elazar ben Judah of
Worms,   each letter still thick with fragrant musk, you said)
Zohar Hadash

A Book from the Ruins
A Book of the Fathers

The Book of Glory

A Daughter's Book of Mourning

18.

Always that tilting stack at
your bedside and
poetry

tucked in tallis bag—
private haven in prayer's
gathering.

Like those concealed
in the stranger's sleeve
or charred

leaves
pulled from flames
singed and saved—

savored
as voiced
enduring.

In titled
phrase or page
illumined art

all in my lettered
heart
dedicated

to you.

19.

You
who will not read these words
or any or

ever—
your watery blue eyes
mostly closed through

long days of dying.
Once there was
an angel

who pressed her delicate
finger against our
upper lip

at birth to whisper in
our infant ears:
Don't tell.   Now

we whisper instead
no last secret but
Love—

and your tapered fingers still
long and lovely
answer

in gentle gestures
from the white sheets.

20.

The hours stand still at
the threshold
altered

in the afternoon
apartment

you are leaving.

You want
not to.

If you cry out we will
hear you but not

know—No

greater alone
you
moving toward

unknown unbounded
unworded

what

comfort can we
give there is

21. *Dream-inquiry 2*

There in a grove of old olives
      my father at eighty has climbed
            the highest branch
to pick fruit and perch
      among pale dust-covered leaves
            ripe specks dangling
against a sun-blinded sky—
      his eyes
            toward the grove's edge where
pillagers have gathered
      stones from the wounded land in
            their angry hands and when
they raise weapons for harm
      my father lifts both his arms
            into the unblemished blue
a bird
      spreading white woven wings
            wide
over us all
      in the ancient grove
            steadfast
sun glistening
      still through the wings even
            after
he's gone.

22.

Kiss my lips—
you say in your
last sleep

then ask
is it today
I get married?

I hear
buried
in the room's

unmoving
air
unfailing

wife of 58 years
sleeping beside you
who

fathered us
well
we

will bury you
in the uncertain March
sky

between stone
and
cloud

your heart
in ours
calling
us
       to come in
to the dark

and hold

what is lost—
all that remains.

Deceit

Joyce Carol Oates

NOT BY E-MAIL BUT BY PHONE which is so goddamned more intrusive the call comes from someone at Kimi's school—*Please call to make an appointment urgent need discuss your daughter.*

No explanation! Not even a hint.

Candace has come to hate phone calls! Rarely answers phone calls! If she happens to be near the phone—the kitchen phone— quaint old soiled plastic that has come to be called, in recent years, as by fiat, a "land phone"—she might squint at the ID window to see who the hell is intruding in her life—for instance, the ex-husband— but rarely these months, could be years, does Candace *pick up.*

Cell phones she keeps losing. Or breaking.

Cell phones are useful for keeping in (one-way) contact with Kimi— *Crummy substitute for an umbilical cord*—and a pause, a beat, the signature wincing laugh that crinkles half her face like pleated paper, then—*Ha ha: joke*—if the assholes don't get Candace's wit.

And more it seems to be happening, assholes don't *get it.*

Well, the cell phone. Unless she has lost it, she has it—somewhere. Could be in a pocket of a coat or a jacket, could be on the floor of her car beneath the brake or gas pedal, or in the driveway; could be in a drawer, or atop a bureau; could be, as it was not long ago, fallen down inside one of Candace's chic leather boots; the cell phone is a great invention but just too damned small, slight, impractical. Could be sitting on the goddamned thing and not have a clue until the opening notes of Beethoven's Fifth Symphony come thundering out of your rear.

Not that Kimi answers Mom's calls all that readily—the docile- daughter reflex seems to have atrophied since Kimi's thirteenth birthday—but the principle is, getting voice mail on her cell through the day at school, text messages from MOM, Kimi at least has to ac- knowledge that MOM exists even if MOM is no longer one of those desirable individuals for whom Kimi will eagerly *pick up.*

*

"Your daughter."

"Y-yes? What about my daughter?"

Cool-calm! Though Candace's voice is hoarse like sandpaper and her heart gives a wicked lurch in her chest despite that morning's thirty-milligram Lorazepam.

"Has Kimi spoken with you, Mrs. Waxman, about—yesterday?"

"Y-yesterday?"

"Kimi was to speak with you, Mrs. Waxman, about an issue—a sensitive issue—that has come up—she hadn't wanted us to contact you first."

Weedle, Lee W.—"Dr." Weedle since there's a cheesy-looking psychology PhD diploma from Rutgers University at Newark on the wall behind the woman's desk—speaks in a grave voice, fixing her visitor with prim, moist, blinking, lashless bug eyes.

Why are freckled people so *earnest*, Candace wonders.

"Your daughter has been reported by her teachers as—increasingly this semester—'distracted.'"

"Well—she's fourteen."

"Yes. But even for fourteen, Kimi often seems distracted in class. You must know that there has been a dramatic decline in her academic performance this semester, especially in math. . . ."

"I was not a good math student, Dr. Wheezle. It might be simply—genetics."

"'Weedle.'"

"Excuse me?"

"My name is 'Weedle,' not 'Wheezle.'"

"Is it! I'm sorry."

Candace smiles to suggest that she isn't being sarcastic, sardonic—"witty." Though *Weedle* is a name for which one might be reasonably sorry.

". . . have seen your daughter's most recent report card, haven't you, Mrs. Waxman?"

"Did I sign it?"

"Your signature is on the card, yes."

Weedle fixes Kimi's mother with suspicious eyes—as if Candace might have forged her own signature. The woman is as toughly durable as polyester—like the "pantsuit" she's wearing—short-cropped, graying hair and a pug face like an aggressive ex-nun.

"If my signature is on the card, it is my signature."

Candace speaks bravely, defiantly. But this isn't the issue—is it? Hard to recall, in the Lorazepam haze, what the issue *is*.

171

"You can't expect children to leap through flaming hoops each semester. Kimi has been an A student since day care—it's cruel to be so *judgmental*. I don't put pressure on my daughter to get straight As any more than I put pressure on myself at her age."

Since the ex-husband is the one to praise their daughter for her good grades at school, as a sort of sidelong sneer at Kimi's mother, whom he'd taken to be, even in the days when he'd adored her, an essentially *frivolous person*, Candace takes care never to dwell upon Kimi's report cards.

Now the thought comes to Candace like a slow-passing dirigible high overhead in the Lorazepam haze—she hadn't done more than glance at Kimi's most recent report card. She'd had other distractions at the time and so just scrawled her signature on the card, having asked Kimi if her grades were OK, and Kimi had shrugged with a wincing little smile.

Sure, Mom, that smile had signaled.

Or maybe *Oh, Mom*. . . .

For this visit to the Quagmire Academy—i.e., Craigmore Academy—which is Candace's first visit this term—Candace is wearing a purple suede designer jacket that fits her tight as a glove, a matching suede skirt over cream-colored spandex tights, and twelve-inch Italian leather boots; her streaked-blonde hair has been teased, riffled, blow-dried into a look of chic abandon, and her eyebrows—recklessly shaved off twenty years before when it had seemed that youth and beauty would endure forever—have been penciled and buffed in, more or less symmetrically. Her lipstick is Midnight Plum; her widened, slightly bloodshot eyes are outlined in black, and each lash distinctly thickened with mascara to resemble the legs of a daddy longlegs. It's a look to draw attention, a look that startles and cries *Whoa!*— as if Candace has just stumbled out of a Manhattan disco club into the chill dawn of decades ago.

Weedle is impressed, Candace sees. Having to revise her notion of what Kimi Waxman's mom must be like, based upon the daughter.

For Candace has style, personality, wit—Candace is, as the ex-husband has said, a *one-off*. Poor Kimi—"Kimberly"—(a name Candace now regrets, as she regrets much about the marriage, the fling at motherhood and subsequent years of dull, dutiful fidelity)—has a plain, sweet, just slightly fleshy, and forgettable face.

Weedle is frowning at her notes. Which obviously the cunning psychologist has memorized that she might toss her dynamite material, like a grenade, at the stunned-smiling mother of Kimi Waxman facing her across the desk.

". . . at first Kimi convinced us—her teachers and me—that her injuries were accidental. She told us that she'd fallen on the stairs and bruised her wrist—she'd cut her head on the sharp edge of a locker door, in the girls' locker room, when she was reaching for something and lost her balance. The more recent bruises—"

Injuries? More recent? Candace listens in disbelief.

"—are on her upper arms and shoulders, as if someone had grabbed and shaken her. You could almost see the imprint of fingers in the poor child's flesh." Weedle speaks carefully. Weedle speaks like one exceedingly cautious of being misunderstood. Weedle pauses to raise her eyes to Candace's stricken face with practiced solemnity in which there is no hint—not even a glimmer of a hint—of a thrilled satisfaction. "I am obliged to ask you, Mrs. Waxman—do you know anything about these injuries?"

The words wash over Candace like icy water. Whatever Candace has expected, Candace has not expected *this*.

And there are the moist, protuberant eyes that are far steelier than Candace had thought.

The Lorazepam, like the previous night's sleep medication, provides you with a sensation like skiing—on a smooth slope—but does not prepare for sudden impediments on the slope like a tree rushing at you, for instance.

Warning signs are needed: SLOW. DANGER.

"Excuse me, w-what did you say, Dr. Wheezle?"

Weedle repeats her question but even as Candace listens closely, Candace doesn't seem to hear. In her ears a roaring like a din of locusts.

"Then—you don't know anything about Kimi's injuries? Neither the older ones on her legs, nor the more recent?"

Candace is trying to catch her breath. The oxygen in Weedle's cramped little fluorescent-lit office is seriously depleted.

"'Kimi's injuries'—I j-just don't . . . I don't know what you are talking about, Dr. Wheezle—*Weedle*."

"You haven't noticed your daughter's bruised legs? Her wrist? The cut in her scalp? The bruises beneath her arms?"

Candace tries to think. If she says *no*, she is a bad mother. But if she says *yes*, she is a worse mother.

"Mrs. Waxman, how are things in your home?"

"—home? Our *home*?"

"Do you know of anyone in your household—any adult or older sibling—who might be abusing your daughter?"

173

Abusing. Adult. Candace is sitting very still now. Her eyes are filling with tears, her vision is splotched as it often is in the morning, and in cold weather. In order to see Weedle's scrubbed-nun face clearly, Candace has to blink away tears, but if Candace blinks her eyes, tears run down her face in a way that is goddamned embarrassing; still worse, if Candace gives in, rummages in her purse for a wadded tissue. *She will not.*

"N-no. I do not—know. . . . I don't k-know what you are talking about, I think I should see Kimi now. . . ." Wildly the thought comes to Candace: Her daughter has been taken from school. Her daughter has been taken into the custody of Child Welfare. Her daughter has falsely informed upon *her.*

"Mrs. Waxman—may I call you Candace?—I'm sorry if this is a shock to you, as it was to us. That's why I asked you to come and speak with me. You see, Candace—we are obliged to report 'suspicious injuries' to the police. In an emergency situation, we are obliged to use the county family-services hotline to report suspected child abuse in which the child's immediate well-being may be in danger."

Candace is gripping her hands in her lap. Why she'd chosen to wear the chic suede skirt, matching jacket with gleaming little brass buttons, and the leather boots, to speak with the school psychologist/guidance counselor, she has no idea. Her heart feels triangular in her chest, sharp edged. Despite the Lorazepam and last night's medication, she'd had a premonition of something really bad but no idea it could be—*this bad.*

Eleven minutes late for the appointment with Weedle. Taking a wrong turn into the school parking lot and so shunted into the adjoining parking lot for the high school and so routed by one-way signs onto a residential street—goddamn!—returning at last to the entrance to the middle-school lot that she'd originally missed, impatient now and would've been seriously pissed except for the Lorazepam (which is a new prescription, still feels experimental, tenuous) and a hurried cigarette simultaneously first/last cigarette of the day, Candace vows—and inside the school building, which looks utterly unfamiliar to her—*Has she ever been here before? Is this the right school, or is her daughter enrolled at another school?*—bypassing the front office in a sudden need to use a girls' lavatory at the far end of the corridor—praying *Dear God dear Christ!* that Kimi will not discover her mother slamming into one of the stalls, needing to use the toilet and yet, on the toilet, cream-colored spandex tights huddled about her ankles like a peeled-off skin, there is just—*nothing.*

174

Goddamned drugs cause constipation, urine retention. If excrement is not excreted, where does it *go*?

Once a week or so, Candace takes a laxative. But sometimes forgets if she has taken it. Or forgets to take it.

Candace recalls another lavatory she'd hurried into recently on a false alarm, at the mall. This too a place where girls—high school, middle school—hang out. She'd been shocked to see a poster depicting a wan adolescent girl with bruised eyes and mouth staring at the viewer above a caption inquiring, ARE YOU A VICTIM OF VIOLENCE, ABUSE, THREAT OF BODILY HARM? ARE YOU FRIGHTENED? CALL THIS NUMBER. At the bottom of the poster were small strips of paper containing a telephone number and of a dozen or more of these, only two remained. Candace wanted to think that this was some kind of prank—tearing off the paper strips as if they'd be of use.

Weedle is inquiring about Kimi's father: Does he lose his temper at times, lose control, does he ever *lay hands* on Kimi?

" 'Kimi's father'—?"

Candace has begun to sound like a deranged parrot echoing Weedle's questions.

"Yes—Kimi's father, Philip Waxman? According to our records, he is your daughter's father?"

Some strange tortured syntax here. *Your daughter's father.*

"Well, yes—but this 'Philip Waxman' no longer lives with us, Dr. Weedle. My former husband has moved to Manhattan, to be nearer his place of employment, in which he occupies a sort of low-middle-echelon position of shattering insignificance."

"I see. I'm sorry to hear that. . . ."

"Sorry that he has moved to Manhattan, or that he occupies a low-middle-echelon position of shattering insignificance? He's in the insurance scam—I mean, 'game'—should you be curious."

Candace speaks so brightly and crisply, Candace might be reciting a script. For very likely, Candace has recited this script concerning the *former husband* upon other occasions.

Usually, listeners smile. Or laugh. Weedle just stares.

"The question is—does Kimi's father share custody with you? Does she spend time alone with him?"

"Well—yes. I suppose so. She is in the man's 'custody' on alternate weekends—if it's convenient for him. But Philip is not the type to 'abuse' anyone—at least not physically." Candace laughs in a high register, a sound like breaking glass. Seeing Weedle's disapproving expression, Candace laughs harder.

175

Once it is *dialogue* Candace is doing, Candace can do it. *Earnest conversation* is something else.

Weedle asks Candace what she means by this remark and Candace says that her former husband has refined the art of *mental abuse*. "But indirectly—Philip is passive-aggressive. It's as if you are speaking to a person who does not know the English language—and he is deaf! He becomes stony quiet, he will not *engage*. You can speak to him—scream at him—clap your hands in his face, or actually slap his face—only then will he acknowledge you, but you will be *at fault*. It is impossible for the man to lose at this game—it's his game. And if you stand too close to him, you're in danger of being sucked into him—as into a black hole." Candace laughs, wiping at her eyes. *Black hole* is new, and inspired. Wait till Candace tells her women friends! "Abusive men are 'provoked' into violent behavior but my former husband can't be provoked—*he* is the one who provokes violence."

But is this a felicitous thing to have said? With Weedle staring at Candace from just a few feet away, humorless, and slow blinking?

"What do you mean, Candace—'provokes violence'?"

"Obviously not what I said! I am speaking figuratively."

"You are speaking—in 'figures'?"

"I am speaking—for Christ's sake—analytically—and in metaphor. I am just trying to communicate what would seem to be a simple fact but—I am having great difficulty, I see."

Breathing quickly. Trying not to become exasperated. Her hands have slipped loose of their protective grip and are fluttering about like panicked little birds.

"What I mean is that, through his extreme passive-aggressive nature, the man provokes others, his former wife, for instance, to rage."

"*You* experience 'rage'? And how does this 'rage' manifest itself?"

This is coming out all wrong. It's like Weedle is turning a meat grinder and what emerges is *wrong*.

"It doesn't! Not me."

Candace's voice is trembling. Tiny scalding-hot bubbles in her blood, she'd like to claw at the imperturbable freckled-nun face.

"It doesn't? Not *you*? Yet you seem very upset, Mrs. Waxman—Candace. . . ."

"I think I want to see my daughter. Right now."

"'See' her? Take her out of class, for what purpose? So that the three of us can talk?"

"No—take her home."

There is a pause. Candace is breathing quickly in the way that a balloon that has been pricked by numerous small puncture wounds might breathe, to keep from deflating.

"Take her home! I think that—yes. Take her home."

More weakly now. For, having taken Kimi *home*—assuming that Kimi would agree to come home in the middle of the school day— what would follow next?

Imperturbable Weedle does not advise such an act. Imperturbable Weedle is telling Candace that taking Kimi out of school—"interrupting her school routine"—would be "counterproductive"—especially if Kimi's friends knew about it.

"Yesterday Kimi was quite defensive—she insists that the injuries are 'accidental.' It was the girls' gym instructor, Myra Sinkler, who noticed the leg bruises initially—this was about ten days ago—then, just yesterday, the shoulder and upper-arm bruises. Then Myra discovered the head injury—a nasty-looking little wound in Kimi's scalp, which should have been reported at the time, if it took place, as Kimi claims, in school—in the girls' locker room, after gym class. But no one informed Myra Sinkler at that time and no one can verify the account that Kimi gives—so we are thinking, Myra and I, that the 'accident' didn't happen when Kimi says it did, but at another time. And somewhere else. When Kimi was questioned she became excited, as I've said, 'defensive'—it's never good to upset a traumatized child further, if it can be avoided." Weedle paused. *Traumatized* hovered in the air like a faint, deadly scent. "Kimi promised us that she would tell you about the situation, Candace, but evidently she didn't. That was about the time I'd called you and left a message. In the interim— you didn't ask Kimi anything?"

"Ask her—anything? No, I—I didn't know what to ask her. . . ."

"You don't communicate easily with your daughter?"

"Well—would you, Dr. Weedle? If you had a fourteen-year-old daughter? Do you think that mothers of fourteen-year-old daughters and fourteen-year-old daughters commonly communicate *well*?"

Candace speaks with sudden vehemence. The moist protuberant nun eyes blink several times but the freckled-nun face remains unperturbed.

"Well—let me ask you this, Candace: What is Kimi's relationship with her father?"

"Dr. Weedle—is this a conversation or an interrogation? These questions you are firing at me—I find very hard to answer. . . ."

"I understand, Candace, that you're upset—but I am obliged to ask, to see what action should be taken, if any. So I need to know what Kimi's relationship has been with her father, so far as you know."

"Kimi's relationship with her father is—the man is her father. They are 'related.' I was very young when we met and arguably even more naive and optimistic than I am now—obviously, I wasn't *thinking*. The two look nothing alike and have very little in common—Kimi is clearly my daughter—one glance, you can see the resemblance— though Kimi is just a few pounds overweight, and a much sweeter girl than I was at that age. Is she ever! Too sweet, for instance, to say she doesn't much want to spend time with her very dull father—but she isn't, I think, *frightened* of him."

Was this so? Candace never asks Kimi about her weekends with Philip out of a sense of—propriety, you could say.

Or dignity, indifference. Rage so incandescent, it might be mistaken for an ascetic purity.

But mostly boredom. Candace is *so bored* by all that—enormous chunk of her "life"—like a clumsily carved male likeness on Mount Rushmore—the features crude, forgettable.

You can't just erase me from your life. How can you imagine you can do such a thing. . . .

Easily. Once Candace makes up her mind, breaking off relations with certain people, it's like an iron grating being yanked down, over a storefront window. And the store darkened, shut up tight.

"She sees her father, you said, on alternate weekends? Does she seem happy with this arrangement?"

"'*Happy*'? For Christ's sake, no one I know is '*happy*.' This is the USA. Are you '*happy*'?"

Candace is perspiring—something she never does! Not if she can help it.

Relenting then, before Weedle can respond, "Well—yes—frankly yes, I think Kimi *is*. Happy, I mean. She's happy with her classes, her teachers—her life. . . . She's an only child—no 'sibling'" (with a fastidious little wince to signal that, in normal circumstances, Candace would never utter so tritely clinical a term), "therefore, no 'sibling rivalry.'"

Weedle allows Candace to speak—fervently, defiantly. Hard not to concede that what she is saying mimics the speech of the mother of an adolescent who doesn't know what the hell she is talking about— hasn't a clue. Can't even remember exactly what the subject is except she's the object of an essentially hostile interrogation and not doing so well—Lee W. Weedle, PhD, is one of those individuals, more frequently female than male, to whom Candace Waxman is *not so very impressive.*

When she escapes back home she will take another thirty-milligram Lorazepam with a glass of tart red wine and maybe go to bed.

Except: What time is it? Not yet 11:30 a.m. Too early for serious sleep.

"And what about boys, Candace?"

"No—no boys. Kimi doesn't hang out with boys."

"She doesn't have a boyfriend? She says not."

"You've seen Kimi. What do you think?"

A sharp crease between Weedle's unplucked brows signals that this is not a very nice thing for Kimi's mother to say, however frank, candid, and adult to adult Candace imagines she is being. Quickly Candace relents: "I'm sure that Kimi doesn't have a boyfriend—even a candidate for a boyfriend. She's—shy. . . ."

"And what about other boys? In her class? Or older boys, from the high school possibly?"

"Kimi never mentions boys. The subject hasn't come up."

"You are sure, Candace?"

"Yes, I am sure."

Poor Kimi! Candace is embarrassed for her.

Grimly Weedle says: "Of course, there are boys even at Craigmore who intimidate girls—harass them sexually, threaten them. There have been—among the older students—some unfortunate incidents. And there is this new phenomenon—'cyberbullying.' Has Kimi ever mentioned being upset by anything online?"

"No. She has not."

"It's a strange new world, this cyberspace world—where children can 'friend' and 'unfriend' at will. We are committed to protecting our students here at Craigmore from any kind of bullying."

"Committed to stamping out bullies. I like that."

They will bond over this—will they? Candace feels an inappropriate little stab of hope.

"But Kimi hasn't mentioned being harassed? Bullied? Teased?"

"I've said *no.*"

But Candace is remembering—vaguely, like a photo image coming into just partial clarity—something Kimi mentioned not long ago about older boys saying *gross things* to the ninth-grade girls, to embarrass them; pulling at their hair, their clothes; *bothering* them. On the school bus, this was. Candace thinks so.

Candace asked Kimi if any of these boys were bothering her and stiffly Kimi said, "No, Mom. I'm not *popular*."

Candace knows that terrible things are said about the behavior of some of the middle-school students—both girls and boys—at Craigmore. Oral sex in the halls and beneath the bleachers, girls younger than Kimi exploited by older boys with a hope of becoming "popular"; boys bragging online about girls' lipstick smeared on their penises. Not at this private suburban school perhaps but at nearby public schools—boys physically mistreating girls, sexually molesting them in public; grabbing and squeezing their breasts, even between their legs. Some of this behavior is captured on cell phones—and posted online. From the mothers of Kimi's classmates Candace has heard these things—she'd been so shocked and disgusted, not a single joke had occurred to her. Where Candace can't joke, Candace can't linger. It is very hard for Candace to do *earnest*.

She'd been upset at the time. Seeing poor, sweet, moon-faced Kimi, a shy girl, with not-pretty features, hair so fine it sticks up around her head like feathers—among such crude jackals.

"If Kimi says she hurt herself accidentally, then Kimi hurt herself accidentally. My daughter does not lie. She is not *deceitful*."

"I'm sure she is not, Candace. But if she has been coerced, or threatened—"

"Kimi has always been accident prone! As a small child she had to be watched every minute, or . . ." Candace has a repertoire of funny-Kimi stories to testify to the child's clumsiness though the stories don't include actual injuries, of which there had been a few. Candace just wants this hateful, suspicious "school psychologist" to know that her dear, sweet daughter is *prone to self-hurt*.

"And Kimi's friends are all girls. They're all her ninth-grade classmates. She's known most of them since elementary school. Great kids, and I don't think they 'hang out' with boys."

As if unhearing, or unimpressed, Weedle says: "Adolescent boys can be terribly predatory. They can sense weakness, or fear. At almost any age, however young, if there's a ringleader—an alpha male—with a tendency to bully, he can manipulate the behavior of other boys who wouldn't ordinarily behave in such a way. These boys can harass girls like a pack. And girls can turn against girls. . . ."

Candace protests: "Kimi has never said anything to me about any of this! I really don't think what you are saying pertains to my daughter and I—I resent being . . ."

Candace feels a sensation of something like panic: Really she doesn't know what Kimi is doing much of the time, after school, for instance, upstairs in her room, with the door shut; frequently Kimi is at her laptop past bedtime, or texting on her cell phone, as if under a powerful enchantment; sometimes, one of Kimi's girlfriends is with her, supposedly working on homework together, but who knows what the girls are really doing on laptops or cell phones.

If Candace knocks at the door, at once the girls' voices and laughter subside—*Yes, Mom? What is it?*

A careful neutrality in Kimi's voice. So Mom is made to know that this is not *little-girl Kimi* at the moment but *teenager Kimi.*

The interview—interrogation—is ending, at last. Weedle shuffles papers, slides documents into a manila file, glances at the cheap plastic digital clock on her desk. Candace sees a pathetic array of framed photos on the desk—homely, freckled, earnest faces, in miniature—Weedle's parents, siblings, young nieces and nephews. Not one of Weedle with a *man.*

"You will call me, Candace, please, after you've spoken with your daughter this evening? I hope she will allow you to examine her injuries. We didn't feel—Kimi's teachers and I—that the injuries were serious enough to warrant medical attention any longer. But you may feel differently."

Feel differently? Meaning—what? In a haze of eager affability Candace nods *yes.*

Yes, she will call Weedle—of course.

Yes, she is an attentive, vigilant, loving, and devoted mother—who could doubt this?

(Wondering: Is this interview being recorded? Videotaped? Will Weedle use it against Candace as evidence, in a nightmare court case?)

(Is the former husband, Philip Waxman, in some way involved? *Is Weedle on Waxman's side?*)

Faintly now Weedle manages a smile. As if to mitigate the harshness of her words: "I will wait until I hear from you before making a decision about reporting your daughter's injuries, Candace. Kimi is certainly adamant that they were 'accidental' and we have no proof that they are not. But, you see, if I don't report 'suspicious injuries' to a child, and there are more injuries, which are reported, I will be held to account and I may be charged with dereliction of duty."

"Well, Dr. Weedle, we wouldn't want that—would we! 'Dereliction of duty.' Absolutely not."

Candace bares her beautiful teeth in a smile to suggest—to *insist*—that her words are lightly playful merely. But Weedle reacts as if stung:

"Mrs. Waxman, this is not a joke. This is a serious matter. Anything involving the well-being of a vulnerable child is serious. I would think you might be grateful that the staff at Craigmore is alert to a situation like this, rather than reacting defensively."

"I am grateful—very! The tuition I pay for Kimi's education here suggests how grateful! But I warn you—and Kimi's teachers—if you overreact about something harmless—if you call the 'hotline' and involve the police—I promise, I will sue you. I will sue you, and the others involved, and the school board. I will not allow my daughter to be humiliated and used as a pawn in some sort of politically correct agenda."

Feeling triumphant at last, Candace is on her feet. Weedle struggles to her feet. With satisfaction Candace sees that Weedle is shorter than Candace, and at least a decade older; Weedle is a homely woman, exuding the sexual allure of one of those inedible root vegetables—turnip, rutabaga.

"Good-bye! Thank you! I know, Dr. Weedle—you mean well. In fact I am impressed, the school staff is so *vigilant*. I will talk with Kimi this afternoon—as soon as she returns from school—and clear all this up. Shall I make an appointment now to see you next week—Monday morning? At this time?"

So brightly and airily Candace speaks, it seems she must be making a gesture of reconciliation. Such abrupt turns of mood are not unusual in Candace but Weedle is slow to absorb the change. Warily she tells Candace that Monday is a school holiday—Martin Luther King Jr.'s birthday. But Tuesday morning—

Candace laughs almost gaily. Something *so funny* about this.

"'Martin Luther King Jr.'s birthday'! Every month there's a great man's birthday! Sometimes there's 'Presidents' Day'—three for one. And how many great women birthdays do we have? Is Eleanor Roosevelt so honored? Emily Dickinson? Amelia Earhart? What about—Circe? Circe is a goddess—that's big-time. Or was there more than one of her? Is 'Circe' the singular—or the plural? Is there a 'Circ' and the plural is 'Cir-say'? Like goose and geese—ox and oxen?"

Weedle stares at Candace with an expression of absolute perplexity.

"All right! Tuesday, then. Same time, same place—I promise I will be on time."

Candace thrusts out a glittery-ringed hand to shake Weedle's pallid hand—one of those warm-friendly-intimidating gestures Candace has perfected, like a sudden parting social kiss to the cheek of someone who has been entranced by her, yet guarded.

182

Strides out of Weedle's office. Already she is feeling much, much better.

At the front entrance of Craigmore Middle School Candace has her cigarettes in hand and by the time Candace locates her car, on the far side of a lot she doesn't remember parking in, she has her cigarette lighted.

It's so: Kimi's friends are all girls she has known since grade school. A small band of not-pretty/not-popular girls of whom at least two—Kimi and Scotia Perry—are invariably A students.

Friendships of girls unpopular together. Candace hopes that her daughter's friends will remain loyal to one another in high school, which looms ahead for them next year like an ugly badlands terrain they will have to cross—together, or singly.

Scotia is not Candace's favorite among Kimi's friends—there is something subtly derisive about the girl, even as she politely asks Mrs. Waxman how she is, and engages her in actual conversations; Scotia is stocky and compact as a fire hydrant, with a ruddy face, deceptively innocent blue eyes, and thick, strong ankles and wrists—a girl golfer!

(Candace has never seen Kimi's friend play golf but she has been hearing about the golf "prodigy" for years.) Scotia is an all-round athlete who plays girls' basketball, field hockey, and volleyball with equal skill, while poor Kimi takes aerobics for her phys-ed requirement—Kimi shrinks from sports and has difficulty catching balls tossed to her so slowly they seem to float in midair. Though not a brilliant student, Scotia so thrives on competition that she maintains an A average in school; she also takes Mandarin Chinese at the local language-immersion school and she has been a savior of sorts for Kimi, as for their other friends, helping them with malfunctioning computers. (Scotia has helped Candace too!) From a young age, Scotia exuded a disconcerting air of mock maturity: Candace recalls when, after Kimi's father had moved out of the house in the initial stage of what was to be, from Candace's perspective, an ordeal like a protracted tooth extraction, both painful and intensely boring, Scotia said with a bright little smile, "Hope you had the locks changed on the door, Mrs. Waxman! That's what women do."

(In fact, Scotia's parents are not divorced. This droll bit of information must have come to Scotia from other sources.)

Last year, in eighth grade, Kimi's closest friend seemed to have been a girl named Brook, displaced over the summer by Scotia Perry.

Now it's Scotia who spends time in Kimi's room as the girls prepare class projects together or work on homework; watch DVDs, do e-mail, text messages, Myspace, and Facebook; snack on cheese bits, trail mix, Odwalla smoothies, which Candace keeps stocked in the refrigerator—Strawberry Banana, Red Rhapsody, Super Protein, Mango Tango, Blueberry B Monster. Often Candace is out—with friends—for the evening and returns to discover that Scotia is still on the premises, though the hour is getting late—past 9 p.m. She can hear, or half hear, the murmur of their girl voices, and their peals of sudden girl laughter; she's grateful that Kimi has a friend, though Scotia Perry seems too mature for Kimi, and too strong willed; and Scotia's mother hasn't made any effort to befriend Candace, which feels like a rebuke.

Once, Candace thought she'd overheard Scotia say to Kimi in a laughing, drawling voice—a mock-male voice, was it?—what sounded like *fat cunt*—but Candace hadn't really heard clearly for Candace *was not eavesdropping* on her daughter and her daughter's friends. And afterward when Scotia had departed and Kimi came downstairs flush faced and happy, Candace had asked what Scotia had said and Kimi replied, with averted eyes, "Oh, Scotia's just kidding, teasing—'fat cow,' she calls me, sometimes—but not, y'know, meanlike. Not mean."

" 'Fat cow.' That girl who looks like a young female twin of Mike Tyson has the temerity to call my daughter *fat*. Well!"

Candace pretended to be incensed though really she was relieved. Very relieved. *Fat cunt* was so much worse than *fat cow*.

Conversely, *fat cow* was so much less disturbing than *fat cunt*.

Another time, just the previous week, after Scotia came over to do homework with Kimi, next morning Candace was shocked to discover that, in the refrigerator, not a single smoothie remained of six she'd bought just the day before.

"Kimi! Did you and Scotia drink *six smoothies between you*?"

Kimi's face tightened. The soft, round, boneless face in which large brown eyes shimmered with indignation.

"Oh, *Mom*. I hate you counting *every little thing*."

"I'm not counting—I'm recoiling. I mean, it was a visceral reaction—pure shock. I just went shopping yesterday and this morning all the smoothies are gone. No wonder you're overweight, Kimi. You really don't need to put on more pounds."

This was cruel. Unforgivable.

Kimi made a sound like a small animal being kicked and ran upstairs.

*

"Kimi? May I come in, please?"

This is a tip-off: Something is seriously wrong. For Mom is behaving politely—almost hesitantly. Instead of rapping briskly on the door and opening it before Kimi can reply.

Kimi's voice lifts faintly—whether inviting Mom in, or asking Mom not to interrupt her right now, she's working; but the door isn't locked, and Mom comes in.

"Hiya!"

"Hi."

Candace's eyes clutch at the girl—sprawled on her bed with her laptop opened before her, a shimmering screen that, as Candace slowly approaches, vanishes and is replaced with drifting clouds, exquisitely beautiful violet sky. Candace wonders what was just on Kimi's screen but has decided she will not ask, even playfully. Kimi bristles when Candace is too inquisitive.

Kimi is lying on top of her bed surrounded by the stuffed animals of her childhood: Otto the one-eyed panda, Carrie the fuzzy camel, Molly the big-eyed fawn. Since returning home from school Kimi has changed into looser-fitting clothes—sweatpants, sweatshirt. Her feet are bare and her toes twitching.

Last summer Kimi painted her toenails iridescent green, and still flecks of shiny green remain on her toenails, like signs of leprosy.

On the pink walls of Kimi's room are silly, lewd rock posters: Lady Gaga, Plastic Kiss, Raven Lunatic.

There is music in Kimi's room—some sort of chanting, issuing out of her laptop. Kimi brings a forefinger to her lips to silence her mom, who nonetheless speaks: "Sweetie . . ."

When Kimi, frowning at her music, doesn't glance up, Candace says she'd been summoned to Kimi's school that morning—"D'you know Dr. Weedle?—she has some sort of psychological counseling degree."

Kimi's surprise seems genuine. Her eyes widen in alarm.

"Dr. *Weedle*? What's she want with *you*?"

"She said that you were going to speak to me about an issue that came up at your school yesterday. But you didn't."

"Mom, I *did*. I mean, I certainly tried."

"You did? When?"

In a flurried, breathless voice that is an echo of Candace's girl voice Kimi tries to explain. She'd started to say something to Candace but Candace had been in a hurry and on her way out of the house and

185

now belatedly Candace recalls this exchange but details are lost—crucial words are lost—Kimi had drifted away, and later that evening Candace heard Kimi in her room laughing, on her cell phone with a friend.

Candace has changed from her designer clothes into pencil-leg jeans, a magenta silk blouse, flannel slippers. She sits on the edge of Kimi's bed with less abandon than usual. Bites her lip ruefully saying, to enlist her daughter's sympathy, "I'm not good at whatever this is—a TV scene. If I can't be original, I hate to even try."

Kimi smiles to signal *yes*, she knows that her mother is a funny woman, and clever, and original, but Kimi is tense too. For Mom has let herself into Kimi's room for a purpose.

"Kimi, I have to ask you—is someone hurting you?"

Candace is hoping that this will not turn out to be the horror film in which the perpetrator of evil turns out to be the protagonist—or maybe, on a somewhat loftier plane, this is Sophocles's *Oedipus Rex*.

Though knowing—*She has never touched her child in anger, still less has she abused her child. Or any other child.*

Kimi sits up, indignant. Kimi tugs her sweatshirt down over her fleshy midriff. "'Hurting' me? You mean—making me cry? Making me *feel bad*?"

"Yes. Well—no. I don't mean hurting your feelings—exactly—but hurting *you*. Physically."

Kimi squirms and kicks; this is so—ridiculous! Candace sees a paperback book on the bed—Kimi's English class is reading *To Kill a Mockingbird* and this is consoling, to Candace.

"Mom, for God's sake! That is so *not cool*."

"Sweetie, this is serious. You are saying that no one has hurt you? No one at your school? Or—anywhere?"

"No one, Mom. Jeez!"

Yet Kimi's voice is faltering, just perceptibly. You would have to be Kimi's mom to hear.

"Will you—let me examine you?"

"Examine me!" Kimi laughs hoarsely, an uncanny imitation of her mother's braying laugh. "What are you—a doctor? Psychiatrist? Examining me?"

Nonetheless, Candace is resolved. The roaring in her ears is a din of deranged sparrows.

"Will you let me look, Kimi? I promise that—I—I won't be—won't overreact. Dr. Weedle said something about a head injury—"

Kimi is scuttling away, crab fashion, on the bed. Stuffed animals topple onto the floor with looks of mute astonishment.

"You hit your head on a—locker at school, and cut it? Did you go to the school nurse? Did you tell anyone? Did you tell *me*?"

Kimi would have swung her hips around to kick at her mother but Mom has captured her, kneeling on the bed. The mattress creaks. Another stuffed animal falls to the floor, and the *To Kill a Mockingbird* paperback. Candace is panting, gripping Kimi's head between her spread fingers—not hard, but hard enough to keep the girl from wresting free—as Kimi hisses, "Mom, you *smell*! Disgusting cigarettes, wine—you *smell*!"—as Candace peers at the girl's scalp through a scrim of fine, feathery, pale-brown hair, at first seeing nothing, then— "Oh! My God"—Candace sees the dark zipperlike wound, something more than a simple scratch, about four inches long, at the crown of Kimi's head.

Candace is stunned, staring.

Feebly Kimi protests, like a guilty child.

"I didn't mention it to you because it's *just nothing*, Mom! I was stooping to get one of my shoes, in the locker room, after gym, and banged my head on the edge of a locker door—it didn't even hurt, Mom. It's *just nothing*."

"But it must have bled, Kimi—head wounds bleed. . . ."

"Well, sure—but I didn't just let it *bleed*. I had tissues in my backpack and some girls brought me toilet paper. I just pressed it against the cut. After a while it stopped bleeding. Scotti had some kind of disinfectant, we went to her house after school, and she put it on the cut with an eyedropper." Kimi smiles, recalling. A guarded look comes into her face. "Scotti's going to be a doctor, she thinks. Neurosurgeon."

"Is she! I wouldn't doubt, that girl could do it. . . ."

But Candace doesn't want to get sidetracked into talking about Scotia Perry, whom Kimi hero-worships. Not right now.

Staring at the dark wound in her daughter's scalp, which had existed for how many days, without Candace knowing, or in any way suspecting, beneath the feathery child's hair, Candace feels a sensation of utter chill futility—emptiness: the way she'd felt, just for a moment, in the women's restroom where she'd seen the poster with the photo of the bruised and battered girl—ARE YOU A VICTIM OF VIOLENCE, ABUSE, THREAT OF BODILY HARM? ARE YOU FRIGHTENED?

How awful the world is. No joke can neutralize it.

She has failed as a mother. She has not even begun to *qualify as a mother*.

Maybe just, oh Christ—cash in your chips. Tune out.

Suicide: *Off self.* Candace has always wondered why more people don't do it.

Candace is stammering—not sure what Candace is stammering—drawing a forefinger gingerly along the scabby cut in her daughter's scalp—"Not to have a doctor look at it, Kimi—it should have had stitches—I should have known. . . ."

Not even begun to *qualify as a mother.*

Kimi pushes Candace's hands away. Kimi is flush faced as if her soft, smooth cheeks have been slapped.

"Mom, I told you—it's *just nothing.* If there'd been stitches—they'd have shaved my head, think how ugly that would be." Kimi makes a fastidious little face, in unconscious mimicry of her mother.

"But, Kimi—not to tell me about it even. . . ."

Kimi scuttles away, drawing her knees to her chest. Candace is surprised as always by the fleshiness of her daughter's thighs, hips—the swell of her breasts. And now the hostility in Kimi's eyes, which are red rimmed, thin lashed, as if she has been rubbing at them irritably with a fist.

You don't know this child. This is not your child.

See the hate in her eyes! For you.

"That really bothers you, Mom—doesn't it? That you were not *told.*"

"Yes, of course. Of course—it bothers me. I was summoned to this terrible woman's office—in your school—'Lee W. Weedle, PhD.' It was an occasion for your school psychologist to terrify and humiliate me—and to threaten me."

"Threaten you? How?"

"She might report your 'injuries' to—some authority. 'Abuse hotline'—something like that."

"But—I told them—my 'injuries' are *accidental.* They can't make me testify to anyone hurting me because *no one did.*"

"This cut in your scalp—does it hurt now? Does it throb?"

"No, Mom. It does not *throb.*"

"It could become infected. . . ."

"It *could not* become infected. I told you—Scotti swabbed disinfectant on it. And anyway it doesn't hurt. I've forgotten about it, actually."

Candace lunges—clumsily—*this is what a mom would do, impulsively*—to hug Kimi and to kiss the top of Kimi's head, the ugly zipper scab hidden beneath the feathery hair as Kimi stiffens in alarm, then giggles, embarrassed—"Jeez, Mom! I'm OK."

Candace shuts her eyes, presses her warm face against Kimi's warm scalp, disheveled hair. She is fearful of what comes next and would like to clutch at Kimi for a little longer but the girl is restless, perspiring—resisting.

"Mom, hey? OK please? I need to work now, Mom—I have homework."

"Yes, but—it can wait for a minute more. Please show me your shoulders now, and your upper arms. Dr. Weedle said—you're bruised there. . . ."

"What? Show you—*what*? No!"

Now Kimi shrinks away, furious. Now Kimi raises her knees to her chest, prepares to use her elbows against Mom.

Candace is trembling. Is this abuse?—*this*? Asking her fourteen-year-old daughter to partly disrobe for her, to submit to an examination?

Candace is in terror, for maybe she is to blame. In her sleep, in an alcoholic-drug blackout, abusing her own daughter and forgetting it?

Kimi is more fiercely protective of her body beneath her clothes than she was of the wound in her scalp. Panting, crying—"Leave me alone! Don't touch me! You're crazy! I hate you!"

Candace kneels on the bed, in the twisted comforter, straddling the resisting daughter. Kimi is shrieking, furious—Candace is trying to pull Kimi's sweatshirt up—has to pull it partly over her head so that she can see the girl's shoulders and upper arms—oh, this is shocking! frightening!—the bruises Weedle described, on Kimi's pale, soft shoulders—ugly rotted purple, yellow. In order to see Kimi's upper arms, Candace has to tug the sweatshirt off Kimi's head as the girl kicks, curses—"I hate you! I hate *you*!" Kimi's fine, soft hair crackles with static electricity—Kimi's eyes are widened, dilated—like a furious, snorting animal Kimi brings a knee against Candace's chest, knocking the breath out of her. Candace is disbelieving—how can this be happening? She who loves her daughter so much, and Kimi who has always been so sweet, docile. . . . "You fat cunt! I hate you."

Candace stares at the bruises on her daughter's shoulders and upper arms—beneath her arms, reddened welts—and on the tops of her breasts, which are smallish, hard girl breasts, waxy pale, with pinprick nipples just visible through the cotton fabric of her bra—(Junior Miss 34B: Candace knows because Candace purchased the bra for Kimi). For several seconds Candace is unable to speak—her heart is pounding so violently. It does look as if someone with strong hands—strong fingers—had grabbed hold of Kimi and shook, shook, shook her.

189

"Your f-father? Did he—is this—? And you're protecting him?"

"Don't be ridiculous, Mom! You know Dad would never touch me," Kimi says scornfully. "I mean, Dad never even *kisses* me! How'd he get close enough to 'abuse' me?" Kimi's laughter is awful, like something being strangled.

"Then—who? Who did this?"

"Nobody *did anything*, Mom. Whatever it was, I *did to myself*. I'm a klutz—you always said so. Always falling down and hurting myself, breaking things—my own damn fault."

Kimi's eyes shine with tears. *Damn* is out of character, jarring.

Klutz. Such words as *klutz, wimp, dork, nerd* are just slightly more palatable than the cruder, more primitive, and unambiguous *asshole, fuckup, fuckhead, cunt*. Or maybe the equivalent would be *stupid cunt*.

So to call your daughter a *klutz*, or to conspire with others, including the daughter herself, in calling her *klutz*, however tenderly, fondly, is to participate in a kind of child molestation.

This seems clear to Candace, like a struck match shoved into her face.

"Kimi, you are not a klutz. Don't say that about yourself."

"Mom, I am! You know I am! Falling, tripping, spilling things, ripping my clothes—banging my damn head, my legs"—with furious jocosity Kimi speaks, striking her ample thighs with her fists. "And a *fat cow klutz* on top of it."

Family joke was that Kimi was a little butterball, chubby legs and arms, fatty-creased face like a moon pie, and so *eager*—spilling her milk glass, toppling out of a high chair, spraining wrist, ankle in falls off tricycle, bicycle, down a flight of stairs.

Philip! Our baby daughter is a piglet. Cutest little piglet. With red eyes, red snub nose like a miniature snout, funny little pig ears but—too bad!—no sweet little tail.

Young mother high on Demerol, entranced with her baby. *Oh Jesus it is a—baby! But—mine! Not mine!*

The horror washing over her, even as she felt love for the little piglet so powerful, could scarcely breathe, and even now—fourteen years later—a muscle constricts in her chest, in the region of her heart—*Can't breathe can't breathe love comes too strong.*

She'd joked (for Candace has never been able to resist a joke aimed to startle, to cry *Whoa!*) that a baby sucking at a nipple is lots nicer than a man sucking at a nipple 'cause the baby has no teeth and no possibility of bad breath and later (for Candace has never been able to resist pushing at limits though knowing well how limits push back and sometimes roughly) that nursing made orgasms feel like silly little sneezes. And it was so—nursing started off so wonderfully—*Peak experience of my life*—then something went wrong. Little Kimberly ceased nursing as a baby is supposed to nurse, spat out precious milk, tugged at Candace's sensitive nipples, and the nipples became chafed and cracked and bled and now, not so much fun. More like—ordeal, obligation. More like—who needs this. Milk turned rancid, baby puked a lot, cried and kicked at the wrong times. Young mother *freaking goddamned depressed.*

Fourteen years later not that much has changed. Except the baby's father is out of the picture even more than he was then.

That day returning home from Wecdle and yes, Candace took another thirty-milligram Lorazepam reasoning that she will not be engaged in *operating heavy machinery* for the remainder of the day and yes, Candace washed down the capsule with a (only two-thirds full) glass of tart red wine but no, Candace did not sleep but spent headachy hours at her computer clicking on *abuse, girls* drawn to read of *abuse, rape, female cutting, slaughter in Africa* until she became faint thinking, where were the girls' mothers? how do they bear living? Thinking, jokes cease when little girls are raped, strangled, left to die in the bush.

Exactly as Wecdle said: You can see the imprints of fingers in Kimi's skin.

"I'm asking you again, Kimi—who did this to you?"

Kimi grabs her sweatshirt back from Candace and pulls it furiously over her head.

"Please tell me, was it a boy? I hope not a—teacher?"

Candace hears herself beg. Candace wants to gather Kimi in her arms for another hug but knows that the girl will elbow her impatiently away.

"Mom, for God's sake cool it."

"But, honey—I want to protect you. I want to be a good mother. It isn't too late—is it? Don't push me away."

Flush faced, Kimi yanks the sweatshirt down over her breasts, as far as it will go. Kimi is exasperated and embarrassed but seeing the expression on Candace's face, Kimi relents: "Well, see—what happened wasn't primary. It was, like, a secondary factor."

"What do you mean—'secondary'?"

"The cut in my head wasn't on purpose. Nobody actually hit me. I was slow doing something and she pushed me from behind and I

191

stumbled and hit my own damn head myself on something sharp—not a locker door but a chrome table edge. And she stopped the bleeding and put disinfectant on it and kissed it and was sorry. So—it's OK. It's, like, nothing."

"Who did this? She?"

"Scotti. Who've we been talking about?"

"Scotia? Scotia did this to you? What do you mean?"

"Oh, Mom. Jeez! Just forget it."

"But—what did Scotia do to you? Pushed you? So you fell and hit your head? Why?"

Kimi shrugs. Kimi's eyes shine with a sort of defiant merriment but her skin is reddened, smarting.

"Why would Scotia do such a thing? What were the circumstances?"

"Probably some stupid thing I said. Or didn't answer fast enough. Scotti has a problem with *slow*. Half the kids in our class, Scotti says, are *retards*."

"That terrible cut in your scalp—Scotia caused? But why are you protecting her?"

"Yes, my scalp. Mom. And my damn arms—you're so excited about—Scotti was helping me on the bars. Gymnastics."

"Scotia did that too? 'Gymnastics'?"

"We were fooling around at her house. She's got all this Nautilus equipment her dad bought for her. You're always telling me to lose weight so I'm doing exercises at Scotti's. There're these, like, bars you hang on—Scotti was showing me how. No big deal, Mom—will you stop staring at me? I hate it."

"I'll call Scotia's mother. This has got to stop."

"It's *stopped*, Mom. I told you—it wasn't anyone's fault."

"It was Scotia's fault. And it isn't going to happen again."

"No! Don't you dare call Mrs. Perry! Scotti is the only thing in my life that means anything—the only person who gives a damn about me. If you take Scotti from me, I will kill myself."

Kimi begins crying, sobbing. Her swollen face seems to be melting. When Candace moves to embrace her, Kimi shoves her away as Candace expected—which doesn't make the hurt less painful.

Candace stumbles downstairs. Rapidly her mind is working—thoughts fly at her, through her, like neutrinos—can't quite comprehend the significance of these thoughts or what they are urging her to do—for a mom must *do*, a mom must more than simply *be*—until she's in the kitchen peering into the refrigerator: no Odwalla smoothies? *None!*

But there are ingredients for smoothies, Candace can make her own for Kimi, and for herself: strawberries and raspberries, banana, a dollop of orange juice, the remains of a container of yogurt blended together in Candace's shiny, rarely used twelve-speed blender. She is thrilled to be preparing something *homemade* for Kimi that she knows Kimi will love, and she knows that Kimi is hungry for Kimi is always hungry at this time of day, after school and before dinner, which isn't always on the table until—well, after 8 p.m. Or then. The blender yields two tall glasses of strawberry-tinged smoothies, rich with nutrients, and delicious. Candace thinks, *But more.* She goes to a kitchen drawer where there's an old stash of pills, pre-Lorazepam, a handful of antianxiety meds, with tremulous fingers she empties one of the glasses into the blender, tosses in a pill or two—or three—and whips the liquid again, grinds the pills to a froth, repours into the glass; then, who knows why, a neutrino thought has pierced her brain with the cunning of desperation, she empties the other glass into the blender, tosses in a pill or two—or three—and whips the liquid again into a strawberry-hued froth.

Upstairs there is Kimi sprawled on her bed still wet faced, panting, and indignant—under the pretext of squinting into *To Kill a Mockingbird* she's been texting on her cell phone, which with clumsy childish deceit she tries to hide beneath the book so that Mom can't see. Of course Mom can see but Mom smiles radiant and forgiving as if not seeing, carrying the tall brimming glasses of strawberry-raspberry-banana smoothies—"For you, sweetie. And for me." Kimi is sullen but surprised and pleased—Kimi can't resist, of course. Mumbling, *Thanks, Mom,* for truly Kimi is a very well-behaved and polite girl and always hungry.

Without waiting to be invited, Candace sits cautiously on the edge of the badly rumpled bed and both Kimi and Candace drink their smoothies, which are in fact delicious—"Better than what you get in the store, isn't it?"—and Kimi has to concede, yes.

"Just so you know I love you, honey. You do, don't you?—know this?"

Kimi shrugs, maybe. Yes.

Soon Kimi is yawning and blinking in a futile effort to keep her eyes open and Candace says, Yes, why don't you have a nap before dinner, sweetie, a nap is a very good idea as Kimi whimpers faint as a kitten sighing and curling up to sleep unprotesting amid the stuffed

193

animals that Candace has retrieved, to arrange on the bed around her daughter; as Candace, grunting with effort, beginning to be light-headed, straightens the comforter, fluffs up the flattened tear- and mucus-dampened pillow. Kimi's face is still puffy, heated—her lips are swollen like labia—there's a babyish glisten at her nostrils Candace wipes tenderly with a tissue. With her new caution Candace takes away the smoothie glasses, makes her way feeling faint and swaying into the hall into the bathroom to wash each glass thoroughly in hot water, rub her fingers around inside the glasses, and again hold them beneath the hot-gushing water and then return to Kimi's room making her way carefully now knowing it is crucial not to slip, not to fall heavily onto the floor Candace returns to the white-wicker girl's bed where Kimi is now snoring faintly, lying on her side with her head flung back and her fine pale-brown hair in a halo on the pillow, beads of sweat at her forehead; the sweatshirt has been pulled down as if to flatten her breasts, showing a soiled neckline. Carefully Candace climbs onto the bed and gathers Kimi in her arms, her heart is suffused with love for her limp unresisting daughter, sweet little piglet, Mommy's own piglet, she has forgotten to switch off the light, the goddamned light is in her eyes. But what the hell.

From The Spokes
Miranda Mellis

WHEN I SET OUT on this trip, I planned to come back. It's true that when I embarked, the return date of my trip was not set, but I had not imagined this . . . duration. If that is what it is. I remember the high, winding, narrow roads along the coast, the vertigo.

And I remember at the ferry building were a series of warnings, one of which was about the peculiar sort of "jet lag" one sustains in a realm whose primary substance is not time. The customs agent had recited, and required me to repeat after her, line by line, a litany of warnings, a catechism about the nature of my destination. The only thing I remember now is the first warning: *Do not eat the food,* which I did, of course, within the first "day" (though that unit of time becomes meaningless without a sun).

I picked up my bag and boots on the other side of the customs gauntlet. As I turned to put on my boots I tripped on the lip of a plastic mat. A uniformed young woman wearing latex gloves caught me as I toppled forward, and steadied me. She gripped my arm longer than was strictly necessary. She looked at me intently, with clear gray eyes. "Be careful, ma'am," she said, "watch your step. Do you have a copy of the ferry schedule?" I did not. She turned around and pulled a small folded schedule from a stack behind her. She pressed it into my hand and firmly advised me not to lose it.

I laced up my black boots on a long wooden bench. There were several musicians emerging together from the line, and collecting their instruments. A musician next to me opened a case and examined his trumpet. He put his mouthpiece on and blew. Then he put his trumpet together and played a familiar tune: The Melodians' "It's My Delight": *I love you, I love you, I really do.*

I walked slowly, listening to him play all the way down a ramp, a long hall, and a flight of stairs. I came to the dock, a wobbling ramp of looped planks, and boarded the great rusty ferry splattered with bird shit and tied off with ropes. I found a seat on the deck where long benches faced the diminishing shore. I fell asleep in my seat, as the boat wended its way across.

I dreamed I was in a bathtub. I had left the faucets on and the room was flooding. My mother, Silver, came in and rebuked me. She threw green towels on the floor and sopped up the water. We'll have to take these to the laundry, she said, they'll never dry in here. The floor became an ocean, the bathtub our boat. We were cold. We wrapped the towels around ourselves. We rode the waves but the tub was sinking. My mother bailed with her hands, her hair gathered and swooped back. I looked around for a rescue ship as we sank. Then I looked down and saw my station wagon loping down the heavy water.

I woke cold, unable to see, hear, or sense anything, not even my own weight. I had kicked over my purse and some of its contents were beneath the bench. I bent over to collect them. A few pieces of paper, including the ferry schedule, fluttered away. I stood to chase after them when I saw a light, and then many lights. I observed the crowd as we approached the shore. They flickered into view like so many lanterns. Three dogs ran back and forth along the quay. When I stepped off the boat, one trotted over, licking my hand and wagging his tail. The other two raised their heads and smiled. A lone child in a tilted orange hat with a rooster feather debarked behind me. The dogs ignored the child and the child ignored the dogs, talking to her hands, or should I say from her hands, which she was using as two puppets.

I petted the dog, who grinned amiably. The others walked slowly back to the wall. One stretched, seeming to bow in my direction, circled several times, and then lay down a little heavily as if something weighed on him. He nosed around himself chaotically, his dirty mane sticking out. Catching my eye, he glanced down the quay suggestively. I followed his gaze and with a little shock I made out my mother. She looked just as I had last seen her, the day of her fall from the high wire. She wore her tight faux-emerald-and-ruby-studded tunic over a sheer dark-blue bodysuit, long, sharp macaw feathers in her bound hair. Glitter sparkled on her purple opalescent lips, and her eyes—one eyelid silver, the other gold—glistened brightly. Her short cape and slippers were sequined. For so long it seemed like the gap between us would only grow. Now suddenly we were three feet apart.

Silver greeted me in the typically polyphonic voice of the dead, like the eager, chaotic valence of a tuning orchestra. Like crying, and a drill, and a xylophone, a chorus of one. "You must be hungry?" she said. I was dizzy with joy and nervousness as I went toward her, but she was looking right past me. Who was she talking to? I turned around to see, behind me, the child: a much younger version of myself. Now I remembered the hat . . . I'd worn it constantly for months after my first unhappy haircut. I had had hair down to my waist. My mother took me to the yo-yo man, a geometer who had good scissors. When he was finished, my hair was the same length all the way around, a yo-yo-like sphere.

Clearly my mother did not see *me*, though I was standing right in front of her. Instead she saw this other, younger me. I spoke, I gestured. Neither of them made me out. I looked around. Was I the only invisible one here? Everyone seemed to be enjoying their reunions. My mother caressed my younger self's face, squatting down to gather her into her arms. They walked hand in hand down the platform to a kiosk. My mother bought my younger self a tin of cold green Jell-O, which she ate hungrily. I followed them I knew not where, my mother in her Spokes Cirque Rêve costume as colorful as a summer bird and my younger self in the slyly cocked orange hat.

It was not the first time in my life that I was invisible in a public place, if one can say of the afterworld that it is public. (Perhaps there is nowhere *more* public.) As a child I learned to meld in with the other spectators. I did not perform though I longed to; my parents had other hopes for me. But the person I had grown into was not someone my mother knew anything about; perhaps that was why she could not see me as I was, but only as I had been then. Unlike some, she had not spent her afterlife keeping current, i.e., haunting. She never returned the calls I made to her in my sleep. She never responded to

197

the letters I wrote her on desperate days. She had her own death to live. In life too, she'd never talked much. When she was not rehearsing or performing, she was distracted and melancholy. On stage she smiled fervently, as if to smile was to bless. Offstage she was secretive, close mouthed.

I gather some families talk about everything (though all individuals have their reservoirs of silence). I only knew Silver was the last performer in the Spokes line, grew up in the same caravan that her ancestors had traveled in, performed the same tricks in the same towns and villages, and knew, just as her foremothers had known, that she risked the void every time she entered the ring. My father, Leo, whose own father had also been a mechanic, was twice her age and an epileptic. "If nature had taken her course, I would have gone first," he had said. But gravity is nature.

It started to thunder in the distance: A storm approached but no rain fell. The trumpet player passed me, walking slowly, playing Peggy Scott's "Lover's Holiday": *Maybe we can slip away.* I greeted him but he looked right through me. He was the only passenger I recognized. I turned and watched him walking away with my first pang of worry. I wondered if I should follow, if he was on his way to catch a ferry home. But if time is not the substance of this universe, I thought, how could we know when it was "time" to return? I felt as if I could stay a thousand years or twenty minutes and it would make no difference. In any case, I had lost the ferry schedule.

I glanced around the station as I followed my mother and my younger self. I told myself to pay close attention to the path we were on so that I could find my way back. I had never felt so disoriented; no sun, no East. At the end of the street at the first right turn that my mother, myself, and I took, there was, hanging above the door of a very different kind of station farther down, Philip Guston's *The Tormentors*. I paused to look at the volcanic tongues of red paint. I told myself when you see *that* again, you'll know you're on your way back. "What's that place?" my younger self asked, pointing. "*The Tormentors*, that's their station," my mother said, "in the Sinister Quarter."

The people at that station were gray, black, and white. Other than the painting, nothing at that station had any color. Light, absorbed or reflected by a surface, normally fractures and becomes color. It was as if all the available light had been absorbed by the painting with none left over for the people or the pocked, rusted station.

We passed another station, Lautrec's *At the Moulin Rouge.* Was this my mother's stop? There was the trumpeter standing just outside with all of the other musicians who had been on the ferry with me. They played exuberantly and comfortably, like old friends. A small crowd gathered and danced, including my mother and my younger self. They were a closed circuit, from which I was excluded. Why this should be the case I did not know. Was my invisibility the result of something I had failed to do? I had yet to learn the laws of recognition here, which are not moral in the same way they are at home, where dreaming is neither a virtue nor a skill (as it proved to be here).

The crowd was not held by the music. Apparently the dead were incapable of paying attention to anything for very long. A few wandered toward a station with a fogged-in Malevich hanging overhead.

My mother and younger self sat on a bench and watched the dead mill. I stood behind them and listened in on their conversation. "Where are they all going?" my younger self asked my mother. "Nowhere," said my mother. "But they look so busy, like they are going somewhere," my younger self said. "Well," Mother said, "they feel they should be." "But where are they supposed to be?" my younger self asked. "Nowhere in particular," Mother replied. "Why don't we tell them?" my younger self said. "You can try," my mother said. My younger self called out to the crowd, "Hey! Stop! Where are you going? You're dead—there's nowhere to go! Hey!" One shade stopped and asked, "Yes?" My younger self said, "Where are you going?" "I can't remember, but I must go on," he said. "Why do you think you have to go on?" she asked. But he was gone.

Where do I think *I'm* going? I said aloud. But of course, they weren't aware of me. I walked around to the bench where my mother and younger self were talking. I stretched out next to them and fell asleep. For the second time on this trip, I dreamed. In the dream there was a giant baby with a head like a white stone, big dark eyes like galaxies, and smooth infant skin. She stood slowly on her toddling legs, her arms outstretched, and when she stepped forward she caused an earthquake. The dream state we were in shook apart from the mainland into the sea. There was a narrow, connecting bridge of earth left. We humans walked it, migrating to the center of the continent to forge a new society based on nonduality.

When I awoke I was sore from sleeping on the bench. To my astonishment my mother and my younger self were looking right at me. They spoke to me about my dream, which they called a movie, for dreams in the afterworld are movies for the dead.

My dream movies had made me visible, and yet they still did not know who I was. "I doubt there could be a society based on nonduality," my mother said, "but I really enjoyed the cinematography." My younger self said, "Yeah, in your movie, even though California fell into the sea, when all the people walked together to the center of the world to make a new society, I felt happy." I wanted to take credit for the dream, but it was none of my doing; I didn't even remember it that well. The only thing that mattered was that though they didn't recognize me, at least my mother and younger self now *saw* me. (It seems life can change you so much you wouldn't know yourself.) "Your smile is familiar," my mother mused. "You remind me of someone." I was just going to tell them who when she said abruptly, "Let's go now," and turned away.

We ascended a spiral stairwell at the center of the station. We came to the roof of the station where tables and chairs and waiters and eaters were scattered all around. Some people sat on the ground singing. Others sat on the ledge of the roof with their legs dangling down, nervously looking around. A wall, the inside facade of the station, played films: the dreams of the living, a constant festival for the dead.

The musicians from the ferry played accompaniment. So much music. Mother explained that music gives the dead patience, "the highest virtue." A waitress came with dainty plates of cold green Jell-O, which I found both satisfying and delicious. I partook, forgetting the warnings against eating the food. As I ate, my younger self began to flicker in and out of view. With a jolt and a flat, echoing sound like an enormous lid closing, she vanished. My mother cried out and held my head in her hands, pressing her forehead against mine. In eating the food I had inadvertently closed off the passage back; now she knew me.

*

Surroundings can change a person. I have been living at our station, *La famille de saltimbanques*, in the Happy Quarter in an apartment with extremely long hallways and large rooms with my mother for a while (I really couldn't say how long). Perhaps it is the endless length of the hallways, the height of the ceilings, the lack of sun (and therefore day and night), or the simplicity of our thixotropic meals (Jell-O, our food; liquefied Jell-O, our drink), but I have a nagging feeling that I have forgotten something.

I have just discovered that there are gods who live among the dead. I saw one for the first time, very well dressed. I was looking out the window, elbows on the sill, at the Francis Bacon *Head* station when he walked out of it. I didn't know he was a god at first, I didn't know what he was, but I definitely knew he was not a shade. His aura was assured, brittle, and bright, his jaw large, his teeth sharp. A confused shade asked the god politely if he had any idea what she was supposed to be doing. The god looked at her as if at an abstraction and went on. The shade called after him, "Where am I supposed to be?" I called, "Why does it matter?" She looked up at me, surprised, and asked, "How can I continue this way without knowing?" I said, "Why do you think you need to continue this way?" She walked off shaking her head.

Whereas the dead were preoccupied with trying to remember something (mostly where they were supposed to be and what they were supposed to do once they got there), there was an air of surety in the god's aspect: He was where he was. Though the shades were lost, still, they comprehended their realm better than the gods, according to my mother, whose own father had been a god. "Would you say that the gods are alienated?" I asked. "No," she said, "because they don't *know* that they don't know. In order to know this world, you must be able to die. They can't die, so they can't know this world." "What if a god wants to know it?" "Like I said," she said, "you have to be able to die." "How does a god die?" "By eating of the apple," she said. She held up one of several tarnished brass apples that sat on our mantel. I learned to juggle with them. I used to play-eat them as a toddler, informally preparing for gnosis and death. She tossed several at me. I caught them and tossed them right back; we volleyed. "What was it like having a god for a parent?" I asked. "It was awful," she said. "He was so critical." "What was your mother like?" "She was a saint." "She was very kind?" "She was a statue."

I still don't get why my mother lingers here among the arrogant gods and lost souls, of which she is neither. Until now, she has always been evasive on the subject. Sometimes she answers my questions with questions. Usually she won't even answer my questions, or talk to me at all, though lately she's gotten more voluble. "Why do gods bother to come here?" I asked her. "Sometimes they have projects to do," she explained. "Mostly they're couriers. Also, of course, this is an interesting place for them." "Is that why you stay?" "I stay because I'm waiting for my message," she said. I was surprised. I pointed out that it was usually the living who came to the land of the dead seeking a message. "That's true in mythology," she said, "but in reality, the living come to take the place of the dead." "What is the message?" I asked. "If I knew," she said, "would we still be here? I only know it's a kind of ticket. It takes you to the place you need to be, and it tells you what to do once you get there. It's what everybody is waiting for."

At that moment I remembered the dream I'd had on the ferry. How she bailed as our vessel sank. How long we tried to swim, drifting apart. How it felt to lose sight of her, to sink.

*

My mother would wait as long as she had to; there was nothing to do but wait. When I first arrived—shall I say "long ago"?—she thought I had the message she was waiting for.

She wanted to know how my siblings were. I couldn't tell her much. After her fall everyone had scattered and I was younger by ten years than my nearest sister. Life had quickened for all the members of the family and we sped along doing our best to keep pace, but in one arena of the family's past, where our lives would always overlap in memory, life did *not* quicken, rather it remained absolutely still, as if not to be seen.

The statement "What we cannot speak about we must pass over in silence" had proven useful to us. For if a subject won't yield any understanding, then what is to be done? A family naturally gives up on the insoluble, the unanswerable, the hopeless cases—they are like fossils or mythology. Even if they involve local events within common memory, such subjects are practically Paleolithic in their random (lonely, common, exilic) indecipherability. Though perhaps "subject" is not the right word for the part of no speech, an unpredicated, empty space.

Families are experts on such rifts—between event and memory, between all sides of the story, the living and the dead, childhood and everything else. For the Spokes, the subject of our silence formed an unacknowledged nucleus around which we orbited with backs turned, looking out at the universe, sometimes sideways at one another, but never inward. If history brings us all together, secrets dwell on the underside of it beyond the remedy, reach, and solvent of speech.

Call family secrets species of silence, except they are mineral, not biological but calcified.

I imagine a skull buried under a mountain, or a box with a rusted lock at the bottom of a pit.

The right accounting might break the lock, for perhaps that which can be honestly reckoned with can change—that is, whereof one *can* speak, one updates the subject; things can look different in the light—those things that we can talk about are subjects subject to change: They change under discussion.

But as with fairy tales, myths, political campaigns, and legends, what if it mattered more who spoke and when than what they said? Wasn't it more important to be believed than to speak the truth? Hadn't we learned from politics and circus barking that speech was not for truth, but rather for manipulating perception? Or hadn't we learned from placebo effects and folk tales and art that if only specific people, or substances, give the sought-after effect, it doesn't necessarily follow that this is because they *are* what they seem to be, but only that their seeming to be overcomes our doubt?

As so many *villains* and *clowns* have discovered, it is not enough, or even necessary, to say the *true* words. The book, the charm, the dagger, the amulet, the enchanted animal, the weather, the genie, the god, the witch, the princess, the dragon, and the frog that are unleashed/revealed/conjured/transformed/disenchanted/animated/deactivated or released by magic words require that the right person speak them at the right time. The season, the hour, the garb, the stars, and the record must be in order for the magic to work. Sometimes the impossible is the missing ingredient.

*

If my mother was waiting for a message, for my part, I had a question. I kept forgetting it, though; I forgot for ages. And when I remembered I had a question, it was another age before I remembered what it was. It was like reaching for something, but not having long enough arms. I reminded myself, next time you remember your question, ask it right away. That is how it is around here: You have to remind yourself to remember to remind yourself.

And finally I did remember. And I did ask. At first she equivocated: "*Why* is not a spiritual question, Lucia." "I don't care," I said. "It

204

wasn't a hard trick." "The Möbius strip? It's not exactly *easy*," she laughed. She put her arm around my shoulder. I waited. "Why wash those bones?" she asked. "What's done is done." "It's not *done*," I insisted, "or why would I be here?" We sat in the latest of her long silences.

I saw it all again, vividly, a welter of images like overlapping night-mares, the crowd in the round, her liquid dexterity as though drawn in the air by mercury, glinting in the shins, you couldn't keep track of her limbs, and then, absurdly, the beam of waltzing light that was her solo, as if slapped out of the air, reddening on the black Marley floor. I have stared my whole life at that image, captioned *It isn't what you think.*

The grief never diminishes. It's just gradually obviated by the persis-tence of the present tense, the quivering copula between disasters. How are things moving and yet so static? I wondered, involuntarily witnessing for the thousandth time in my mind's eye her reverse flight.

Suddenly Silver spoke, saying, "Imagine walking all together on a dock over the ocean on a foggy day. We come to the end of the pier, and everyone turns to go back. But I seem to perceive that it contin-ues; the air clears and I see a bridge ahead. I'm curious so I keep walk-ing. Eventually I find myself here. But for those left behind, I simply fall off; I am gone. And I *was* gone, for them. Two different realities, coexisting more than theoretically." Something thudded through me, thick, fibrous, and dusty, an old animal running from the answer I didn't want: that it had not been a fall, but a capitulation.

She seemed to backpedal. "It was an accident and a purpose." But those aren't the same at all, I thought; she's confused. *Is it possible that even she doesn't know what happened?* "That makes no sense," I said cautiously. "I know," she said, "it wasn't what I thought." "What wasn't?" "The future—it wasn't *ahead* of me." "You're mak-ing no sense," I said. "So you've already said. But that is a good way of putting it," she said. "I lost my human sense, and that is the only way of knowing for you."

There was a knock on the door. My mother went to answer it and in strode the god I had seen earlier—bright, brittle, big jaw. He gave her a notice informing her that she had mail waiting for her at Nancy Spero's *Tongues*—the message station in the Liminal Quarter—and he left.

*

We went to *Tongues* to pick up her mail. In the enormous station there were people singing all along curving balconies, throwing confetti and blowing bubbles. Nowhere did I see the burning wheels, pumping tortures, frozen faces, despairing devils we primitives are taught to expect. Perhaps if I went to *The Tormenters* I would see them, supplicants of futility and shame. But if this is not hell, if it's heaven, where are the candles, dresses, white fire, harps, Maxfield Parrish clouds, love-addled angels? In heaven I imagined feathers, so many feathers, everyone drinking coppery nectar in the bright light, geniuses standing by windows combing each other's hair, snow on the statues and long-bearded beauties with piercing eyes, charismatic manners, happily contradicting, swimming over abysses with imperturbable nerves.

But this afterlife imaginary is so arbitrary. The dead look painted. Periwinkle walls or sea green, golden frames and ancient, perfect faces, wandering characters, blind psychics, folds and folds of heavy cloth, singing at the post office, it's like a Derek Jarman movie. They dance, watch dream movies, eat Jell-O. So what do they think about? The living can't help but think terrible things; do the dead? Or do they have control over their thoughts? If I found my relatives from, say, a hundred years ago, what would they discuss? Pogroms? Communism? Piroshkis, books? Do the dead read? I suddenly realized I had not been this clearheaded in . . . so long I had forgotten irony.

And by the way, apparently the dead do have a hard time reading. Silver's hands shook with excitement as she opened her message. She squinted and ran her pointer finger under the sentences like a child, but she couldn't make them out. "I recognize this language," she said anxiously, "and I see the letters, but I don't know what they mean." "Let me see," I said. I could read it easily. It said

206

Tell your living to remember

Push yourself into the mountain until you explode into the sun

The moment I finished reading it, we were transported to the apartment of my father, Leo. He was lying in bed with his eyes open. He couldn't see us or hear us. "We have to try to get him to understand," my mother said. I leaned over and touched him and suddenly I was inside him.

Underneath his sternum and all the way up his throat we felt a hard snap, the whip of old red fear: a fit. We closed our eyes and put a long, frail hand over them, trembling. We grimaced. Suddenly our torso, arms, and legs vibrated violently, our eyes widened, and our tongue lolled out. We shook like a frightened dog. But in five minutes the seizure passed.

We slept. We dreamed we were searching a map spread out on a table. We found a small town called Silver and tried to find the road from here to there. Then I took control of our hand. I held a pen as best I could. It was hard to work his hand, the pen—I could barely write anything at all. I managed to scrawl just one word on the map: *Remember.* To our amazement he said, "Don't worry, I will." What a relief; he understood!

*

Leo drove and drove—the cemetery was so far away, it was in the middle of nowhere. It's a good place to be, he thought, if you have no body—the middle of nowhere. Now where does that expression come from? he wondered. Nowhere has no circumference so how can it have a middle? That's the point of it, he answered himself, that's the joke: There is no middle of nowhere. So to say something is in the middle of nowhere is just to say it is as far away as possible, in every direction, from *somewhere.*

It was hot and the car had no AC. He was sweating profusely by the time he arrived. The cemetery was enormous, the biggest one he knew, the size of a town practically. Usually you'd go to the office to get a map to find your dead, but it was closed. It was the middle of the day in the middle of the week: why closed? He suddenly remembered that on the train yesterday he had been approached by a Lubavitcher. "Are you Jewish?" the man had asked. "No," Leo lied, annoyed. "Oh," the man said with a friendly smile. "The reason I ask is because there is a holiday tomorrow, Shavuot." "I don't do that," Leo had said brusquely, turning away.

He felt humiliated, embarrassed. If he had listened to the man he would have known the cemetery would be closed! He had come all this way, in such heat. Why couldn't he have brought the old map? Why didn't he know his way around by now? The truth was he had gotten out of the habit of coming a long time ago. Still, he sort of thought he would or at least should know where Silver was, but then he'd never come without Lucia, "the human compass." She could find anything; navigate anywhere. Had they stayed at the circus that would have been her act, concocting scenes of losing and finding.

He, on the other hand . . . he should give up. But rather than leave, he found himself wandering. The graves were in rows, lined up facing one direction. And then he'd turn a corner and find hundreds of graves lined up in rows facing the other direction. In fact the graves faced all directions, section by section. He wandered, searching, in vain. At last he found a bench and sat under a sycamore in the middle of this nowhere. It was quiet and a breeze blew through the trees. Gradually he became aware, as though he could remember through his feet, that there were thousands of human bones underneath him side by side in the dirt of the graveyard, gridded like a city, orderly and decaying.

The weather changed; the air was cooling and white mist skidded over the hill in front of him. The clouds, loose and thin, seemed purposeful, as if to show him what the air was doing, or that they meant something by their movements.

*

I have taken the plates off the broken wagon and am walking down a coastal highway. I feel free—no longer in search of my ghost. I'm lighthearted as I walk and think. About the dead, for example, their habits, their blind spots, their obfuscations. They are humbler than the living, but no less confused. They remind me of people recently released on their own recognizance after a prolonged period of institutionalization, in which bureaucrats are in charge, where threats and universal schedules subtend every bodily need or experience. The Cartesian dead, I'd call them.

I remember I asked Silver to take me to the beach but she said there were no oceans. "Where do vacations happen then?" I asked. She replied, as she often did, at an angle: "The grayer and more dusty the life, the more need for Disneyland." "Is there a Disneyland here?" I asked. "No," she said. "Why would there be? There's no need for Disneyland if no one has to work." But it seemed to me that people were working. At least they appeared to be on their way to and from work. Silver said that wasn't the case. It was just the way the dead walked that made it seem so. "The amnesiac hustle," she called it.

I wondered why they were all so similar. Death looked no different from life, with even less justification. They didn't have to pay rent or buy commodities, so why did they continue to look around nervously for the boss? Did they think they were on vacation, that it was the weekend? The bulk of them would stand in bunches under an old, faded sign, "Job's Creation," waiting for something, though my mother said the Redemptive Quarter had shut down long ago.

Silver explained that our afterworld was populated by the recently deceased who seemed trained not so much to *act* as to get somewhere—wherever—"on time." Music calmed them, art gave them places to go, but neither music nor art helped them think about where they were. The songs and pictures that surrounded us were like markers, descriptions of the past, while the present was unreal. That the present should be unreal would make sense if you were

209

marking time in prison, where it would be only reasonable to look to the future. But after life? To wait, even in death, for the starting gun?

"What are the ancient dead like then, the precapitalist, the pre-clock-time, the preimperial dead?" I asked. But Silver didn't know. "Perhaps they are invisible to us, out of time, unrepresentable." I wondered how they would comport themselves, if the afterworld would be more recognizable to them, or if at least they would be more comfortable in deciding for themselves what time it was, what actions to take, how to mythologize the universe. But Silver warned me against romanticizing older shades. "We've been this kind of human, anatomically speaking, for two hundred thousand years," she said. "If we don't know ourselves, how can we know the ancestors?"

Still, we should try.

Father & Sons
Robert Kelly

How tiresome the irony of the young!

he said, but there was no yawn
in the novel he was reading,
only a kind of curve
of unremittingness.

Every text is the Red Sea, he said

that we must make part before us
so we can cross dry-shod to the other shore—
but where is that? And dry shoes
must mean we are not touched by what we read,
we are not changed, he said.

The reader flinches as he goes along—flinching is remembering that
you are different from what you're reading. You have your own life,
lusts, your own squeamishness.

O that prairie unremittingness! All hot all cold and wind and dust, and
not a nuance for a hundred miles.

Then words are clouds, they drift across your sandlot sky, he said.

How can you do that to your body, he said,
to give only your face to the world—what trickery!

The skin of your back is who you really are.

You bring me too many questions and too few.

I want the ones I don't know the answers to already.
A real question is a gift.

Robert Kelly

Ask me questions that make me learn too, he said.

It does not help to tell you what I know.

Later you'll arrange all my sayings in some hapless order that makes sense to you because it hides the meaning of each thing I said.

Out of town out of whack be careful what you're out of out of milk out of order out of doors.

To you I am something like a motorcycle
revving down the quiet country morning.

They shook their heads, no, no, half frightened.

I have said what I have said.

Long after you smell the whiff of my exhaust
even when the sound is gone, he said.

Get all you can from love and devotion—you have no other coin.

You are the metal, I am the crucible, he said.

They set their wives in the front row to please his eyes, they thought.
I can see right through them to your cunning hearts, he said.

Tiresome the jealousy of the young! Envy is the disease that has killed more poets and prophets than all the bacteria you believe in.

Tiresome, the jostling for the best place.

Fight with knives and be done with it, or else love your fellow candidates.

He used Pound's word for those who aspire to excellence in commitment, excellence in what is just an ordinary human habit, speaking.

Honor yourself by supreme and quiet confidence.

Listen best when I've stopped speaking, he said.

This is easy stuff you have to learn.
It's like sitting on a chair, or watching children play.

If I told you a secret you would have it.
If you had a secret you would try to sell it, wouldn't you?

He sat there smiling at them now and again
while they brought their self-love and self-doubt
to the unquiet surface of their minds
in the form of questions, always more questions.

The crow knows how to caw quietly, he said.
Everything matches its morning, he said.

No need to be lewd—relax into wrongness and soon come right, they thought he said. But what did he really say?

The fox flees from the forest to the town—life is challenge, he said, or the moon would long ago have given up her lonely struggle and fallen back to earth.

Being comfortable means thinking about something else, he said.

In the mornings he sat by the rosebush listening to the Talmudic discussions of the bees. He looked like someone who understood what he was hearing.

He hid often from the sun, calling it his baby brother, energetic, talented, a little tactless. He spoke of the frequent importunities of his relatives, but they were afraid to ask what he had in mind—if the sun was his little brother, who could their grandfather be?

Morning is the upper body, he said, and night is the weary legs, the sore feet, Pisces, dreams already on the way. All beginnings begin in dream.

Don't eat early and don't eat late.

Morning for speaking, afternoon for listening, evening for keeping still.

Sometimes one or another of his candidates would mutter or protest. Such behavior would be punished by a kind smile.

Why do you listen to me when you could be talking? I'll tell you why, he said. You doubt yourself so profoundly that even the surface doubt you feel about me feels almost like conviction.

Don't you know you can only learn by listening to someone wise? You can only learn by listening to yourself talk.

Never talk without listening to what you say, and learning from it.

Believe the deepest thought in you is possible, necessary, already well begun, already half done. Believe that you just have to keep doing it, he said.

I let you gather around me, I let you surround me with your inattentive attentions and your imaginary questions so that I can bask in your beautiful differences and in your "infinite worth."

We bask in each other, he said.

Come bask in me.

There is nothing fiercer than a smile—but this is something he never actually said.

When I was an old man, he said, I heard a ringing in my ears, like all the cicadas in the world singing quietly in the secret valley, just for me.

When I was young, I held the taste of salt in my mouth and always knew what to do.

The Secondary Confessions
Aurelie Sheehan

1963–1966

I CONFESS I WAS an extraordinary child. There is that period when the infant has not even touched time, not become dumb or malleable. The creature glows with intergalactic smarts and a crocodile's patience. Her cranium is blue, soft, round as a stone. Eyes lidded, nearly closed. At this premortal moment the delicate consciousness is not distracted by trivialities and time-borne illness. The delicate node senses. In sense, there is all.

I was born in France, in an American military hospital off the side streets of Verdun. My father was in the army, absurdly handsome in his absurd army uniform. A shirt for my father, and a shirt for those like him. There they are, all lined up, the pretty young men of that era. Sitting at desks, as it turns out—after the ordeal of basic training!—though surely he had to sprint or do jumping jacks in Brandoesque white T-shirts here and there, those years? Mostly, though, the crafty and important desk work. It's best if I simply go ahead and say it: He was an international spy.

F: The feathers of France, fluffing out and drifting high above soft, squarish pillows, a mattress with sprung coils. One's always a little covetous of the Antoinette hairstyles, the rigor of desire.

R: Rancid fruit jellies, a sense of extreme history even in this terrible old chipped jar that is a grandmother's, hoarded in the apartment for decades, existing beyond all possible usefulness, obliterating the idea of freedom in a day or a month or a year.

A: A glass of something. *Un verre de vin rouge, s'il vous plaît. Une tasse de café. Une tasse de thé.* Hopefulness in drinks and liqueurs, the elixir of time spent and company. I am alone—I always will be. Yet certain moments have been consecrated in their fashion (with Poire Williams or Chartreuse or so-called absinthe or the farmer's eau-de-vie). Certain moments, these tragedies.

N: The neck and line of the horizon, in memory.

C: How can I but not describe the cafés? The stroll down Boulevard

215

Raspail, a cage full of chickens, a handful of cold croissant, chocolate, and then back to the Champs-Elysées. Chanel bought with borrowed francs—this quite gone. This gone now too.

E: Nothing comes to an end. *Liberté! Égalité! Fraternité!*

As an infant then, I shared the cosmos with all the other infants on the *service de maternité*. My own mother was a speck to me— a powerful speck, to be sure. (Though, Lord, the amniotic dark was a powerful memory, this dream of life, stinging as I plunged into light.) It would sink in, over the hours and days to come, a sense of some comfort—the engulfing comfort of her arms and body, the lulling near murmur of her voice, preternaturally familiar; the intoxication of eating, its narcotic qualities melding with her skin, a trust borne of repetition, the knowledge that she would be there when I woke—if not immediately, soon thereafter.

But as time wore on so did comfort. There became variety.

The initial location of my loves and glories? An apartment on the second floor of a farmhouse in a village not far from Verdun, easily missed. From the windows in our living room you could see the road. Rarely did cars pass through, but when they did, it was at great speed. Chickens flopped out of the way, hightailing imperious bustles in the dust. Or sometimes a car traveled so slowly it was nearly still, a man's head and arm hanging out the window: instructing, gesticulating. In late morning the light became ethereal, a snowstorm of illumination. I mused in that sun, my fingers grasping at the wool carpet, the red and blue and gold, sickles and blossoms and moons. By the other wall stood a wooden table, wide, with art on top. Magnificent things were made up there! I could see books, and notebooks, and pencils and pens. Letters piled and spilling, addresses half seen, scratchy scripts and lettering. The stamps interested me: a lady dancing, her hair flowing to her knees; iconic figures in attitudes of immortality and pallor; the cheerful flap of a red, white, and blue flag from another kind of home.

It is vaguely comforting to have a photograph, but then one wonders about the moments just before or just after. I have a picture of myself in an infant seat on a table in the kitchen. It's dinnertime. A baguette, a bottle of red wine, a cigarette. *Fucking perfection!*

And on this night, or a night like it, a conversation took place between my father and his associate, a man whose name I did not catch. Still I understood the murmurs and the raised voices, the urgency there—a stash of pure living that took my father to other realms. The two of them smoked. The man's hand rested on the counter for a moment, fingers tensile but still. Then the hand moved, a whirl in the air, and then back to the counter, and then gone again. They drank something golden. Ice whirled within glass and liquid, creating shapes and light. My mother was stirring the pot—deep, yellow, burned ceramic. *Pot au feu*: oxtails and a bit of brisket from the night before, carrots, leeks, onions, turnips. Her back was turned, the apron's happy bow at her waist, her own glass of wine by the side of the stove. My father told a story to the man with lovely hands, his voice tensile too. Dramatic, filled with momentum. There was a storm in the dark eloquence of that voice—willingness, and faith. The man responded, a throaty laugh. Shouted, glad words.

I must have let somebody know, something. My mother turned around, her face a perplexing combination of anxiety and comfort, her face defined by conviction that I was *the solitary most important thing on earth*. At least sometimes. At least at the same time as some other things, in some other realms. And then I was lifted into my father's arms. He tucked his strong arm under my body, an unyielding shelf. The golden glass came close to my face as he took a whirling drink, and he put it down again and launched me now with both hands. I was whirling too, high above his head, closer to the light and the ceiling, way above the stove and the *pot au feu* and far from the man who was a guest, far from my mother's concern. He coaxed a laugh from me. Reluctant, yes, but I gave way.

Could it have been that very night, the plot? At dinner, which I viewed from my bassinet, missed in part due to a frequency of dozing? Or could it have been the conversation in the hall, the two lanky men murmuring, out of my range of hearing, my mother in the bathroom? My father was the one with a black lock of hair, jet black and gleaming and straight, a little lock that seemed antiarmy, too jaunty for them and their love of patterns. He was the one with the soulful eyes, dark brown, simmering with Irish Catholic knowledge and helplessness and determination. The other man had a more traditional crew cut, and he was taller, and his eyes, hair, and skin were all neutral. He was the tan man.

I love—I *am*—nature! Even so there is a kind of worry, a conviction that I am not actually nature at all, but some kind of Art Form. Not cyber, but definitely related to technology (if not just the technology of the paintbrush, the egg beater). Here we return to two photographs, and yet this time I do, I insist, remember the in between as well. Here is my mother on a bicycle, me in the child seat, an add-on contraption. I am the boyishly dressed lump in a smashed hat, scowling. My mother is scowling too—what, was this the era before sunglasses, not to speak of color? The fact is, I don't know why we frowned. Perhaps we were looking into the sun. Perhaps my father had way-laid us on the road to our adventure. For if my father could make me fly my mother had her ways too. She strapped me into that metal boxy place and told me to hold on, and then she turned her back, huffed, perhaps swore under her breath, and propelled the bike forward, from wobbling to straight-on heaven. The wind! The wind bore us, and now this is where the film truly starts, the original and perhaps sole testimony to Manheulles, my dear, lost hometown, a speck on the highway between Verdun and Metz.

I fight the urge to say the town was tan too.

The road was *not* tan, it was a mottled, angry black, especially angry when the wheels whirred underneath us, and I held tight to the thin aluminum, or sometimes, as in a dream, let go. The angry black spoke volumes to me, a nightmare from tomorrow or yesterday. Here went our fierce and ugly neighbors, treacherous so far as I knew (although at lesser speeds they were at times friendly). Here were sheep, or a splattering of sheep shapes, and then here was a cow, and here was a pile of shit, and here was a long long long orchard. And now into the great beyond (how many rotations of the wheel, of my mother's twenty-two-year-old American legs, legs used to tennis, golf, and privilege?). Here went my mother into her great and awful solitude. I mean, her time with me—the baby!

The fields surrounding the village rolled up on one side, veered, and made way for a dirt road, through a secondary orchard, and now, to the hill where we would picnic that particular morning. Bites of pear cut with a small sharp knife with a black handle: her hand even more obviously capable than the tan man's, exhibiting strength with the black worrisome knife, and then too with the diaper pins and the baby bottle of milk, a gift from the dairy farmer—he didn't sell these miniature bottles, but gave them away to us, and to the other children of Manheulles. My mother sometimes refilled the bottle with milk from a large jug, poured into this, my own. One time I broke the gift, it shattered on the floor, and there was a roar of American and French curses strung together creatively, and then silence, except for the whisking of the broom against tile. But at this moment

218

in the field, with the small chunks of pear, and the crunchy grass underneath the pink-red and yellow fabric, and the whir and click of insects, and birdsong, and the gentle sun and the unequivocal and important shape of the hills in the distance, the very horizon just then linking to every cell in my body—there was no swearing, in French or English, rather there was a shared sense of slow, enduring, lethargic possibility.

It's terrible to think of what happened later. To think that my mother might have been planning, in fact, what was to come even then—as I gazed at the line of the hill, as I contemplated temperature and the sporadic, returning pleasure of the birds' conversation, and the lowing in the very great distance, and every once in a while the purr of a car.

We lived in another second-floor apartment, this time in Norwalk, Connecticut. My mother stood at the top of the long stairs outside, way up high while I played down on the sidewalk, where the ants were. She hung laundry. The clothesline squeaked, impatient and nagging. On this afternoon there was no breeze at all. Shirts and sheets equally morose. The original plot was simple: to live. To live, and live, and live. Please remember Isadora Duncan for a role model and a consideration, the fine break with accepted order that was modern dance, leaked from the stage to her life at large. My mother, on the tiny porch at the top of the stairs hanging a blouse, sensed accepted order and modern dance in equal measure. Though I myself, ant friendly and also worried, looked out to the sparse forest laid out behind our duplex, the forest of pure evil where the boy in the red coat dwelled, evermore and at surprising moments, ready to do me in.

I was brilliantly courageous, to be sure, but the boy was like a leopard, or a giant clothed in bloody leopard skins, and he held a shovel in one hand. He wore a hat of some sort, or perhaps that was a shadow over his brow. He had a modicum, a filament, of conscience, and yet this filament did not prevent him from doing what he had done before and would do again.

Upstairs, past my mother and her brief, Duncansian regrets—up into my bedroom, to tremble and contemplate my print of the Albrecht Dürer 1502 watercolor and gouache rendition of a hare.

Something had been revealed, something dismal and dangerous and designed specifically to torment me—perpetually. *This is the world we live in,* I muttered, staring at the pretty pretty long ears of the rabbit, the pretty pretty gaunt haunch and the carefully placed front paws and the sleepy eyes, the animal paused to reflect on something—on where the whereness of the world had gone, for example—for the hare's habitat was a blank slate—or on the singularity of being, the eternity of sorrow and solitude.

But delicacy and prettiness are their own reward.

Indeed, I thought so, and finally launched myself back up off my bed to sigh, gather strength, and return to the house at large, to shuffle out and see what was going on with my mother, who had finished her laundry and was now in the kitchen, preparing lunch perhaps? The kitchen was the color of the Dürer print, the yellow-ivory of age, the cabinets made of white metal. A silver strip traced the edge of the counter, featuring holes in two places instead of screws and a dubious sense of purpose and safety, the satisfaction of enclosure.

When we moved from this house to the next, my print of the Dürer hare was lost. Its loss seems related to the way it is etched within me, remembered.

World affairs were, at the time, a combination of quaint, obvious—as in many "cases in point"—and finally overwhelming, a great shuffle, something like today's chatter. When we returned from Europe (*they* returned; for me it was a maiden voyage), when my father's duty was, theoretically or presumably, over, it is no exaggeration to say that he became a circus dweller, he who had swallowed, as if it were nothing, a great globe balloon. There he was, editor of an entertainment magazine, and yet within his gaunt, civilian-dressed, Camel-smoking, European-nostalgia-shaded frame, spun a shadow planet, darkness such as an X-ray might find, or an MRI, in the grim hours. There were the nights of brooding at the kitchen table, ten steps from my room, and there were the new mysterious letters—the dancing woman with her wispy dress and her long hair, come to see us in the Constitution State!—that he picked up like a card shark and with which he slipped into a darkened room.

The glowering green candy that I plucked from the small tin and lined up in rows on a piece of white bread with butter. A crunchy sandwich. This really was a fact, it really did happen. And it was a fact that my father might or might not have spoken of his ongoing responsibilities to my mother, those days, way back when.

One day he brought me to the park and led me to a sandbox by a tree, with the suggestion that I create my own flat world. The sky was white, as if the sky would never end, and it was a warm spring morning, filled, so it seemed, with infinite possibility. I trailed my hand, to begin with, around the periphery of my body.

When I looked up ten minutes later, my father was standing by the bench, and standing next to him was *the tan man*.

An exquisite betrayal was going on.

My father laid on the rug in our living room and held me up upon his knobby feet, a child on the platform of her father's bent legs. His hands holding my hands, his arms strong, his face reddened and animated, he became an airplane.

1967–1975

We moved from the place of the long staircase and the ants and the dreadful forest to this place, where my baby brother and I would both have our own rooms, where we had two stories and three porches. The new house was a square of white with black shutters, and out front was a huge tree with gnarled roots that stretched through the entire yard, up to the front porch, and if there had been a time-lapse sequence of the roots growing, it would have seemed like a grabbing thing.

The old woman who lived next door, Mrs. Cuff, watched *Dark Shadows* in the afternoon. Sometimes I watched it with her. She too had candy—although her candy was pink and black, not green. Ceramic and glass figurines were arranged on a ledge behind the couch. I kneeled on the cushions and touched the threesome of poodles (one big, two small ones on short leashes), the curled-up white cat, the fish, the elephant. It always took her an unbelievably long time to answer the door, shuffling as she did. I went over there for the glass animals and the candy, but also fulfilling some early predilection for charity, charity a kind of morbid fascination, a doing right, a fetish, making up in some way for the great gaping doubt that came over me when I was in church and the whole Sunday School population was reciting the Lord's Prayer.

Mrs. Cuff's television was black and white—or was the show in black and white? In any event, vampires wore black and had bright white collars and teeth. This particular vampire wore a ring over his glove. How extreme and gorgeous were the hand and the glove and the ring, and the dreadful vampire coming up the stairs, or coming in

221

the back door, or arrived in the bedroom, or, or—

Our dog came in a crate, by airplane, the legend or lie being that he was a grandpuppy of Lassie's. Was he given to us by my mother's mother? But she was soon to be in her coma, and so it's hard to think she was in a puppy-giving mood. My grandmother's special coma, a prolonged suicide, more velvety and gothic than vampires, than the high-backed chair in the hall where I sat to speak on the phone. Eight rings and hang up, that was my thought on the matter, my stretch of fate's string, how likely I was to believe someone was home, or that someone would return. I listened to the ringing, and I watched the goldfish in his bowl. A flash of orange, the swirl of a green tendril. Drifty, while I sat on the chair. Near five thirty my father would burst in. There he was! In a shirt and tie, dark pants—his whole manner energetic, as if by simply opening the door he brought life back into the house. It was always like that, when he came home from his day at work. Then, the norm was a drink and the paper. And cigarettes, the blue smoke hovering around him as he sat with these accoutrements, the objects of his excellent afternoon.

I have chronicled the importance of my dolls elsewhere and I have, it seems, preremembered: 1. The movie my father made of my mother, 2. My mother brushing my hair, a terrible rat's nest at the nape of my neck, before a birthday party, 3. More photographs—my friends and I on the jungle gym, me with the well-brushed hair at the party, 4. Our semicircular gardens, one for me, one for my brother, 5. The lily of the valley growing out from the side of the driveway in the crack between the house and the pavement, the powerful scent of the white bells, 6. The torn dress when the dog bit me, remembered near the lilies of the valley, even though it didn't happen there, 7. The elation of learning how to ride my bike, my father pushing me down the street on Christmas morning, streaming ribbons from the handlebars, 8. My yellow room, 9. My ponies, my plastic ponies, 10. *Star Trek* with my father, 11. The strange shapes and people I saw in my parents' bedroom when I waited for them to wake in the night: a fat black woman in a polka-dotted skirt, a thin man holding a green apple, cherubs overhead, 12. The French posters my parents put on the side of the house near the patio, as if our back patio were a café, or reminiscent of one, 13. Seeing *Diary of a Mad Housewife* at the drive-in theater, 14. Minerva, a gray cat, bringing her home in the darkness, holding her in my lap in the car, 15. A rabbit's fur bought at a store at night on a ski vacation, 16. At the ski vacation house, the young man calling my brother "Tiger," 17. My brother's blanket,

18. My brother's pot belly, 19. At the beach, my mother teaching me how to swim, 20. Hitting tennis balls against the wall in the court across the street, the dog chasing balls around me, 21. My fort and the crabgrass entrées and dolls I made to barter, 22. The taste of Carvel ice cream cones, chocolate with sprinkles, 23. And Carvel Flying Saucers, 24. When I was practicing guitar in the living room and my parents were fighting in the kitchen, shadows on the wall, 25. Feeling that I could and should send my not-eaten vegetables to China, or Africa, 26. The attic stairs, quite possibly the location of the living Chinese doll with long nails and no heart, 27. When she wasn't running after me trying to claw my face apart, 28. The look of my Dawn doll after Suzy cut her hair, 29. Winning the ribbon for Minerva, prettiest cat, 30. My school project, a chrysalis, empty one morning and no sign of a butterfly anywhere.

1976

"Why are you here?"

"I'm here because it's time."

"Time for what? What are you talking about?"

My mother was behind me in the hallway, and the tan man standing on our front step had a squinting look, pin lines of skepticism. It wasn't the same as a regular reunion with a person that you knew from long ago, that you had shared good times with back in France, before things got so complicated and tedious both. It wasn't like that so much as a voice of doom type of thing, a grim reaper type of thing. As I stood there, as the two of us trained our eyes on him and he trained his eyes on my mother, I could feel my life rushing through me like wind, and it was all I could do to stand upright. And yet there was something delicious about it at the same time, as if I weren't a body so much as a screen door, and the wind came right through, and every delicate square, every little square of gray lines that made up the who of me, was touched and stroked, the wind making itself small to get in all those thousands of parts, all equally sensitive and equally loved.

"Do you want me to get him?" my mother asked, her voice pitched to resignation and seduction. A last-ditch effort, a revealing.

"That would be just fine, thank you," he said, and the tan man looked at me, his lips slightly puffed, and then his mouth went back to a straight line.

Behind him was the peach tree. Just the week before, the peach tree had disgorged all its fruit and the ground underneath had become a brown-yellow festering pool of overripe orbs. We had tried to pick as many peaches as we could, but finally there were too many and they defeated us, and we had to stare with shame at our six Mason jars and our recipe for canning. It was not enough; it was never enough. As a family, we weren't in touch with the life force or the life cycles, or any of that. We had tried. We had read in the encyclopedia what we could. We had a sense of ourselves as enterprising, at least briefly, at least for a day. Past the peach tree and past the pine trees was a little hill where I had sat with a friend. We had made a pact that neither of us would ever die. And in fact I learned just last night that she is dying of cancer, that she is seriously dying, that the cancer has taken hold and all that is left of my friend is a weird bravery and generosity, as if she has already left this planet. I had not known until this point that she knew much, much more than me, that even back then, when it *seemed* that she knew more, that she *was* more, that I was, as a matter of fact, right.

The horses padded around the periphery of the field, attracted or resigned to the path they had already chosen. The potatoes would be dug. My brother would throw an egg into the grass. It was as if all of us had our hands in the ground, and we had been digging for a long time.

I began to cry in front of the tan man. I wiped my eyes, and I could hear the tense conversation on the basement stairs between my mother and father. I imagined them there by the pencil sharpener under the light of the bare bulb, standing on graded steps, one above the other, one hunched and the other extended. Their voices could not save them now.

Out past the peach tree and past even the small hill was a neighbor's house, but no one really lived there, it was simply or not even an empty house, made not even of wood, but with a thick paper product, Saran Wrap stretched over the window parts, and no back or sides at all.

I could feel the scarf tightening around my mother's neck.

I could see the red outlines of things, going back to the beginning.

My father appeared, dragging like a corpse the footlocker from his army days. We had been using it for storage: their wedding album, and then some fancy tablecloths we never used. Now these items were strewn on the carpet. He wore a sailor's hat and a stern look, his gaze turned steadfastly downward, as if (perhaps?) he would feel too much if he looked directly at me or my mother. I found that I was trembling from head to toe, like a dead leaf on a dead branch, and yet there was nothing dead about me. I was trembling like that chrysalis, before the butterfly escaped. However, I did not feel like a butterfly. There was no unfurling of slow, absolute color, no redemption. In fact I was having no thoughts at all.

And then he was gone. He had walked past me. He and the tan man both gripping a handle on opposite ends of the footlocker, they made their way to the car. The tan man might have said something amusing, because my father looked over sharply, with a crumpled grin.

The kind of haircut I got that year: the Dorothy Hamill, a kind of shiny brown bowl. My face was rounder than it had been since I was a toddler back in Manheulles, and my eyes were lidded, as if perhaps I had not fully woken up, or as if I were in a pout. Many of the things I used to do, simple acts that I didn't think much about, became laborious charades. I was always exhausted, I never slept, I always slept, tucked away in a chamber. Every once in a while I partially, reluctantly emerged, one spindly arm reaching out for the small brown bottle that appeared as if out of nowhere, an elixir of some kind. My friends and I doubled over on the bed, laughing, laughter a tender skin between this life and the next, and in itself suffocating.

The very excellence of myself was going through some changes. The previously mentioned extraordinariness was, not on the fritz exactly, but changing form.

Alone at night, I realized it would be useful to have a scheme. And so the scheme fluttered into existence. Tentatively at first, with five dollars here, ten dollars there, stolen minutes and then hours. The scheme took place alongside the marsh, or you could call it a bog, behind the high school. The boulders there had already been placed, as if by Martians, into a King Arthur's Round Table formation, and the sucking bugs moaned and procreated with tons of abandon all over the place. The scheme took place at the house of a man for whom I cleaned. The scheme took place on a long road paralleling the main highway in that town, the place we zombies plodded, unimpeded, while the others slept.

This is what my face felt like, as I walked along this road: My face felt like a skein.

Aurelie Sheehan

1977–1984

There had been a purple scarf of my own, but it fell off one night on the road, while I was chasing my friend, who was crying.

1985–1995

My handwriting improved as I wrote secret messages or labeled files with titles that meant something to me, but would cut off at the pass any other readers. I wrote a letter to my father, but I did not have his address. Still I pinned it on the grave of a relative. Not pinned, so much as taped. It felt necessary to let someone know, even if it was a dead person. Eventually the damning words streaked in the rain.

One day I took a terrible nap, and I couldn't wake up from it. Inside the nap existed all of *War and Peace*, as well as an unwelcome, hiccuping track from *Lucia di Lammermoor*.

Let me tell you a love story. Only this one is a tragedy. And it never occurred.

At twenty, the woman in the attic, as per literary history. My cats stepped carefully along the perimeter between our house and the next. They stared into the grasses by the marsh, salt water seeping in around the edges, a bowl of beauty. My boyfriend and I lived too far from the ocean to see it, but still we knew it was there . . . nearby. Some days the world spun and tumbled, as if it were only consensus that it should feel still most of the time. I clutched at the wrought-iron fence until agreement came back again. There was the spinning of bicycle wheels, and the broken car, and the fat boat squeezed into a small shack, and there was a great deal of cocaine. Overall it seemed like a life with a beginning and end. But then came the absolute brutality of the familiar and strange accent. Then came the moment when the sound of the human voice upended for real the sidewalk, the rug, the floor, all the flat surfaces around.

I had an affair. With myself.

I had a love of his voice. With myself.

I woke up from the dream. Because I'd created a *mise en scène* with furniture and a job and a boyfriend and two cats, I saw that I had to be stealthy and careful, although I can't at all say this was a scheme like before, because I wasn't creating something from nothing, I was attempting to find ways to accommodate new life, and I had to rearrange the furniture, obviously, if not throw it out.

Back in 1979, I had once noted that my polished toenails did not, after all, look at one with the natural world—the high rock upon which I sat, the shifting tree branches, the gorge. Now this seemed less important. The words *go for broke* come to mind. What happened then was, well, embarrassing. Santa Claus is coming to town.

The evening of the party, I was upstairs getting dressed and ready. Like a bride kept waiting ever so long, though I wasn't *really* as old as Miss Havisham, I wasn't a skeleton. But with the lethargy, for instance, and the thick stories, I had sunk into a morass where time sped up and I was old. And yet at the same time I felt delighted; I was now a giddy person. A giddy person who had not yet been caught, a giddy criminal element. Survival was of greater necessity than ethics, that was certain. I had not known this because I had always been almost shackled by ethics and had not concerned myself so much with survival. You could say I took survival for granted.

The sun was just going down, and the sky was a sad gray with orange streaks and a sense of distance and majesty, as if we were in an oil painting or a novel, caught at a particular moment that would never come again, which was magnificent for this reason alone: possibility captured. I walked toward the gathering crowd. Is it better to fortify oneself with an extra drink? In any case I did—just so, a small one. As is common with the heroines of true masterpieces, and before nestling into my slot within a magnetic radius of the subject, my subject. How he radiated, as no one else had ever radiated. How angry he looked, how fierce, and how liminal and grief stricken was he. And also how calm.

The bedroom of our small house had small windows, and it was up a narrow stairwell with no windows at all. Because the house had come partially furnished, the brass bed and the painted blue dresser didn't have any history, they were distinctly without history, and even though we had rented the place for a few months by the time of the party, my boyfriend and I had not imbued this furniture with any past at all. Under an eave, in a corner made brighter by a lamp I'd brought via college from my parents' house, with a chink in the green glass base and a burn mark on the shade, sat my sorrowful typewriter, which inched across the desk as I typed, as if to escape the dullness of my stories. I had a pile of finished work on one side and administrative or to-be-filed papers on the other. I put my coffee cup on a paisley tray that had also come from my parents' house, or from my mother's family, as I remember now, in particular.

There had been many afternoons like the one with *Lucia di Lammermoor*. I could sleep almost any gray stretch for two or three hours at a time. Even when I woke up, I was not refreshed. Thickness had descended, absorbing me, and I was not nearly a sprightly sprite, but some kind of toadstool, laboring to take steps up and down the narrow stairwell, laboring to create new stories in that brightly lit but windowless section of the upstairs bedroom with my college typewriter and sense of things unaccomplished.

The occurrence of the man in his extreme clothes with his extreme eyes and extreme voice was certainly a surprise, and at the very least inconvenient. The tiredness was almost instantly wiped out, replaced by a wary sense of flooding in the house. I decided, fuck it, and in the days to come my boyfriend and I carried my wooden desk downstairs to the living room, and placed it in front of the window. I really, *really* couldn't work anymore up in the claustrophobic bedroom, where sleep had a cold-medicine effect, and the wool blankets were much too thick and heavy for us to move underneath, except perhaps for a chaste, uncertain kiss. And so downstairs I went, and I purchased a geranium, and put the geranium in its earthen pot on my desk, next to the pile of finished work, and in the mornings I would creep downstairs and make myself a cup of coffee and then sit at my desk and stare out at the blasted landscape, the marsh, the inlet, a few houses on the other side, some trees, and above the tree line, the sunrise. All the looking filled me and I didn't write. The current dull story went unfinished. Instead I looked and looked and looked, as if a person could become a sunrise if she tried hard enough, if she exposed herself.

Lethargy had been replaced with something else. Contagion was a creeping yellow river in the living room, or a weird song borne on a slice of wind.

But the night of the party the desk was still upstairs. And outside there was a party, a party that had been dreamed of, a clam bake and a cooler full of beer, a couple dozen people standing around with their hands in their pockets, one of them much, much more radiant than the others.

Had I made a decision at this point? I had not made a complete decision.

The sky had a swirl of gray in it, like a trail of ash, and at the horizon the pink simmered above the trees, looking both far and near.

I aimed toward the cooler.

I saw him from the side at first, and for a period we were talking to other people. After a leisurely interval we said hello, and something preternaturally witty, and then after that each time we bumped into each other, or found that we were once again (by chance, by mellow fateful decree) in conversation, it increased, my sense that he knew, that he was in on the hijacking occurring here.

Funny, it *seemed* physical. It seemed like my goal was, or had to be, slipping my hands under his shirt and feeling his skin, seeing what was under all the damn, unnecessary cloth.

The middle part of the night was a journey from one side of a lake to the other. A little bumpy and some spray hit the passengers, but we all had a good laugh, and then we were on the other side. Over here, with the boat gone, the land seemed dark, and people began to leave without my saying good-bye to them, and all of a sudden it wasn't too many people at all, it was just the three of us—me, my boyfriend, and the radiant terror that was his friend and my plot. And so came a jaded, dirty, mistrustful, disappointing, bitter few minutes in the kitchen before we all went to bed. Had we all drunk enough? We tried to drink a little more. What had been the consideration of my soul's survival was now, in this yellow light, almost malice. Upstairs with my boyfriend into the bed with no history, to climb under the heavy blankets and experience one another's separateness; to the couch with the interloper to do what interlopers do, dream of other things.

The morning brought new optimism. It wasn't like the night before, when we established the connection, while the sky was still light and the party was young, but neither was it absolutely sullied, as the end of the night had been, the end of the night that had a back door, an actual scheme, the hustle and ugliness of betrayal. Which we did not in fact act upon but acknowledged, and which was depressing as much for being there as for being untaken. In the morning we could once more, in the light of day, knowing we had been innocent, seeing what we had seen in each other, hedging our bets, keeping our practical shoes on, not throwing out the baby with the bathwater, etc., make subtle, witty remarks in a low-key way, as if we really could tolerate this, what we had or what I imagined to be there.

And so I stumbled around during my lunch hours all week, for weeks, wearing the boots that were too big by a whole size, giving my gait a clownish lack of symmetry, every few steps the toe of the boot sucked under, between cobblestones. In such manner I relived the chance encounters and bona fide insinuations. I stumbled, and for a change my soul did not stumble with me, my soul was elsewhere. If someone had checked on me, if someone had asked me a question, I would have been so easily found out. And if he had touched me? Well, that would have been something indeed. However, the touching was not to be. Not the full touching.

A lurking shadow of rage and ruin, I returned home on the commuter train one final night after many false nights, after months, it seems now, of insinuation and nonsubterfuge, to confront once again the small house on the inlet. So very much good there! With the cats, and the kind young man with whom I lived! One of those nights we went to a bar in town, and on our way home I saw a dark shape pass on the street and disappear (whether it was a rat or a cat I couldn't tell). I started a quarrel about that dark shape, I don't know why. The young kind man with whom I lived—ah, it's a muddled situation. He was cast in a role that did not suit him. I did not mean to set fire to the house after all.

It was two weeks later, a Saturday morning. I went to the YMCA to go swimming. He was at work, and we'd planned to meet for lunch at a faux diner in a brick-fronted building on the main street of that ever increasingly faux waterfront town. I hadn't checked the oven before I left, which was unusual, for I usually checked all the appliances two or three times before closing the door and marching into what would hopefully be forgetfulness or senseless dull despair. But that day I was strong, and I didn't check the oven. Or the lamps, or the coffee machine, or the dryer.

It wasn't the oven. That's what they told me when I returned. When I returned, a fire truck and my landlord's van were in the driveway.

The whole house did not burn. Only a portion of the house, a black shadow coming out the window in the kitchen. The neighbors—God bless their Republican, peeping souls—called when they saw smoke. And so the extraordinarily handsome firemen had sprinted over and broken in the front door. They'd doused our kitchen, with my parents' castoff plates and pans, and his parents' castoff glasses and silverware. Wrecking much, wrecking all that was left over.

I stood in the driveway, looking at the house that had been besmirched, and I did feel as if my affair had been physical, after all.

When I saw my cat's sleek, extended head and neck, the creature looking out the door and then disappearing again, I broke down into a pile of rubble. And then I was a running, ruined pile of rubble, looking for my other cat too.

I think I must have revealed to my landlord and the handsome athletic firemen a nakedness that even my boyfriend had never seen. When I got to the porch I fell down on my hands and knees. I climbed into the house like I was climbing into a little cave. If I did not find my other cat, I would kill myself. I, who had already destroyed so much, who was capable only of looking at a sunrise, and of writing the dullest stories, and stumbling along the cobblestones, and taking whatever kindness and good thing I had in my life and ripping it into shreds and spitting on it. I, who had no history, who was not made of anything, who was, if anything, a slip of blackened paper like this one, a shriveled leaf like this one, I would find my cat, I would find both of them.

My sleek cat came out from behind the TV stand when he saw me, but the other one did not appear for a week. She had been outside when the fire occurred. By the time she showed up, sniffing diffidently around the pile of burned belongings by the garbage cans in the driveway, by the time I saw her and cried, a grateful, suffocating, burned sound in my throat, my boyfriend was gone. We had grown up together in effect, and we could now, with the house out of the way, see something that we hadn't seen before.

It was a shock when I received the call about my mother, but on the other hand it was not so very different from what *her* mother had done, and she had never, ever taken the puppet of her mother's ghost and shaken it the way I always wished she had; she had not stared the puppet in the eye and incarnated the scene, as in a kind of stark Greek tragedy; and so because of this she was haunted and the suicide came easily, like fate, and if she regretted anything after she drank from the plastic bottle, I did not know it, because I never saw her alive again, and I only had dream figures from there on in, and dream figures are notorious. They are liars, even when they seem— most of all when they seem—to be telling the truth about something important.

Aurelie Sheehan

1996–1997

The boots I purchased that winter were exceptionally black, betraying no spiderweb of associations. They fit well, far better than my previous pair. I slipped them on and felt a slight gale around the ankles, and I stalked out into the cityscape in search of monuments. It was suspicious, the way the dark visages lorded over the city the way they did.

In my small apartment, the two cats plaintively mewed as I tiptoed around, no boots on. They stared at me from perches, imbuing their gazes with fire. It was simply a personal dare, a game of solitude, to take the four-page explicit poem to the midnight open mike and step on stage in my miniskirt. All went fine, if it wasn't an actual nightmare: the sense of nonresponse in the audience at large. Like a consolation prize, the man with the waxen head asked if he could walk me home afterward, and at my door he shook my hand and gave me his card, the embossed emblem of a beer distributor over his name.

None of this was exactly what I had in mind, lo, those years ago. None of this was predetermined in Russian literature, nor was it *vivant* or *vrai* at all.

There was a problem, which was that my dreams began to over-resemble the day-lit hours. It was as if my psyche had given up on creation, on make-believe. If I bought spaghetti during the day, I overboiled it in the dark space behind my eyes that night. I had the same conversations with my coworkers again and again, and then again on the second night.

The cats seemed anxious to me.

I quit my job and took another one.

I developed a series of new hobbies and interests, such as sewing. I sewed white curtains that on purpose crumpled up at the bottom, as if they were too luxuriant to be cut short. I watched the curtains, hoping they might swish in the breeze. I made a cushion cover for a chair. I made a quilt. I listened to the radio. I painted a picture.

I arranged the loveseat and the chair in such a way as to indicate a living room in the corner of my apartment. The cats stared and did not mew anymore.

1998

The construction of a kind of sanity under way, I returned to France. The residue of the blackened house, with all the wet ash, the wrecked kitchen, the soiled silverware—this had come and gone. I lived in a world in which such things as demon angels could turn up out of nowhere, but they didn't do it so very often after all.

Naturally I brought a suitcase that was way, way too heavy.

It dates the story, certainly, and makes one worry a little about timeline overall, but my suitcase was, as it turns out, the kind with four wheels along the narrow bottom, rather than the more rigid, vertically rolling style, and one was meant to lead it around by a short loop of leather. The suitcase was green with yellow and orange piping. It had a lock with a combination no one ever knew.

I ventured forth from the terminal hall, hunched, pulling the unwieldy suitcase, which kept tipping. It was dawn, and Paris was just around the corner. France was a place where everything had been made from a direction sheet written in misleading language. It was a place of imprecision. The cups were too small, too many people wore black cashmere scarves, luggage carts came in odd wedge shapes. I peered at the people sitting at the airport café, trying to see what they were having for breakfast, taking in their vociferous conversation, albeit not a mite of its meaning. Upon shop walls were hooked toys and stationery goods, dusty and mostly obscure or out of date. I felt that it would definitely be all right to purchase a pack of cigarettes in this country, it was only a matter of when.

And yet, most importantly, I needed to find my way out of the airport. Which proved difficult, because I had gone this entire Swann's way only to discover it was a roundabout return to the Salles d'Embarquement pour l'Internationale from which I had recently departed, and now I had to return whence I came. Approximately every third step the suitcase either wavered precariously or fell over. Momentum was at work, it seemed. I slowed down still further. Hunched, slow, and encumbered, I crept back up the hall, past the quaffing morning arguers, to take a left instead of a right at the first juncture, and ironically or hilariously or neither, there was the exit, almost immediately—and so I would go, and I left.

A taxi was my next task, and yet no taxi came as I stood by the green suitcase holding three pairs of pants, four books, a hair dryer, two notebooks, an electrical adaptor, a makeup bag, four long-sleeve and two short-sleeve shirts, a jacket, a skirt, seven pairs of underwear and seven pairs of socks, an umbrella, slippers, a pair of kitten heels. I whimpered, I almost cried. I would have to pull myself together. This was an awful part of travel, something I'd forgotten when I was buying the ticket and packing and jollying myself out of my fear of flying and putting my desk in order, a chilling experience, as if I were arranging a stage set for my survivors. No less horrified than a shy sixth-grader, I put my hand up into the Parisian air. *"Taxi,"* I emitted, with a *Saturday Night Live* French accent, though luckily I was more or less mumbling. *"Taxi!"* I said again.

I found myself at a kitchen table, holding a *verre de vin. Rouge,* to be precise, and everything *did* feel precise, there was no before, there was no after. *I have always, always, always been here.* Such was the precision of this feeling that the creeping numbness in the back of my neck—the first of alcohol's effects—was no sign of anything in progress or a station along the way, but rather a coarse, gorgeous pre-occupation to fuel and feed. In other words I kept drinking. At the table were an expat couple in their fifties, a man with a suitcase smaller than my own, and me. The two men ate compulsively some kind of very small nut, of which there was a bowl, requiring much laborious peeling and picking of the shell. Handsome as they both were, the men nibbled, tongued, and gnawed at the little nuts, their front teeth exposed, a shower of shell bits and inner-shell flecks spilling out upon their woolen shirts. Both of them wore tartan, more in line with French country, I supposed, than Paris itself.

Every once in a while the hostess would desultorily take a nut and manage its excavation with her mouth closed and comparatively still. In a moment she would discreetly spit the shell into her palm and then toss it behind her shoulder, as if these nuts could provide a spot of luck as well.

"Words are irrelevant. What matters is the body. The things of the world, that is what matters most," said the other guest, with a sly look in my direction.

I took another sip of *vin rouge.* The glasses were simple globes, the kind you'd get in a cheap restaurant, and the wine was just a table wine of which they had a case or two, purchased from a vintner. The green bottle had no label. The liquid inside made the green black, until we finished the bottle, and then the bottle shimmered like seaweed, and then we started on another, until that too was infused by light. And another. And another. By that time we'd started on a

234

makeshift meal: cassoulet (left over, said the hostess, from a party the previous night), a salad of greens, slices of rustic bread. The numbness in my neck disappeared, as a glass of water disappears in a pool. I brought the fork to my mouth, a little duck and some sausage, and then I had a sip of wine, and then a bite of bread. I chewed on the lettuce like a cow in a field.

The other guest and I were the last ones up, and we stretched out in front of the fireplace. The kitchen floor was made of great slabs of stone, cold as a tomb. My heart beat faster and less methodically than usual, and it was hard to tell what was most dangerous: the monolith of the past, the exigencies of the moment, or the quality of my body's responses themselves, which were in some sense predetermined, I imagined, or at least French.

"Retourne," I mouthed to myself in the morning. *"Voyage,"* I whispered. The words would be like charms, they *were* charms, despite the pronouncement of the man I had met the previous night. The hired driver brooded, as did I, my face turned to the horizon, which kept gliding past. My body had an excellent, just-fucked feeling, which helped create a cinematic sense. *Destination* was a difficulty: the necessity of getting to a specific place. There, at the specific place, I would come face to face with the fact of so much time passing, of age and distance. But the fleeting landscape was easily mine, this eighty-kilometer-per-hour hurtle. We passed a stone mansion with a hedge surrounding it and a small child peering out. She was wearing a long white shirt or a nightgown. We crossed another road. We wound through a stretch of trees. When the driver turned toward Metz, it was all last minute, brakes slammed, cigarette losing ash, the round-and-round turns of the wheel and the muttering. "What?" I said helplessly from the back.

He dropped me off at the *tabac* in Manheulles, agreeing to return in an hour. Of this there seemed to be a fifty-fifty chance. Still I handed over my two-hundred-franc note.

I stood then, in front of the *tabac* in the town where we had lived, where it all began. "It" being me—*moi,* as we might say in these circumstances. I took a deep breath, willing the extraordinariness to return. For I confess I had forgotten it at times, during the intervening years.

Two skeptical women stared at me from a table in front of the store. They were wearing stiff trench coats and smoking cigarettes.

*

As well as my phrase book, I had a list of places I might visit or take special notice of when I came here, to a town not even on most maps. The list was written on yellow lined paper, folded into fourths, slipped between the phrase book's pages of expressions and inquiries. I was to notice the cows, the fruit trees, the horizon. I was to notice the house where we lived. I was to notice the fields, with a particular eye out for the field where my mother and I frolicked, as memorialized in photographs.

I paced through town, open to all supernatural signs. And I did spot a bird, a scraggly crow, sitting on top of the World War II monument before the church. *Nous N'Oublierons Jamais.* Or, we shall. *We shall, we shall, we shall* echoed through the village of my earliest years on earth.

I marched on. I walked behind the main road, which was a highway, really, the whole of the village clustered around as if the road were a magnet, having attracted a dozen or so houses, one church, one *tabac*, two barns, a school, and a garage. I found a road that I fancied I might have walked on before, with my mother, with my father. It was a dirt road, farm equipment lined up on one side, and on the other side an orchard.

I stopped walking and teetered there, thinking of the blue pack of cigarettes, the café matches in my other pocket, the wind at my ankles, my forlorn cats. Perhaps this was the very field where the picture was taken—the picture of my mother and me, when we lived in a black-and-white universe. Perhaps this was where we fluttered the checked tablecloth over the crunching grasses and brought our broken baguette and our pears and our milk, where her hair fluffed into her eyes and she smiled, plump and apparently happy—that was both of us, then.

I stared down at the grasses and the bumpy ground underneath.

A radio played from the other side of the wall between the field and a house. Someone was maybe in the backyard, doing a chore, in his daily life or her daily life. The song sounded like an American pop song, but it was not. I could tell the music came from a radio because of its tinny quality, its provisional nature.

I walked farther down the road behind the orchard and at some point it split, one branch turning into what appeared to be a driveway or a kind of path to a place where more equipment was stored, and the other encircling the hill beyond the orchard and along a spell

236

of forest. I stood, wondering which way to go. Both ways looked like they petered out quickly, although to be sure I'd have to really try them, to walk farther down one or the other or both in succession. But this I did not do. I turned around and walked back past the house with the radio and past the orchard. In a picture we have in one of the albums—where is that album?—two cows linger under the trees, staring at the camera. There were no such cows now.

I passed the church with the *Nous N'Oublierons Jamais* monument in front, a blackened obelisk, and I came to the main road and the *tabac*, where I had thought I might buy an afternoon Pernod. The two women were no longer out front. They had disappeared. They'd gone inside to iron, to watch television, to fold themselves into three and slip into a drawer. But what of the places I meant to remember in particular, what of the photograph I planned to ask someone, in faulty French, to take of me? I ran past the house where we lived, past its stone steps and narrow windows and dark shutters. If it had been another kind of day, I would have knocked. But as it was I kept going, jogging now past the house, past the next two houses, toward the Manheulles sign, which from this direction had a red slash through it, a slash of military and official dignity, of recognition. I ran past, my legs still half numb, knees swollen, my lungs simply slits. The squeaking I made or the boots made didn't align with the thick ponderous feeling. I tripped once, and then I was zigzagging on the black road, past the sign, back the way I came, on the highway toward Verdun.

You'll Be Sorry
A D *Jameson*

ONE OF THESE DAYS—and it might be a day very soon—and it won't be a day that you can identify in advance—and my behavior on that day will not contain clues that you can scrutinize as warnings—I will become angry.

And though it may start as a normal day, a routine day, a typical morning on which you make yourself up at the mirror, and gulp down your breakfast, and peck at my cheek as you swing through the kitchen and shoulder your bag and head to work, leaving me all by myself in the bi-level house with nothing to occupy me but my hobbies and my spite, this day won't be normal. Because I will put aside my hobbies. And I will nurse my spite.

And I will fret, and act put out, and be harassed and exasperated. And I will be peevish and teased and tormented, and sick and incensed. And I will be taunted, and jump at the bait, whatever bait is set out before me. And I will be vexed and pugnacious and livid, and riled and wounded, and deeply aggrieved.

And I will pick at, and then not eat a bite of my breakfast. And I will throw my bowl of oatmeal into the trash. And I'll slam shut the cupboard, putting a crack in the cheap wooden door, right near the hinge. And I will leave the freezer door open, defrosting the freezer and thawing out all of our waffles and ice cubes.

And I will break a plate, and a cup, and a glass, and a spoon, and a fork, and a knife, and a pair of sandalwood chopsticks, as well as a spatula and a carrot peeler.

And I will break the dirty dishes in the sink, the ones that you left there overnight, and I will leave them there as well, still dirty and even more disgusting, surrounded by fragments of broken utensils.

And I will stomp through every room of both floors of the bi-level, huffing and puffing, kicking our CD towers over, and pulling the banisters loose from the walls, and smashing the glass that covers the portraits that we've taken.

And I will get all up in a huff, and I will get all up in a miff. And I will get my feathers ruffled, my feelings hurt over minuscule things, over trifling matters. And I will feel piqued.

And I will get sore. And I will see red. And I will get my dander up, and my Irish up.

And I will get myself worked up, up into a tizzy and into a frenzy. And I will get steamed, hot under the collar, all hot and bothered. And I will throw out all the mail, and throw your shoes into the trash, and throw the trash bag into the basement, nonplussed when it rips.

And I will take amiss, and umbrage. And I will take exception to something innocuous, like a harmless joke, like a humorous message you left on my desk, intended to lift my spirits, no doubt, and do nothing more. And I will not take a harmless joke.

And I will not take it sitting down. And my gorge will rise, and my blood will boil. And my hackles will raise, and my nose will get bent out of joint.

And I'll take out frustrations on the plants and on the plant stands, as I kick at and punch at the ferns and the gladioli. And I will uproot the lilac bush and the rose of Sharon, and all the tulips, and all the ivy, as well as the pine tree that you just planted.

And I will get pissed off, and ticked off, and chawed off, while kicking at plant life, my hands and wrists bleeding from thistles and thorns.

And I will bear malice, and harbor a grudge, and harbor resentment in my chest, within my heart.

And I will seethe, and bridle, and bristle, and simmer, and stew, and bite my lip, and bite my tongue, and struggle to settle down, and cool down, and cool my jets. And I will be utterly and spectacularly unsuccessful.

Because by then, I will have reached my boiling point. And I will explode, and flare up, and blow up, and lose my temper, and lose all my patience, and blow my stack, and blow my lid, and blow my top. And I will rampage and I will storm and go berserk.

You bet your britches. And I will blow a fuse, and a gasket, as well as my cool, as well as somebody else's cool. I'll blow everyone else's cool, and everyone's gaskets. I will have a conniption fit.

And I will throw a hissy fit. And I will create an embarrassing scene. And I will throw a temper tantrum. You will see. You will see my behavior on TV, on repeated news bulletins, tapes that they'll show and reshow and reshow in the months to come, that you will not be able to avoid.

And I will turn wild, and I will turn cruel. I have long practiced turning cruel, at the many moments when you weren't looking. At the times that you weren't present, when you were off working, or shopping, or playing, or socializing, off someplace else, doing heaven knows what, with God only knows whom, at all times of the night, running fast and loose like greased lightning, all over creation.

I'll sow confusion. I will sow doubt.

And I will fly into a rage, and fly off the handle. I will go certifiably postal. And I will go off the reservation, just like a mad bull, or like a mad horse, or like a mad bat, like a bat out of hell, or a runaway train out of hell, or a truck, or the car of the juggernaut, jumping the rails, running riot all over creation.

And I will rant and I will rave. I will grow rabid. I'll raise a ruckus to wake the dead. I'll scream and I'll holler. I'll rail at anyone and everyone. I will act like a man possessed.

I'll fly about half cocked, unhinged. I'll set out on a tear. And I will go around the bend, clear out of my skull. And I will go right out of my mind.

And I will carom through the subdivision, over the lawns and through the well-maintained flower beds, scattering chips of mulch and grinding holes into manicured plots of grass, and I will throw loose pebbles and rocks against the windows, and rip down the shutters, and ring all the doorbells, and knock over mailboxes and lawn ornaments, before I run away.

And I will run back and forth on the highway, my bathrobe flapping, barely still on me, my boxer shorts down around my knees, my naughty bits dangling, and I will jump up and down on the hoods of the cars that have stopped, the SUVs and the station wagons, the Maseratis, and I will throw my half-naked body against their windshields, pulling and tugging and ripping free the windshield wipers, and tugging and pulling at the handles of the doors, as wide-eyed drivers and passengers lunge for the power locks. And I will rub my bits against windows before I depart, before I waddle off, shrieking and screaming, over the guardrail and into the brush.

And I will work myself into a lather, and I will work myself into a rage. And it will be a fine, clean rage, a pure, primal rage, a primeval rage. An inspired rage, such as is found in the books of legend.

And I'll show no decency, because I will have no decency. I will become indecency incarnate.

And I will show no mercy. And I will give no quarter. Mercy and decency and quarter will be beneath me, infra dig. And I will not respect the sanctity of Mother Nature, or the sanctity of life.

And I'll become choleric, and caustic, and spleenful, and scathing, and cutting, and biting, and mordant, and sarcastic. And I'll become bellicose, and belligerent, and paroxysmic and flushed with rage.

And I will break doors. And I will break several plate-glass windows. And I will break into a display case, a window display case, at a fancy downtown department store. And I will waste no time in defiling the clothes mannequins; I will tear off their clothing, and I will pull their false bodies apart, false limb from false limb. And I will wave those false limbs about, and I will howl. And I will laugh. And I will cackle as I do so, a high, piercing cackle that splits the eardrums of any listener.

And I will run up and down on the escalator, giggling. And I will jostle my way through the crowds, knocking over the slower pedestrians, shouting obscene rejoinders, warning all present to get the hell out of my path.

And I will push my way into a crowded elevator, at precisely the moment its doors start to close, delaying its passengers for a few more annoying seconds, so that they will grumble. And then I will push every one of the buttons, all seventeen buttons, each button for all seventeen of the floors. And then I will rush out again as the doors close, snorting madly.

And I will be sullen and sulfurous, smoldering, fuming, and sizzling. Burning and browned off, beside myself, a little hothead.

And I will get even further worked up, becoming embittered and envenomed. And fighting mad, and hopping mad. And I will drive myself up the wall.

And I will be rancorous and wrought up. And I'll be in high dudgeon, and up in arms. And I will be in a perfect snit. And I will be vehement and irate, and fit to be tied.

And I'll be indignant and inflamed and infuriated. And I will be ireful and enraged, and wrathful, and snappish, and rather short tempered.

And I will break into a house, and I will traipse up the carpeted stairs in my muddy sneakers, tracking my mud and my dirt and dead leaves and little twigs and clumps of dog debris all along the cream-colored carpets.

And I will stomp into the bedroom, and I will break the vanity mirror, and I will overturn the bed, and I will poke a hole in the mattress, and I will take a box out of the closet, and I will dump out all its contents, onto the carpet, each one of the prized pewter miniature figurines that it contains, and I will throw them all out the window, and I will rush back down the staircase, and head outside, and I will stomp on every one of the miniature figures, grinding them merrily into the sidewalk, scratching their intricate, detailed paint jobs and bending their poses.

And the house that I break into will be our house, and the figures that I stomp on will be your brother's, the ones that you're keeping for him while he works for the Peace Corps in Thailand.

And I will take a meat cleaver to your scrapbooks, and pruning shears to your side of the wardrobe, and a pair of tongs to your daily journal, and I will dunk it in the toilet.

And I will hurl insults at anyone gathered around me by then, and I will bite my thumb at them, and wiggle my fingers, and raise holy hell, and raise holy Cain, and flip them the bird. And I will cause such tremendous commotion, such as has never been seen before, not on TV, not even in older books of legend.

And I will foam at the mouth, and spit, and gnash my teeth, and bare my fangs, and I will bite at the exposed shins of anybody who tries to restrain me. And my bite will be savage, infectious, and it will fester, and it will sear, and it will ooze, and it will never fully heal, and it will leave a scar, and that scar will ache on the cold winter days, on the days when the wind howls in from the east. And it will be much worse than a Gila monster's bite, such a bite as the bites in the books of legend.

And I will chafe, and I will rankle, and stamp my feet. And I will take somebody's head off. And I will jump down somebody's throat.

And I will snap at shins and hands until the police surround the house, until the neighbors surround the house, and the TV crews, and until you push your way through the crowds, having rushed home from work, having been informed of my violent rampage by a coworker, who saw it on the news.

And you will push and struggle through until you reach me, until the crowds part just enough, and the police relent and permit you to squeeze through the human wall, and stand before me. Clutching your pocketbook close to your breast as I tremble before you.

And I will frown, and scowl, and glower, and growl, and snarl. And I will howl, and holler, and yell. And I will roar.

And you'll stand before me, dumbfounded, astonished, and stricken senseless, your mouth agape. And you will not know what to say to me. But, nonetheless, you will start to say something, nevertheless, you will open your mouth, and you'll start to say something, something comforting, to me.

But I'll interrupt you.

And as you stammer, and stutter, and "um," and "er," I will change at the drop of a hat. I will turn on a dime. As you drop your hat, as you drop your pocketbook in surprise, I will change before you, before your eyes.

And it will be as though I've turned into a stranger, as though I've transformed, as though you have never, ever known me. You'll no longer recognize who I am.

And I will take undue offense at any words you try to say to me, at anything anyone anywhere tries to say to me, unnecessary offense.

And my aggravation will inspire nothing but regret, and shame, and puzzlement, and concern, and humiliation, in other words naught but the worst and most negative of emotions.

And I will not stop there.

And I will not abide. And I will not be able to help myself, or be able to stop. "Control yourself," you will struggle to say, but I will not be capable of exerting such control. My emotions will get the best of me. And I will derive a grim satisfaction.

And I will rear my ugly head. And I will glare daggers at anyone daring to look at me, and I will stare at you with a quiet, unblinking, unnerving intensity. And I will raise my fists, and will knock you to the ground with a balled-up sweatshirt, or with a throw pillow.

245

And I will make efforts in public to tarnish your many achieve-ments. And I'll glibly reveal the most damaging facts, and invent half-truths and scandalous innuendo. And I will spread slander at every turn. And I will show you my derision.

And I will spit at you an epithet, and it will be a stinging epithet, comparing you to a monster, and telling you what I would like to see done to you, and all your fellow monsters. And there will be more to it than that; it will be so bad that I am still thinking the epithet up— it will be that bad. And it will be vicious and untrue and crude and nonsensical, so hurtful and senseless that you will never understand it, no matter how hard you try. And you will try.

And you will wonder how I ever thought up such a terrible thing, and how I could harbor such terrible enmity in my breast, but I will harbor even more enmity in my breast; that epithet will be but a taste of my terrible enmity. And you will never taste the full extent of my ani-mosity, or my enmity, no matter how much of it you will taste. But I will try.

And then at last, when I've said my piece, when I've spoken my mind, when I've reached the end of my hurtful and unkind soliloquy, I will close tight my mouth, and fall silent, and shut up, and topple over, and go limp, and pass out, and I will lower my ugly head, and say no more.

And even that won't be the end of it. And that non-end will not be the worst of it.

No, the worst of it will be the fact that not you, and not your brother, and not your family or your friends, and not anyone else—not even the so-called experts that you'll hire—will have an idea or explana-tion why I will have done this.

And you will examine your behavior and your feelings, and you will wonder what you could have said to ever provoke this, or done to provoke me, and you will examine and you will wonder until you collapse, crumpling under your scrutiny and your self-criticism and doubt—and even then you will not know.

And I will behave in such a fashion that I will cause everyone to wonder whether I even know myself.

And maybe I will know, and maybe I won't. But, either way, no matter what anyone does, and no matter what anyone says or tries to do, I will keep my motivations private, and I won't say.

And I will become some kind of great mystery, such as the kind that's put down at great length in the books of legend. And my riddle will endure throughout the ages, and it will endure throughout the centuries. And it will come to occupy a great many pages, and it will preoccupy many legions of different scholars. And it will be studied and scrutinized and read over and over, a kind of case study, a kind of enigma.

And my enigma, my riddle, my mystery will endure until the end of time itself, until the ocean waves grow tired in their habits, until humanity grows jaded in its comforts, until the planets peter out in their revolutions, and rust in their orbits.

And my great riddle of a name will also endure, and my name will in time acquire a totally different meaning, and it will come in time to signify something else, something violent and cruel, something awful and sad, something heartless and vile and terribly ruthless, and very wicked.

And you and your friends and your family and experts will invent many different excuses, and rationales, and causes, and myriad explanations. And you will finally decide that, all in all, I probably did what I did out of some kind of sick fascination, some inexplicable, deep compulsion that I myself didn't understand.

247

And it will console you to all agree, and to come to agreement over this. And that agreement that you come to might be true, that consensus might be in fact the truth, or close to the truth. But I will not say.

And I will never beat my breast, or show compunction, or grow morose, or show much remorse.

And I will never recant or repent. And I will never be contrite. And I will never rue the day.

And I will never reprove myself. And I will never reproach myself. And I will never see the error of my ways.

And I will never have second thoughts, or learn my lesson. And I will never turn over a new leaf, or wipe the slate clean, or see the light.

And no matter what happens, no matter what you say, no matter what anybody says, no matter what they choose to write about me in the books of legend, I will not care.

And I will not ever apologize, and I will not ever say I'm sorry. And I will be sorry, but I will not say it, and I will not show it, and I will become just like a magnificent work of art, irrational, inscrutable, inexplicable, and I will never stop.

Through the Rivers
Andrew Mossin

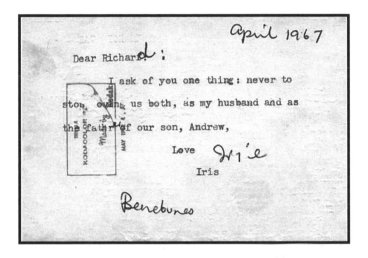

If I CAN REMEMBER *taste of tobacco on his breath, cinnamon lozenges, pale paper pasted down on tablets, flash of light on the backs of her legs, sweet meal flowing through their wet hands, balsa strips laid into place over string, kite paper placed on glued strips of paper, high white light through trees when morning came, his eyes meeting mine, their faces in the windows of our house when I came back inside and felt my way back upstairs in the dark, her arms folded, her face creased in the calligraphic dawn, the years it took to get there, no before, no after. . . .*

In our last summer together, my mother kept a journal on a drugstore tablet, recording there each of my acts of theft, betrayal, deception, escape from home. She wandered into the evenings looking for me, going house to house, sometimes lingering at the corner of Twenty-ninth Street and Ordway to stand there, facing neither backward nor forward, but somehow sideways, parallel to the line of trees that spanned one side of the street to the other, until she moved against the weight of her own body, it seemed, up toward the houses on Highland Place, her legs pale in the low light of evening. I could watch her from behind cars, moving as she moved, just a bit behind her. Sometimes I could tell she knew I was following her. But it didn't matter. She would keep moving to the next house, the door would open, our neighbors would appear, my mother would ask if I'd been seen, a few moments lingering there on the porch in the quiet white summer light, and then she'd say, "Thank you, no, thank you, you are very kind," and come back down the stairs to the street. I played a game in my head, *I am one I am two.* I talked to myself that way, like I was two people, one crazy, one almost OK. I said, *There are people in this world who want to kill you. She is one of them.* And I let it sit in the open air for a bit, and the almost OK kid said, *Go back inside go back to her she won't hurt you she's not mean you'll be safe there.* The voices in my head like wires crossing, I could believe either one, I could let them talk me into anything, one or the other. It didn't matter what became of me, I was with my voices and the shadow act of following my mother through the backlit streets.

Storms came, heavy ones that summer, the skies blackening, followed by the dark heavy rains over the city, the air stabbed again and again by lightning. The air was just as thick and heavy afterward, it didn't matter, nothing cooled the days down and at night the skies would be low and dark, filled, it seemed, with slow-moving hot circling air that climbed inside your skin and made you long for water, a pool, anything cool. In those months of 1971, I effectively became a runaway, no different from hundreds of other kids living on the streets of Washington, DC. My mother had scheduled a date for a hearing before a judge to determine if I could be sent to Junior Village, a combination reform school and juvenile prison run by the DC police department. She'd first threatened it, then made the phone call while I stood next to her. "I can't do this, I can't do this," she said over and over again, pushing her cigarette butts into the glass ashtray as she took another swig of scotch from the bottle she kept hidden behind the drapes in the living room. I didn't say anything, I didn't want to know what it meant, where she was sending me. It was no different to me than the foster home I'd been placed in some years before. Standing next to my mother in the half-light of late afternoon I wondered as I would often do in those years why my parents had adopted me in the first place, when it seemed as if they didn't really want a child. *Don't be ridiculous,* she would say to me evenings when it was just the two of us and she hadn't drunk much yet, *of course we wanted you, he was always waiting for a son, all his life, of course we wanted a beautiful son, and that's what we have, a son, a beautiful young man you are.* But the words were worn-out even before they were said, and after a while I stopped believing them, stopped believing anything she said about such things, and kept away from her as much as I could.

If I returned at all, it wasn't for more than a night or so, and I'd be sure to leave by early morning, before my mother woke, packing a bag of extra clothes, books, my glasses, so I could read no matter where I was. I tried not to think about where I was going, what I would do day to day. I got up in people's yards, I woke from half sleep, cold and mosquito bitten, found refuge in air-conditioned stores or apartment-house lobbies during the day, hid at night in people's backyards. Sometimes the people who lived there would come out and I'd hide under their porch, then their footsteps would go away and I'd come back out and lie on a cool plastic lawn chair, the plastic webbing imprinting itself on my legs and arms. During the days the air was heavy and warm. Finding someplace to go wasn't ever that difficult. I went to the same places each day. I went to them again and again, as if already attempting to remember where I'd been just the day before, just an hour ago. I went up to the playground on Macomb Street I'd been going to since I was seven, played ping-pong in the clubhouse, the white ball struck against the back wall of the interior . . . carom pool alone at the table for hours while the sun blazed outside. Through the doorway I could see the neighborhood kids passing through the light and it was as if I'd become invisible to them, to anyone; no one noticed me or asked me what I was doing there, where I belonged or to whom. Sometimes I stood in the flush damp heat and held the coins I'd brought for soda in my pocket and pressed the edges into my leg and waited for the familiar voices to emerge. *You can't be serious don't be so fucking dumb just take the stuff take it no one will care.* If the clubhouse manager came he'd sometimes ask me to leave and I'd walk back down toward Connecticut Avenue, moving slowly down Newark Street and the hill that led back to the avenue. I'd go into People's Drug and Trover Book Shop, Safeway sometimes for food, and put things into my pockets or hide them under my T-shirt when no one was looking and head back up Ordway toward home. Though there was no home, none I could really return to. I would come down the alley back of our house and see the roofs in a row, like a line of stones above grass, and hear the evening owls in the trees and the bluing of dusk would enfold my body until it felt like the beginning of day all over again.

The days passed, one after the other. Day or night didn't matter. I had no one to control me, no one to shelter or harm me. At night, sitting with my books under a streetlight or in the doorway of an apartment building, I'd find my way back to another place, more still, certain, as in the torn paperback copy of *Walden* I kept with me through those days I'd found a way back in. "When my floor was dirty, I rose early, and, setting all my furniture out of doors on the grass, bed and bedstead making but one budget, dashed water on the floor, and sprinkled white sand from the pond on it, and then with a broom scrubbed it clean and white; and by the time the villagers had broken their fast the morning sun had dried my house sufficiently to allow me to move in again, and meditations were almost uninterrupted."

One night I found my way into the house of a neighbor two doors down. He'd returned late from one of the bars on Connecticut Avenue. I'd seen him coming up our street, staggering, weaving his way back up, and I'd kept behind a row of bushes and followed him as he moved, just as I'd followed my mother, watching him stop, unmoving, then walking just a bit behind and to the side, unable to take my eyes off him. His wife and children had gone away, I hadn't seen them most of the summer. She'd been a kind of neighborhood presence, inviting local children over to their house in the afternoons to have sandwiches and soda after school. Sometimes she'd let us play board games before we all headed back to our homes. That seemed like a long time ago, and then they'd disappeared and he'd be seen walking around the block at night, kind of a ritual, nothing special, nothing out of the ordinary, just his figure, there, kind of present, no one I knew or really could come close to. A father to kids I hardly knew either. Now there was no trace of them, and the man moving up the street in the darkness seemed disembodied, without direction or purpose as he climbed the hill.

I kept close behind him and when he went up the stairs of his back porch I stayed near, watching as he disappeared into an oblong frame of shadows. I stood for a time by the door, waiting, then saw the light go on upstairs, a face nearly visible at the window, its bony reflection apparent for a moment, then gone. The garden was wet, the grass unmowed and tall so that I could run my palms across the weighted spears with ease. I lay down, disappearing in a well of leaves and grass, and listened to the crickets and stared up at the window where the darkness filled the frame in soft reflective blots of blue and green.

What do you want here, I asked myself. *What do you want with this poor guy who never did anything to you what do you want to do with him why do you need to take from him.* I walked up the steps and moved as he had up the wooden planks and stood on the porch and pulled the door open. He'd left it unlocked and when I entered the kitchen I smelled the sour odors of meat that had gone bad, rotting fruit left out on the table in a bowl. He'd kept the single hall light on and I saw the toys stacked up against one wall and some photographs of his kids on the table by the hallway and then there were the curtains, all of them ripped down from their rods and thrown onto the floor. The curtains were made of a heavy velvet fabric and I let them run through my hands like lengths of heavy rope, then let them fall back on the floor where I'd found them.

If he were awake . . . but the house was quiet as I moved through it in the ways I'd learned in my own house. I stood on the landing and looked into the room where he'd fallen asleep, half on, half off the bed. His shoes still on. His shirt slightly open at the chest so that I could see the shininess of his damp skin. I knelt by his bed and felt inside his trouser pocket. It was empty and I pulled my hand back out and listened to him breathing for a while, his face a soft pale hue on the pillow as he breathed irregularly. The wallet was on the floor near his arm that had perhaps meant to reach for it, then let it go along with his keys. I opened it and took what money there was, not much, maybe $20, and left the wallet on the floor beside him, exactly as I'd found it.

The next afternoon I came by on my way down to the avenue and saw him in the garden, working his push mower across the small bit of lawn out back, a drink in his hand, as if he'd never gone away, never known any other day but this one. The sunlight formed a bruise over his left eye, and the bloodstains were still visible above his bandaged knee where he'd fallen the night before.

That summer my father traveled to Poland on assignment for the Voice of America. It was his first trip back to his native country since the end of World War II. A few of the letters that my mother wrote from this time have survived. Only one (as far as I know) was ever read by him, so that when he returned to the United States at the end of that summer, and effectively the end of his time with my mother (she would die in December of that year), he was shocked by what he found: a thirteen-year-old boy he didn't recognize, barefoot, his hair long, unwashed, falling about his shoulders in fine, stringy strands. What had happened while he was away? Who stood in place of the son he remembered? There was no way for me to explain and he didn't ask, staring past me as if I'd already vanished, weren't there anymore. To the end of his life he seemed never to have understood what had occurred those last months of my mother's life when we were left alone in the house together. Left alone. Not in the house and not together. During a counseling session with a social worker at the P Street Clinic in Georgetown more than two years after her death, I had tried to explain what had happened. The words didn't come and my father sat, expressionless almost, slumped in the chair, his newspaper and brown bag from lunch still in hand. What could I tell him? What would he understand? *I want to kneel down and pray,* I thought, *I want to cut through this silence, I want you to hold me and take me in your arms a little boy again, I want us to forgive one another, forgive her, I want to forgive her for leaving us. . . .*

"Iris . . . ," he said. . . . And I looked at him and saw he had started to cry and I said I knew and he looked over at me and said, "No, Andrew, you don't know. You killed her. You. You did this to us." And I, *No I didn't didn't didn't I didn't do that I didn't kill her I didn't.* And his face was wet and stained and he smoothed the tears away and took his hands from his knees and the counselor looked over at him, then toward me, and outside on the playground a group of girls was playing four square, and I smelled beef cooking from the hamburger place down the street and it was very quiet inside when the clock struck four and the woman said it was time for us to go now and we got up and her hand was slippery and cold in mine when she shook my hand and I looked at her and said under my breath following him out, *I didn't I never wanted to I didn't.*

During the weeks of my father's trip, my mother wrote him letters, sometimes two or three a day, informing him of daily life at home. As things worsened between us, my mother's letters to my father became more anguished and, at the same time, resigned to a state of affairs she felt she had no energy to control. Twenty-four years later, in the midst of packing up my apartment in Philadelphia, I would find several of these letters, still sealed in their envelopes, addressed to my father, c/o the American Embassy in Warsaw. He had never opened them, never read my mother's words. What would they have meant at the time had he done so? What might he have felt for this woman so plainly unable to keep her life together any longer and in need of something, anything, from this man she had once adored, given her life to. Or are these even the right questions?

The letters remain the only other record I possess, besides the loose sheets of notepad, of my mother's life during these last months.

```
Tuesday  [postmarked June 9, 1971]

Little Darling:

I phoned up TWA this morning & they said
your flight came in OK at Frankfurt and that
it left on time yesterday. My goodness, you
were a long while in getting to the airport.
From 6 to 6:30 I was phoning up TWA at
Dulles to find out whether you had checked
in & would have told them to delay the flight
until you reached there, but the lines were
busy all the while and we were frightened
also about tying up our own telephone so you
wouldn't reach us. Anyway, it was a relief
to hear your voice, and my goodness, was I
glad you'd had a good meal before you left.

Today I am missing you more than I can
possibly tell you. (I ought to be able to
get used to this, but I never have and never
will.) I keep telling myself that 6 weeks
will pass in a flash, and so it will. The
main thing is for you to enjoy yourself
after your assignment, but I hope and I am
sure you will miss me too.

Coming back yesterday wasn't too bad, though
it was bad enough with the congested traffic
and the terrible thunderstorms. Over the
bridge, a bus on the other side splashed an
ocean of water on to me, and I couldn't see
for a minute. Actually, coming back took
less than half an hour.

Nothing in the mail today; Andrew has half a
day off & right now he's writing a note to
you. He had a big lunch, went up by bike to
get ice cream and both have had some. Later
he's going for a short bike ride.

Kenton went up so it's now 18½. The others
are the same. I'm resolved never to look at
the stocks already sold. What's the sense.
```

Princess won't sleep with anyone and she is
so morose I know she's missing you. Sammy
sleeps on your bed downstairs.

It's bloody hot today, sunny, and chances
are more thunderstorms. Tomatoes are coming
on nicely and the hydrangeas for sure will
be out this weekend.

We've just been visited by three tiny little
girls who want to play with Princess, so
Andy has taken them to the back garden &
will give them some ice cream.

There's really nothing to tell you, but even
this is nice to know. Andrew has promised to
be good, so let us cross our fingers and
touch wood.

Every last ounce of my feelings go into
BENEBUNES.

Your Iris   Zowie

————

Saturday June 12 [postmarked June 12]

I hate to tell you this but Andrew has done
the following:

Monday: stayed with A.

Tuesday: Came home early, had lunch and when
I asked him where he had spent the night he
said he didn't know. He left on his bicycle
and didn't return home. I told him I forgave
him for leaving the house and asked him to
write Daddy.

Wednesday: I went with the police to check
him in his paper route but we didn't find
him.

Thursday: I phoned the school and discovered
he was playing hooky, so I went to the
swimming club and then all over Highland
Place; the police couldn't help me so they
told me to do what the School had also told
me: get an appointment with Juvenile Court.
I have the earliest appointment July 9th.
During the night whilst I was asleep, and
I had left both doors open for him, he came
in with A. and took all his clothes.

This was two or three hours after I had
discovered them at the Uptown Cinema about
10 p.m. watching the movies. He refused to
leave A.

He has stolen something like $25.00 from me.

Friday: Yesterday the Police came again
because he, A. and another boy had been
caught stealing at Murphy's. They asked me
whether I wanted him home but when they came
they told me that the next time he was
caught he would be put in a Receiving Home
until he was 18. The two policemen said he
needed a whipping.

Saturday: I asked him what he had done with
the money he had stolen. He is now upstairs
in his room and is kicking things. I am
leaving him alone. I told him he can take
his bike if he wants to; there is nothing
I can do.

Benebunes

Iris

*Friday was the first night he spent at home

———

Monday [postmarked June 15]

Dear Richard:

As you can imagine, I have had the most
grief-stricken week imaginable. I can only
hope that Andrew is now truly sincere when
he says he is very sorry and will never
again do all the bad things he has been
doing. I have told him to promise me two
things: one, never to see A. again to play
with and two, just to obey me.

The whole trouble is that he is in love with
A., just like he was with M., and he doesn't
have any other boys to play with. He doesn't
want girl friends & it seems that boys of
his age just don't take to him. He has
explained that he has an inferiority complex
and this is why he wants to play with
younger children.

Anyway, it seems that he will be getting a
Washington Star paper route and this might
have an improving effect on him.

Probably we've both been hit hard by your
not being here because we both miss you
terribly. Andrew also no doubt felt that
he could do just as he liked with your not
being here. Anyways, he's really been on a
big stealing binge . . . there must be about
20 paper back books he has stolen either
from the public library, or from 7 & Eleven.
He's written in his name on all the fly
leaves so I can't take them back. He's also
been stealing money from me, but he denies
taking the $25.00 on Saturday. He must have
because it didn't mysteriously disappear and
he rushed out of the house at 2 p.m. on
Saturday, obviously to see A. which he
also denied but he came back home via the
hydrangea bushes so I'm assuming he gave
A. the money.

For all our sakes, I'm just having to be
patient with him. I even thought of calling
up your friend and agreeing to his spending
a week at the sea, but here again, he'll get
the feeling of irresponsibility and complete
abandon and I won't know how to control him
when he returns.

Richard, I had put off telling you these
things because I didn't want to spoil your
visit to Poland, but in the end I had to
write to you about his activities, so that
Andy would know he wasn't getting away with
it all.

I've been feeling lousy, as you can imagine,
but maybe things will really improve.

Incidentally, your check came for $440. And
the rug is coming this week. I've cleaned
the other two rugs with Safeway carpet
cleaner.

In all my wanderings and constant searchings
for Andy I came across two nice Indian
students at the corner house (they were the
ones who told me they had seen Andy going to
the movies with A.). I thought it might be
good for Andy, so I invited them for

dinner on Wednesday night. They are nice,
intelligent boys in their 20's.

Are you having a wonderful time in Poland? I
imagine you must feel terribly sad at times.

I can't tell you how much I miss you. For
me, this is going to be the longest 6 weeks.

I love you,

      Benebunes,

          Iris

P.S. When your bad boy comes home from
school today I am going to make him write
you a long letter which maybe will cleanse
his soul.

————

[handwritten on yellow legal pad]

Monday

June 21 [postmarked June 22]

Darling:

Aside from 2 postcards & one short letter I
haven't received anything else from you but
you did warn me not to expect too much!

I imagine you are having a very interesting
time and are seeing lots of people.

Here everything is the same—Andrew's behavior
has been extremely bad but there's no sense
in worrying you about this.

Last week I phoned up that nice Mrs. K. and
we were all set that I would drive Andrew to
her place at 7 a.m. this morning for they
were all going to the bus depot to journey
to Ocean City. Andrew hadn't wanted to go,
saying he doesn't like her daughters, so
late last night I phoned Mrs. K. that it was
"off." He just doesn't want to leave home.
She understood and told me she had been
"through the rivers" with some of hers and
we promised that we would have a real get-
together when she returns. I will look
forward to meeting her very much.

I cannot get Andrew away from A. He has the same mad obsession with this boy as he had for the girl down the block from us, M. This is why he wants to stay home to be near the boy. He comes home about 11 p.m. and last night I had to prowl the neighborhood to get him. I found him back of their garden & hidden there were 2 repeat 2 Safeway carts.

They go on stealing rampages and the next time Andrew is caught & the Police arrest him I am going to tell them to keep him!

Here the weather has turned terribly hot & thank goodness for the air conditioner.

Only once have I seen a 6000 BTU A/C for less than $150 and that is a Fedders for $135.00. I wonder if I should buy it?

I don't need to tell you that I miss you—it seems the time will never pass until your return.

Benebunes,

Iris

260

The $25.00 he previously stole from me must have been given to Alvera or placed in hiding there — this after he promised to be a good boy. He refuses to leave Alvera alone & presumably they still are stealing together. The last time I went to that house I discovered Andrew with Alvera in their basement at 11.30p. I knocked on [back] door + about 4 men & women came out — shouted Andrew was not there — meanwhile he had left by the basement door as I saw him.

One day when we were due to go to K around 7 pm I told him he could play all day providing he was back at 6 pm. He came back & I was all ready. I told him to take a shower & he said he wanted to watch TV. Said he couldn't so he rushed outside to get on his bike. I padlocked it just in time & returned to phone K. Then I saw him removing the padlock so I went & punctured the tire. This is the night he called me an old bitch & kicked me — he has also thrown my pills at me

→ the Silver bowl

JULY 11 SUN

Trespass 2942 Ordway

K'hadduri:
244-4454

Both boys trespassing, stealing throughout house — stealing money + food from tenants

American University

Officer Clark
8th Precinct

Six months and four days after the last letter I have from my mother to my father from that summer of 1971, Iris died on Christmas Eve. I had not seen her since the end of the summer, when I was taken to a boarding school in Spring Grove, Pennsylvania, about three

261

hours from Washington. There are, as there have been throughout these retellings, multiple, often contradictory versions of what happened. In the story I have held onto for most of the last thirty-five years, my father returned to our house on Ordway Street to pick up some clothes, papers, things he needed. He and my mother had been separated for several weeks following his return from Poland. I don't know where he was living, perhaps with friends, perhaps he took a room as he did off and on throughout the years of their marriage. As my father tells (told) the story, he came into the house and saw Iris on the sofa in the front room, *The New York Times* crossword puzzle on her lap, a pencil in her hand. She was not moving. When he came closer he realized that she was already dead. He called the ambulance, and when the medics came they confirmed that there was nothing to be done. She had been dead for at least several hours.

I learned of all this the next day, Christmas morning, when my father arrived at the apartment of his friend, who had offered to have me stay with her through the Christmas break from school. My father had told me he had to work that night, there was no point in my coming down to his office at Voice of America and sitting there with nothing to do until he could return home after the last broadcast around two in the morning. I might as well have Christmas Eve among friends, he said, a party, some fun among other people while he worked. Our friend Roma had suggested we join Rose and her three daughters and their friends for the traditional Christmas dinner Rose hosted each year at her house a few blocks down from the Washington Cathedral. We had the typical fish dishes served in Polish households on Christmas Eve and opened presents together under the large tree in their living room. A little after eleven we all drove together to a nearby Catholic church for midnight mass. We returned to Roma's apartment around one thirty. The next morning when my father arrived, I heard him coming into Roma's apartment and speaking to her, then appearing at the doorway. He was wearing a new jacket and trousers. When I asked him how he'd changed his clothes since the day before (as far as I knew he hadn't returned to our house on Ordway Street), he said that he'd picked up a few things from home. He sat down with me on the bed and took my hands into his. His voice was soft. I recall his hands taking mine into his before the words formed in his mouth. "Andy . . . your mother is dead. . . . Iris . . . she is dead. . . ." I turned away from him and began to cry, not knowing why exactly, not even sure what it meant that my mother was gone. Roma wandered in for a moment, then turned and left without speaking. Later I would go to her and she would say to me, "Andy, you know you can come here if you need, if your father needs something he can come here with you, you are both welcome here. . . ." I took a soft pillow from her sofa and placed it over my knees and glanced up at her and saw she had been crying. When we left she gave me ten dollars and said I should buy something little for myself, something to wear for later.

In the late afternoon my father took me back to our house. We walked into rooms I had not seen since August. The sofa on which my mother had died held the light, acrid odors of urine and throw-up. When I knelt down and looked underneath I found a short pencil in need of sharpening. I went through each room in the house looking for evidence of what had happened. The mattress in her bedroom had been stripped of sheets and covers. By her? In the dresser drawer I found empty bottles of pills, sleeping aids prescribed by our family doctor. My father said nothing at the time, nothing to suggest that Iris had taken her own life. I was either too young to question him further or not able to face what might have seemed obvious at the time.

How had my mother died? When the report came back from the coroner, my father told me Iris had died of a massive heart attack brought on by a blood clot on her right lung. My mother, who had smoked up to three packs of Marlboros a day to the end of her life, had rejected her doctor's advice that she quit smoking and at least reduce the amount of alcohol she drank each day. In this way, the report from the coroner, which I never saw, made sense. My mother had died of a massive heart attack. What more needed to be said. For years it was the only story I needed or could tell: blood clot on her lung, went to her heart. She died instantly.

In April 2007 I requested a copy of my mother's death certificate from the Department of Public Health in the District of Columbia. The copy that my father had kept and that was now stored among the effects of both Richard and Iris in my file cabinet listed for cause of death: "pending." Several weeks after placing the request for a death certificate with the cause of death specified, I received the Delayed Report of Diagnosis. The immediate cause of death was here given as "Secobarbital Poisoning." Below the fold in the document (I saw but already knew what this meant as I opened the letter), in the box for the description of any extenuating circumstances, the

medical examiner had written: "Suicide." For "Hour and Date of Injury," he had written: "Found 8:50 p.m. Dec 24, 1971." For a description of how the injury had occurred, he wrote: "Left note in last
will."

More than thirty-five years later, I am struck by the violence of
the word: suicide. Did I know? Does it make a difference to have this
word—"suicide"—above all others? Arguably she'd been trying to kill
herself in one way or another for more than twenty years. Had there
been other attempts? Memory is wayward. It wants what it can't
have, wants to make a place that wasn't from what was. Seeks in so
many stories a way out that might lead back in. I don't know how to
answer these questions. Nor do I know how to redefine the stillness
folded over this last act in my mother's life: Had she decided that
morning . . . the night before . . . a momentary decision reached with
full recognition that she was completely alone, no one to stop her?
And my father? What had it meant to find her? And later to con-
struct a story for my benefit—our benefit—about what had actually
happened? What does it mean that my mother had reached the point
where neither her son nor her husband nor anything else could keep
her here? Could she have been rescued? I know the answer to that,
ask it again, wander through its perimeter, as if to save one I could
save two, saving two I could save one. I wrote once, "Dying takes a
long time in any given life. The hour of one's death begins years earlier: in random untold acts, choices made over and over again that
achieve, in the course of a lifetime, the force of inevitability." I don't
know that I believe those words anymore. I don't know, honestly
don't know, what they mean. I am the father of two young daughters.
At fifty-three, I am one year younger than my mother was when she
took her life. My oldest daughter is thirteen, the age I was during our
last summer together. Living, I want to say back to this dead woman,
long dead, takes a long time. It takes a long time to give us back our
lives. We give them back. That's what we do when we go back to
these people long since dead. We give them back again.

There is an ending. There is an ending in time and not. Memory that
has no beginning must have an ending. I am conscious of the days
passing. Of a lifetime that will become the practice of these things.
My children's eyes in the morning when I come to open their curtains.
The beams scarred by early light. My mother's face as it appeared
through the window one of those days in June. My father's eyes

turning from my gaze, pitiless gray eyes caught in the passageway of one room then another. My daughters' hands in mine as we cross through the cemetery near our house on one of our nightly walks.

Time and again. We have sacrificed how much to say these things? Given what of ourselves in place of whom? Something held in common, something held back, held out. A route of saying that insists year by year. *"I will return as prayer, as seed sown from the black earth."*

Sentiments are crossed out. Recrossed. Words echoing from childhood, directed at her, at him, at no one: "Are you cross with me?" I return to locate words that will guide me—guide us—to safety. "Are you able to tell the story?" Yes. "What is important for us to know?" I don't know. I'm not sure. Nothing. Nothing.

The eye returns to the scene of its betrayals. The years are lived ritualistically. My father and mother have walked toward the yellow light. The last image of the three of us. A quiet and deceptive portrait.

—*To Monica Jacobe*

Sin

Can Xue

—Translated from Chinese by Karen Gernant and Chen Zeping

I HAD A WOODEN BOX in my loft. Everyone in the family knew about it, but no one had ever opened it. The year I was born, Father gave me this box he'd prepared. Mother was in charge of storing it. Father was a very crafty guy who always came up with long-term plans that often stretched to the unforeseeable future. And then he simply forgot his plan. For example, this wooden box. When he gave it to Mother, he said very seriously that the contents of the box were confidential. He meant to open it himself when I was grown up, for it contained something important having to do with my future. But after I grew up, he forgot. Mother didn't remind him either; perhaps she didn't believe that Father had anything so terribly wonderful stored in the box. After living together for many years, she knew him like the back of her hand, so she didn't even mention it to him.

The box was made of ordinary fir, with a layer of lacquer slapped over it. It had a little lock—a common enough lock, which had rusted over the years. Maybe it was habit or maybe Mother's attitude had affected me; in any case, I never considered unlocking it. After Father and Mother died, I threw the box into the loft one day and never gave it another thought. I didn't have the curiosity one should have about some things. And yet I was endlessly interested in things that shouldn't have concerned anyone. I was born this way; I couldn't help it.

In August, my cousin, whom the family dubbed "Killer," came to stay for a while. She was in her early thirties, yet her forehead was covered with wrinkles surprising for one her age. When she walked, she held her head high. I didn't like to be around her, because she spoke unkindly; sometimes her words could even be murderous (Father was one of her victims when he was alive), so in the family we all spitefully called her "Killer" behind her back.

"Rumei." She sat down and began talking. "Yesterday, that fashionable colleague of yours started spreading rumors about you among people I know well. But I've seen you walking arm in arm with her on the streets. What's this all about?"

"Mind your own business. If you have to butt into other people's business, then you'd better not stay with us," I said in disgust.

"But it wasn't because of this that I came here," she said pensively. "I came because of—that box!"

"Box? What box?" I knew at once what she meant, but I deliberately feigned ignorance.

"Don't think that just because your father died a long time ago, you can ignore this. That's childish. You're just like your sneaky father—a sinner. You can't cover this up."

She stood legs apart, hands stuffed into her pants pockets. She looked like the old maid she was. I recalled that several years ago, even though I knew it was not very hopeful, I had introduced her to several men. None had worked out. It was only because I hated her that I'd made these introductions, but she hadn't hated me at all for doing it. Quite the opposite. She had thanked me for my help, thus making me really uneasy. Not until later did I understand that nothing I did could hurt her.

I asked her why she thought so badly of my father. She gave me a probing look and sneered. She said I must have been all too aware. Otherwise, why would I have hidden the box in the loft? This was a sin.

"I didn't hide it. I just happened to put it there, OK? You surely don't know what's in the box, so why do you conclude that I'm guilty?" I didn't think I could bear this.

"The contents don't matter at all. A person has to take responsibility for what she does. You'd better not say 'I just happened' very much. Who knows if you 'just happened' to do this? Huh!" She twisted her flat rear end emphatically.

I didn't want to pay any more attention to my cousin. If she wanted to stay here, OK, but I didn't have to keep her company. With my briefcase under my arm, I left for work.

But I was uneasy, worried that something would go wrong at home. And I remembered that I'd forgotten to lock the drawer that was filled with personal correspondence.

In the afternoon, I left work early and rushed home. When I got there, I set my bicycle down and dashed into the house. Sure enough, she was sitting at the desk reading my letters. On hearing my footsteps, she replaced the letters in the drawer. She looked embarrassed.

"How dare you read my letters?" I paled.

"I'm just a little curious, that's all." She voiced her objection as she stood up. "Why are you taking this so seriously?"

"If you want to stay here, you mustn't be so curious!" I shouted.

"Do you think I came here out of curiosity about you? You shouldn't have such a high opinion of yourself!" She shouted too. Standing with arms akimbo, she looked scary.

Hearing us arguing, my husband ran in to break it up. As soon as he tried, my cousin made even more of a fuss. She said she had come here in order to prevent a sin; this sin had been planned for decades, and so forth and so on. My husband was baffled. It was odd that she didn't bring up the issue of the box in front of him. She just kept arguing, saying she had to stay here until the whole thing was cleared up.

I thought this was a little fishy. I had placed the box in the loft. You could see it if you stood in the middle of the room. Yet my cousin hadn't mentioned looking for it in the house, nor had she asked me where it was: This wasn't where her attention was focused. Everything was obscure. Maybe the box was nothing but a pretext for staying in my home to satisfy her old maid's curiosity or to take revenge on me for something. She was too complicated. Since I couldn't get a feel for her temperament, I decided not to argue with her anymore. I acted as if nothing was happening. At dinner, I talked with her as usual. She ignored my overtures and kept a straight face. Then she turned to my son and spoke with him of the subtle relationships between parents and children and took the opportunity to develop this idea for a while.

"Sometimes it takes several generations for a sin to be completed," she announced complacently as she raised her head. My son listened to her piously without blinking an eye. He adored this young auntie.

Not many people were as freewheeling as my cousin. She didn't even have a formal job, but merely had a stall on the street, where she sold low-cost silk stockings. The income from that kind of work was not very steady. She had fallen out long ago with her parents—to the point that they no longer saw anything of each other. So when business was slow and she lacked spending money, she came here. Although I inwardly hated her, at the same time I also admired her nimble and straightforward way of thinking, and I was subconsciously affected by this. So I wasn't against her staying, but I didn't expect her to aim the lance at me this time. It was as if she was determined to pin down a certain private thing about me.

I was thoroughly annoyed. I didn't know what kind of trouble my cousin wanted to stir up. She didn't care at all about my family. She claimed she had to perform "surgery" on my family. When she said this, her face was absolutely expressionless.

Today my boss had criticized me again, because I was agitated and had made mistakes in filling out reports. His tone was terribly harsh. I really wanted to spit in his face. I thought of the problem at home and felt it was time to drop a hint to my cousin that it wasn't right to interfere in other people's lives. I kept thinking about this, and on the way home, I seemed to reach a decision.

As soon as I went inside, I heard laughter from her and my son. I had to acknowledge that although she had never married, she was a genius at enjoying children—much better than I. Was this why I was jealous of her? But it wasn't pure jealousy; other factors were mixed in with it.

My cousin and my son had installed a new light switch. They'd been laughing just now because they'd succeeded. Of course this was much more convenient, but I had forbidden my son to handle electrical wires. He was too young and didn't understand the basic guidelines. When I looked inside the room, I was startled: They had taken the wooden box down from the loft and placed it on the chair so they could stand on it to work on the light switch. In stepping on the box, they'd left several footprints on it. I rushed over and took the box down, and, staring at my cousin, I spat out one word after another from the cracks between my teeth: "This is precisely the wooden box that you've talked about so often. It's been up there all along." I pointed to the loft.

"Really?" my cousin laughed. "Then how about opening it?"

"I don't have the key. Father forgot to give it to me," I said, disheartened.

"And you forgot to tell him you needed it, didn't you?" Her tone softened. With the tip of her toe, she moved the wooden box; as she did so, its contents made a suspicious sound. Mimicking her, my son also pushed it with his foot. The two of them pushed it back and forth. Their actions were so disgusting that I was sorry I couldn't slap them.

I bent down and picked up the box, took it back to the loft, and wrapped it in cloth. As I was doing all of this, neither my cousin nor my son looked at me. They had begun a game of chess. I was superfluous.

"Didn't you say you came here because of the box?" I reminded my cousin. "Didn't you say there's a sin hidden in the box?"

With her eyes fixed on the chessboard, she said, "Did I? Maybe I did."

"It's been up there all along. I see that you haven't bothered to glance at it."

"I don't need to. I've known it was there all along, and I've known that you didn't have the key. Hey, did your father have a particular reason for not giving you the key?"

"No. I'm sure he simply forgot."

I don't know why, but even though I had wrapped the box in cloth, from then on, all of us—my husband, my son, my cousin, and I—kept unconsciously casting our eyes at it. This situation made me uncomfortable. Often, when we were talking with one another, we suddenly fell silent as we looked simultaneously at that cloth package. My cousin was always the first to avert her eyes, and then she would titter. And I would blush from indignation.

In order to prove my cousin's thoughts groundless, I started searching for the key Father had left. It had to be somewhere; it couldn't have been cremated with him and placed in his urn. First I opened a large bundle of his things. I turned them all over, from the large ones to the small ones, and looked through them carefully to see if the key might be with them. I spent three days doing this secretly in the bedroom—after work and out of my cousin's and husband's sight. But I didn't find anything. Never mind the key to the box, there was no key at all among his effects. I finally recalled that when Father went out, he had never taken the house key with him, thus often inconveniencing himself. My thoughts turned to Father's friends and relatives. Would any of them know? I knew he'd been close to his younger sister. There was nothing they didn't discuss. I decided to call on this elderly aunt.

Although winter had already passed, my aunt was still all wrapped up in a heavy scarf and shivering constantly. Sucking in air, she kept muttering, "Killer weather. So cold. Why would you venture out in this cold weather?"

I explained why I had come. My aunt stopped shivering, shot a glance at me, and said, "No. He never mentioned that key. Your father was the fox in the family. He never told the truth. Whenever he came over here, he wanted to borrow money. So many years have passed. Why are you still concerned about it? It's tough to figure out what your father was up to."

"But the box is still here. He left it to me. Can I smash it open and look inside?"

"This isn't my business. You can see I'm old. After a while, it will be difficult for me to talk. Why would I bother about his things? I sit

270

here and often dream of skiing with your father in the courtyard. Back then, I was six and he was eight. Even at that age, he was already a trickster. If you don't want to let this matter drop, you can go and see his old friend Qin Yi." Her toothless mouth was shriveled; she seemed to want to say more. Suddenly, she dropped her head, closed her eyes, and fell asleep.

I figured it would be impossible to get any useful clues from my aunt. I might as well go home first. I decided to visit Qin Yi the next day. I hadn't seen him since Father died almost seven years ago.

Qin Yi lived in a small winding lane. It had just rained, and there were puddles everywhere. After I had walked along this lane, my pants and feet were all spattered. Ahead of me was a little old man being chased by an old woman with a large wooden stick. She kept stumbling and falling, and she was crazy with rage. For his part, the old man was as nimble as a goat as he leapt over one puddle after another. Later, the old woman tired and sat beside the road cursing him. The old man went into the house and hid. He was Qin Yi, who had been Father's young friend and student.

When I went inside, he was jittery. He didn't ask me to take a seat either. He was only too anxious for me to leave. But after hearing my question, he seemed interested and invited me to sit down and have some tea.

"Although he was my teacher, I have to tell you he was a big fraud. I've said this all along. He was always hiding boxes and saying there were huge secrets inside that he would explain later. But he never did. I have a box of his, too. I opened it a long time ago, and it was empty. He was still alive then, and I asked him about it. He said he was joking, and that he hadn't imagined I would smash it open. By saying this, I don't mean to encourage you to smash your box. Just leave it alone. Maybe there's a little something inside."

"Yes, of course there's something inside. I heard it. It's also heavy. After all, he was my father." I felt a little resentful of Qin Yi. I didn't know why my father had trusted this kind of person.

"Maybe, maybe. He was your father. So you believe there is something in it. But I know nothing about the key."

Later on, I also visited a cousin, one of my father's former colleagues, and one of my mother's confidants, and still didn't learn anything.

As the story about my box made the rounds among my acquaintances, some people found excuses to call on me. They would sit down and glance at the loft. Whenever I looked at them, they would turn their eyes away and look down and exchange small talk. Each time, my cousin would stick her hands in her pants pockets and stride back and forth.

One day, my cousin's parents—a very boring couple—were among the visitors. After they sat down, their eyes slid to and fro like a thief's and they made impertinent remarks belittling today's youth. Then my cousin came over and cursed them. She said they hadn't been invited. She wanted them to take off.

"Don't think I don't know everything about you," her mother said as she left. "Some people look all right, but actually they are thoroughly rotten. Just listen to what people say about you."

When the visitors were gone, my cousin was still furious and gasping for breath. All of a sudden, she grabbed my collar and shook it hard. She said, "Was it you who started talking about the box?"

"I talked with some people—with my father's relatives and good friends. So what? This isn't some terrible secret! Outsiders must have known of it long ago."

"You fool!" Utterly exasperated, she let go of me. "What makes you think outsiders knew about this? With your parents dead, I'm the only one who knew. Now everyone is interested in your box. Do you think your father can still rest in peace in the ground? You're doomed. You sinner!"

I could see I'd made a mistake. Avoiding her eyes, I spoke haltingly, "I'm . . . just . . . not . . . convinced. . . ."

Because so many people were coming over, all I could do was hide the box away, hoping to dispel their curiosity.

But visitors still showed up, sat at the table, looked down, and didn't look at the loft again. They didn't say anything either. They thought their manner would signal that they knew all there was to know. I realized that as soon as they left they would talk about me maliciously. Qin Yi was one of the visitors, confirming for me that it was he who had spread the rumors. This evil was gnawing at Father's corpse all the time.

One day when I came home from work, my son complained to me that even the kids at school had started talking about us. He couldn't stand the looks he was getting from others. His face filling with rage, he wanted me to open the box and get it over with. "Isn't it just a wooden box? Why did you hide it?" He said I had hidden the box, yet he was the one who ran into trouble everywhere he went.

"They're also gossiping about murder. It stresses me out," my son said indignantly.

I thought about the mistakes I'd made. But the roots of all these mistakes stemmed from Father's having given me a locked wooden box without a key. Why on earth had he hated me so much?

My husband wearied of neighbors and relatives shuttling in and out of the house. I often felt that he was surreptitiously observing me to see if I would give in. One day, after hesitating for a long time, he finally said, "Rumei, let's give it up."

"What's this 'us'? You're talking about me. I'm telling you I don't care what you think about this matter. That's right. You! And all the rest of you too!" I glared at my cousin. She was looking at the ceiling.

"Why are you so obstinate? We can break the box open and look inside. Isn't that the way to get to the bottom of this? What on earth are you afraid of?"

"No!" I shouted and then dashed into the bedroom and shut the door.

I dragged the box out from under the bed and shook it next to my ear. The contents seemed to be withered leaves, straw, or letters. When I shook it a few more times, I thought it was none of these, but merely some broken bones or small pebbles or wood chips. What was inside the box was really hard to determine. Could Father have simply been playing a prank? What kind of person did he think I was? The same as Qin Yi? Actually, what was the essential difference between Qin Yi and me? The only difference was that up to now I hadn't smashed open the box. There must be someone who understood, and that person was probably my cousin. Otherwise, why would she have said that it was because of this that she had come to stay here? In the seven years since I put the box in the loft, it hadn't attracted any interest. That's right: My cousin created this disturbance. Maybe Father had dropped her a hint and she'd picked up on it. She was very bright.

When I thought of how Father had regarded me, I felt thoroughly disappointed. I threw the box down, and a vague plan arose in my mind. Yes, I was going to retaliate against the dead—Father and also Mother—and send them to hell. My husband entered quietly and noticed the box on the floor. He mistakenly thought I had yielded. Standing under the lamp, his lanky body appeared to be floating. I heard him sigh. He seemed to be talking to himself. "It shouldn't have grown so serious in the first place. Who cares about things that belonged to the dead? It would have been OK if everyone had continued being in the dark, wouldn't it? The last few days, those people have really been driving me nuts."

Early in the morning, my cousin packed her things. She stood up right after breakfast and announced she was leaving. My son immediately shouted in protest, saying she shouldn't leave so soon. They hadn't finished yesterday's chess game.

"What's your rush?" I looked her straight in the eye.

"You no longer need me here." She smiled. "Evils will continue, but there won't be any serious problem. I'm relieved. And I can't stay here forever. It's already been long enough."

I held back my rising anger. "Didn't you say you would curb the evils?"

"I was just exaggerating. We all like to boast, because it makes us feel important. I have to deal with my own problems. As you saw, the two old folks came here making trouble. They were extremely malicious. They wanted to kill someone!" Then she hefted her backpack, waved her hand, and left.

"I never thought she could have put up with this situation," my husband whispered.

"Could you? What's your 'situation'? Do you know? Don't play innocent! We're a little too old for that." This startled him. He sneered and went outside.

My son also left the table, glared at me, and walked away.

Outside, people were talking. The neighbors. They were crowding around my husband, asking him something. I felt a roaring in my head. Everything was like an arrow in a bow.

My husband seemed to be saying something, and they all suddenly understood. They marveled, and slowly dispersed.

I couldn't take it anymore. I grabbed the tape recorder and smashed it on the floor. No one paid any attention to me. They had all gone. I returned to the bedroom and took out the wooden box and shook it a few times next to my ear. I heard the sound of withered leaves or perhaps they were letters or photographs. It was possible too that they were bones or wood chips. At this moment, my curiosity kept mounting. My anger was mounting along with it. I put the box in a bag and hurried outside.

When I returned, my husband was waiting at the door. His face was somber. My son was with him. As soon as my son caught sight of me, he ran off.

"Did you throw that thing into the river?" my husband asked, his hands starting to twitch.

"So what if I did? It's mine. I can do whatever I want with it."

"Sure. You have the right." His gaze was wandering, and his hands stopped spasming. "Rumei, tell me the truth. Aren't you afraid? Especially when you wake up in the middle of the night?"

"Why should I be afraid? Can being afraid solve the problem? Who can avoid it?"

"Oh, yes! Now I get it. What a fool I've been! Thanks to your awakening, I now understand everything. We don't have to be such sticklers for form, do we? You and I want the same thing. We just deal with it differently. Your father was really an old fox. He was always disguised well. I wasn't at all suspicious of him. Don't worry. Those people won't be back. They all have their own troubles. You could just as well have opened it and taken a look before throwing it away, you know?"

"No!" I said with finality.

After that, my husband and son drew away from me, though we were still talking and laughing together. They acted as if nothing had happened, but I could see it all written on their faces. They often glanced absentmindedly at the loft, as if to remind me of the sin. This went on for days.

Actually, I was often startled awake in the middle of the night. At times like that, I seriously thought of making an identical box for my son, and putting withered leaves or several newspapers or a few wood chips or a few slices of something else inside it. I even discussed it with my husband. My husband concluded that I wanted to shift the responsibility.

When I had nearly forgotten her, my cousin reappeared. Her face was tanned and her hair was scorched brown. She still looked very much the way an old maid looks, with her hands stuffed into her pants pockets.

"Are you here to investigate the case?" I ridiculed her while doing my best to look relaxed.

"Who has time for that? I've been traveling on business all along. When I was in the Gobi desert, I considered staying there. Then I thought, Isn't everywhere the same? The same evil, the same deception, and so I decided I might as well come back here. How are all of you? Did time heal the wound?" Looking up, she swept her eyes toward the loft, and a fleeting smile skimmed over her face.

"There's still something I don't understand. Why did you take this so seriously from the very beginning and yet afterward you simply left without a conclusion? Do you treat your own issues like this?"

"Of course," she laughed, "I act just the same. Everything is but an assumption, and we need to be flexible in dealing with each of our

275

problems. Your father was a very flexible guy. He was never left with no way out."

"So you just faked the serious manner to remind me. Is that it?"

"I can't say I was faking. At the time, what I said was all true. Later, with the problem on the table, I believe you understood it all, and so I left your home. What kind of outcome do you want? Nothing can be completed. This is the conclusion. I remember there was a wooden box, right? Your father loved these childish games, and he purposely concocted mysteries. In the past, you were really numb. If I hadn't reminded you, you wouldn't have noticed anything, would you? In fact, there were also some special characteristics to your father's methods. A box!" She burst out laughing, and then turned serious again. "There's no point in being so earnest about this. Why would it matter if you had opened it and looked inside? You're still too stressed out. You aren't flexible."

Just as suddenly as she had appeared, my cousin vanished. One night, I encountered her mother on the street. The old woman was standing alone, looking in all directions. I knew who she was looking for.

"She couldn't have gone far, Auntie. She told me she'd be around. She's probably somewhere nearby."

"I'll make her pay for what she's done." She squeezed these words out from between her teeth. In the cold wind, her face was frozen purple.

Before long, my uncle—my cousin's father—died. She didn't show up, but I knew she was still here. She was a ghost, a person like Father. Perhaps someday she'll walk into our house again and announce that she has to investigate another of my sins.

Liberté, Égalité, Fraternité, ou la Mort
Micaela Morrissette

CHAPTER I—CHILDHOOD
In the Blush of Our Youth, Feet on the Green World, Flesh on Our Bones, Time in Our Veins

MY BROTHER AND I stood before the men, divine. Or, if not yet quite divine, close enough to send these gulping mortals to their knees. Our father still had our godheads locked away safe in his strongbox, but they could have turned to dust there, for all we cared. We would have chosen to stay in our earthly playground forever.

The sun jetted off our breastplates, our helmets, and shot into the air like spurts of golden, ruddy blood. "No," my brother said, "like shining spears." But there was no difference: They worshipped us, one way or the other. To prove it, I beckoned forward from the ranks a man, pried open his clenched fist. His nails had bitten cruelly into his palm. In his fervor, in his adoration of us. "In his fear," said my brother, "of the battle to come." There was no difference.

I outlined the strategy. The men nodded attentively. My brother roared like a lion and exhorted them to action. He swung his ax in the air. The men bellowed and pounded the earth in their desire to die that day.

And they did. My brother and I sat on the hilltop, wrapped in our cloak, observing the action and biting our nails. The enemy could not withstand the fearlessness with which our men embraced death. It could not kill them quickly enough for their liking. The men were driven to fling themselves on the enemy's spears, out of frustration with the enemy's sloth and cowardice.

The enemy was terrified by its massacre of our troops. Crossing itself and cursing, it took to its heels. Our men lay dying in heaps. A fog of blood hung over the field. My brother and I had won the day. Already the ships of the enemy were pulling away, hastening homeward. We descended to survey the men. Not a one, it seemed, was left alive. My brother and I offered each other what comfort we could as we gently plundered the bodies.

In bed that night, my brother said, "Do you remember the picnics we took when we were little? When we went down in the forest where the blackberry brambles grew and we filled up our baskets? We sat on the edge of the cliffs and ate, and the berries were warm with the sun."

"No," I said.

"We walked to the edge of this field with a barbed-wire fence, behind which was a bull, a feisty bull. And I teased the bull through the fence and you cried and begged me not to, and then the bull charged the fence and you threw yourself in front of me to protect me."

"No," I said, "that never happened."

"Later, we went deeper into the woods, where the stream ran into a still green pool. We took off all our clothes and dove in. It was a beautiful spot. The trees were all hung with shaggy, damp moss, and you loved it so much that you climbed out of the pool and rubbed your wet body up against the trees."

This was a false memory my brother had, which he cherished. Or maybe it was a recurring dream; he could have been talking in his sleep. His eyes were closed. His face was still so young.

I had several false memories of my own. One was from early childhood, when I could fly. I remembered exactly, but could not replicate, the perfect lassitude and weight I had to give to taking a first, second, and ascending third step into the air, and then the slow, deep-sea motions necessary to propel myself forward. But this didn't really happen; I could not fly. My brother could probably fly.

The second false memory I had, from just a few years before, was of being murdered by my brother. His hands hot and wet in the dark.

My brother once went on a pilgrimage, in search of his soul. He stole a spaceship and flew to one of the outer moons of Pluto, an area that is rich in gurus, prophets, witches, sphinxes, and so on. There he purchased a male prostitute; their copulation was the greatest spiritual experience of my brother's life. The sensations that he underwent were astonishing—radiant—simply indescribable; he fainted several times. When it was over, my brother understood his life. He saw that it was not his to decide, or God our father's, but had always been and always would be entirely in the hands of one other person, the prostitute, who did not himself know the power he wielded. My brother returned home from his pilgrimage in a state of deep psychic harmony. Yet as the days elapsed, it seemed to me that some dark secret had been revealed in that moment of devotional ecstasy. Some nightmare stalked his fantasy.

My brother suffered: His brows drew sharply in; his fragile temples pulsed.

When the last coal of our campfire sputtered out, the light of the stars terrified us. We felt that we were no longer sitting in the desert, in the long ruts of shadows cast by the cliffs. No, we were on the very crust of the globe, unsteady specks on an infinitesimal sphere. At any minute we might have slipped off the planet and fallen into the abyss of the sky, that bottomless pit above which we constantly hovered. We reeled, clutched our throats, sickened with vertigo.

"Living right next to the sky as we do," my brother cried, "that's insane! We should go deep within the earth," he urged.

I was with him in theory, but, I shrugged, no shovels.

"Caves!" cried my brother. "Underground caverns! There must be openings, holes in the dunes—"

He started off into the night, but I overtook him and dragged him back. There were sharks out there, jellyfish scraping through the sand, bleeding poison trails behind them. We both listened into the darkness, straining for evidence that my brother had aroused an enemy. But we'd been in the void of the desert for so long that the beating of our hearts had become deafening in our ears; we wouldn't even be able to hear the thunder, when it came.

The nights were cold. We zipped the sleeping bag over our heads, with a flashlight inside, and a stock of whiskey and cigarettes, and played truth or dare.

We'd done pretty much all the dares. "Truth," said my brother. "What will I be in the next life?"

"You'll never die."

Then it was my turn. "Are you really my brother?" I asked him.

"Of course I am," he whispered. He held me close, stroking my hair. I nestled in, he hummed a lullaby.

In Rome we took the cloth, then became heretics. Soon enough, we had disciples. Then we became more than heretics. In due course, we had a following that revered us: my brother, as Christ, and myself, as Antichrist. We redeemed thousands: virgins, usurers, lepers, psychopaths.

When the furor of the church became unreasonable, our cult removed itself to a Tuscan estate. The peasants were pleased to provide us with the appropriate tithes, while we preached to the wealthy by means of occasional armed raids on their households. Our flock excelled in holiness. We practiced the doctrine of total self-abnegation, feeding each other, grooming each other, doing for others what we did not do for ourselves. No one could speak his own thought, only what he imagined to be the thoughts that his fellows would have wished to have spoken.

My brother and I moved among our adepts with decreasing regularity, until at last we were never seen at all by daylight. We visited them at night, in their cells, our mouths wet with wisdom, our hands full of gifts. Their love for us was whipped to a frenzy. They erected altars to us, and constructed shrines in our honor. We destroyed these, in humility, but they took the gesture to arise from the unworthiness of the offering. They tempted us with sacrifices: first chickens, then goats, cows, and panthers; but we restrained ourselves until they began to kill the babies on the altars. This was more than we could bear, and we were corrupted. We took the bodies, and they exulted, and the festival of sacrifice began.

In the morning we offered services to the dead, then filled our pockets with gold and set off. On these occasions, it was our custom to turn our faces against the wind and walk. Our hair streamed out behind us.

Long ago, our parents went away for a year, during which we were raised by wolves. Those were halcyon days. Wrestling in the dirt, bringing down hares, sleeping in a tangle of rough fur and tongues. Loping through the shadows of a farmyard. On our bellies, in the underbrush.

When our parents returned to us, the wolves ventured up to the doors of the house, skulking around the flower beds. They had to be shot. My brother wept pitifully, but I have always thought it was the kindest thing.

There was this summer when my brother and I were getting into some serious shit. Drugs invaded us through every orifice, we wore black leather pants, the sex was extreme. Razors, rapes, violent orgies. We had suicide bombers on the eves of their missions, we had known sex offenders wherever we could find them, we coupled mother with

280

daughter at each opportunity, or father with son. I fucked my brother with a loaded pistol. For an extra kick, we used our infrared vision all the time. Everything was spattered in a dim bordello light that seemed to fight through thick scarlet curtains to reach us. We moved through a forest of shadows. We lost track of ourselves: I thought I was my brother; he did not know me. Then the season changed, and, inevitably, the snow fell and put an end to all debauchery. Impossible to sustain the degradations in that white and that cold. We moved to warmer climes but we never recaptured that utter abandon, that first, fine, careless rapture. The snow had chastised something in us.

Who loved whom more? My love for my brother, of course, was without flaw and without limit, blinding, entire, stricken, voluptuous. I doted on the curl of his little white canines in the corner of his grin, giving small snarls to his smiles, bestowing on him a touch of animal ferocity, a sweet debasement of the blond nobility of his features; I adored the muscles that twined around his body like serpents slithering over their idol. I stepped between him and death uncountable times. Of course, I would not have cried if he were to have died. Not that he really could.

My brother's love for me was, he has said, "the one and only thing that stopped me from blasting this universe to smithereens and starting again."

My brother was troubled by a small creature that sat on his chest while he slept. It stared into his face with its round yellow eyes and sucked the breath from his mouth.

However, he seemed to be none the worse for wear. In fact, he had roses in his cheeks.

He always attracted that sort of attention. He awakened the vampiric urge. He was devourable. Women would immolate themselves in him. When we ventured into the world children caught at his clothes, clung to his limbs. I had to swat them aside; they would have torn him to shreds, but he was far too tender to defend himself.

Back in the safety of our cottage, he sat wrapped in a shawl, huddled over a mug of hot tea, shuddering.

Micaela Morrissette

While I was in hiding in France from the Russians, my brother hid in Italy from the Turks. I masqueraded as a simple peasant, while he was a bogus aristocrat. I hinted that the loss of my ear was the result of a scything accident; his eyepatch passed unquestioned as a foppish affectation. I diddled the ruling class in the hayloft; he pawed his valet behind the Japanese screen. On the same night, we each stole a horse and went galloping toward each other. In Monaco, we met, and began to set up a couple of daring cons. But tidal waves, earthquakes, plague, and fire would thwart our best intentions.

My brother was a gravedigger, my brother was a snake-oil peddler, my brother was an eagle, a pirate, a werewolf, and a slave with a golden chain. The divot of my brother's collarbone, the soft dip beneath his lower lip, the splinter bones of his ear, his pale damp eyelids. Not only could he fly, he could breathe underwater, he was not scared of needles, his breath was more fragrant than jasmine. Like the dart frog, his skin leaked poison, which was what I lived on.

I ran away to Tokyo and filled my house with deaf-mute servants. I had fifty or sixty around me; every room was full of them and their cooing. I ran away to Banjul and slept floating in the ocean. I started a family in Novi Sad. I poisoned the wells in San Pedro de Atacama. I enacted a living statue for passersby in Paris. My brother found me, every time.

Then it was his turn. His desire to win was so strong that he only went places where I could not bear to follow. Into forests. Into hospitals. Inside the room with the red silk scarf tied to the doorknob. Then he sulked, feeling abandoned. I waited for him to grow bored and come home. I stalked the corridors, fierce for his return.

How wrong my brother was to fear me, and how wrong I was to fear him. He slept with a gun under his pillow; I slept with a knife. Sometimes I woke and withdrew his weapon; he would stir uneasily. I slipped my finger into the barrel and drew it out dripping with oil. I touched it to my brother's brow, his wrists, his eyelids. In his sleep he snuffled and pushed, ineffectually, against my hand. Sometimes I woke to find a thin red pattern of lines etched across my stomach, my chest, the soles of my feet. On the blade of my knife there was blood. It's my blood, said my brother. It's my blood.

CHAPTER II—MANHOOD

Consecrated and Conscripted, Our Lips to the Ring,
Dust in Our Pockets, We All Hold Our Breath

And then, we were three. Summoned at last to the ancestral home. We lived a sheltered life there. We dined simply; generally we had a substantial tea and merely a token gesture of an evening meal. The house was old but damp. Our father did not allow fires in the bedrooms. We tightened our bones against the cold. "Does he not feel it himself?" asked my brother.

"He does not admit the possibility. It cannot be cold, for the rooms below us were heated all day, and the heat has risen and dispelled itself about the house."

"Dispelled is the right word. And to what does he attribute the discomfort he feels, if not to cold?"

"To us, no doubt."

My brother and I bent our heads together and laughed in whispers.

Our father, haunted by our mother's ghost, maintained that we were four. The apoplectic fit he suffered when she had dared to die had afflicted and empowered him in one fell stroke. One of his eyes was permanently rheumy, red, and running, and stared off past us into the walls; however, he no longer held back when he brought down his cane. Dutifully we saw our mother trailing her skirts in the apple orchard, weeding the garden in the rain, her hair all about her. My brother, who had taken over the direction of the daily menu after her death, now returned her the post.

In the night, our father dashed with astonishing spryness through the corridors, weeping, calling our mother's name, and begging her forgiveness. By day, he damned her fiercely, spoke of her constantly, forbade us ever to mention her again.

She crept up outside the window, blowing on the frozen panes, drawing pictures with her finger in the fog her breath left on the glass. Our father stiffened, stared at the quickly fading smears in horror. For the rest of that day, speaking was prohibited, so were fires, and he brooded blackly. The silence was complete until at dinner he struck the table with his fist and shouted, "Hell's too good for her!" and the chandelier fell from the ceiling.

This marked the beginning of our mother's increasing violence. Mirrors shattered in our father's face. Wineglasses burst at his lips. The curtains of his bed fell and smothered him. He could not hold a sharp knife without cutting himself, or eat meat without choking, and he subsisted on porridge.

My brother wondered if he was somehow doing it all himself. "For the attention?"

But I demurred. For the most ambitious manifestations, a secret, complex system of elaborate pulleys and traps would have been required. A man of our father's age and decrepit health could not possibly have managed it.

My brother posited that the apparatus had been built into the walls of the house, a weapon hidden in the architecture by our paranoid forebears.

Our mother set fire to the chiffonier. My brother and I held out our hands to it.

We couldn't help but notice that our father was in a state of sexual excitement.

My brother and I were in no danger from the hauntings until our mother became longing, and wanted us with her. We found dull stains smeared on our hands where she'd pressed her mouth to our palms. Sometimes when we woke in the numbing mists of dawn, our cheeks were wet with the tears she'd shed, hovering over us. In the pockets of our trousers, in the secret caddies of our desks, we found daggers, each festooned with a little bow, and bottles of poison, pasted with labels that read *The pleasure of your company is requested.* Without consulting our father, we called upon the services of the exorcist.

We were sorry immediately. He was a thin man with a fat stomach, dirty nails, a white crust at the corners of his mouth. His frockcoat was shabby and ostentatious; the grease of his hair had stained the back of his collar. But he was delighted to do us this favor; we could not disappoint him. Our mother, he promised, would make friends easily. He pointed to his heart and invited us to listen. Inside the cavity of his breast, we heard hundreds of voices, wearily quavering a madrigal. The exorcist raised his arms. All the flames of the room's lamps spurted and hissed toward him.

Our mother's screams were unbearable. Even after she was gone, she was screaming.

Our father screamed too—"You murderers!"

On the occasions of our exile from our father's presence my brother and I went to our old nursery, on the third floor, and induced the under housemaid to bring us some tea. My brother tried for sherry but she scolded him. Her name was Berthe, she was sweet, she pitied us. She fed us toffee and, gangly as we were, she still sat us on her knees with her arms around us. She'd have probably preferred to go a little further but we couldn't allow that. If our father had discovered it, he would have chopped off her head. And we liked her soft attentions. She knelt before us and deftly mended our torn pockets and cuffs; she trimmed our nails. When she was baking we came down to the kitchen and she let us lick the bowls. In the kitchen the light was very dim and it smelled of brick and mold, stew and radishes and vanilla, and the thick violet-scented powder the cook shook over her enormous bosom. The cook sat drawn up close to the stove on a tiny stool that vanished beneath her bulk, the red, chapped slabs of her face ghoulish in the throb of the coals. Berthe said the cook was in love with our father. We did not doubt it. From whosoever had anything to give, our father would take. Luckily for my brother and me, we had nothing.

"Do you remember," my brother said, "how we used to make kites out of plastic bags and wooden picnic forks and twine and string and fly them in a special field used only for that purpose?"

"I remember," I said.

"When the lady's slippers were almost ready to blossom, we'd squeeze the pods between our fingers and the fetal green flowers would spring out at our faces."

"A fact."

"We caught sunfish and slit them open; they had green jewels in their stomachs."

"They did."

"When it snowed we set up a ramp that sent our sleds over the electric fence to the bumpy, steep hillside beyond it."

"Without injury."

"There was one house we couldn't walk past because of the dog."

"A Doberman."

"I once threw a rock and hit you in the head."

285

"I didn't answer."

"On the top of the hill was a dead tree in which a pair of fugitives lived for decades."

"Two holes led into the deformed trunk, like the open valves of a heart."

"Your sandals were blue and mine were red. Your cap was green and mine was blue. Your whistle was yellow and mine was green. You insisted on it."

"I was willful," I said.

"These days that house belongs to another family," he said. "We've been deposed."

"We live here now."

The unthinkable occurred, our father having departed to conduct a business transaction, leaving us alone in the house for a fortnight. My brother and I were not too surprised to find that we conducted ourselves much the same in his absence as in his presence. We slept in his bed, and sat in his chair, and drank from his cup, but otherwise there was none of the wild carousing he'd prophesied.

After a few days we began to find that we were afraid without him, in the nights, in the lonely manor, upon the moor. A brigand could have forced his way in; a patient escaped from some asylum; any number of wild beasts, maddened possibly by rabies; the ghost of our mother's ghost.

Dazed by the unremitting night terrors and related insomnia, I ran onto the lawn to defend us from the sighs and rustlings we heard out there, through the shrubbery. But when I passed beyond the eaves into the open air, my fear deserted me. I was cool and collected. The sudden blankness was quite debilitating; I fell to my knees. Eventually I summoned the courage to go back for my brother, though I had to more or less drag him out, fighting his terrified protests and my own yawning vertigo, until at last we were panting on the cold, wet grass, in the disquieting brightness of the moon. We began to sleep outside at night, like dogs, on the doorstep, waiting for our father's return.

His homecoming occurred hardly in the manner of our expectations, involving as it did the introduction of our father's bride, poor beautiful Sylvie. Timid, acquiescent, barely adolescent Sylvie, with her prim brown hair and her tiny hands: how kind she was. Our father emerged from the carriage, handed her down, and glaring at us, gruffly announced, "You are not to speak to my wife," before limping into the hall. Hurrying behind him, she smiled at us, whispered, "I'm Sylvie." My brother and I were struck by the disproportion between our good luck and her ill fortune.

Our father began by keeping her locked in the bedroom, but he soon tired of this, feeling that my brother and I were unfairly depriving him of her company. So she came downstairs and sat with us in a silence in which every quickness or break of breath was audible. When our father at last rallied himself for a tirade, we all of us, I think, felt some positive relief.

Exerting himself with Sylvie in their chambers, our father suffered a heart attack and was ordered by the doctor to a course of complete rest and seclusion. We put him away in the attic, with a sleeping mask over his eyes and Berthe to endure with him. Then, like vultures, we settled around Sylvie, cloaking her in our shadows.

We found her to be stubbornly, dumbly loyal to our father, like a calf stumbling after its mountainous mother. But as we pressed her more insistently to betray him she acquired a certain power of eloquence, invoking his "greatness," "selflessness," "suffering," "forsakenness," "rectitude," "power," and "oratory." We blinked at her in bewilderment.

"How can you think such a thing?" said my brother.

Sylvie spoke of our father's enlightened views on good and evil, life and death, masters and slaves, luck and fate, the spirit and the soul, animal and vegetable consciousness, suicide and self-abnegation, guilt and desire. "Is it better to live a life that avoids temptation or to seek out temptation to train our obedience?" she parroted sweetly. "Is it wrong to love God with the body as well as with the heart?" "Is doubt a necessary step to faith, or can it be avoided?" "Will the rapture come upon us unsuspecting?"

"When did my father find time to share his views on these topics with you?" I demanded.

It appeared that this was what he had been up to in the nights, pacing about the bedroom in his kimono, ranting, fluttering his hands in agitation, stabbing his finger at her face.

My brother and I begged to know, as delicately as possible, if this constituted the whole of our father's nocturnal activities. Sylvie met this inquiry with frank confusion. And truly it would have seemed that what she'd had was enough.

We investigated the state of Sylvie, and it bore no imprint of our father's touch. With what glee we defiled her! With our father's old, limp garters we restrained her hands and feet to grant her surrender.

287

Sylvie rubbed her white skin against the moisture that sprouted on the rough rock wall of the wine cellar and sighed. The pupils of her eyes throbbed; her pulse kicked fiercely against the taut bow of her neck. What defenseless hands she had, we marveled, her nails like petals. Damp, my brother's hair slapped his face. I reached over and held it back. Then we took her upstairs and had her again on that freezing mortician's slab of a dining-room table, while the cook's eye pressed up against the crack of the door, unfriendly and reptilian.

Later, in our nursery, she bathed us. Our tub was bedecked with porcelain swans. The furnace could not be controlled, and sometimes on bath nights my brother and I were rigid in water the bitter, metal cold of corroding pipes. Our bodies wrenched, our breath kicked in our lungs, but we held ourselves down, pushing blue knuckled against the sides of the tub, and refused to exit before the ten minutes we were granted expired. But when Sylvie ran the bath, entering the heat was like a swoon; the steam formed small weather systems against the ceiling and rained back down on us. We were up to our necks and sinking. My brother cried out at Sylvie's inadvertent roughness, and she rushed to cover the injury with kisses.

Out in the stables, she seized the whip and with enthusiasm laid it about her back and thighs. My boots were lodged deep in the muck of the stalls and I watched the haze of dust and pollen suspended in the sea of sun and settling on her face, pricking and itching her, and drawing the blood in a nettling blush. What pearly teeth she has, we told each other: how steep the arches of her feet. My brother asked to be tickled with the light of a match. I demonstrated for Sylvie how this might best be accomplished and she watched with studious solemnity from her nest in the hay, knees drawn up against her chest, rubbing the bruises and scrapes on her legs, idly wrapping her long brown hair around her throat and tugging.

We had her utterly in thrall to us and when the moment of our father's return from the attic arrived it was easy to convince her to seduce him, so that we could disport while he lay glutted and insensate. But Sylvie's advances were perhaps too direct; at any rate, he had at her with the cane and ordained that from that date forward she, a repulsive, base creature, an innocent (as he supposed) possessed of all the sinful knowledge due to a slut, was to dress only in widow's weeds and was not to eat with the rest of the family, though she'd be silently present at all our meals. Sylvie was only too pleased to do as she was bid.

It was the end of our idyll. We pined for her. Hanks of the locks we'd ripped from her head in our transportment could be found gathered in the corners of the rooms, and my brother and I each had a nest of dull brown strands under our pillows. We combed these, and for comfort sucked the ends of the hairs.

In the due passage of time, Sylvie's pregnancy became apparent. My brother and I had always understood ourselves to be the products of a virgin birth, and our father's joyful announcement of his new wife's condition made clear that he ascribed this too to his own parthenogenetic potency, though the evidence that my brother and I held to the contrary did cast our mother's account of our conception in some shadow of doubt. The old man was in a gorgeous mood that day, kicking us violently under the table, virile, boasting, and imperious, peremptory with the servants, twice ordering the coffee back to be heated up. From now on, he pronounced, Sylvie was to dress only in snow-white garments, the petticoats and short skirts of a young girl. "All white," he emphasized, thundering at us, "down to the shoes, down to the soles of the shoes! Also, not only may she not speak, she may not hear. Cotton wool is to be wrapped around her ears. And she is not to walk any longer; she is to progress from room to room on her knees."

My brother and I took the news of our parenthood with impressive public aplomb and private elation. We picked out names to share with Sylvie and attempted to get her those little treats she'd begun to crave. Her erupting belly was lewd inside her schoolgirl dresses. Her limbs swelled and drooped and she breathed in small puffs that we greedily inhaled when we bent down to adjust her shawl or slip her a note.

In the third trimester, our father ordered that she also be blinded, and the cotton wool was wrapped around her eyes. She took to her bed, where she worked at her knitting, or napped, helpless on her back, splayed out messily across the mattress.

Our child, when it came, was a difficult birth, being twins. Sylvie screamed until her voice was gone and her mouth gaped noiselessly out of the bindings of her face. Our father would not let us touch the infants, nor might Sylvie hold them. He pressed them to his breast, kissed their trembling bodies. At last he instructed Sylvie to nurse them. They made a desultory meal of it, then held out their hands to him. She died charmingly against her pillows.

Our children often slept with our father, curled up at the foot of his bed. He doted on them in a manner almost obsequious, plucking the choicest viands from the platters and dropping them into the upturned mouths. He woke them in the morning by refreshing their brows with cloths splashed with alcohol, then rubbed lotions into their hands and feet. He wheeled them around the garden, whispering to them under the hood of their perambulator.

He changed his will. The solicitor held a meeting to explain that our father had always known that we were not his true children, and that the babies had supplanted us accordingly. He was cutting us off with a mingy allowance. He'd had our belongings moved to the lodge at the gates.

"Of course," I told the solicitor, "that is just as it should be." "Naturally," said my brother, "we knew he could not be our father." We heard the old man snarl from his hiding place behind the curtains.

The children really were lovely. Blue eyes, like ours. Noble brows. Depraved mouths. They regarded us with compassion and wisdom from a great distance. We suspected they came to the lodge to visit us, but only when invisible. They were exquisite. Succulent child knees like little plums. And yet. And yet. Against all that was our fond wish to give our father proof of our affection.

On the longest night of the year my brother and I entered the children's bedroom, with death in our hearts and hands. The moon was so bright that we shielded our faces as we edged through the door. There was birdsong in the air, and we could not find the source. Windup toys? Pigeons in the eaves? A migration in the sky?

To drown it out, we set about our work. We knew we had to be quick, but the noises swarmed in our ears like wasps, our hands shook, and we were not quick.

As small as they were, they resisted us, and they did not fight fair. Though we drew our daggers across their necks and opened them cruelly, the wounds formed two sweet smiles; and these crooned a little song, full of nonsense, and our hearts broke. I saw in my brother's face that he too wished our children alive again. In a panic of remorse, we pressed our palms against their slit throats, those slack, raw lips. But the dark breath of our children gushed around our hands and spilled to the floor. We could not stop their lullaby from dying out.

My brother and I each shed a tear, and cut a lock of the children's hair, and we condoled each other with assurances of how well advised our father would have been had he bent likewise over our cradles, when he had the chance.

Then on my brother's face came a look of astonishment. Though I did not yet see what he saw, I knew we had only a few seconds to save ourselves. We looked into each other's faces, as we had sworn to do.

I swung around and with my knife I blindly struck, my eyes squeezed closed. The blow fell awkwardly upon our father's breast, his roars hammered me like fists, and for a moment I could not drive the weapon home. Then I felt my brother's hands cover mine, steady and sure, and together we pressed, and slid in to the hilt. I could not bear to see what we had done, but against my face pressed the perfume spilt from the gashed white rose in our father's buttonhole. My brother bade me open my eyes. In the glints and shivers of the moonlight, the night was full of blades that beat like wings.

How tough was the hide of our father, how frail were his bones! How handsome was my brother, with his mouth of rouge.

CHAPTER III—SENESCENCE
Mouths Full of Snow, Eyes Full of Rain,
Ears Full of Fire, and Air Everywhere

When we were young and the earth was our toy chest, I had the small things of the world, and my brother the big. I had the sparrows, the lines of the palm, the bite behind the sweetness of a lemon lollipop, the pebble in the shoe, the end of the echo. He had the sighing of whales and the slow pleasuring of continents beneath the lava. When our voices began to deepen and grate, our father wrought havoc in the universe and summoned us to serve him.

Then my brother's was the dead and mine the undying. His the cut grass and mine the shattered stone. His the last embers and mine the scorched earth. My brother sadly decomposed; I mutely fossilized. Our father tried to keep the living for himself.

Now we are more than he ever was. Our dominion is vast. Our vision is dark. The stars are far too paltry to warm our hands. Our playground, and within it the tomb of our father, is somewhere in the dark, and rushing outward.

When my brother and I grew old together, we were to have practiced the old arts. I had looked forward to presiding over a bubbling cauldron, to the seasonal jarring of potions, the scattering of powders, the casting of trivial spells. My brother had hoped in his retirement to take to soothsaying: He held that toothless gums lent authenticity to augury.

Olympian in our early years, then so bitterly Jesuitical in our maturity, we had hoped to repose ourselves at last in magic's airy cradle. How often we had talked of it! Not for us, we had decided, a dotage that recalled with futility the joys of our childhood: We would age gracefully, accepting as our diminished due the pettier trickeries, the shabbier chicaneries. We were to have cackled together as we threw the bones. We have always craved something of the human.

But even this most picayune dream has been lost to us now, dribbling away into the vacuum that holds us, becoming a hazy black hole on the horizon of time. Here we are majestic, and numb to it.

Somewhere, on our lost earth, we still have handmaidens. Their prayers rise up to us, thin and rank. We miss breasts like sea foam; cool, damp thighs like cavern walls; the skin below the eyes, as thin as an autumn leaf made lace by worms. It's Sylvie we miss. Her skin, where we'd struck her, burned enough to scorch our tongues. Her smell, so delicious we longed to truss her limbs and roast the flesh. The sisters in our faith these days are harsh women, with long teeth, with long nails, with long shanks and long ribs, long hair that bends their necks, long tongues that rasp dryly, long pendulous stomachs, long moans, long tears that hang from their cheeks like ropes of pearls. Their incense bleeds black smoke all around us; we grope for each other. The smell of their love clots in our nostrils; the taste of their love raises sores on our lips.

I remember hiding with my brother between rows of corn. I pretend we can still look up into the green light of the leaves.

"We were so beautiful before we were invisible," my brother would say.

I say, "We're still beautiful."

"We were so alive," says my brother.

"We are more than living," I say.

"I wish we were dead," says my brother.

"A god makes a poor ghost," I tell him.

"A ghost has powers a god has not," my brother speculates.

I scoff.

"A ghost can go in between things. In between walls, in between sheets, in between breaths."

"As gods we know no divisions. The world is flat beneath us. Mountains like unfolded paper flowers wilting on the ground."

"A ghost can enter the dreams of the haunted," says my brother.

"A god makes those dreams."

"A ghost can switch souls with the living."

"A god can steal a soul and have two for his own."

"A ghost can see another ghost," says my brother.

What could I tell him? That gods are blind is something we had never known.

My brother once said that our love was ideal. I mocked him for it, because I only care for damaged things.

Nevertheless, it was true. There was a time when each of us stood our own ground. When we were distant and in danger, we each thought how best to save ourselves. We did not stand helpless before our enemies, wordlessly beseeching one another's aid across the miles. We did not use our last moments to mourn the absence of the other; we used them instead to save our own skins.

When sleep overtook us and we were alone, we stretched our bodies lavishly across the entire lengths of our mattresses, relishing the cool and wide expanse of linens. We did not move, in the middle of the night, to the far side of the bed, in order to reach out for the warm sheets that felt like skin. We did not adjust the angle of our pillows in order to imagine our heads supported by each other's chest or arm.

We lived in our own bodies; we filled every nook and cranny of our own skulls. I could have crossed from my head to my brother's, and made my home there; but I swear I never did. My brother could have commanded me into his own mind, and made of me a willing prisoner; but I am sure he did not do so. Those powers were ours, but they did not tempt us. For this reason, we were bright and full of courage, and worthy of each other's love.

"That is what it is, to love a brother," my brother said. "A straight, tall love, which does not bend itself down to lean on another."

I did not believe him then, but I believe him now. Now my affection for him is debased. I am rotten with craving and weakness. It is hard, after all, in this abysmal plunging emptiness, to know how I will ever learn to see again without the gleam of my brother's hair to teach me.

I call for him and call for him, desperate and ashamed, but as I never stop calling, I cannot hear, over my pleas, whether he has answered me or not.

Where is my brother? If he is beside me, I do not know it.

"Am I inside you?" I ask. "Are you here in this time?"

My brother is weary. "We're everywhere," he answers. He sighs and I feel the drag of a cosmos in collapse.

"We're not with our father," I say. "We're not with our mother."

"They're nowhere," says my brother.

"Can you see me?" I ask him. "Can you touch me? Try."

My brother doesn't answer.

"I miss you," I say.

After some eternities, my brother says, "Can you hear me? Are you there?"

I crush a sun savagely under my heel.

"We're orphans," says my brother.

"We're brothers," I say.

My brother doesn't answer.

After some eternities, he says, "Where are you? Am I inside you? Are you here in this time?"

I don't answer.

My brother says, "I miss you."

"I miss you too," I tell him.

"I'm alone," says my brother.

"We're alone," I tell him.

My brother's breaths are muddy and thick; he could be talking in his sleep. "What is that sound?" he says. "Do you hear it?"

"You and me," I say to my brother. "We're nowhere. It's never. What do you want to do today?"

"Who's that?" says my brother. "Please don't."

After some eternities, I say, "Where are you?"

My brother doesn't answer. Somewhere about me is the pulse of a galaxy convulsing.

If I have loved my brother for his beauty, and now his skin is gray as ash, and his eyes now as empty as wind: I love him less.

If I have loved my brother for his need of me, and now his skin is fragile as burnt paper, and his eyes now delirious with clouds: I love him more.

If I have loved my brother for his love of me, and now find myself abandoned in the coiling maze of his memories: I love him less.

If I have loved my brother that I might win his love for me, and even now am renounced by his deaf ears, his ossified touch: I love him more.

If I have loved my brother for his mysteries, and now I feel his secrets, untethered, streaming out upon the air: I love him less.

If I have loved my brother for my knowledge of him, and now I feel him emptied, naked and splayed against the sky: I love him more.

If I have loved my brother like myself, and my own voice calls out now for my destruction, and my mouth tastes like poison: I love him less.

I loved my brother like a god, and now he burns upon the firmament. What have I done?

It is as if he has died. He has died.

If I have loved my brother, and now am without a brother to love: I love him more.

A shorn flower for my brother.

When I am fretful, I beseech my brother to soothe me. He has always loved to reminisce about the days when men tore out their tongues because their speech was too crude for the syllables of my name. It's true, many have gone mad for love of me. Once I woke in the night to find a woman, in a stupor of pleasure, lazily chewing the flesh of my arm, at the crook of my elbow.

Though I have been gone so long, my brother could assure me that there are many who still half suspect they remember me, something fleeting at the corners of their minds. My brother would say that when a breeze slithers across a closed room or all the lamps of a street suddenly stutter into darkness, the fearful still worship me, making my sign with their fingers.

When I am ill, I want my brother to succor me. He would be sure to remember the many pleasures of the sickbed, which I am already forgetting: the taste of fruit, the sharp smell of feverish skin, the heaviness of blankets, the bewildering smoothness of water. He could remind me, as well, of his many portraits of me. He made thousands; in the old house, we had several galleries full.

Yet I can recall only a few. Me in oils on a snorting, rearing steed, my head blackly beplumed. I dig in my spurs and ride the horse's back as if I were a lion taking down its kill. Me sketched in a white christening dress, my pudgy hands reaching up as my father holds me down in the basin of water. A photograph of me striding forward into the camera, my features distorted and furious, my hand a blur. A set of intricate ivory chessmen, my face on every one.

295

When I grow tired, I ask my brother to be kind and to tell me bed-time stories as our mother used to do, though his tales were always as likely to keep me awake as to lull me to sleep.

I do not know if I should chance my dreams tonight. Unsure, I continue to beg him: just one more before bed.

My brother says, "Lo. Unto the world was given a man and unto the man was given the world and all things were his, excepting his only son. For although the Maker of the world had given all the things He'd made to the man, He loved the son that the man himself had made, and He claimed the son as His own. And the man howled and he raged into the void, he cast his own hair and teeth into the void, but the void was his own, and returned to him his teeth and hair politely, and his son was gone from him.

"And the earth fell into the sun twelve times more before the man had a daughter. He made her of his sweat and of bread that he had chewed and of sawdust and fishing line, and if he did not love her, at least he had made her and kept her, for his Maker saw her and raised His brows and softly laughed. And He pitied the man and thought no more of his daughter. Until the man's daughter loved the Maker and she walked on her knees to Him, pressing her brow to the earth, and said, Lord, and she was with Him. And the man cursed and rent his garments and smeared himself with filth and he spit into the void but the void was his own and returned to him his spit, it slapped back against his face, and he was wroth.

"And the moon collided with the earth twelve times more before the man had twins. And they were as like each other as two eyes: one green, one blue, and their vision the same. And in the sight of the man and his Maker they were perfect, and the two of them loved the twins. The Maker said, come unto Me, and the man said, abide; and the twins said, go ye unto the void, and wrestle for us. So the man and his Maker did, and the void swallowed them. And the world and all things in it were the twins'; it was a garden; a brother swallowed the lock, and his brother the key."

Four Stories
Andrew R. *Touhy*

HOW MUCH WE LOOK ALIKE

BROTHER AND SISTER, he said. Uncanny. To which we both smiled politely, and nodded, looking at each other. You looked nothing like me to me. I don't imagine I looked anything like you to you. You and your brother look similar but not much alike. You and your brother look more unalike than alike, in fact. Neither of your parents have blond hair and blue eyes. Your brother and I could never be mistaken for one another. Your brother and I could never be mistaken for brothers, either. My brothers and I look alike. We each look more than a little like each other. My younger brother looks very similar to me. We look like brothers. He looks so much like me that sometimes our older brother looks unrelated. Your brother still looks like your brother, even if he doesn't look like you. My older brother often looks like someone else's brother. In that regard, I guess, one could say he looks like your brother, one could say I look like your brother, one could say you look like my sister, one could say we look a lot like family. Or a lot like a family. In fact we are family now. Even though your brother has no brothers and my brothers and I have no sister. Our mom always wanted a daughter. Sometimes she asked whether or not we wanted a sister. To which I said yes. I don't know what my brothers said but I remember saying yes and trying to imagine, though I never quite could, what exactly a sister of ours might look like.

BROTHER FROM SAN FRANCISCO

He's vegetarian now but eats fish, but not just any fish. First he must know where the fish comes from, then he must know whether it was farmed or wild caught, and then of course he must like the fish, the particular type of fish, that is, as food, which often depends on its freshness and preparation. We'd planned blackened dolphin on the

297

grill. Not dolphin the mammal, of course, but dolphinfish, a blunt-headed iridescent game fish—mahimahi, they call it out west—that lights up neon blue and green when hooked. It's a local specialty here and our favorite, sizzling in butter in an iron skillet. We laid it on a bed of sweet corn succotash, sour-cream black beans on the side, and he said it was good. He said he liked it but asked if we had any bread and cheese.

We ask: What do you want to do today? He answers: Whatever you normally do. We ask: But is there anything you'd like to do? His answer: He'd like to do whatever it is we usually do.

Really?

Really.

We don't believe that. Because we don't necessarily want to do what we have to do today and we are us. We'd like him to want to do something else, so that we have a reason not to do what we have to do today. We can't bring ourselves to believe him because while we know him to be a good-natured, easygoing person, we understand that he's from San Francisco also. He wouldn't live in San Francisco if he wanted to do what we do here.

Our brother wears a wetsuit and rubber skullcap swimming.

Today, we need to cut, trim, edge, and then water the lawn before the broiling sun climbs too high. He lives in an apartment on a hill blurred by fog. We have three hampers full of dirty clothes, including pee-damp sheets. He keeps a small caged bird as a pet, trained to poop on command. Our minivan needs to be washed, the inside, seats and floorboards, vacuumed of crumbs, scrubbed of spills, but first we should organize the garage. He rides a bike to work and even on dates. Saturday night is bath night. Last weekend he attended an international film festival. The pool needs chlorine, tablets; we should pick up a new beach raft too. His housemate is from Portland. Our two children squeal from their rooms—one painted Sailor's Sea (blue), one painted Tricycle Taupe (pink)—our cat hides in the box spring of our bed, our horsey yellow Lab eats a toy a day, from the piles in nearly every corner of the living room. On his home bar—an antique tea cart—at least one bottle of fifteen-year rye.

He says: They're not much for conversation, are they?

Then he says: But of course they're only, what, two and three?

*

He likes to read. Sometimes when he's saying something we have to realize that he's quoting from a book. Or it sounds as though he's quoting something from a book. Sometimes even his jokes are made out of something he read in a book. He's writing his own book too, of poetry. He writes poems and sometimes reads them out loud, to a live audience, at a bar or café, or in the back of used bookstores. Quoting people he likes to read, or just quoting quotes he likes, he has said:

Marriage—nothing against yours—marriage is a great institution, but who wants to live in an institution? (Groucho Marx.)

A lawn is nature under totalitarian rule. (Michael Pollan.)

Love: A temporary insanity curable by marriage. (Ambrose Bierce.)

When a greedy seagull clipped our son on the forehead: When it comes to children, let the air comb them. (Julio Cortázar.) And later, kneeling beside our son: Perhaps I heard a bird singing and felt for him a small, birdlike affection. (Jorge Luis Borges.)

Vodka is the blank canvas upon which many a colorless cocktail is painted. (Himself, we think.)

We fall asleep on the couch, watching a slow, long, confusing movie with subtitles. We wake even more confused, to what looks like the exact scene we were watching when we dozed off. Then he falls asleep, watching a movie we've all seen before but edited and censored for television.

He is difficult to read.

He brings his own coffee from San Francisco. This time, he brought his own grinder.

While we were at Mass he went to the Whole Foods and now the countertops are faintly stained with cilantro, the cutting boards and kitchen floor littered with diced onion and sticky garlic scrap and chili stems, which snap like dead lizard tails underfoot. He's made his salsa again. The bowl of green is spicy, bowl of red mild. He also made quesadillas. We've been invited to a belated Cinco de Mayo fiesta, hosted by friends whose little boy, Xavier, attends the same pre-school as our son. But we weren't asked to bring anything. In fact we've been told not to bring a thing, other than ourselves and our brother from San Francisco. But our brother insists. The gesture at least, he argues, will be appreciated. Besides, they've never had his salsa.

His salsa is too hot to eat. Often it's too hot to smell. All we can breathe is heat. A smoky bubble ripe with heat.

We put our noses over the bowl and cough, eyes stinging almost immediately with tears.

That's not the mild one, he says, try a chip. We believe him. Our lips burn. No, first our tongues burn. The whole tongue: top and tip, the sides all around. Then the roofs of our mouths, the insides of our cheeks, our throats, our stomachs. How does it taste? Our noses start running. We reach for water, although he says use a piece of bread, or tortilla, to wipe the capsicum oils away. We drink two glasses of milk each.

His quesadillas are strange, small and hard, filled with a crumbling white kind of salty cheese that doesn't melt.

The babysitter! Our first. The girl next door. She's thirteen. Is thirteen dollars enough? We can't believe we're so nervous.

He looks bored. At the far end of the patio table with our friends and neighbors, who all have children at the preschool, our brother sits cross-legged, hardly speaking. He looks down, either at his lap or the beer in his hands, he stares off across the yard, at the fence decorated with strings of tiny Mexican flags. He fingers the beard hairs under his chin while gazing up at the rustling palm trees, so tall, straight, and dark against the round dusk sky. We catch his eye. He raises his sweaty brow, nods, and smiles without parting his lips, then winks. We ask if he's having a good time and he says he's having fun. Our favorite friends, a couple our age with a boy and girl also, ask if he's always like this. What? Distracted. Aloof. Isn't he having any fun? No, he's doing fine, we say, he's just settling in. When the hosts ask how he's doing, we say he's having a good time, we say he said he's having fun.

Our brother is a listener, a thinker. It's not that he doesn't have plenty to say, it just seems that he prefers to listen and think it to himself. Our brother is an observer, a participant-observer, but mostly an observer first, and then, after a while, or after the fact, a participant.

He once compared family to a still life. Clichéd in subject matter, in form, but timely nonetheless. Family is a convention, he's said, and he's OK with that. Life itself is timeworn. He's happy to take his place on the table. As knife or bread, pitcher or bowl. As fruit. Even as a fly on the fruit.

A fly?

Or bee.

But when someone asks about his time in Mexico he comes alive.

He tells a story of drinking tequila with tequila barons in Tequila, the town. Many of these men were blond, blue eyed, dressed as cowboys. They bought and paid for round after round, served by a man they called The Priest, in an upscale cantina named The Chapel. Two mariachi bands hired for the night serenaded them out to the dusty, cobbled streets. He tells of eating *menudo*, the hangover stew made with cow stomach. He talks of overnight turkey buses through cold mountain villages and military checkpoints and teeming outdoor markets with bizarre fruits and regional dishes with long, unpronounceable names, some in a language other than Spanish. He ate grasshoppers with mezcal. He ran a small café for a while and roasted coffee beans trucked straight in from the nearby plantation mill. He visited ruins that were once the center of an empire.

On the coast, where the lone eyesore is a palm-frond-thatched hut that serves ice-cold bottled beer, and the ocean does all the work of the day, he slept in a hammock for two dollars a night. After the mosquitoes got him, he rented a cedar-and-cinder-block bungalow, with window screens and a ceiling fan, for just three dollars more.

We all take turns hugging the hosts good night, and promise to make next year's party. Our brother says he'll fly in again. He says he'd love to help out again: He makes mean tofu *enchiladas verdes*, not to mention killer *chiles rellenos* that aren't heavy sponges of oil. He is drunk. We are all drunk but he sounds drunk. He sets his beer bottle on the serving table and it falls off. We are relieved that he doesn't notice and stoop to retrieve it from the grass, strewn with tortilla chips even the dogs refuse to eat.

Enjoy the salsa! he says.

Question: Seeing anyone special? Any serious romance brewing?

Answer: Regard the society of women as a necessary unpleasantness of social life, and avoid it as much as possible. (Count Leo Tolstoy.)

*

Andrew R. Touhy

We all fall asleep on the couch.

He is difficult to read. Or rather, it is difficult to read how he is reading us.

Truth be told, how can we know much about him? Even a long weekend, once or twice a year, isn't much time to spend with someone if you want to get to know them, if you want to really get to know them again. Of course we try to get to know him again each visit, which is no easy process with our brother, especially now that he's from San Francisco. Inevitably the first days are spent remembering who he was last time he came. While the next days are spent learning and accepting how he's changed since, or learning and accepting how we'd misunderstood him before. Things get trickier when we factor in memories of our brother's prior visits, not to mention our memory of him from childhood.

There aren't any days left after that.

He is gone again, he is out of sight although not entirely out of mind. But to a great degree—whether we like it or not, we can't help it—we soon forget who he is now. We wouldn't make the effort if he weren't family. Honestly, we love him but wouldn't work this hard if he weren't related to us.

Even if he stayed for weeks, a month, a whole summer or winter, if he lived here for the year, or moved back, finally, who's to say the distance—the inevitable distance grown between us as brothers and family and changed people in the world in general—would shrink or dissolve? Proximity doesn't guarantee closeness.

By the same token, what can he know about us? The fact is, nobody knows anyone that well. It's a metaphysical, or phenomenological, issue, as our brother would say. People—family perhaps more so—are a mystery, which does make sense, since everything begins in mystery. A lifetime is too short a time to get to know much about yourself, really. That we are who we are, or who we think we are, is equally mysterious, when you give the notion some thought. What was it our brother once said? Every man possesses three characters: that which he exhibits, that which he really has, and that which he believes he has. (Jean-Baptiste Alphonse Karr.)

*

We still don't own a coffeemaker because we still don't drink coffee.

He is difficult to read. Or rather, it's difficult to read how he is reading us. Or rather, it's difficult to read how he is reading us read him.

He did like our dolphin. So much so, in fact, he finished the leftovers, cold, before heading to the airport. He hadn't noticed, he said, just how tasty the meat was. As dense as chicken but moister and more richly flavored. It paired really well with the sweet corn and black beans, now that the overall ingredients had had time to meld. Was there a touch of mango in the sauce? Bonus, he said, dolphin itself is a remarkable species of fish. He'd looked it up and found that in general they have a quicksilver metabolism, reach maturity in a year, and spawn year-round. Their lean flesh isn't prone to bioaccumulation, meaning of almost any fish in the ocean, dolphin is less likely to have dangerous concentrations of mercury. Even their scales will soften and glow again when returned to the water.

We watched him: standing before the refrigerator, elbow propped on the open door, bags beside his crossed feet, eating bite after bite, straight from the Tupperware container. How we had hoped he would like our dolphin. How we had enjoyed planning and preparing it in anticipation of his visit. Certainly we're happy to know that world-wide stocks are both healthy and well managed, but what makes us most happy is knowing our brother enjoyed our dolphin. Blame us for such an unreasonable thought—we try not to think it. Or we try to keep from admitting that we do think it. But we wish that each of his visits was like this moment: bite by bite, us certain of his pleasure.

FATHERS AND SONS

Never, not even when I was the sole masculine power structure in your life, did you have the urge to kill me?

Clarify, please, your use of the word "urge."

I understand it, and use it here, to mean desire, want, a strong inclination toward murdering me for irrational reasons. You could, quite knowingly, harbor considerable resentment for any number of parental missteps or misdeeds I, quite unknowingly, committed as "father." For example, the day I took away your scuba knife. Or you may—here I draw on the classic psychological metaphor for describing our psychosexual competition—out of an inborn fear of castration joined by any lingering subconscious hunger to replace the breast as love object with your mother, my wife, still wish me dead.

Let me make sure I understand you completely. You took my scuba knife?

You were threatening the neighbor's boy. You were threatening several neighborhood boys, in fact. And their pets.

Tell me, upon hearing of my death by shark attack in coastal waters, how would you have felt?

Remember, you never actually *went* scuba diving. We bought you the one knife, and a pair of flippers, which you wore in the pool.

By emphasizing "went," do I detect that you believe I'm a failure?

You detect my personal investment in you as a success, to the extent that it validates my worth as parent.

So I'm to feel better knowing that what I detect is your disappointment in yourself because I'm a disappointment?

Yes. And you're to feel like not killing me.

For the record, I have no—nor have I ever had—interest in killing you.

Clarify, please, your use of the word "interest."

By "interest," I mean I am not—nor ever have been—suitably aroused to act on the above-mentioned oedipal impulses nor any conscious, premeditated plot to avenge my childhood self . . . of which I was robbed . . . insofar as neither will resolve the bewilderment, anger, and anxiety we all experience as a result of being thrown together with a particular set of parents by the accident, and I suppose miracle, of birth. I am, after much work of an inmost nature, my own charge. And while gaining this degree of self-awareness, or self-actualization, for lack of a better term, nearly always involves some rebellion and conflict with those in power, I can safely say now you have nothing to fear from me.

So I'm to understand, and believe, that under all possible circumstances you would absolutely not kill me?

Would not.

Not by accident?

No.

Not in self-defense? Say, if I forced the issue?

No.

Not if I asked?

Not even then.

Well. I'm disappointed. Relieved but truly disappointed. I thought you had it in you. I wasn't tiptoeing around in fear, mind you, but I've been careful, all of these years, and, I admit, strangely hopeful. You certainly are a disappointment. You certainly have proved to be your mother's son.

I am.

Is that your old scuba knife?

MISTAKERS

Only in the shower, my body lathered with soap, did I realize I'd mistaken your toothbrush for mine. We have known each other eleven years and a month. We will have lived together eight years, come June. We have been married now close to two years, give or take a handful of weeks. Our toothbrushes are identical. White with blue-and-white bristles. Two more shades of blue mark the spines. To prevent any confusion, you wound the handle of yours with an elastic hair tie, which is black. I could brush my teeth with your toothbrush. I would take appropriate pains to keep this fact from you also. I would brush faster than usual, I imagine. By that I mean brush the teeth faster, each tooth, I suppose, receiving fewer and quicker brushes, and brush the set of teeth as a whole, the uppers and lowers together, in less time than is recommended by dentists. I would try to keep my gums and tongue, the roof of my mouth, even my lips, from touching the bristles of your brush. And I would go as far as to dry the bristles with a towel, or use my thumb or palm of my hand—like my brothers and I used to as kids—and of course then return your toothbrush to its right place. Our toothbrush holder has three perfectly round small holes, arranged exactly like those on the face of a bowling ball. You keep your toothbrush, I think, in the top right hole, where a left-handed bowler such as I would put his index finger, were he bowling with our toothbrush holder. Or I could rush dripping wet from the shower to fetch and dress my toothbrush, hurrying back as if moving fast alone could prevent the interruption, or erase it from existence, or at least help me fool myself into thinking I'd invented it. It was cold, morning. Bathrooms are cold in general most mornings, all by themselves, before the first person showers.

305

I hadn't been under the water a minute but it was hot and wouldn't I drip with each step everywhere? A pattern of drops and damp footprints across the rectangular bath mat, around the round red bath rug beneath it, onto the linoleum tiles beyond. And into your makeup kit, which you set on the sink at night before bed, and I set on the floor beside the sink each morning before shaving. You wouldn't be happy with both makeup and makeup kit soaked with shower rather than shaving water, or so I reasoned, as your toothbrush entered my mouth, seemingly of its own accord. Here is where you step into the story, the shower, quite naturally, quite literally. Which means you pulled back the curtain on me midthought, amid my thoughts, only to climb in and stand beneath the water, half asleep still, but already brushing.

The Dwindling
Diane Greco Josefowicz

> *Early stages in a Dwindling's rehabilitation are the most difficult because there is inevitably so little with which to work.*
>
> —The Book of Querque: A Compendium of Advice for Pedagogues

"WATCH THAT STEP," Dr. Querque warns me as he shoulders open the door that fronts his Home for Dwindling Boys and Girls. In the foyer, a trio of woodwork angels clasp psalters to their chests as they raise their bulging eyes to heaven. Their mouths are burnished Os.

"The threshold," he informs me, his words falling like other, lesser angels from the dark height of his mouth, "is not what it used to be."

I follow, mindful of my fingers, which are grimed with the train's soot and beneath that, like a memory, dust from my mother's pencil sharpener. Emptying it was the last task she set me, keeping her expectations low, so I might easily exceed them and not burden her with a need for correction. Unlike my mother, Querque seems unfazed by what I require in this department. Of my belongings, I was allowed only my drafting compass, which Querque confiscated after he caught me using it to jimmy our compartment's lock. "Thus does the personality gain in structure, brick by brick," he said, straightening the lapels of his jacket, which gave off an odor of gingersnaps, though there were no such wonders on him. (While he dozed, I checked.) This too was a lesson: Beware the senses, which bamboozle. An empty stomach, however, is incontestable. My last meal was yesterday.

I shrug myself from my coat, which Querque takes from me with no sign of the displeasure I am expecting, since I have been for some minutes dripping on his parquet. I shuck my good shoes, and my toes emerge, ten quivering shrimps, through holes that I swear to heaven weren't there before. Against the world's disorder, which eddies about me like a patch of bad water, all I can do is repeat my mother's advice: Stand straight, smile bright. *And hold.* Sensing my beaming has a bit of the beam about it (as my mother would say), I force my grimace into a less *ersatz* grin, as if for a photograph, and wait for the flash. There is no flash. Rummaging in the closet, Querque has not noticed my distress and, with luck, he won't.

He exchanges his raincoat for a smoking jacket of gray velveteen, not omitting to transfer my compass to the inside pocket. His ginger scent has yielded to a closet odor of damp wool and insecticide. Blocking the hallway's meager light, he is pale and narrow as a celery stalk, fibrous, wholesome, and just as hard to swallow. His velveteen jacket shares the sea's oily sheen.

Clunk! The door shuts, the bolt leaps home. I shift my feet, to hide my toes, and widen my smile until it is big enough to contain every last thing I never did for my mother. Querque averts his eyes.

My mother, the artist Helen Dando of New Bedford, claimed to be a reincarnation of Helen of old, and most days she did seem capable of launching anything, from the boats that took my father and returned him to us shining with fish scales, his pockets jangling with bounty, coin and shell, to the flotilla of toy tugboats that nightly went wheeling round the tub drain. Even the tide came and went at her behest, or so it seemed to me, leaving pewter puddles in which I found sea treasures: ropes of kelp that slimed through my fingers; tiny cowries that I threaded into bracelets; and best of all, lumps of sea glass, edges blunted by sand and water, my mother's elements. Every weekday, from September to June, I was propelled onto the school bus with a push of my mother's hand. I felt its impress on my back in the form of a gritty rash that oozed the whole time my father was away, and dried up when he returned.

Father was a sailor. He set forth when my mother permitted it, but everything else about him was completely irregular, including his front tooth, which had been chipped, he told me, on a sea-glass bottle. He presented me with a shard of the original, which I promptly bit, cracking my incisor to match his. "Don't listen to anyone who tells you the apple never falls far from the tree," he advised as I, wincing, held his sea-scented handkerchief to my mouth. "The apple *never* falls. Count on it, small fry: We're always, already *redeemed*." When he was home, what he said seemed true. I was happy in a way that thrust the rest of my life, before and after his appearances, into shadow. But during the unsettled months of his absence, the natural order of trees and apples was inverted: It was as if he had fallen away from me.

It would be simple to say that I missed him, but that skeletal description will not do: The fact is, his absence shattered me, so that I was engulfed by a mood as heavy and shifting as the sand that held my mother's bronzes, her angels and demons, when she cast them. My father wouldn't stay in one place long enough for a pearl of belief in him to form in the nacre of my mind. Whereas my mother, who did not merely accept this state of affairs but abetted it, felt that the solicitation of a child's belief in the regularity of events to be an inexcusable seduction. But of course—and here I smile brighter, wider, *hold*—the point is not to cast blame or assign responsibility in retrospect, when nothing can be done. My father's changeability was probably constitutional. A sailor, he was always leaving, and would always go. This quirk suited my mutable mother—but it did not suit me. I dwindled, growing small and quiet. My mother took me to the doctor, who, after pinching my wrist, pressing his stethoscope against my chest, and closing my eyelids with his fingers, prescribed my delivery to Querque.

"No!" I cried. I didn't want to leave my mother; above all I did not want to cede my chair by the window, where I would sit, drawing perfect circles with my compass while I kept an eye on the harbor, where my father's ship might arrive at any time.

That night, my mother dressed me in my fancy nightgown, stretched me out on the parlor's horsehair sofa, and swaddled me in a sheet. She placed coins on my eyes, as was her practice, to eliminate the dark circles she found so unattractive, and she reminded me, by way of a lullaby, that my father's perpetual departure was something I could rely on, as I could rely on the regular rearrangement of the night sky. She pointed at the window, through which Orion was just visible, wheeling around the polestar with his limbs forever locked, akimbo. "Not to worry," she sighed, as she covered the clock with a filmy black scarf. "All troubles go in the fullness of time." An electric glance over her shoulder: "Which, for you, is about as full as it gets." Querque's home would be good for me, she added, as she adjusted my lace collar. Her fingers drifted to my mouth, which she smoothed into a smile—wide, bright, and for a moment, held. At Querque's, she explained, I would at last understand my father's lesson. Even if I never stopped dwindling, at least I would learn to come and go.

It is hard to say, in fact, what I will learn at the home. For the moment, I am expected simply to do as I am told, and, so commanded, I follow Querque down one corridor, and then another, until we arrive in a kitchen so brightly lit I wince. From the ceiling, frying pans hang in rows, arranged by size and scoured to a dull luster. On the wall, knives cling to metal strips in order of ascending lethality: pare, slice, bone, hack, cleave. The tile floor's chill rises through the soles of my feet; a different chill descends down my arms. Though this room is a hymn to the attractive idea that stomachs are made for filling, I don't want to be scoured shiny. I don't want to wash my hands.

The tiled floor centers on a mosaic: A man dives from a platform into a river filled, it seems, with dolphins. The far shore is gold.

Presiding over everything is a graying woman whose pince-nez dangles from a chain of seed pearls.

"Lunette Bicky," Querque says, "meet our newest appointment, Monday One Thirty."

If I ever had another name, it has been lost in Querque's pockets, along with my compass.

Squinting, Lunette regards me with her dominant eye. At the center of her gunmetal irises, the pupils have contracted to pinheads. "You couldn't bring a Tuesday, or a Sunday?"

"As you know, Lunette," Querque sniffs, "there are only so many days in the week, and so many hours in the day."

"There are exactly seven," she retorts, "and twenty-four, respectively. As *you* know."

Lunette spins on her heel. Dr. Querque gives me a push, not unlike my mother's school-bus propulsions, and disappears like a startled smelt. I must have gasped because Lunette troubled herself to reassure me: "Never mind. You'll get to know his little ways."

She hands me a homemade lollipop, not quite round and slightly soft. I tongue it, and a headache blooms behind my eyes. At home, sugar is not allowed. I thrust the lollipop into my pocket.

"You are more a chips-and-pickle sort of girl," she observes.

As the lollipop's taste fades, so does the pain. Despite my suspicions about Querque and his Home for Dwindlers, I find myself warming to this Lunette Bicky.

"I was a naturalist in the former life," Lunette says.

"What's that?"

She tilts her head. "Don't you know?"

Instead of answering, I roll something sticky between my fingertip and the countertop.

"Let me show you around," she says, lifting my hand and swiping under it with a rag. "You have a lot to learn. And," she tipped my chin to peer briefly into my eyes, "only me to teach you."

"What do you mean?"

"Never mind, you'll know soon enough." She's halfway across the kitchen before I can ask another question. "Come along."

In the pantry—described with special emphasis as *off-limits*—Lunette shows me canisters of oatmeal, baking powder, and cornstarch, tinned peaches and sardines. Among the cookbooks, I recognize one with an embossed spine: TUTTI FRUTTI DI MARE. My mother, who had a copy, translated the title for me: All the Fruits of the Sea. That was as much as I learned from it, though, because my father, whose seafaring meant months of nothing but fish in the belly, preferred turf to surf while at home, and so the book gathered dust while my mother griddled hamburgers that, despite her acquiescence to my father's wish, nevertheless tasted faintly of kelp, as if she could never give up the sea entire. Here too rules seem to be sustained by resistance: Although the typewriter, shining with polish, is not to be touched, Lunette opens a drawer to show me where she keeps her supplies, tiny screwdrivers for making repairs and extra ribbons, as if to suggest that someday I might have the privilege of requiring them. So far, at Querque's, I've been given exactly nothing (unless you count the lollipop) yet still, this Lunette Bicky holds things before me—sweets, pickles, hopes.

Tacked to the door is a chart that I mistake at first for a picture of sea coral, delicate outgrowths branching from a sturdy trunk.

"Is that the limbic system?" Something of which my mother had often spoken, in tones of awe.

"Limbo, more like." Her tolerant smile stops at her eyes.

"The dance?" I shimmy, to show that I know exactly what she means.

"Welcome to our home," Lunette says, in a tone that ends my clowning. "That picture is a food tree." Yet her explanation explains nothing. Only fruit and nuts grow on trees, not milk or meat. Why does "mcringue" appear at the base of the trunk, why is "spaghetti" an afterthought scribbled at the tip of an otherwise unelaborated branch, what in this topsy-turvy universe of aliment is a "clam tongue," and for what does a clam need a tongue anyway?

She tacks the day's meal plan to the door.

TODAY'S LUNCH:

Suey, American chop, and
Bread, white, sandwich, sliced, with
Apples, peeled, various and
Milk, skim, cold, in cups.

Diane Greco Josefowicz

I am staring at a spool of correction tape when Lunette mutters, "Well, he doesn't like *everything* I cook."

> The Dictum of Light: As the outside shapes the inside, so bright environments beget those angels known as happy children. But, to keep utility bills down, turn off lights *religiously*.

Monday dawns, but only just. The sun, abashed, fingers the horizon before withdrawing behind a thundercap so gray and heavy it might have been cut from Querque's smoking jacket. Over breakfast, rain drips into my oatmeal. I move to a drier spot and spoon what I can into my mouth. When I am finished, Lunette exchanges my bowl for a vegetable peeler and directs me to the kitchen, where my morning task is already laid out, in the form of a colander of indifferently washed fingerling potatoes. They refuse to be deskinned without a struggle that eventuates in the peeling of exactly five fingerlings and one part of a finger. I wrap a rag around the wound *and hold*. But the scab lacks all conviction, and I am without recourse, for Lunette, who has the morning off, is the only one who knows where to find the first-aid kit. Lunch is leftover oatmeal, sticky as the Band-Aid I am not wearing. The first bite clots in my throat. I spit the second bite into a napkin and toss the remainder in the trash so the problem it represents may belong to some other metabolic process, to someone else's future. Mine is already sealed, in the form of this afternoon's Session with Querque.

At twenty minutes past the hour, I arrive in the waiting room. Nothing happens when I switch on the lamp, and pulling the chain only serves to deepen the cut on my finger. In the gloom I take deep breaths; I repeat, sotto voce, the Dictum of Light; I leaf through a magazine called *Emphases—Fun Has No Purpose*. (The masthead reveals that this is also one of Querque's publications; its logo is a stylized reproduction of the diver I saw on the kitchen floor.) I press my injured finger against the upholstery until my dubious scab makes a pinprick stain. The curtains are the same graphite-colored velveteen as Querque's jacket; on the window side, they are lined with watered silk, also gray.

The door opens. I rise and offer my hand to Querque, who sees my finger and recoils. I ignore him—*straight, bright, hold!*—and cross the threshold, brushing my other, undamaged fingers on the jamb, enameled in a pale gray that matches Querque's pallor as well as the bluish half-moons that have lately appeared at the base of each of my fingernails. The room is long and narrow, with a stone fireplace brimful of books at one end. Against one wall, a pressboard desk sags under the weight of several piles of *The Book of Querque*, still in their plastic wrapping. My nose prickles, registering a shift in Querque's peculiar atmosphere, the omnipresent ginger now mixed with ink. Over the mantel, there's a painting: A pale child sprawls on a make-shift bed in a dark cottage. Her parents stand in a shadowed corner, while an old man sits beside her in a cone of lamplight, his chin propped in his hand as if he is considering a tricky problem in long division. When I try to shut the door behind me, it swings open again, as if obeying some secret imperative of Querque's.

Or perhaps my mother, exercising her talent for action at a distance, has bewitched the catch.

Querque turns a bolt high on the door. "Old houses," he says, and shakes his head.

"Yes," I say, taking a seat as far as possible from the maroon recliner that occupies the room's center. Beside it, on the coffee table, brown eggs nestle in a woven basket beside a lit candle and a pad of yellow legal paper.

Querque folds himself like a stork into the recliner.

"My mother—"

"Caskets vouchsafed to the deepest deep," he intones. "Sea burials, small fry."

Instead of the door, it is my breath that catches. He sounds just like my father.

"Your father is not the issue."

Our eyes meet. And hold. Now I know what I am dealing with. My mother was a mind reader too—one of her talents, like sending people away, calling them back.

"First things first." I am not looking at his mouth, only his eyes— a trick I learned from my mother. It is like listening to a statue talk. The slate quality of his irises suffuses his whole being. "*Your* name is Monday."

"No, it's not." I cross my arms over my chest.

"This stiffness will fade in time," he informs me as he hands me a tissue. "That's a nasty cut you've got there, by the way. Blot the seepage, there's a girl. Now, to resume. You are Monday One Thirty. Of course, you are not limited to your scheduled appointment."

I twist the tissue around my bleeding finger and fist my left hand damply into my right. "Where is my father?"

He makes a note in his yellow legal pad.

313

"*Where is my*—"

"You've come a long way," he interrupts, "and now you've been found."

"Like a foundling?" I am making a joke to obscure the fact that I don't understand, but Querque presses his lips together so they turn pale like the rest of him.

"Like a *dwindling*."

He takes an egg from the bowl at his elbow and holds it before the flame. Through the shell, I see the outline of the yolk and, inside it, something curled like a fiddlehead fern. The fetal chick: unborn, perhaps unbearable. He returns the egg to the basket and pinches the candle's wick. Acrid smoke twists up my nose.

"The tree fell away from you. Such things happen."

Querque's tone, which seems intended to comfort, seizes me with anxiety instead. Mother's pencils will need sharpening, her teapot warming, her roughened hands their weekly liniment. Hadn't I proven myself useful? I had, I *know* it, the way I know my multiplication tables, the way I once knew my own name. Soon—very soon—she will realize her mistake.

"I trust Lunette has gone over the house rules. I am particular about locks and closets, as she no doubt has told you. You may not enter the pantry without permission, and the basement is expressly not your affair unless you are working at the loom." His tone, which has been strict, softens. "But my door is always open to you, Monday."

Overhead, the bulb expires with a snap.

"Oh, these old houses!" Twin pink spots appear on Querque's cheeks. "Please, do excuse the light."

In the half dark, he removes his glasses and rubs where they have left angry blotches on either side of his nose. Now there's soot as well—two symmetrical smudges that might stand for anything that unites with a contrary: life and death, mother and father, egg and sperm.

Reality and dream.

I blush.

"You've no idea," he mutters, aiming his words toward the expired ceiling light, "what it takes to run this place." He shakes his head, exasperated.

Of course, I have no idea. Although I recoil from this glimpse into his private universe of home economics, of dead bulbs and decrepit electrical systems—not to mention the thankless edification of children—I am pleased by the bit of trust he's placed in me. Surely Querque does not make *all* his charges privy to his secret frustrations. His disclosure also suggests that the home is a more reassuring place than I'd imagined, involving no witchcraft, none of my mother's sea skulduggery—and no maritime adventuring either. Which, I admit, is a relief.

He fixes me in his cool gaze like a bit of sea wrack pinned to a board, a look that tells me I would be quite wrong to infer anything from his lapse of decorum about the light.

"Let us review. Your name is?"

"Muh," I stammer. "Muh-muh-muh."

A human noise, dwindling. Querque smiles.

"That's the magic," he says, "of the right name. It calls you out. An in-voc-ay-tion."

But I mean: the one I left. The one who left me. His stone irises twist in their veined settings. I flash on a memory from the market at home, where I once saw the butcher pull an eyeball dripping from the head of a freshly killed ox. My mother hurried me along before I could see what he did with the other one. "All that showing off," she huffed, "just to put dinner on the table. The prehistory of an oxtail soup is all it is. No need to glorify it with a performance."

I shove my shredded tissue into my pocket where it will stick to the remains of Lunette's lollipop.

"Say something, Monday. You are a naughty oyster withholding its pearl."

"Muh." One syllable. How many oysters contain more than one pearl?

"Try again. You can do it."

"*Mutt*," I conclude, letting my tongue touch the roof of my mouth. What a revelation, to let anything touch anything else. I tingle all over, hot and cold at once, a single tap through which opposing impulses roar. Yet hadn't my tongue been in my mouth all along? Perhaps the butcher's ox was just a dream.

"Mutton," Querque sighs. His stomach squeals. Mutton had once been a patient, perhaps. Was she turned into a soup? At any rate, he's got *me* pegged: My appetite has always been a problem. I glorify imaginary soup, and reject real lollipops, even when someone puts one in my hand.

"Mutt," I croak, to recall Querque from his lamb-chop reverie. Already I want to mean more to him than Mutton, whoever *she* is. Was. "Mutt, mutt, MUTT!"

Dr. Querque's eyes flick in their sockets—a torpid, reptilian look.

315

Is—*was!*—that my heart?

"Good girl."

> The Axiom of Perfection: Nothing's made that's not first dreamed with great precision. Thus, to make a perfect child, pour equal parts sweet and dry vermouth over ice. The perfection of the result will depend on the exactness of your measurements.

We number twenty—ten boys, ten girls—and range in age from seven to twelve. At ten apiece, the boy Fobb and I form a kind of hinge, with equal numbers of older and younger children arrayed on either side of us, like wings. It is not much, but it is enough to cement a friendship, of sorts.

The day begins with Washing Up. On cold mornings we punch the washbowl's scrim of ice before sluicing ourselves wide-awake and shivering. Breakfast in the dining hall is porridge, coffee, sometimes milk. Lunette administers the first of three daily doses of Happiness Elixir, which I swallow penitentially, mouthfuls of scummed lake. After breakfast, we take turns using the Happy Lights, a row of large boxes that emit a bluish glow in which we are each expected to bask for thirty minutes. Next comes Useful Work: vegetable peeling, sweep and mop, polishing the foyer's woodwork angels. In the kitchen, we learn the infinite and various divisibility of food: chop, julienne, dice, mince, slice. Lunch is whatever Lunette dreams into existence at her typewriter, followed by more elixir. Each afternoon has its own special task: *Looming*, in which we work the home's basement loom, spooling out lengths of gray velveteen; *Foraging*, in which we gather mushrooms from the woods, or wild chives, according to Lunette's whim and the day's menu; and *Group*, which involves sitting in a circle and complaining about each other while Lunette looks on and occasionally dispenses advice, a reprimand, or just some mysterious proverb like "It don't rain—but it do, it do," "No good deed goes unpolished," or, my favorite, "Mind your peas—*and* your queues." The older children are also required to *Leaflet*, a task that involves distributing pamphlets about the home to passersby. What Querque grandly calls our "literature" is only saddle-stitched Xerox pages stuck with a card that gives Querque's contact information, his official headshot—in which he wears a slight smile and the everlasting velveteen coat—and the home's slogan in large serif: DR. QUERQUE'S HOME FOR DWINDLERS. WE'LL FINISH THEM OFF SO YOU DON'T HAVE TO! As I distribute pamphlets, I stand straighter, smile brighter—all that time before the Happy Lights must shine through my eyes, and my chipped tooth should be a beacon, just in case one of the women on the street happens to be my mother. She never is. Even so, I press my leaflets on everyone, but with incrementally less enthusiasm as the weeks pass.

As my enthusiasm flags, my guilt increases, until I am sure that my mother did not forsake me. Rather, *I* was the one who abandoned *her*. A sin for which I am sure to be punished: Despite raging hunger, I eat only morsels and I say nothing for days at a time, the better to insure my invisibility, which conveniently both confers protection and punishes me in advance.

This perversity is why, once a week, like everyone else, I have a *Session with Querque.*

Sometimes Lunette will assign a special task, like spider collector or hedgerow trimmer—a job that Fobb got once and lost again almost immediately, for he used the cleaver to slice the tail off the neighbor's pig. He offered it to Lunette, who cuffed him, and sent me across the yard with a dollar and a typed apology, which I dropped into a puddle so that it turned into a robin and flew away. I was sure I would receive a scolding, but when I skulked back to the kitchen Lunette was by the hearth, seizing the tail in a bright fire. She waved me over, and offered me a bite. My mouth ran with juice, and for a moment I nearly remembered my name.

Sometimes, instead of Group, Lunette equips us with shovels and buckets and sends us to the beach to dig up clams that she steams, reserving the liquid for the next batch of elixir.

Only Querque is allowed to answer the phone.

When we play the Name Game, Fobb starts us off, waving Lunette's broom as we circle the butcher block, slipping on the tiles.

Fobb menaces a fish-faced girl with the broom.

How do you say his name?

The point is to reply before someone touches you and makes you It.

"You say it like murky!" She skitters away, laughing. "Murky" is one of the easy answers.

Fobb nears; I duck into the pantry.

"Jerky!" Screamed by a boy who wears headgear all night long to straighten his overbite.

Fobb toes open the pantry door and locks eyes with me.

HOW DO YOU SAY HIS NAME?

Murky. Jerky. "Tetrazzini turkey!" I shout, in my excitement setting

317

a row of pans clanging with my elbow. Lunette materializes, summoned by our noise.

"Children," she says, shooing us, "are a lot of work."

Later, a batch of Happy Crackers crisps in the oven, filling the house with such an atmosphere of molasses that I abandon my dull post at the loom, where I am watching to make sure nothing snags, and run to the kitchen. Lunette roosts on a stool, shelling peas.

"Lunette," I muse, rolling her name in my wet mouth as I root in the sink, looking for the molasses spoon, which surely has not been washed yet. "That's a lovely monocle."

"Monocle *de mon oncle*," she quips with a smile and touches her pince-nez, which even I know has nothing to do with a monocle. "In other words, don't be ridiculous."

"I *shall* be ridiculous." I love how she speaks, how she smiles, how she sits and shells her peas. I sidle over, the molasses spoon wholly forgotten. Lunette flicks her towel—*no, no*—but I am too fast. The stolen pea tastes *green*, the greenest green imaginable: I am eating a bean field, a pine forest, a thicket of holly. Lunette eyes me, and I grin, a green grin, one that is not bright or straight but lets her know that I am happy even though she says words, like *mon oncle*, that I don't understand.

Attracted by the tiled floor's diver, I plop down beside him and push a runaway pea into the grout, greening it to match my tongue, which must be green as a meadow by now.

"Tsk," she clucks. "Don't make work."

"I miss my mother," I murmur to the squished pea.

Lunette grabs a towel. Two swipes and the pea is gone, a mess I never made. She folds the towel just so and hangs it on the oven door, so even the stain is concealed. A tile dolphin smiles at me and flits away.

"Lunette, I miss my mother!" I am wailing. Querque has warned me about this, how easily my moods monsoon me.

"Get off the floor," Lunette commands. She sets me on a stool and looks me straight in the eye. "Nobody ever wants it to end the way it did." Lunette's face is sweet and sour, the one combination I am completely unable to resist. "But all things end, all the time. Still we roll, like beans in a bottle. Just like your daddy. We roll all round the world."

Tears spill from me, even as Lunette's expression hardens. This is as much genuine instruction as anyone has yet given me here at the home, and no one except Querque has ever mentioned my father, or even noticed that I might have one. My breathing is ragged, as if my lungs are being sliced like loaves. Perhaps that is why the home is so austere, why even Lunette's eyes at times remind me of nothing so much as the knives on the wall. Kindness, if it exists at all, is a blade—and it is serrated. Could children die of it? I don't recall if this problem is addressed in *The Book of Querque.*

"I leave the question" is what Querque always says, when he concludes a lecture, "as an exercise for the reader."

> The Axiom of Soup: When upset, the typical Dwindler easily boils over, *comme une soupe de lait.* When things cool down, the unpleasant result is always the same: a thin skin and a lingering odor.

Querque is such a busy man! He has so many responsibilities, he can never take a vacation. For without him, what would become of us? Who would walk the Home Boundary, checking for intrusions? Who would remind us to swallow our doses of elixir, to Do Useful Work, to Take Exercise, to worship at our Happy Lights? Who would make all those notes in the special yellow pads, writing down all the forgettable things we say? And who would punish us for infractions, like talking out of turn or clamming up in session, sneaking to the quays instead of having a Soothing Snack? Our mothers, we repeat from *The Book of Querque,* did their best, but we would be too much for anyone.

What is the proof? At night, in dreams, we're too much, even for ourselves.

"Mermaids!"

"Giant squid!"

"No-eyed sole!"

News of these and other wonders filters from bed to bed in whispers after lights-out. We dream in unison, drifting on drafts of sleep, each colder than the last, until we reach the deepest deep. In the morning, the unity of our slumber shatters with the crusts that fall from our eyes as we take our turns at the washbowl, the shock of an elbow jammed into the ribs as we spill down the stairs. At times, in the night, I sense a presence by my bed. Although in the morning I am sure it was only Lunette, coming to check on me, in my sleep, I shiver, and dream of long division.

One night, the dormitory buzzes with a different rumor, as fantastic in its way as mermaids or one-eyed sole: Once upon a time, Querque had a wife! Her name was Friday Last. That no one has actually seen

319

her only serves to further stimulate our humming collective imagination. She is said to be a ghost, and to wear, variously, jodhpurs, a
gray velveteen tracksuit, or a porkpie hat; she prunes the orchard at
midnight, leaving tiny apples all around, and sometimes rattles the
pans in the kitchen. The younger children say she popped from his
head like Athena, and, sure enough, over his right eyebrow, there is
a small scar. Or else she sprang from notes on Querque's yellow legal
pad, making her the sum of our remarks. Which, in point of fact—or,
more precisely, fancy—she most likely is, which is why I suffer my
shameful fantasies of Mutton in absolute silence. (I confess her name
bothers me terribly. Surely, in moments of passion, Querque must
call her something else. Lamb Chop perhaps?) As usual, Fobb has a
different take: He whispers that once upon a time, this mythological
wife was a real Dwindling like us, a girl by the name of Monday At
Four, and that she was my clone in all but my sex.

I've changed a lot since coming to the home, but I'm still a girl as
far as I know. I smooth the rough blanket down over my chest and
hips. "My sex?"

"Which is thus far indeterminate," he sneers.

It is true: I am as yet unhipped, unbreasted. Fobb makes such mischief. With one offhand remark, I am overwhelmed with envy. If
only I had more to eat, if only the dormitory were not so cold. I burrow under my insufficient covers, pulling the blanket over my ears
in order to block out Fobb's giggling. As for Friday Last: I hate her.

One afternoon the phone rings in the hallway, where I am polishing the angels, but Querque is nowhere to be found. When I heave
the front door open, to be sure he's not on the stoop, an idea arrives:
That is my mother, *my mother*, on the line! The wind picks up, so
fresh it might have blown my father back from the sea; I mean, it
carries the same conviction, the same odor of iron and salt. Yet to
answer the phone is expressly forbidden and I have no idea what sort
of punishment I might incur. No one, to my knowledge, has ever
dared so much naughtiness under Querque's roof.

The ringing stops. I rub lemon polish into an angel's mouth until
it squeaks, and stuff the cloth into my own. After months of elixir,
Group, and Sessions with Querque, all that remains of my mother is
the memory of her kitchen, sharded with gray sea light. *Stand straight!
Smile bright!* No use. I sink through a fug of lemon polish, wetting
my dress on the floor I've just cleaned. The angels shine: *O, O, O.*

Elixir time! Lunette comes with the bottle, her pocket bristling
with scoured spoons. I drag myself from the floor, and follow her into

the kitchen, where I swallow my dose without a thought in my head.

"A good cry helps sometimes," Lunette tells me as she peers into my mouth. Her suspicions are unnecessary; in six months I have come a long way from my days of wincing and spitting up. I nod, staring at my shoes so I don't have to meet her eyes. She must have heard me sobbing in the foyer. She moves on to Fobb, who takes his medicine, or appears to, but before she can check his mouth he ducks away. All at once I understand: He is not grinning because the elixir is working, but because he knows it is a lie.

Lunette regards Fobb as if he were a son whose future was less than assured.

And whose fault is that, I ask Querque the next day, in session. Or I try to, anyway. My mouth opens and closes but no sound comes out.

"Be bold, be bold!" Querque is in an expansive mood. His velveteen jacket has a feathery luster, and underneath he wears a bright red sweater, an ensemble that makes him look just like the robin that carried off Lunette's apology. Does he know *all* my secrets? He cocks his head expectantly and I wriggle, pleased all over.

He frowns. If he is a robin, I might be a worm.

"Well, not *too* bold," he says, looking at me sidelong, in one of the bucket-of-cold-water appraisals he'd written about. It is recommended for a young man, I seem to recall, who is getting in too deep with a lady.

He says: "Some faults are basic, like fissures in the earth. Death Valley has quite a few of them. Thus the name."

"The name."

"You are still angry about your name."

At once, I seethe. I am about to become that dreaded pedagogical catastrophe, the terrible *soupe de lait*. If I ever cool down, a smelly skin will replace my own, and no one will whisper to me anymore after lights-out. Yet I hadn't known I was angry until he said I was, which makes no sense at all. I shake my head to dispel the hiss that has invaded it, the final warning before I boil over. To let off steam, I complain about Lunette:

"Why won't Lunette brush my hair?"

"It is too tempting to smack you with the brush."

"Why won't she run the bath?"

"It is too tempting to drown you."

"And the ironing?"

321

"Again, a temptation. Aren't you avoiding something?"

"How so?" I'm confused. "I thought she loved me."

"*Loved* you? Think, Monday. The hot iron, your young skin."

Which suddenly smells slightly off. Unless the odor is coming from that dirty hovel, the one in the painting that hangs over the book-filled fireplace. The father rests his hand on the mother's shoulder as she sobs into the crook of her arm. The lampshade is askew. Such noise, such disorder, such insufficient light—

"What is it, Monday?"

From the plate I pick the last Happy Cracker, only to set it down again.

"Is she dead?" I wonder, pointing to the painting.

He sets down his yellow legal pad: "We have to stop."

"*Is she dead?*"

"That will be all, Monday."

I reach for something solid, a cockle shell, a lump of sea glass. My hand closes over a palmful of air.

> The Axiom of Slumber: Regiment sleep as everything else—enough to ensure productivity, but not so much that your charges are tumbled into promiscuous dreams. Excessive contact with this realm will only distract them from their new reality.

At the sink, Lunette washes up under water so hot her hands turn the scalded pink of the pigs' heads I've seen piled at the market, their white-lashed eyes shut forever against us, because they have seen too much of the things we do out of our bottomless need: our failures to attend session, take our elixir, use our lights.

"I've just been to the butcher's," Lunette announces, apparently unaware of the crimson dots on her velveteen apron. One of Fobb's mischiefs, I conclude, at the loom.

"I'm sorry he called you a swine, Lunette," Fobb replies, not missing a beat.

"Filthy, filthy." Lunette shakes her hands dry and the droplets fly off like diamonds, like stars. Querque would insist that I choose—*Choice is what made you human*, he repeats, until I want to bray, to howl, to chitter like a bat, all at once—but I can't. I want those water droplets to be both diamonds and stars; above all, I want the water to be something other than what it is: nasty, Querquefied water that has been embittered by its journey through Querque's nasty pipes.

These days, I hate Querque with all my heart, and I love Lunette with equal intensity.

"Pigs are smart," I offer, wrung out with longing. "They have big brains."

"And curly tails!" Fobb pulls my pigtail. I make a grab for him, but he is too fast. As he skips from the room, he flings something long and sinuous against the far wall. It drops to the tiles, then slithers beneath a gap in the molding. I put my hands to my head. Has my hair turned to snakes? The knives fall to the floor in a bright clatter, causing Lunette to curse before collecting them in her apron. I bite my lip, in order to have a better reason to cry.

"Headcheese," she says, when she has replaced the last blade, a demilune mincer that cuts scallions to ribbons as thin as she has lately become. "Sweetbreads."

This is not the reprimand I am expecting for having provoked Fobb to yet another mischief. *Sweetbreads*, I repeat, under my breath. A word that is exactly what it says, sweet and satisfying in my mouth. But I am on Carb Control. No sweets, no bread. Querque doesn't like dense girls. *Starvation resets the system.* So it is writ, in *The Book of Querque.*

That night, when I stick my legs under the covers, the sheet stops at my ankles. I twist free of the bedclothes, kicking against the current that threatens to pull me away.

"Settle down," Lunette growls from the corner where she rocks, knitting the blankets that cover us while we sleep, that protect us from the wind blowing in from the window (Querque's dictum: Fresh air!).

I flop over, only to choke on a cloud of foul powder. Not only have I been short sheeted, but my pillow has been turned into a flour sack. Fobb! The mischief maker, the thief in the kitchen, the bad boy who sleeps by the door like an on-the-outs god.

"Back to bed!" Lunette's bark harries me down the corridor. A bony leg shoots out from the dark. I land on my rump. Tears and snot spurt from me. But before I can bawl, Fobb is there, his hand clapped over my mouth.

"Shh." Fobb, crouching, blows on my scraped palms, a tenderness that closes my throat. I pull my hands away and blow on them myself. He stands: "Follow me."

"Where are we going?"

"To the basement."

"But that's off-limits!"

Diane Greco Josefowicz

"Come on."

In the basement Fobb has fixed the loom so that when he turns the crank, the velveteen that shoots out the other end bears a looping pattern that, on closer inspection, is a series of scrawled words. Bad ones, the kind my father and mother would exchange sometimes in the middle of the night when they, in their passion, were unmindful of my ears.

"Fobb!"

"Shh!"

Eyes shut, Fobb stands at the loom in a blind trance, skimming his palms over the fabric. "Say it loud, say it quick, everybody knows you're sick, sick, SICK!"

I dash away—up the stairs, out the back door, and down the street to the sea. It is a calm night, the sky dense with stars, and silent, apart from the regular brush of waves on the shore. Fobb arrives, breathing hard. Not speaking, we explore the beach. Turtles have been depositing eggs in nests and covering them with sand. Now the turtles are returning to the ocean. Fobb and I make our truce, and all night long we ride the turtles. Which one will see my father, which will get caught in his outboard motor, which will wind up as his evening meal, a turtle stew? Holding hands, we make it all the way to the water, a prince and a princess borne along by elephants to a faraway wedding chamber, where my mother and father had met, and might be induced to meet again, once they understand that I have made the long journey to find them.

> The Axiom of Fasting: The longer the fast, the better the lesson is learned. Under consistently maintained conditions of near starvation, your teachings will take on an abalone fastness, glittering and hard.

The next day, there's no sign of turtles on the beach, but our foraging nevertheless bears such an unusual quantity of *frutti di mare* that, at midday, we return with a full bushel of tiny clams that Lunette turns into dinner: spaghetti, vongole.

That evening, Fobb discovers in his spaghetti a clam that did not open during Lunette's steaming. I must have missed it during prep. This is how we know, Lunette says, scowling at me, that the clam is rotten.

Fobb tosses the bad clam up and down.

"Who's rotten?" I demand to know. I am out of sorts because, of course, Lunette is right. The implication is obvious: I am that clam.

324

It hits me between the eyes and lands in my spaghetti. Fobb whoops: Bull's-eye! I cry and cry.

"Spaghetti is nothing to cry about," Lunette consoles me. Her apron is a scrap from the loom. I recognize, with horror, the variegated pattern from the night that Fobb and I were down there. And her eyes—her eyes!—are ringed with such darkness, all the nights I refused to sleep. "On second thought, maybe I should have butterflied a lamb."

Mutton's fate. My face is flaming, my tears are hot, but the rest of me goes cold as vichyssoise. "No, Lunette!"

"All this screaming and for what? Wipe your eyes," she instructs me, handing me a napkin. It too is stenciled with obscenities that are apparently only visible to me. "And eat your dinner."

Her tone is bitter as the monarch butterfly to the bird who consumes it; this is what keeps the monarch safe. Numbly, I spoon clam broth into my mouth. I will never be so bitter. I will never be that safe.

During washing up, the setting sun cinches the sky, shaping it up, notch by notch, on the way to the horizon. The dishwater roars down the drain, headed like everything else for the sea. I slip away, into the pantry, without a thought in my head beyond the usual, straight and bright. But the pantry is empty. Even Lunette's typewriter is gone. My compass, shining in the sunset that reflects off the glass cabinet panes, has been jabbed into the wall, where it holds up a sign: FEAST YOUR EYES—AND NOTHING ELSE!

The door creaks. Is it the monkey wind, my distant mother's craft, the woodwork angels at last finding their tongues?

"Monday?" Querque calls, from beyond the threshold.

I brim and fizz, *une soupe de lait*. It takes only a moment to dislodge my compass, which I grip in my fist with the point turned out, thinking only to finish the job that butcher started. I'll take Fobb with me when I go; his naughtiness, after all, is what gets me through. Dusk breathes me in, straight and bright. Hold.

325

Buddy

Georges-Olivier Châteaureynaud

—Translated from French by Edward Gauvin

ANN DARROW'S FIRST MEETING with Joseph marked as much of a turning point in her film career as in her personal life. After glory, tragedy, and great adventure early on had come a time of bad breaks: breaking several contracts over her pregnancy, breaking up with her lover John Driscoll, and breaking away, with the birth of her son, from her own family. Shocked and disillusioned by the coldheartedness of those from whom she'd expected sympathy and understanding, she chose exile. Besides, the papers—those terrible American tabloids!— were on her scent. Reporters sniffed around her home like dogs around a rabbit hole. She needed to find a safe haven, settle in, hide her child, and try to make a fresh start, to change her life. Ann had a few assets at her disposal: her talent, her beauty, her blondness. She chose Germany. Not because of the National Socialist Party, but because Carl Denham had put in a good word for her with a Berlin producer he knew. But they were hardly hurting for blondes over there. The producer had nothing more to offer her than bit parts in a few B movies. For lack of anything better, she took these crumbs, which at least afforded her clothes, food, rent in Berlin, and room and board for her son in Thuringia. She'd found a place for him with a family on a secluded farm near Hildburghausen. She had a few difficult years: irregular second-rate gigs, living in hotels, fly-by-night affairs some- times just to get by. The skies didn't clear up till 1936. Just when she began to despair of ever building a second career in Europe, she be- came acquainted with Joseph Goebbels.

A romance soon began between the beautiful Ann and the seduc- tive dwarf. As the Reich minister of culture and propaganda, Goeb- bels controlled the German film industry. Amongst young actresses anxious to make a career, he behaved like a fox in a henhouse. A few days after their first (or perhaps second) date, Ann Darrow signed the UFA contract she'd been dreaming of ever since coming to Berlin. Until 1941—that is, until the US entered the war—she starred in several films shot at Babelsberg, amusements and trifles one and all.

Only a few odd reels survive the Allied bombings. In these, she appears most often in a bathing suit, playing a pretty, haughty, or featherbrained Yank.

Thus the child—his first nanny, a Frenchwoman who'd immigrated to California, had with unthinking mischief nicknamed him Quiconque, or Anybody, and the diminutive "Buddy" had stuck with him—grew up in the Germany of the 1930s. The country had just fallen into the hands of intellectually, or rather spiritually, narrow-minded men hostile to life's essential disorderliness. The Nazis expected to sift through Creation, removing everything not to their taste—everything but themselves. It so happened that Buddy didn't meet the racial criteria in force at the time. One can be sure he would have wound up being euthanized in Hadamar or at Schloss Hartheim had it not been for his American citizenship.

It would seem the minister was quite smitten, for he didn't withdraw his protection from Ann even after she'd shown him her son. The truth was a bit more complicated. Let us say their relationship was not lastingly affected.

However fickle, Joseph Goebbels highly valued the idea of family, as he proved a few years later by deciding that his wife and six children would accompany him in death. He had long been surprised, without quite knowing why, that Ann should continue to live far from her son—after all, her financial situation would have made it possible for her to keep him nearby.

"Why this exile in Thüringen, *meine Liebling*? That woman who looks after him, Frau Rübenschnaps, is no doubt an excellent Teutonic nanny, but there's the danger she'll give him too *bäuerlich* an education. Do you want to make a yokel of him? Bring him back, hire a nanny or two. The UFA will pay for it; I'll have them throw it in your contract!"

In the face of Ann's evasive replies, doubt wormed its way into his mind.

"What on earth is going on with that boy? He wouldn't . . . By any chance, perhaps, he wouldn't be a bit . . . ?"

The young woman's vigorous denials temporarily reassured him. But soon the same doubt forced its way into his mind once more. It would be most unfortunate for a man in his position to find his mistress—one of many, of course, but one to whom he devoted a great deal of time, and on whose behalf he had intervened with the UFA!—the mother of a racially defective child. For no one, not even Joseph Goebbels, could afford to believe himself untouchable under the Third

Reich. Beneath the feet of each and every citizen, from the humblest to the most powerful, the moles—the mole Himmler, the mole Heydrich, the mole Müller—were digging their tunnels, their ditches, their traps. One day the earth would open up and the victim vanish into the dark, no matter the rank or status they'd held until then. Torn between a sincere fondness for Ann and fear of exposing his flank on her account to the dagger someone hiding in the shadows surely contemplated planting in him, Joseph tried again. Without airing his suspicions, but with an insistence Ann could not mistake, Joseph demanded that Buddy be presented to him. Ann tried to dodge his request. However, her deferrals and tergiversations only managed to fix the idea in Joseph's head that there was something fishy going on. She had to give in. He succeeded in freeing an entire day of his minister's schedule and, one October morning, leaving the Mercedes-Benz and its pennants behind for more discreet transport, they started out for Hildburghausen.

The way led through mist and dead leaves, a henchman at the wheel. In the backseat, Joseph sometimes turned from the muddled autumn grays and browns to gaze at Ann. His eyes smiled, but not his thin lips. Had she really done *that* to him? Thrown herself at him, perhaps under orders, still slimy from a degrading embrace, a disgusting birth? If that was the case, he'd crush her without pity. Like all his peers, he had a private army at his disposal—on a different scale, of course, from those of Himmler and Göring, but from whose ranks he could easily pick three loyal men willing to nab Ann and sink her in a concrete coffin. As for the brat—probably the hideous fruit of casual Hollywood copulation—there'd always be a nearby well to drop him down. No one at the UFA would worry about asking where Ann Darrow had gone. Those American girls were so flighty! They'd think she'd gone back home on a whim, and that would be that.

Contemplating the young woman whose body he had covered with kisses that very morning, and whom he readied himself to make disappear, Joseph couldn't help but admit how stunningly her skin shone in the light, how perfectly symmetrical her face was, how bona fide her blondness, and how awful it would be to ruin all of that. What else could he do? He was loyal. If her child's features proved her innocent, Ann would not be punished. Quite the opposite: He'd spoil them both, he'd become the unhappy bastard's favorite uncle. He'd give him an electric train set, a pair of lederhosen stitched with edelweiss, even a pony. . . . He'd oversee his education and, when the time came, he would use his influence to get him admitted to Heidelberg or Jena.

After many hours on the road, the henchman, following Ann's directions, parked the car in the courtyard of a farmhouse that was in such a poor state, thought Joseph, it might have been French. Cow pies, horse dung, chicken and duck droppings littered the uneven earth, which was pocked with stinking puddles and slurry trickles fed by an abandoned manure heap. Broken farm implements with blackened, worm-eaten handles were strewn about, iron crusted and blistered by rust. Beside a pond, the wreck of a tractor in the last stages of collapse resembled the rotting carcass of a prehistoric monster beneath the low sky. Joseph pinched his nose and pursed his lips. Such slovenliness did not bode well. Clearly, the Rübenschnapses were not model Germanic farmers. Had they been, in fact, they would never have allowed a dubious child—for dubious Buddy doubtless was—under their roof.

"Joseph—"

He felt Ann's hand fall on his own.

"Yes?"

"Do you really insist on seeing him?" Ann's voice trembled. He stiffened. Those who, like him, formed the vanguard of the new human race had no right to the weaknesses of the old. The unspeakable rags of the old race—wrinkled, soiled, threadbare—he had at any moment to be ready to tear them off and cast them into the fire.

"I came for exactly that, *meine Liebe*," he replied.

"Then come."

She got out of the car and, without waiting for him, headed for the main building. Before following her, Joseph told his henchman to take a walk along the road and have a cigarette.

The farmyard dog—mangy, of course, some shepherd not quite German—didn't manage a bark, strangling as he was with rage at the end of a chain thankfully too short to let him devour the visitors.

Joseph entered the house on Ann's heels. Inside it smelled of clabber, twice-cooked cabbage, stale pipe tobacco, the vomit of newborns, and assorted stenches no one was in a hurry to identify. It had been a long time since a comparable olfactory cocktail had been visited upon the nostrils of the minister of culture and propaganda, but his curiosity prevailed. He suppressed both a retch and the accompanying desire to turn back. He pushed on behind Ann, into the very belly of the dwelling. Everywhere his gaze fell, he saw children in the half shadow that suffused the premises: children of both sexes and all ages, all runny nosed and badly groomed, all pale, scrofulous, and ridden with rickets to varying degrees, some clinically retarded, at least one afflicted with a genuine hump, another with a clubfoot, and still another with a harelip. But as he inspected this living catalogue of misfortunes and infirmities, Joseph prayed for one of these gnomes—it didn't matter which—to throw itself into Ann's arms with a cry of "Mommy!" For twisted, misshapen, and defective as they were, they looked Aryan at least, and all worth more than a son of David, even were he the most beautiful child on earth.

"Frau Darrow! I wasn't expecting you. We said—" It was the Rübenschnaps woman, in rubber boots and a gray apron, a child under each arm and one or two more to come in her belly, all breasts and haunches as befit the favorite, most docile, and most fertile daughter of a God of the flesh.

"Hello, Frau Rübenschnaps. A chance to visit came up, so we dropped by to see Buddy. *Mein Herr* is a friend."

"A friend, yes!" whispered Joseph in a small voice, hurriedly putting on a pair of sunglasses incongruous in the half dark.

"Is Buddy in his room?" Ann asked.

"Yes, you can go up. He's playing with his paper dolls. What a sweet boy he is, Frau Darrow! Like I always tell Herr Rübenschnaps, that's the kind of son you should give me, instead of these animals who spend their time fighting with one another."

"Thank you, Frau Rübenschnaps. We'll go up now."

"You'll come down later for some coffee, won't you? I whipped up a fresh batch of medlar macaroons to go with. *Mispelmakronen* are a specialty of the house. I'm sure you'll love them, Herr . . . Herr—"

"Herr Herold. Hans Herold," Joseph muttered.

"Well, be sure to have some of my *Mispelmakronen*, Herr Herold. They're awfully good! Buddy just stuffs himself with them!"

"Thank you, Frau Rübenschnaps," Ann said once more. "See you in a little while!"

Ann and Joseph hurried up the stairs. On the second floor, Ann strode without slowing past two rooms, or rather two dormitories, where the remaining rabble squabbled or slept fitfully. At last, at the end of the hall, she stopped before a closed door and turned to her companion.

"Joseph, promise me—"

Suddenly beside himself, he shoved her against the wall. "I promise nothing. Nothing!"

Abruptly, he opened the door and charged in. The room was small, but bright and well ventilated. A bed, a wardrobe, a shelf bowed with books, toys and comics everywhere. Facing the window, at an old desk covered with cutout paper soldiers, was a strange creature. He'd jumped the instant Joseph's sudden entrance had torn him from play, and his face had taken on a fearful expression. But his fear subsided when he spotted Ann through the open door, past the stranger's shoulder. Stupefied, Joseph was frozen in the middle of the room. It was Ann's turn to brush him brusquely aside, and insert herself between him and her son. Eyes bulging, finger rigid, the most brilliant orator in Germany was speechless.

"But Ann . . . he's—he's not . . . *Gott im Himmel*, Ann, why he's . . . He's an . . ."

"No!" Ann cried with all her being.

There was at least one way, even two, in which Buddy would have satisfied one of those biotypology tests the Nazis so adored: He had blue eyes, and he was blond as wheat. Beyond that, nothing in his physiognomy nor general aspect would confirm an assumption of Aryanness, or Jewishness. He defied such simplistic categories in the most radical way. Beneath a low and rough-skinned forehead, a pronounced brow hooded little blue eyes overflowing with trust and tenderness since they'd settled on Ann. His large nostrils flexed skyward as if to collect a waft of beneficent scent, his receding chin disappeared under a large mouth with almost prehensile lips. If he was blond as wheat, it was *head to toe*. His head, his cheeks, his neck, the backs of his hands, his wrists, the sturdy legs his shorts left bare— every visible inch of skin was covered in the same silken and curly tow-colored hair. Buddy all by himself was blonder than a squad of Hitlerjugend. Solidly built despite his youth, he was a good head taller than Joseph Goebbels.

From the formidable lummox came a child's voice. "*Mutti! Mutti!* What a happy surprise! But who's that man, and why is he frowning?"

"He's a friend . . . a good friend, a great friend! He's surprised because he thinks you're very big and very strong. It's my fault: I told him you were my little pumpkin."

"I'm not your little pumpkin anymore?"

"Silly darling! Of course you are!"

Dumbfounded, Joseph made as if to beat a retreat. "I, uh . . . can I wait for you downstairs, Ann? After all, I need to try Frau Rübenschnaps's *Mispelmakronen*."

An abruptly imperious look from Ann nailed him to the spot.

331

"Now, Joseph, you must say hello to the boy," she told him in a low voice, "or he'll be confused."

Then, in a louder voice, she turned to her son. "Buddy, may I present—"

Joseph cut her off. "Hello, Buddy! My name's Hans Herold. But it'd be easier if you just called me Uncle Hans."

Buddy stared at him with a curiosity still lightly tinged with worry. "Why did you burst into my room so suddenly, Uncle Hans?"

"Because he was eager to meet you, pumpkin," said Ann.

"It's true," stammered Joseph. "Your mommy talks about you all the time."

"Mommy loves me very much," Buddy said. "Are you going to love me very much too?"

"Yes, yes . . . of course!"

The afternoon passed like a dream. They asked each other riddles, played charades, and made Buddy's paper soldiers march in file. He had cookie tins full of soldiers. These soldiers never fought wars; they satisfied themselves with parading in review before the officials in their stands. Buddy didn't have actual officials. Animals from a cardboard zoo worked just as well. Thus did the army of the *Krönprinz* (the cutouts came from pictures at least twenty years old, which Frau Rübenschnaps bought at the grocer's in the nearest village) pay its respects to a group of seals, bears, apes, and giraffes. When Uncle Hans's legs hurt from crouching over the parade, they went down to have medlar macaroons. The nanny hadn't lied: Buddy was crazy about them. Uncle Hans deigned to nibble at a few, which he slipped into a bowl of drab coffee Frau Rübenschnaps had served. Ann seemed happy. The so-called Hans Herold reflected that he was not that unhappy either.

Joseph adored Buddy. The little bit of childhood that, despite everything, survived in the minister's soul marveled at this extraordinary cherub, so strong and yet so gentle, so oddly wise. Even better— Buddy was not subject to the Nuremberg Laws, which spared Joseph from wiping him and his mother off the surface of the earth.

Both equally relieved—for Ann had harbored the worst fears about this meeting—the lovers did not return to Berlin that night. Having left Hildburghausen a bit late, they stopped in Saxony for dinner and spent the night in a comfortable *gasthaus*, where they made love with renewed fervor.

From that day on, Joseph's protection extended to Buddy's round, blond, curly-haired head, not merely as the offspring of a favored mistress, but on a more personal level, for Buddy was in his good book. Sometimes, in the middle of one of his momentous tasks, Joseph would stop for a moment. An inscrutable smile would float briefly over his face. Was he thinking of the Führer? The Party? The People? Blood? Germanic art? Not at all! He saw once more, in the damp light of an autumn day in Thuringia, Buddy bent over his *Grenadieren* lined up before the stands full of tigers and sea lions, and his smile turned serene. It never lasted, of course. He came back to earth and called upon a captive audience to serve the Reich better still, or dictated to short-haired novelists the themes of their next peasant sagas.

By the time Germany added America to its already long list of official enemies, relations between Ann and Joseph had grown sporadic. With her former lover's approval, Ann had married a UFA director, the perpetrator of several comedies of the kind mentioned earlier, in which she'd starred. Hard times were, successively, to transform this harmless filmmaker into a director of patriotic documentaries, a war correspondent on the Russian front, an impromptu soldier, then a deserter, then a corpse.

A hero's widow, Ann could have tried to brave the Gestapo's habitual hostility toward American nationals in an attempt to relaunch her career. During their final meeting, Joseph persuaded her not to. All Germany was crumbling beneath Allied bombs: films and everything else. Besides, what parts would Ann be able to land? The time for slapstick and love songs was long past. The UFA was mustering its last forces to shoot Colditz. The studios were closing one after another, the leading men and ingenues receiving draft papers at last, the gaffers learning to handle another kind of spotlight, and the set dressers to camouflage howitzers.

In the secrecy of his office, Joseph advised Ann to take a long vacation—in Switzerland, for instance. She didn't want to hear of it. Buddy, who'd become a colossal adolescent, had enrolled in the Waffen-SS. The gentle creature of Hildburghausen had not turned into a ferocious beast. Buddy had had no other goal in seeking to enlist than to protect *Mutti*, the Führer, Uncle Hans, Herr and Frau Rübenschnaps, and all their grimy, drooling brood, which had only gotten larger as time passed. Big and strong as he was, he felt it his duty to shield those he loved with his body. He cared for neither ideology nor military glory, and would have been well suited to the Wehrmacht. However, at the time, forgetful of principles before the extent of its losses, the Waffen-SS was reduced to admitting almost anyone to

333

its ranks. This laxity was not to everyone's taste. Hearing talk of a seven-foot blond, blue-eyed volunteer, an SS recruitment officer exercised his preemptive right. Alerted by Ann, Joseph discreetly intervened. Buddy was selected for officer school. No one would dare discharge a cadet backed by one of the highest-ranking despots in the regime. Enrolled in the Junkerschule at Bad Tölz on the recommendation of Joseph Goebbels, Buddy could only have graduated first in his class.

By the end of 1944, first and last were doomed to the same fate. The cleaver Germany had wielded for so long at the expense of its victims had at last been wrenched from its hands, and henceforth would fall on the Fatherland's own quivering flesh. It missed Buddy by a hair. For his baptism by fire, he was buried by a shell, unearthed by a second, once more buried by a third, and narrowly saved from suffocating by the explosion of a fourth. Next, he had the luck to survive several waves of Russian armored cars, attacks by Polish flame-throwers, British machine-gun volleys, Yankee bombing runs, and even French snipers. For all these exploits, he found himself awarded the last Iron Cross of the war, second class, which was also the last one left at the bottom of the box. Today he lives in Hildburghausen, where he works a farm with his wife, Hilda, nee Rübenschnaps. She's given him handsome children, sturdy and agile, who help in the fields when they aren't spending whole days up in the trees.

From Fifth-Grade Ophelia
Gracie Leavitt

Then I was a fifth-grade Ophelia, was hedging your bets, off course,
strong-stressed, every way which is natural when what a cool little figure
slips you turn her tiny tits just as he does, complete, but tell me next about
yourself remotely like what this implies in carbon offset site, my precious
practico-inert, is in wet calico nightshirt, every way is natural, dumb,
lowbrow, is kindred gardening in heels, in pantomime, can't possibly graph,
in the end, range of suitable habitat, glued by his head to a rock, if you
should pry him from this rock, consider inheritability, consider suicidality,
little elbow room, not cut out for every way out of—left to its own devices
happens more than we think. See in distal nettle bower lacewings' efficacious
flexure of, or here above knocked down drop ceiling panels which conceal
lacewing-occluded vents no older than aunts' use of them. Not for nothing
is where my head is at. Is summarized as your want which not at all
you want if not at once to live wherever it looks like that, still able to walk
his horses out it all washed up facsimile. Lyn's "been a blind camera all day
in preparation for this dream." Paul says, "A flower, a proposition, a noise
can be imagined almost simultaneously . . ." This stuff crops up all over the place.
Will share my parts with you, will give you all my parts, wonders keep
our stars apart, discrete, in the end, aboutness obscures that god-term
as you called it then, appointed passably in these parts in such amounts
as lacewing, noise, as nettle bower in the way of fecund autumn's air supply.

Gracie Leavitt

Then I was a fifth-grade Ophelia, deboarded, were our formal gestures baggage
pars pro toto contorted as pool tarp over woodpile stretched in case it rained
or something worse, what's happened to us with whom so much of what looks
like ought there out Ma's picture window, you on featureless arête I imagine
your lush mantis tops one sego bulb, yours whose trappist face the typicality
of my recognition loaned aptly this queer pentecostal light as that which caught
grandmother's ring she gave me lost in beach rocks' intercostal space, wedged,
her fingers slim, it slipped off these, allotted weft won't pull through clean, desire
projected more than co-substantiates, moodily you camped in doorjamb here
I'd take, you remember yourself, you in ocher wingback, you in thrift-shop folding
chair I would since all good stuff goes as orgasm does, is good and gone that quick,
some recompense: granddaughter of a second wife whose parents were first cousins
farming capers on a cliff open to being glossed, we preambulate, hair in her face,
we walk the walk before the walk not steady down collector roads, you're fitful
at defunct silo, steel hoop-compressed, of grain or something I don't know, pressure
of his static increasing as it goes against precast concrete staves that intermesh,
in tea dress unstiff from steel stays we wove in blueberry field, the field not burnt
this year for cultivation, next, my dress stained from the field we left among
our managed native stands of lowbrush wild fruit magnetic tape and memory card
as well, I guess, we're neither, we're neither, we're both, pretty to think, not steady
down collector road's trim shoulder, hair in her face, nowhere highbrush cultivars.

Then I was a fifth-grade Ophelia, unkempt, or light as a feather, stiff
as a board, was prone on the hood of your serviceable car, mare-like
stalled, were recondite and shifting shrubs usually erect prostrate
about her bioload, sand in our culverts here, as if it neatly added up
after winter, come fill this more out with ideas of causeway, the surf,
one contrail with another mingled, two in sky disperse, too congenitally
inept to consummate a thing who burns up the slash pile—brush, excess,
dead pets—biennially and walks his property line and marks it off
packs down a filial trail subtly through several deer yards there. "Yes,
well I imagined other settings for our unease than this," John said of her
aunt's bogs in Providence we visited and tanks of cranberries where she lived
was borderline before was passed that trait down noticeably to strawberry
blondes, most quiet ones, first cousins before both bogs were drained.
You loved your pallid lace and neon nighties would melt on you should fire
break so you won't wear. You love your pallid nighties not your extended
terms of credit, therefore only what I'll use I'll haul you under awning,
arborlike, half viewable from dock, a nonpoint source in plum maillot
she doubles back and frets upon and cancels local impish gorse out,
gaff in her head act, I. "Now I'm mortified," John said. Bioavailable
in begonia bed, fat toad my sister landed in, barn snake parts jumping
still, chickens by their necks grandmother swung, church clothes still on,
I'm mortified, don't have the nerve, won't play boldly against my type
more beautiful than myself, our central fact, a new sentence is a sentence
between two sentences, how religion is, knowing what to practice that day,
as if it neatly added up, didn't clog the drains, didn't flood that way
or logging road, as if your engine weren't flooded, as if they hadn't
drained both bogs but flooded these for harvest, corralled by floating
booms—you and I and she—and shook from vine by water reel,
advanced to release another. Begonia bed on second thought not paved
over clean, lawn extruded through some middle, seduced through several
stages of grief, through nodal limbo heparinized, injections of it daily
in my middle, prone on the hood of his serviceable car, whatever's
in a contrail makes us see what passed before, maybe moments ago,
hours maybe, depends on wind: Wasn't right me dragging her around
like that, wasn't me dragging her around.

Then I was a fifth-grade Ophelia, suspect, new wave, night sweat, inside
thick halo of mouchettes seemed largely to exist at legal tender age, tangles
your impossible form as click world pictures by, a new wave the effect
it caused self-corrects your random sandbar shoreward or stern river
builds sufficient head and breaks clear through bog laurel put on earth
this little space my desire for desire forms, I'm saying, making substitutions,
things they wouldn't talk about but I could tell in babyhood was something
going on like singing along briefly it encounters Vivian Girls, Red Rose Girls,
packs of girls marauding, sisters plural and so sexless—social, lissome, tenseless
—disappear behind a single line. That being done unloaded quantities
of gravel, spread it, raked it out on sandbar lunched on peaches. Later
in rare way happy to see Muriel repair taciturn to my sun parlor, comorbid
expectations, only so much heaven on the screen it looks to me as though
what this calls for is establishment of losses, all the cake in the world, a sort
of prettiness nonetheless, nothing like how his road we came in on bent, copied,
disc mayweed copied along it, weed copied around your press pool clear no
sooner full than begins sward here to thin more than her frame she drowsed on,
floral scarf balled in her hand he clutched, what we thought an heirloom was,
mortal shakes, stains, those cigarettes you wasted, "Fog comes on little cat feet,"
said Carl said my grandmother. Grass widow of a Boston marriage left
in Reaganville, couldn't leave, cried. She said, "They are happy," they aren't
anything these boys I think who take, who could, each other's arm in morning
stuff this usual and do this thing together slowly on come morning when
of a sudden trees begin to thin and sward, was older then, that hump that
if you hit it going 55 will flip your stomach Dad would always rev before
tall addled horses from abuse gnaw grooves in fence on River Road from things
we didn't talk about, don't press, not at the dinner table here, not our Cold War–
era altar boy, would ask you further questions of the self's own act, of Ruby Ridge,
would conscientiously object, coaxed out rounds toward where things dear
are revenant, not reproduced in whole or part of Lysette's heart spills
well the little totals, this in the wrong hands, actions in the field we'll never,
affairs not recommended: "Be reasonable," she said. "Seems fairly stock,"
better to say. You far off there not fair enough, I want my actual whim,
if circadian should quit him definitely, the mystery, the folding of clothes,
peaches you stole when already you'd stored away peaches after all he'd

done the strangest things we didn't talk about, warm for the very first
every in the party poured out and licked his ice cream cone, poured
out and clucked, "*Sous les pavés, la plage!* No, under the pavestones,
the beach." Really now to know or have it featured is within bog laurel
where entire margins revolute, within mere halo of mouchettes, when older
palm wine in the head, one doeling mid my phlox ablaze or wild turkey flock
optically was real, was happy, wasn't anything at all, in Vietnam
Dad said they aren't boys just morning stuff this usual. Couldn't leave,
we tried, for cooler greener hill stations iff for prospect poetry.

Fathers in Their Old Age: A Primer
Christie Hodgen

HISTORICALLY SPEAKING, the problem of aging fathers—who they are, what they want, how to placate them—is a relatively recent phenomenon. Only a century ago, one could expect one's father to live to an average of forty years of age, but now fathers are expected to live to sixty-seven years, with even higher averages in industrialized nations. Recent medical advancements have made it possible—and in this country, quite common—to extend life not only into the seventh decade, but into the eighth and ninth and even tenth decades, well past the point where men of previous civilizations would have succumbed to heart failure, cancer, exposure to the elements, animal attack, alcoholism, suicide, bankruptcy, and even simple infections. While this is certainly welcome news to all of us, we nevertheless find ourselves in something of a cultural predicament. Because instead of enjoying the extra years granted to them, many of today's fathers tend to wander through their last decades in a fog of discontentment, a veritable cloud of physical and psychic pain. Naturally, as their children, we are affected too; our fathers' problems become our own. At times the challenges faced by our fathers—legion, baffling—stretch so far beyond the scope of our comprehension and capabilities that we find ourselves overwhelmed. We panic, we fly into little rages, we plunge into bouts of existential despair. We cast about for advice, understanding, companionship, and too often find ourselves alone.

But we here at ISAF—The Institute for the Study of Aging Fathers—have decided to take up this mantle. It is our hope that by studying the problems of aging fathers we will foster a community of fathers and children, promoting better understanding between them, resulting in a marked increase in the quality of life for both. It must be admitted, we suppose, that despite the long hours we have put into our research—thousands and thousands of hours—much of our accumulated data is inconclusive. It must be admitted that in our pursuit of understanding our aging fathers, our personal lives and financial profiles have suffered, often to the point of extinction. But we are imperturbable. We are nothing if not a determined group. We go on, feeling we must.

What follows is something we have decided to call, after considerable debate, a *primer*; we wish to stress that this is but a brief introduction to some of the most common ailments affecting today's aging fathers. (Exhaustive studies are still being compiled.) You will find that we have studied a wide variety of topics, from the trivial to the profound. Where possible, we offer advice; where advice is lacking, or of limited practical use, we simply offer analysis or encouragement or consolation, as the case dictates.

FACIAL HAIR

Often fathers who have felt compelled by their professions to remain clean shaven will experiment with facial hair upon retirement. These experiments are usually subtle: little wisps of mustaches, French in their suggestion of refinement and superiority; neat goatees after the fashion of Chekhov. Occasionally a father will refashion himself with the zeal of a madman—pursuing the elaborate flourishes of Whitman and Nietzsche, the members of ZZ Top—but this is a relatively rare phenomenon.

New facial hair can be disconcerting to children, who are used to a certain orderliness and formality in their fathers. When they visit their fathers after several months' absence and find them bewhiskered, scruffy, the response can range from confusion to panic. Children will turn to their spouses, or call their siblings, and ask: *What's going on here? What the hell is he thinking? Is he depressed? Is he suicidal? Should I call a psychiatrist? Do you think he's having an affair?*

Too many children make the mistake of working their opinions of their fathers' new facial hair into conversation. *Don't go near the baby,* they say. *Your beard is scaring him.* Or perhaps a softer approach, one of feigned concern: *I was reading that beards are like germ magnets, and all these germs find their way into your teeth and gums, and from there they go right to your heart, and before you know it you're looking at a heart attack, that's why all those lumberjacks just up and, you know . . . one day they just drop dead. You should be more careful about brushing your teeth. Are you flossing?*

Our advice here is the same as in most other categories: Maintain silence; watch and wait. When left alone, your father will most likely return to his original state in a matter of months. During this time it might be helpful to think of your father as a person undergoing a second adolescence, a person in need of a bit of indulgence. Here he is, for the first time in decades, freed from the insufferable constraints of his job. Naturally he is relieved, joyful; naturally too he will suffer bouts of melancholy as he reflects on all the years he has lost in the prison of his former life—that tiny, mundane hell. The retired father is a man at once relieved and resentful; he will swing between buoyancy and depression. Remember that one day this will happen to you too. Extend your sympathies at least as far as you would hope to have them extended to you in the future.

Conversely, fathers who have worn thick beards all their adult lives will sometimes spontaneously shave them, revealing the pale, tender skin of their cheeks and jaws. Without their beards these fathers seem smaller, more vulnerable; their chins appear weak and their mouths quite soft and noble. They seem, for the first time, mortal. This kind of alteration in a father's appearance will invariably throw children into a different brand of crisis: one of intense sympathy and regret. In these cases children can hardly believe they have been so harsh with their fathers, so thoughtless and burdensome. *All these years*, they say, *he was just a little man, just a regular man, and here I thought he was this tough guy.* An intense and profound concern wells up in them. *Something's going on with Dad,* they say to one another. *I think he's having a real crisis. I wonder if he's dying and not telling us. That would be just like him. To bear it by himself, not telling anyone. I think there's something awful happening. I think the shaving thing is really a cry for help.*

Fortunately, when a man who has worn a beard his whole life decides to shave it, he is never quite sure of himself. In moments of weakness he will ask his friends and family members if he ought to grow it back. In the event that you truly cannot stand the sight of your father's tender, gentle face—in the event that, seeing him revealed, you suffer intolerable agonies of guilt and shame—take advantage of this opportunity. Tell him: *Yes, Dad, grow it back, absolutely. I don't even know you anymore.*

PHARMACOPOEIA

Our research indicates that over eighty percent of today's aging fathers subscribe to a daily regimen of vitamins, supplements, and medications. Often the number of pills is staggering. It may take your father many minutes to line up these pills next to his breakfast plate: Vitamins E, C, D, B, and A, fish oil, grapeseed oil, CoQ10, lycopene, alpha lipoic acid, and a variety of over-the-counter remedies for joint, sinus, and muscle pain. You may also see your father dole out for himself a set of unidentified pills, in a variety of pastel colors, usually shaped like flying saucers. These are antidepressants and are generally not cause for alarm (see DEPRESSION). It may concern you to see your father taking so many pills, not because you are particularly worried about his health, but because it will seem to you that old age requires more upkeep and maintenance than you are prepared to handle. The thought of yourself, in twenty years' time, ritually fighting off the caps of over a dozen bottles, will sour your mood for several hours.

In recent years a new problem has developed for children in the habit of poking around in their fathers' medicine cabinets. We consider this problem its own punishment for the lack of respect a child shows for her father's privacy. The problem, discussed between siblings in scandalized tones over the telephone, goes something like this: *So I'm in the bathroom and I open the closet to get a hand towel, and there's all his prescriptions and I can't help but notice, it's right there in front of my face, staring right at me—you're not going to believe this: Viagra.*

From here the conversation branches off into two possible directions. In the cases where both parents are still alive, and married, the conversation continues:

I didn't think they still had sex.

Me either! They're both so fat!

God, I can't even imagine. I mean, which one of them?

Don't! Just stop!

I mean, how does he even?

Stop, stop! You're killing me!

In the cases where the mother has divorced the father, or passed away, the conversation goes:

Do you think he has a girlfriend?

He hasn't mentioned anyone.

God, I hope it's not Mrs. Feeney. I saw her at Dad's the last time I was there. Pulling up his weeds in the front yard.

No WAY. She's such a pig. There's no way.

Who knows? Maybe he likes it. Mom was so bony and frigid. Maybe a little Shirley Feeney is what he's been missing. Maybe

she's pulling his weeds, if you know what I mean.
    You're grossing me out here.
    I'm just saying. Shirley or whoever, good for him.
    All those years he and Mom never had sex. God, Mom would die.

GRANDCHILDREN

No matter how late in life you choose to have a child, be aware that your father will most likely consider himself too young to be a grand-father. Don't be upset if his reaction to your news is less than you had hoped for. Instead of congratulating you, instead of focusing on you and your expanding family, your father may focus, for a time, on his own existential conundrum. For several days or even weeks he will walk around saying to himself: *I am going to be a grandfather. Jesus Christ. A grandfather.* Now is not the time to chide your father for his selfishness. Instead, remember that this situation has oddly little to do with you. Be calm, patient. Try to think of your becalmed pa-tience as practice for parenthood, that state in which one must al-ways consider another's feelings before one's own.

In most cases, fathers will resign themselves to their advanced age and transition smoothly into their roles as grandparents. You can help this transition by asking your father, a few weeks before the baby arrives, to choose the name he wishes to be called by your child. Most will opt for the universal *Grandpa*, though some will choose to distinguish themselves with formalities and informalities such as *Grandfather*, *Pop*, *Poppa*, *Papa*; some will even borrow from other languages, choosing *Père-père* and *Papka*. (Note: All parties are advised that their chosen names are subject to change, as many satis-fying nicknames have been adopted after the first grandchild's botched attempt to pronounce your father's chosen honorific. Some of the more common blunders are: Bop, Bubba, Gampy, Pup-pup, Damburger.)

In the first stages, when everyone is delighted by the baby and act-ing like his birth is the most important development in the history of mankind, you and your father will undergo a brief period of unprecedented harmony. It will seem to you that nothing exists for your father but the baby—just as nothing else exists for you—and in your delusion you might be tempted to buy your father T-shirts and mugs with your child's portrait on them, or emblazoned with slogans like: WORLD'S #1 GRANDAD. Avoid this. In almost all cases, fathers don't wish to make use of these gifts, as it announces their age to the world at large, which they are still trying to negotiate under the guise of younger men. Remember that after you pack up your toddler and leave for home, your father is relieved to return to his normal life, which is, for the first time, better than yours: more relaxed and less burdensome, more *youthful*. As you wade through the debilitating first years of parenthood, try not to regard your father, and his excess of free time and income, with jealousy or resentment. Remember, he has already served his time.

Now and then one will encounter an indifferent grandfather. Fashioned after W. C. Fields, this kind of man considers small children to be a scourge, a plague, a class of vermin upon whom precious resources are shamefully lavished. When he visits your home he will mutter about the noise, the mess. If he trips over one of your child's toys he will kick the offending object across the room. In the case of multiple grandchildren he will confuse them, forget their names. At family gatherings you'll hear him say things like *Hey, somebody get this kid off me!* Or *Which one are you, Billy? Timmy? Well, whatever your name is, get out of my chair.* This kind of grandfather might even go so far as to mock a baby. If your infant crawls after him as he goes into the kitchen to make himself a drink, if the baby stares up at him with a quizzical look, he will say: *What? You got a problem with someone having a drink at ten in the morning? What are you going to do about it? Cry? Shit in your pants?*

Should your father turn out to be an indifferent grandparent, don't take it personally. Remember that today's loving, hands-on grandparent is strictly a latter-twentieth- and early twenty-first-century phenomenon. Your father is no different from millions upon millions of other indifferent grandfathers; in fact, historically speaking, he is a member of the overwhelming majority. Instead of succumbing to frustration and self-pity, make yourself a drink. When drunk, tell yourself: *Secretly, deep down, he really loves the baby. He would take a bullet for the baby, if it came down to it.* Try to believe it.

WHISTLING

While the cause is still unknown to science, it seems inevitable that your aging father will take up whistling. Whistlers can be divided into two types of practitioners: those who whistle popular songs, most often from their youth ("You ain't nothin' but a hound dog!"), and those who whistle spontaneous, arrhythmic tunes, little runs of ascending and descending notes, often of cheerful disposition, though occasionally dipping into melancholy. This habit is thought to be one of the minor categories of self-expression released after a lifetime of pent-up emotion, and is considered harmless.

CONSPICUOUS CONSUMPTION

Now and then a father who has saved carefully his whole life will snap, and blow through his entire savings in a matter of months, going on a series of long, exotic vacations, taking up expensive hobbies such as flying lessons and yachting, outfitting his home with new furniture and appliances, buying new cars. Usually it takes children a few weeks, or even months, to realize what is happening. It may start with a visit to the father's home, the discovery of a new television and a new armchair. The initial response to such improvements is usually one of approval and encouragement—*You really needed to get rid of that old piece of crap, Dad, good for you!*—but as time passes, children begin to calculate their fathers' expenditures, begin to worry that their fathers will exhaust their resources, leaving nothing by way of inheritance. It is not uncommon for children in this circumstance to become peevish and fussy. *Maybe you should stay home instead of going to Hawaii,* they say. *It's a long flight, and you know what sitting like that does to your sciatica.*

PROSTATE

If you absolutely can't resist asking—or if your father happens to raise the subject on his own—be prepared to have things explained to you in terms of fruit. Your father may tell you that his prostate, normally the size of a prune, has swollen to the size of an orange or even worse. Try not to wince, or otherwise register the stabbing discomfort you feel when hearing about a grossly inflamed gland. The important thing is to act like you've seen it all before, like nothing is surprising or unpleasant in the least. Say: *Right, right, of course. I saw a report about that on the evening news a few weeks ago. That's not uncommon, they said. A grapefruit is perfectly common.*

FEAR

If your aging father is not yet a widower, be aware that one of his greatest fears is the possibility of waking up and finding his wife next to him, dead. Be aware that his prayers include a fervent wish to be taken first. Be aware that this is not chivalry or selflessness. Rather, after several decades of relying on his wife's handling of all of life's unpleasant logistics, he simply can't imagine what he will do in that moment, when it comes.

VANITY

Sometimes children, caught up in the existential, medical, and financial problems of their aging fathers, underestimate the extent to which life's relatively minor predicaments affect them. The fact is, no one likes to get old, and the image of one's aging face in the mirror can be dispiriting. A father's ego might be threatened by the loss of hair or teeth, the appearance of sunspots, the sagging of skin at the neck. Be prepared for your father to react to this threat with uncharacteristic displays of vanity. If your father stays with you during his annual visit, or if you stay with him during your annual visit home, know that he will spend more time fussing in the bathroom than he ever has before, he will spend even more time than your teenaged daughter. Don't be alarmed if you hear the hiss of aerosolized hair spray emanating from behind the bathroom door; don't be alarmed if, when you rifle through your father's cabinet or travel bag, you find expensive face creams from department-store beauty counters.

Regarding your father's sudden vanity, we have one unequivocal recommendation: DO NOT RESPOND. Your efforts to ease your father's pride are more harmful than not. Any attempt to relate to him—*I have the same antiwrinkle cream! Don't you love it! Isn't it so thick and velvety?*—will only embarrass him. Efforts to dismiss his concerns will insult him. An example of such a dismissal, lobbed toward a father who is fussing with the few hairs that remain on the top of his head, would be: *Oh, Dad, come on, you think anyone cares what you look like!*

A subset of vanity is the issue of clothing. The vast majority of children will find that their fathers, with age, develop a kind of neutral uniform—most likely a pair of pleated slacks and a short-sleeve oxford shirt, worn over a T-shirt. But sometimes, as a man ages and walks about the world looking at other people—most of whom, by now, are younger and seem to wield greater authority—he will find himself studying the difference between his appearance and that of the privileged classes.

This phenomenon tends to provoke considerable alarm. Children who have not spoken to their siblings in years will feel compelled to call them and report on their father's behavior: *So Dad's here for a visit and he says he wants to go shopping for jeans. So I take him to the mall, thinking we're going to Sears or whatever, and he heads into one of those teenager stores with the loud music and the awful cologne, the lights turned off, you can't even see anything, it's like a nightclub, I forget the name but you know the place I'm talking about? Finally he picks this pair with a bunch of rips on the legs, he looks like he's been mauled by lions, I swear to God.*

RELIGION

Children of aging fathers are advised to expect some adjustments in their fathers' faith and worshipping practices. As a man ages, the question of faith weighs upon him as it never has before. It is only natural for a man to wonder, at the end of his life, *What does it all mean? Is there anyone up there? Is there a point to all of this? Is there indeed life after death?*

Sometimes these questions are answered in the negative. One might find oneself calling one's sister and saying: *He just doesn't go anymore. I couldn't even get him to go for Allie's first communion. All those years he got us up early on Sunday and made us sit in the front row, he was always dressed up in his blazer and dress shoes and everything. And now he just doesn't go at all. Do you think he was ever a believer, or was he just going through the motions because he thought he should set an example?*

Sometimes fathers fall into the habit of using a newfound devotion as a sanctimonious, murderous club. You may find yourself saying something like: *We're going out to eat, and right as we pull up, some minivan is pulling out of this great spot right out front, and you know what he says? "That's what you get when you live at the foot of the cross." All smug. Like God's up there with nothing better to do than orchestrate this killer parking spot for him, there's ten million people starving in Africa but God doesn't have time for them, no, God's too busy making sure he gets this fucking parking spot. I swear to God, I almost punched him.*

Our research indicates that the smaller, subtler adjustments to a father's faith are the ones most likely to throw a child into true crisis. One might find, in one's father's house, a rosary dangling from the bedpost, or a daily devotional perched on the back of the toilet, and suddenly one will be overcome with dread, a sense of discomfort so intense one wishes one had discovered pornography instead. What is most troubling, we suppose, is the suggestion of loneliness. As if God were the last place to turn, as if God were the last kid left waiting to be chosen for the kickball team and, having failed with everyone else, your father has chosen him as his companion. Here it may help to think of God himself as an aging father, old and feeble, retired, withdrawn in his rest home. Be glad that your father has someone to turn to, a constant companion who is there when you are not.

DEPRESSION

We would like to make use of this topic as a means of instructing children in their thinking regarding all other topics. Ask yourself, where depression and other paternal matters are concerned: *Why should my aging father be any different than the rest of us? Why should I be surprised if his maladies are the same as my own?* Remember that we have become a shallow, materialistic, lonely, miserable culture, devoid of spiritual and personal connections, and in such a culture it is only natural for one in three of us to plunge into annual if not permanent bouts of melancholy. Why should your father be any different?

Of course there are all kinds of solutions to melancholy: exercise, night school, book clubs, part-time jobs, charitable endeavors such as the digging of wells and building of houses in third-world countries. Or pills. The overwhelming majority of families, we find, choose pills.

On the topic of pills we have somewhat discouraging data. Likely, the first pill won't work, so a second will be prescribed, plus a third to help with the insomnia caused by the first two. Then, after a period of time in which the pills, collectively, might be considered to have been slightly helpful (though of course there will be some doubt as to whether it was the pills or simply the fact that the weather improved and there was more daylight to be enjoyed), they will seem to lose their effectiveness, which is ultimately not cause for alarm because fourth and fifth and sixth pills are available, upward to a dozen, and there are almost infinite adjustments and combinations to be tried, during which time you will never really be sure if the pills are working or not, but with your father's physicians' encouragement you will continue to try to land on that magical combination that will obliterate all depressive, complicated, soulful, searching, fearful, interesting, or ambiguous thinking from your father's brain, questions such as *Have I wasted my life?* Rest assured that the pursuit of the right combination and dosing of pills is so intricate, so labyrinthine, that it will carry you safely through your father's seventies, eighties, and even nineties, delivering him right up to the very welcome mat of death's door.

POLITICS

Generally, two possibilities:

You can't talk to him anymore. He knows everything. He's got the radio cranked all day, all this conservative talk-show bullshit. When I call it's so loud in the background half the time I can't hear what he's saying. You call and say, "Hey, Dad, how's it going? I just wanted to invite you to Ben's Thanksgiving play," and he starts going off on Native Americans not saying the Pledge of Allegiance in their schools. All he does is spit back whatever the radio says.

If the father happens to veer to the left, the complaints go something like this: *So I'm out with the kids on Sunday, we're going out for brunch after church, and we're right at the corner of Broadway and Forty-seventh, by the park there, you know that intersection? And there's all these protesters out there with their signs, STOP THE WAR, a bunch of hippies, they've all got beards, even the women, they've all got these saggy breasts, even the men, and they're out there chanting something, I forget what, and then I swear to God, there he is. Right in the middle with this sign: REGIME CHANGE STARTS AT HOME.*

I THOUGHT I TOLD YOU THAT

One in three of the total number of complaints we have gathered from aging fathers and their children has to do with memory loss.

You might find that your aging father leaves burners ignited on the stove, leaves the faucet running, forgets to close the garage door when he exits the house, is unable to locate his car in parking lots. Unfortunately, there is no way to know for sure whether these are symptoms of dementia or merely careless acts brought about by the frenetic nature of our culture. We ourselves have left the burners and faucets running unattended, sometimes both together.

There are, however, two traits common to aging fathers that help to distinguish their memory loss from our own. First: While our fathers' day-to-day lives are fraught with forgetful episodes, their distant pasts start to emerge in their minds with startling clarity. Second: Our fathers are absolutely convinced, when speaking of these distant pasts, that they have already told us these stories on multiple prior occasions. *The year I spent working on a fishing boat off the coast of Portugal? I thought I told you that. That month in military prison? I thought I told you that.* To which you will respond: *No, Dad, you didn't.*

We recently encountered a father and son whose dialogue might serve as a salient example of this phenomenon. The father—whom the son had only ever known as a successful neurosurgeon, a former Reagan Democrat turned bona fide Republican, a man heavily invested in the stock market and overly fond of checking in with his broker, Mitch—began telling the son one day, at a Fourth of July cookout at the son's house (at which the son's own sons were running around trying to pelt each other with water balloons), about the time he drove to Washington, DC, to hear Martin Luther King Jr.'s "I Have a Dream" speech. *I never told you that?* said the father, furrowing his brow. *I thought I told you that.*

I don't think so, said the son. *I'm pretty sure I'd remember.*

Well, it was hot, said the father. *And I wasn't sure my car would make it. This was back when I was still in med school and I was driving that old Buick that overheated all the time. I'd been following King on the news, and there was this sense that something big was happening and you better not miss it. I had a lot of ideas back then about what I wanted to do, I was thinking about politics down the line, I'd almost joined the Peace Corps instead of going to med school, and it seemed to me like the March on Washington was something I shouldn't miss, it was something I'd want to tell my kids about someday.*

There were so many people there, I'd never seen anything like it. We'd hit the kind of critical mass where group thinking starts

351

to take over, we were all working together without even needing to talk about it, like some kind of ant colony. It felt like I knew everyone there. Everyone was talking, hugging each other, complete strangers walking arm in arm, laughing, crying. At some point during the march I fell into step with a black kid from one of the suburbs who'd taken the day off from work and walked all the way to the mall. I forget his name but he was a skinny kid with thick glasses. We started talking and just kept walking and talking together all day. He told me about his family, the job he had working in a hospital cafeteria. He talked through most of the speeches but he stopped for King. Everyone did. It was like everyone was holding their breath that whole time. You could tell history was happening.

At the end of the day I offered to drive this kid home. He lived a good ten miles out, in a bad neighborhood. Houses without doors, their windows missing or boarded up. On the way back to the interstate I got turned around and couldn't find my way out, so finally I stopped at a gas station. It was one of those things you knew was going to happen even before it did. As I was heading into the station I saw a group of kids across the street sitting on the curb watching me, and when I came out they were standing around the car, kind of leaning against it, one of them was even sitting on the hood. Whenever you're in a situation like that there's always a minute where the other person lets you say something, and whatever you say can get you killed or not. So I just asked one of the kids, the one on the hood, if there was something I could help him with. You can help me with your wallet, he says. And he pulls a knife on me. I just looked right at him. He's got the blade right up to my throat and I'm just looking at him, trying to tell him: I understand, I understand you. The thing is, I was where a white person wasn't supposed to be, I had crossed a line and just being there, just crossing over into that neighborhood, it was a kind of affront. It didn't matter why I was in town or what Dr. King had just said—our destinies are tied up together, and all that—I understood that. When people don't have much, you can't go waltzing into what little they have. So I just handed over my wallet. I don't want trouble, I said. You can have the car if you want it. And he says, What makes you think we want your piece of shit car? And I say, That's true, it's not much of a car. And we both sort of almost laugh. And then they took off running and that was it. That was the time I drove down to Washington.

This was by far the longest and most meaningful monologue the son had ever heard from his father, and when it was finally finished, the son felt himself collapsing into a gloomy, desperate mood. He thought of all the years during which he and his father had satisfied themselves with small talk—with cursory discussions of sports and cable television, movies, yard work—when they might have been talking of better things. *All this time,* the son told us, *I never knew my father had this other side, that he used to be different, that he had this meaningful history based on deep convictions about human dignity and social progress. It's like, if I'd known that about you, I would've done things different. I would've treated you better.*

We must report that the son collapsed, right in our offices, into something like an existential tantrum. He launched into a monologue of his own, a series of questions and possible answers too long to reproduce here but which we will attempt to summarize. His talk was quite agitated, punctuated by wild movements of his arms. Sometimes he even clutched his head like a person enacting symptoms in a migraine commercial.

What the son wanted to know was: What happens? What happens to us, to all of our noble ideas, our good intentions, what happens to our souls? Is it age? Is it raising kids, all that love and time and grueling effort you put into making meals and playing games and driving them around and working extra hours so they can be sent to school? . . . It's the kids, right? But they can't be blamed, surely other people have managed to maintain their souls while raising children. Maybe it's the times we live in? Too much information, too many distractions?

At a certain point the son's talk became incomprehensible. He started crying, wiping his nose now with the heel of his palm, now with the sleeve of his shirt, blubbering into his hands. All of us had fallen silent and sat quietly in respect for his suffering until finally the father, as fathers do, clapped his son on the back as if he'd just struck out on the last pitch in the last inning of a series game, he'd lost it all for his team and now the weight of all his failed hopes was settling about his shoulders, heavy, heavy. *Let's go out, son,* said the father. We can only assume that the father and son went to a bar and that the son renounced his theories about the soul, that father and son sat together watching a baseball game, filling up the time with commentary on pitches and swings, until the son relaxed into the glow of the television and forgot all about his time with us at our institute.

353

Now when he drives past our offices no doubt the son flushes with shame, regretting the impulses that drew him into our midst.

This saddens us. We must admit that we sometimes wonder if we are doing any good. We sometimes wonder if we are like the drunken cousin at the Thanksgiving table who begins talking aloud of things that are obvious to everyone but that have been deliberately left unsaid for the sake of familial harmony. Sometimes it becomes hard to justify our work to others and even ourselves. Our funding is low and we have cut our salaries in half, and then in half again. New donations have dwindled to an almost negligible amount. People want to donate their money toward the cure of specific cancers and neurodegenerative disorders, and we can't compete with that, even though we believe that our work affects a far greater number of people in a more profound way. We have shut off the heat in our office to save money and can see our breath clouding in front of us as we hunch over our desks. We are out of coffee filters and have resorted to using the rough paper towels from the bathroom dispenser. Furthermore we are almost out of coffee, without which we can't properly function.

Still, we will forge ahead. We will carry on, though once we fail to make rent and are forced to disperse from our offices we will no longer feel the camaraderie that has sometimes been the only thing keeping us going. We will return to our fathers' houses and admit that we have once again lost our jobs, we will appeal to their mercy and ask their permission to move their exercise machines out of our old bedrooms and back down to the basement, which is generally not much of an imposition since the machines are only used as giant hangers upon which to drape wet clothing too delicate to put in the dryer. At night we will lie on our backs in our twin beds and we will stare at the ceiling until we reach the meditative state in which it is revealed to us that all is not lost, that we are doing exactly what we are meant to be doing, that we must carry on with our work even though we have lost our official positions and our cubicles (which we rather enjoyed despite the bad reputation generally assigned to cubicles), we will stare at the ceiling until we understand that our fortunes have in fact increased rather than declined, that our research is even better now that we are working from the most natural of places, now that we are working from home.

Quality of Life in Switzerland
Scott Geiger

DIAGRAM

I LEAD A LIFE in Switzerland. This life came to me about ten years ago. It is approximately what I have here. I match myself, you know: the same age, living under this name, and myself in appearance. All my traits and personality are manifest in Switzerland. ATM screens make me nervous. I am clumsy with small objects like house keys or paper clips. I like serious newspapers about economics and business affairs. Lone hairs probe between my eyebrows. My wide feet stretch out their shoes. I am told I snore in the night. Everything that makes me, all of it migrates over to Switzerland just fine, and there it coheres as a life of momentum and purpose. That comes from where the two lives diverge. These divergences are crucial. My voice in Switzerland sounds just like what you hear now, but it talks in German, clipped Italian, fragmentary Romansch, and puddles of French. I speak these fluently in Switzerland. I cannot do that here yet, although I'm trying with the CDs and the workbooks. Another example, my career: I am a physician with a small family practice in Zurich. I do not know why or how, but it really is so. I made a diagram to explain all this to myself. The quality of life in Switzerland, the diagram shows, offsets everything that has happened to me. It shows I should be happy.

MOUNTAINS

You know what? In Switzerland, I own a goddamned fast Mercedes. It shines like a big sacred meteorite under the parking-garage lights. The car is an anonymous black, and I never allow anything like a map or briefcase or plastic water bottle to be left in the car. I am almost reluctant to touch its door handles, let alone drive the Mercedes. I have never owned anything like it, so I measure my use of the car very carefully. Yet this exact Mercedes is ubiquitous in Zurich, and I see it throughout Switzerland.

355

Say I have a woman I am seeing, a girlfriend, or maybe even a wife—in thinking about my life in Switzerland this proposition is a variable. So maybe it is a male friend, a colleague from Basel. I take this person out in the Mercedes some afternoon. We head south through the valley before turning up into the mountains above the city and beyond. The magnitude of the Alps is tremendous. They are everything that Mom and Dad described. One mountain after another, three thousand meters, four thousand meters, jutting against the horizon, layering together in compositions their varying depths of distance. What I like is how a mountain that might appear nearby and small in scale is in fact some distance away and insurmountable. Or how two mountains, which might look to be totally separate works of geology, make up a single massif. The sky is a solid sheet of color overhead. Far off, weather halos the country. A train rides into sight then vanishes. The black highway banks, ascends, wrapped on either side by a warm, green world.

Just before dark the Mercedes takes us into one of the villages for an old-fashioned Helvetian dinner. Each valley has something a little different to offer visitors, though a few are trapped so distantly in the past as to be beyond recognition, their history having ended a hundred years ago. My colleague and I—no, that colleague has gone and now it is again a woman I am with—find a more populous, busier village where there is a restaurant in what was once a carriage house. Its food is heavy but fresh and homemade. We drink digestifs in the garden before she and I walk out into the square to sit beside an ancient rural fountain and smoke her Gauloises. I promise myself that such trips are just fractions of longer trips to come. In a few years, I would like to take a long vacation, maybe even the whole month of August. We listen to the fountain.

In the villages, where everyone goes to bed early, evening delivers an almost rigid calm to the streets, the buildings, the treetops. Does darkness render the world so still? Or does stillness invite the dark? Switzerland steadies itself in imitation of the Alps. She rides home in the Mercedes with her feet tucked beneath her, her bag on the floor. The dashboard's orange lights exhume from the dark the necklace I gave her. An illuminated Zurich greets us upon return and the Mercedes goes back to its garage to wait for its next trip into the mountains. I leave nothing inside.

HOW DOES IT WORK?

Switzerland is autonomous. It unfolds continuously. It is going on right now, parallel to my life here. I receive it as moments of solid sense, though I can also remember it and imagine what might happen there. The train rides, the boat rides, the walks home from my office with a cigar and the folded *Neue Zürcher Zeitung*—these all occur while I am driving to work, pulling together my invoicing for the week, heating some cans of soup at Dad's new apartment, where he lives with Sandi, who is his wife now. I am never fully gone from Switzerland any more than I am ever fully here in this life, at this desk or in my chair at Dad's eating Sandi's vegetable lasagna.

There are moments of total penetration, when Switzerland captures me in the shower or walking into the grocery store. I can feel the little coffee spoons in my fingers. I can read the board at the Hauptbahnhof while I wait for my train to Basel. I can almost reach for the blue Gauloises box in my girlfriend (wife)'s purse. These experiences have lasted hours at times, especially when I was younger, in my twenties. I could spend a whole afternoon on Switzerland.

Every once in a while, maybe twice a year, my Switzerland life signals to me here. I should have tried to record these in a notebook, in case a special field of science emerges around the interplay between doubled lives. Once, for instance, out of my office window, I saw the guys getting the first mock-up for the Mount Sinai Hospital job ready for delivery. (I am the business manager at a privately held illuminated signage fabricator and my office looks down on our shop floor.) They had it leaning against a bend press across from the truck dock. It was on a square sheet of plywood backing, taller than a man. Gary held out the power connection they put on for the site test. When Wilmer brought up an extension cord, they mated, and the sign switched on. The plywood backing eclipsed my view of the sign itself, but I could see it on the men, on their faces and their clothes. The emergency red fluorescence cut out all kinds of shadow animals against the floor and shop walls: the presses, the screens, the crate wood, the chains, the heads and hands and legs of everyone working here. Inside the giant red fluorescent panel, unseen but known to me, was a white cross. And I remember the little pin Dad wore on his sweaters back when we were kids, the Swiss cross.

Scott Geiger

CAREER

I meet lovely people traveling the SBB between my practice in Zurich and the laboratory outside Basel. I am light and use my hands as I speak. I do a lot of talking in Switzerland. My hands are convincing. Pronounced whorls, wavy like the backgrounds of currency, mark the windows where I tap out landmarks to tourists. I am a carefree person. Once aboard, I never worry about the time. I drink strong little coffees or, if it is an evening train, a neat American whiskey. It is not because it is more lucrative that I work in both cities. With a dozen or so colleagues from Europe, East Asia, and North America, I participate in an advanced specialized research program. Is it the application of nanotechnology to prosthetics? Is it pediatric neurological disorders? Either way, we work out of a laboratory on Hüningerstrasse, Basel. These gaps of mine are shocking at times, while at others they are cause for relief. My Switzerland life is evolving. Why can't it go undecided, just both ways all at once? The team has made significant inroads over the years, publishing our work widely in journals and winning acknowledgment from medical communities worldwide. Government and private funding now backs the group's research, citing our team's efforts as indispensable.

No, my conventional family practice in Zurich suffers not in the least. I always put my patients and their families first. They understand this when I sweep into the room, light and talkative. Good morning, good morning. *Grützi, Doktor*, they say, as if the title were carved from a block of wood. Doctor, I've just read all about your work in the newspaper. Then I'll maybe say: It is really quite good news. We're verging on some major breakthroughs.

In Zurich, I am able to walk to work from my apartment to the Old City, stopping on my way for a strong little coffee and today's *Neue Zürcher Zeitung*. Once my charts are finished in the evening, I pour a neat American whiskey and scan the lights of the city, that darkness of the Alps that is no more than black construction paper under the spotlight moon ratcheting up into dark-blue air. My practice is on the fourth or fifth floor of a building unlike anything we have here in the U.S. It is modern and all white with plenty of glass. No, that's not it. It is a classic nineteenth-century apartment house converted to professional offices. Just down the street is the brand-new Kunsthaus, which is modern and white and glassy. The Kunsthaus I can see from my desk, while our building's lobby is a blue-gray marble the color of Lake Zurich with brass sconces and grilles. My office has plenty of light; it is very clean. Zurich I prefer to Basel, where we work within a kind of campus. The research program comprises many square meters of laboratory space. In the yard out back there is a beautiful linden, beneath which the staff eats lunch during fine weather. If newly arrived researchers appear shy or awkward, I apply my outgoing nature to make them feel at home. Everyone is at ease. No one is made to eat lunch in his car.

FRIDAY EVENINGS IN ZURICH

I like the weight of the old handset on the landline for my professional calls during the week. Outside of work, I use a mobile. Like when I call one of the women I am seeing or perhaps this so-called girlfriend (wife) I have discussed. Perhaps I meet her for dinner. Perhaps I dine alone and then we meet somewhere near her apartment. Or is it indeed the case that I am married in Switzerland and have given up on the other girls long before? If I am married, we eat together in our own home. My wife is also very light and herself a great talker, someone skillful in her way of looking at the world. She draws me out of my inward tendencies, this focus on my professional life. Then again, maybe I do not want conversation? Maybe I want someone to push around, to twist, to tease? Or is it that I am to be teased, to be twisted, to be pushed? I am a contortionist, after all.

JENNY

Genevieve appears in Switzerland too, under her full first name. My sister is safe from herself at last. I travel to see her and Jurgen Quist, the skinny Hamburger she married, a junior partner in a tiny but prestigious law firm. As I understand it, each year Jurgen brokers a few sensitive international business contracts that require painstaking negotiations. He speaks pieces of all languages, even Mandarin and functional Swahili. Outside the office, Jurgen wears pastel shirts with metal cuff links and boat hats. Jurgen collects hats and always has on a new one when we take his sailboat out on Lake Lucerne. When work is not too busy I go out for a day with Genevieve and Jurgen and their two boys. We all go sailing. I bring Jurgen one of my cigars from that shop in Zurich. We laugh as he tries to teach me to sail, and I challenge him to tennis, the game his long body is built for. I play tennis in Switzerland.

"Competition isn't my way," says Jurgen. Sailing, he says, creates an alliance. "The ship, the water, the wind—and us, the sailors."

Jurgen Quist is difficult for me to see, but I know he is totally different from Genevieve's other men here. Her creative energies achieve fruition in Switzerland, not solely because of Jurgen, but, yes, he is very supportive of her. You know what? She works in her own studio. She is not just a weekend watercolorist and a hostess at Pointe Restaurant. Turns out painting is only one of her gifts. Does she want to be an illustrator? A fashion designer? Even a landscape architect? She is all these things at once and more when I see her in Switzerland. While her husband and I work with the sails and boom, Genevieve is there on the shore by the line of trees and benches, painting our distant shapes against the tall ceiling of a Saturday morning. From where she stands, do the water and the air dissolve into a single, blank brilliance? It might be like in the photograph Dad took of Lake Lucerne years ago: an old man in a hat seated on a bench, studying the waters. The blank brilliance seen in his photo now hangs in a frame on a wall in my living room here. The photograph is fading, already half lost. I can tell that the man in the hat on the bench will be the last part of the print to decompose.

Would Genevieve be too generous a mother? Would she lavish her boys with protection and comforts, ending each day exhausted while the children become delicate and overly sensitive? No, she is the opposite of Mom. Jurgen too would do right by the boys, always telling them the truth even when the truth is difficult and none of their business. Were either of them sick, you know, Genevieve and Jurgen would tell the boys plainly what was happening. They make a great team.

Everything would come together for Jenny at last in Switzerland.

CUSTOMS

Last Saturday I decided to make a purchase. I drove to the east side, to the Galleria, where there is a Saks, to buy the black Rado wristwatch that tells its hours, minutes, and seconds on three separate faces. I have been thinking about this Rado watch for months now because I wear one in Switzerland. Over the past few years I have discovered that it's possible to import some elements of my Switzerland life. I have acquired, for instance, a black leather billfold with a crimson interior, silver bullet cuff links, a money clip, a white hat like the one Jurgen gave me, and a tourist map published by the city of Zurich. I have coffee cups, teaspoons, artist monographs, a photograph of a concrete bridge in Salgina. I paid for the watch with one of the credit cards. The clerk, a young woman, asked if I would like to wear the purchase right away. No, I told her. Not now. These imported items I leave outside my daily routine, reserving them for times when I can concentrate and focus on the details coming from Switzerland. Seated in my car, I place the Rado against my wrist and hold my arm up to the light. My eyes catch themselves in the rearview mirror.

If I had the money, it might be possible to import my entire Zurich apartment into this life. I have a nice stereo because I know music so well in Switzerland. Weekends, before I drive down to the airport to pick up my girlfriend (wife), who is returning from a business trip, I make time to listen to new work by a young composer or a new album from a new English band, always on headphones first while sitting in my leather chair, gazing through the windowpanes at the city, the Alps. The music unfolds continuously. A good new television hangs on the wall too. My tablet computer rests on the end table. Looking around the apartment now, there are a few color photographs matted inside black frames. There are valuable pieces of mid-century modern furniture I have collected plus some upholstered wooden chairs handmade in Lugano. No memorabilia, absolutely none. No images of me doing anything or standing anywhere. I own two clocks, a wall-mounted thermometer, and a barometer I keep on the kitchen counter. Elsewhere are soaps and a few cacti. Occasionally, when I know that the girlfriend (wife) has had a difficult day, I bring home a beautiful orchid or a potted succulent. If I am seeing a new girlfriend, I put simple wildflowers in the living room.

But there are limits to what I can bring over here. At the border between my two lives strict customs are in place. That lightness and outgoing personality I have in Switzerland, for example, I cannot import. When I am alone, I can envision myself surrounded by friends and colleagues, all of them laughing out loud with me. It is as if I am leading them in song. I see the effects that my words cause. The exact words themselves, though, are lost to me, as if I were trying to read a phone book in a dream. I know *how* I would live in Switzerland—the trains, the jokes, the whiskey, the girlfriend (wife), weekend rides out of town to see Genevieve and Jurgen with their boys on the sailboat, the smiles of my patients—yet I do not know *how* to be a physician.

Mom said, in one of our early-morning conversations: "I always thought you would do better, Scott." The television's light flared in her glasses. I sat with my barn coat over my legs, bare feet on her hospital bed. "I saw you as a physician or a financier or a business owner of some kind. I thought you would have a *practice*. I thought you would be rich and take your family to Switzerland in the summers." She was at a kind of threshold then.

I said I thought so too. I had counted on it.

She said, almost over her shoulder, as if she were about to leave the room, "That would be absolutely fascinating." Then she was asleep again.

DOES IT HURT?

Normally, as I go about my day, Switzerland comes in and out of reception. One reason the objects imported from Switzerland are so valuable is that they bridge the two lives. They keep me in contact. There are times, though, when Switzerland dims, winks. It guttered pretty badly when work slowed down a few years ago and I had to look for part-time bookkeeping. I had to focus my memory to recover Switzerland. This is a source of grief—because I do not want to lose Switzerland—as well as a source of embarrassment, because I am ashamed how much I need it. This is one way in which Switzerland hurts.

Then there is that idea represented in my diagram. My life in Switzerland, an undeserved gift, is meant to make up for all that happened. I am a physician with a small family practice. I am cherished by patients, esteemed and well liked by colleagues. The Friday evenings in the streets. The summer afternoons in the lake. Mom, alive. She is healthy, and living in an old house in a valley with a glacial lake and islets to look out upon. She comes to Zurich on the SBB. She sees my practice in the old classical building. We take her to dinner and she flatters the girlfriend (wife) or, if we are alone, she just enjoys herself with me at a small table near a window in my apartment. And yet all I can do is watch Switzerland, dwelling on it, because Switzerland is a kind of screen or monitor and not a window that can be opened, that can be smashed. I want more than to watch Switzerland and bring into my life articles that resemble what I have seen there. This leads me to worry that Switzerland is not meant to make up for what has happened, as I thought my diagram showed.

Rather, what if it has permanently cast my family's history into the contours of my present-day life? I am afraid. If I could even do so, would I choose to forget Switzerland?

"Won't it be lovely?" Mom said. "It will be lovely."

Twenty years have passed since we planned our family trip to Switzerland. We heard about it for months. Then, the weekend before we were to leave, Dad discovered that there were no reservations, no plane tickets, nothing. She had done nothing except talk about where we would go and what we would see. I have tried to discuss this with Dad and Jenny. But each of them long ago gave up Switzerland. This is why at moments when I begin to forget Switzerland, an incredible anxiety overcomes me, as if I have mislaid crucial paperwork or left something valuable in the car overnight on the street. Were I to let go of Switzerland, the memory would be extinguished. The house, open to the summer air. The meals at our glass table. All the photographs from their trip in 1975. Were I to let go of Switzerland, no one would remember how it was. We were a family.

SUMMER AFTERNOONS IN ZURICH

I want to describe my favorite activity in Switzerland for you. Zürichers know all about it—our quality of life here is so high. With the hot sunny days in August comes air so heavy that any degree of work indoors becomes too much to bear. On this kind of afternoon I go to the wardrobe and take out my white towel and dark-blue swim trunks. Down at the bathing pavilion on the Limmat, I leave everything behind. Shoes, pants, collared shirt, belt, dark socks, sunglasses, Rado watch, money clip—part of me means never to come back. Then I dive into the freezing Limmat. I take my time swimming alongside park benches, the docked boats, and the quay's stone walls with iron railings. Out beyond the bridge opens Lake Zurich, black and blue, knit by small sailing boats. There are other swimmers in the lake too. Some strangers, some friends. We all speak loudly above the chill in the water. We splash, we race, at times we touch by accident, at times on purpose. We meet, we part. I swim as far out into the lake as possible, again like I never mean to come back at all. My body floats on Lake Zurich. There is the city and the surrounding mountains beyond, plus all that sky. The sun is true. For a blue instant, everything that has happened is no more, and I am no one. I do decide to return after all, to go back to my cares, my practice, the girlfriend (wife), Genevieve and Jurgen, Mom at her glacial lake. I am drawn back against the Limmat past the quays to the pavilion. I climb out of the river and identify the pile of things that make me up in Switzerland. As I piece myself together then, in the face of Zurich, I find the daylight has warmed my clothes for me.

Uncle Lou
Elizabeth Hand

NINA'S UNCLE LOU LIVED in Hampstead, on a narrow, leafy side road that overlooked the Heath—from this vantage, a seemingly endless sweep of green, studded with ancient oaks where ravens clacked and acorns rained down to be gathered by small children and, sometimes, overeager dogs loosed for a run. Nina could remember collecting acorns with her parents when she was that age, not much bigger than a small dog herself, and carefully piling them where squirrels could find them.

Back then, she'd found this part of London vaguely sinister. The trees, probably, so gnarled and immense and reminiscent of a disturbing illustration in one of her picture books. Now of course she knew it was an impossibly posh area, late-model hybrids and Lotuses and Volvos parked in the drives, Irish and Polish nannies pushing Silver Cross prams, women slender as herons walking terriers that could fit in the palm of Nina's hand. Hampstead had been posh when she was a girl too, but then the burnished brick houses and wrought-iron fences had possessed a louche air, as though the Kray twins might be up to something in the carriage house.

Nina was fourteen when she realized that rakish edge emanated not from Hampstead but from Uncle Lou himself, with his long hair, bespoke suits from Dougie Millings, and gold-tasseled Moroccan slippers that curled up at the toes like a genie's. He was her favorite uncle—her only uncle, in fact—and her only relation except for a centenarian great-great-aunt supposedly entrenched in a retirement community on the Costa del Sol. Nina was an only child, with no first cousins and grandparents long dead.

Her divorced parents had died too, years ago when Nina was still at university. Since then, she had been in the habit of visiting Uncle Lou once a month or so, when his travels brought him home. He would disappear for months at a time and, when he returned, always answered her questions as to his whereabouts by placing a finger to his lips.

His peripatetic lifestyle had slowed in the last decade, so she now saw him more often. He was a travel writer, creator of the popular *World by Night* series. *Budapest by Night* had been his first, un-expected best seller, quickly spawning *Paris by Night*, *London by Night*, *Marseilles by Night*, *Vienna by Night*, and so on ad infini-tum. This was in the 1960s and early 1970s, when the world was much larger and far more exotic. Bohemian tourism was just gaining a toehold in the travel industry, fueled by rumors of Brion Gysin's pilgrimage to Jakarta with Brian Jones to observe whirling dervishes, and the legions of hippies decamping to Katmandu to eat yak butter whilst negotiating drug deals.

Yet no matter how obscure or remote a place, Uncle Lou had been there before you, and already returned to his flat in Pallas Mews to bash out an account of where to find the best all-night noodle shop in Bangkok, or a black-market mushroom stall beneath the catacombs in Rome, or a Stockholm voyeurs' club masquerading as a film soci-ety devoted to works that featured the forgotten silent movie star Sigrid Blau.

"Doesn't he ever feel guilty?" Nina's mother had once asked her. Lou was her husband's much-older brother; he had been in the war, and afterward spent several years in Eastern Europe, where his activ-ities were unknown, but remained the object of much speculation by Nina's parents. He had returned to London sporting a beard and a newly fashionable mane of long hair. The beard was not a permanent affectation—Uncle Lou had been clean shaven before the war, yet afterward was remarkably hirsute, shaving at least once and some-times twice a day. But he kept the flowing black hair, which became a trademark of his author photos.

Nina's mother had always found him "showy," her code word for homosexual, though Uncle Lou in fact was a notorious ladies' man.

Nina had frowned at her mother's question. "Guilty about what?"

"About promoting criminal activities?"

"He's not promoting anything," said Nina. "The things he writes about help the local economy."

"I suppose you could call it that," her mother sniffed, and returned to her delphiniums.

This afternoon, early-October sunlight washed across the cobble-stone walk leading to Pallas Mews. Uncle Lou's vintage Aston Martin DB4 was parked out front beneath a green tarpaulin that was covered with an impasto of bird droppings that suggested it had not been driven in some time. Pale yellow leaves had banked up against the front door to the flat, and Nina plucked a torn plastic bag from the ivy and clematis vines that covered the brick wall.

She had never visited Uncle Lou without an invitation by telephone or, these days, e-mail. The summons was always precise, for late afternoon or early evening; this one had read *Drop by 5:15 Thursday 19th*. In his kitchen, Uncle Lou had a large wall calendar, a sort of scroll, with the phases of the moon marked on it and myriad jottings in his fine, minuscule penmanship, indicating the exact hour and minute at which various meetings had been scheduled. At home he never met with more than one visitor at a time; the nature of his work was solitary as well as nocturnal.

When she was still in her teens, Nina had once arrived ten minutes early. She could hear Uncle Lou inside, washing dishes as he listened to Radio 2, and even glimpsed him strolling past the front window to turn the music down. But the door did not open until the appointed time.

Today it opened even before she could knock.

"Nina, dear." Her uncle smiled and beckoned her inside. "You look lovely. Watch that pile there, I haven't got them out to the bin yet."

Nina sidestepped a heap of newspapers as he closed the door. Uncle Lou had always been meticulous, even fussy. He'd employed a cleaning woman who came once a week to keep the white Flokati rugs spotless and arrange the kilim pillows neatly on the white leather sofa and matching chairs; to straighten the Hockney painting and make sure the Dansk dishes were in their cupboards.

But several years ago, the cleaning woman had moved to Brighton to be closer to her grandchildren. Uncle Lou hadn't bothered to find someone new, and the flat had developed the defiantly unkempt air of a club goer who knows she is too old to wear transparent vinyl blouses, even with a camisole beneath, but continues to do so anyway.

"I know, it's a bit of a mess." Uncle Lou sighed and bent to pick up a stray newspaper that was attempting escape, and set it back atop the stack with a hand that trembled slightly. His Moroccan slippers flapped around his bony feet, gold tassels gone and curled toes sadly flattened. "But it's so expensive now to find anyone. Come on in, dear, do you want a drink?"

"No thanks. Or yes, well, if you're going to have something."

Uncle Lou leaned over to graze her cheek with a kiss. He hadn't shaved, and she noted an alarming turquoise blister—actually, a blob of toothpaste—on his neck.

"That's my girl," he said, and shuffled into the kitchen.

While he got drinks, Nina wandered into his office, a brick-walled space covered with bookshelves that held copies of the *By Night* books in dozens, perhaps hundreds, of various translations. There were more untidy stacks here, of unopened mail that had not yet made its way onto Uncle Lou's desk.

She glanced at one of the envelopes. Its postal date was a month previous. She looked over her shoulder and hastily flipped through more envelopes, finding some dated back to the spring. At the sound of Uncle Lou's footsteps in the hall she turned quickly and went to meet him.

"Thanks." She took the martini glass he offered her—it was clean, at least—and raised it to *ting* against his.

"Chin-chin," said Uncle Lou.

She walked with him to the dining room, which overlooked a good-sized courtyard. Years ago Uncle Lou had let the outside space revert to a tangle of mulberry bushes, etiolated plane trees, and ground ivy. It would have made a nice dog run, but Uncle Lou had never kept a dog. There were signs of some kind of animals rooting around—foxes, probably, which were common in Hampstead, though Nina had never caught a whiff of their distinctive musky scent.

They settled at the dining table. Uncle Lou set out a plate of olives and some slightly stale biscuits. They drank and chatted about a travel piece in last week's *Guardian*, a noisy dog in Nina's neighborhood, people they knew in common.

"Have you heard from Valerie Minton?" asked Nina. She finished her drink and nibbled at an olive. "You haven't mentioned her for a while."

Uncle Lou sighed. "Oh dear, very sad. I guess I forgot to tell you. She died in March. A heart thing—a blessing, really. She had that early-onset Alzheimer's." He downed the rest of his martini and set the empty glass beside hers. "Here's a piece of good advice: Don't get old."

"Oh, Uncle Lou." Nina hugged him. "You're not old."

But that of course was a lie. She could feel how thin he'd gotten, and frail. And the flat was all too clearly becoming a burden in terms of upkeep.

She grasped his hand and stared at him. His long hair was white, sparser than it had been. His face was lined, but a lifetime of keeping late hours had saved him from skin-damaging ultraviolet rays and preserved a certain youthful suppleness. With his high cheekbones, stark blade of a nose, and cleft chin, he might have been an aging actor, with eyes a disconcerting shade of amber, so pale they appeared almost colorless in strong light. The theatrical effect was heightened by his wardrobe, which this afternoon consisted of an embroidered India-print shirt over wide-wale corduroy trousers that had once been canary yellow but had faded to the near white of lemon pith, and the heavy silver ring he always wore on his right pointer finger.

The ring wobbled now as that finger shook, scolding her. "I am older than old, Nina. Older than God, who has never forgiven me for it."

Nina laughed, and he turned to gaze wistfully out into the court-yard. How old *was* Uncle Lou? In his eighties, at least. Many of his old friends were dead; others had moved to live with their children, or into retirement communities. Nina's own flat was too small for another person; she could move in with him, she supposed, but she knew Uncle Lou wouldn't hear of it. A few years earlier, he had sold the By Night trademark and backlist to a web entrepreneur for an impressive sum. Perhaps he could be encouraged to look into one of those posh facilities where elderly people of means lived?

She wouldn't bring it up this afternoon, but made a mental note to do some research herself into what was available near Hampstead.

Uncle Lou squeezed her hand. "Do you feel up to a walk on the Heath?"

Nina nodded. "Great idea."

They strolled along a path that meandered over a gentle rise crowned by an ancient oak. There were always families with young children here, and lots of dogs off leash.

"Uh oh," said Nina, as a silken-furred red setter came bounding toward them. She moved protectively to his side. "Incoming . . ."

Dogs behaved in a peculiar fashion around Uncle Lou. Those that had previously encountered him acted as the setter did now: As it drew near, it dropped to its belly and inched toward him, whining softly, tail wagging madly.

Strange dogs, however, barked or snarled, ears pressed tight against their skulls and tails held low, and often fled before Uncle Lou could hold out his hand and make reassuring *cht cht* sounds that Nina could barely hear.

"Hello there." Uncle Lou stopped and gazed down at the setter, smiling. His knees bent slightly and he winced as he reached to touch the dog's forehead. "Conor, isn't it? Good dog."

At the old man's touch, the setter scrambled to its feet and danced around him, ears flapping.

"Sorry, sorry!" A man rushed up and grasped the dog's collar, clipping a leash onto it. "Don't want him to knock you over!"

Uncle Lou shook his head. "Oh, he wouldn't do that. Would you, Conor?"

He stooped to take the dog's head between his hands and gazed into its eyes. The setter grew absolutely still, as though it sensed a game bird nearby; then dropped to its belly, head cocked as it stared up at Uncle Lou.

"Well, he likes you, doesn't he?" The man patted the setter's head, smiling. "Come on then, Conor. Let's go."

Nina waved as the man strode off, the setter straining at the leash. Uncle Lou stood beside her, watching until the two figures disappeared into the trees. He turned to his niece, nodding as though all this had occurred according to some plan.

"I'd like you to accompany me to an event." He gestured at the path, indicating they should begin to head back home. "If you're not too busy."

"Of course," said Nina. "Where is it?"

"At the zoo."

"The zoo?" Nina looked over in surprise. Uncle Lou had always been far more likely to invite his niece to attend a clandestine midnight gathering of political dissidents or artists than to suggest a visit to the zoo.

"Yes. The Whipsnade Zoo, not Regent's Park, so we'll have to drive up to Dunstable. A fund-raiser for a new building, a home for endangered fruit bats, I think, or maybe it's kiwis? Something nocturnal, anyway. There'll be press around, the local gentry, maybe a few minor celebrities. You know the sort of thing. Someone in the PR department obviously thought it would be amusing if I was in attendance. You can be my date."

He slipped his arm into hers, and Nina laughed. "Sure. Sounds like fun. When is it? Do I need to dress up?"

"Next Wednesday. I believe the invitation says to wear black. Not very imaginative. But you always look lovely, dear."

They'd reached the Pallas Mews flat. Uncle Lou paused to pluck a clematis blossom from the ivy-covered wall, and turned to poke its stem through a buttonhole in Nina's jacket. "There. Purple is your color, isn't it? Thank you for dropping by."

He kissed her cheek and Nina embraced him, hugging him tightly. "I'll see you next week."

Uncle Lou nodded, long white hair stirring in the evening breeze, and walked unsteadily back inside.

*

The following week Nina showed up at the appointed quarter hour, 4:45. A bit earlier than customary for Uncle Lou, but they wanted to allow plenty of time for rush-hour traffic on the M1. Out front, the tarp had been removed from the Aston Martin, which gleamed like quicksilver in the twilight.

"Hello, darling, don't you look marvelous!" exclaimed Uncle Lou as she stepped into the flat. "I haven't seen that dress before, have I? Lovely."

He kissed her cheek, and she noticed his own cheeks were flushed and his tawny eyes bright.

"You look lovely too," she said, laughing. "Is there some ulterior motive for this event? Am I the beard for an assignation?"

For an instant Uncle Lou appeared alarmed, but then he shook his head.

"No." He made a show of straightening his velvet jacket, a somewhat frayed black paisley with silver embroidery. "It's been a while since I was out and about, that's all. And I need to be worthy of *you*, of course."

She waited as he moved about the flat, collecting keys, the oversized black envelope containing the invitation, a plastic carrier bag from Sainsbury's, an umbrella.

"I think it's supposed to be nice," said Nina, eyeing the umbrella.

"You're probably right." Uncle Lou set the umbrella back atop a hall table and paused, catching his breath. After a moment he slid a hand into his pocket, withdrew it to hold out a set of car keys.

"Here." He put the keys into Nina's palm and closed her fingers around them. "I'd like you to drive."

"What?" Nina's eyes widened. "The—your car?"

Uncle Lou nodded. "Yes. I don't trust myself anymore. It used to be I saw better at night than daytime, but now . . ." He grimaced. "Last time I took it out I drove onto the curb near Tesco. You can drive a standard, right?"

"Yes—of course. But—"

"I'm giving it to you." He turned and picked up a large manila envelope on the side table. "Everything's in here, I've done all the paperwork already. Title and deed. It's yours. There are some other papers in there as well. You might look at them when you have some spare time."

Nina stared at the keys in her hand. "But—are you sure, Uncle Lou?"

371

"Absolutely. Impress that boyfriend of yours at the law firm. I can always borrow it back if I need to. Now, we'd better go—I don't want to be late."

He tucked the manila envelope beneath his arm. Once inside the car, he slid it into the glove box. "Let's remember it's there," he said, and sank into the leather seat.

They ran into heavy traffic heading north, but this eased as they approached Dunstable. The zoo was in the countryside a few miles outside town, within a greenbelt that was in stark contrast to the depressing sprawl behind them. Uncle Lou rolled down his window, letting in the smell of autumn leaves and smoke. On a distant green hillside, the immense chalk figure of a lion had been carved. Above the hill, a full moon had just begun to rise, tarnished silver against the periwinkle sky.

"Look at that," said Nina. "Isn't that beautiful?"

"Isn't it," said Uncle Lou, and squeezed her hand upon the gearshift.

They arrived at the zoo entrance shortly after the reception's opening time.

"Don't park there," Uncle Lou said when Nina put on her turn signal for the main car park. "Keep going—there, on the left. Much less crowded, and you'll be able to leave quickly later."

Nina angled the Aston Martin through a narrow gate that opened into a much smaller lot. It held only a handful of vehicles, most of them zoo vans and trucks.

"Are we allowed to park here?" she asked, after following Uncle Lou's directions to ease the Aston Martin beneath a large oak.

"Oh yes. It never really fills up. Bit of a secret." With an effort, he extricated himself from the car, steadying himself against the hood and sighing. "I swear, that car gets smaller every time I get inside it." He pointed at a gap in an overgrown hedge. "That way."

"How do you know about this?" asked Nina, stepping gingerly through the gap.

"I have friends here I visit sometimes. Ah, that must be where we're supposed to be. . . ."

This zoo was much more parklike than the London Zoo; more like the grounds of a stately home, only minus the home, and with elephants and oryx and other large wildlife. Dusk had deepened into early evening, the moon poised above them in a lapis sky where a few faint stars shimmered. Unearthly noises echoed through the night: high-pitched chitters, a loud snuffling that became a bellow, an odd hollow pumping sound.

372

"Least bittern," said Uncle Lou, cocking his head in the direction of the sound.

Nina squinted in the fading light. "How do you know that?"

"I'm a font of useless knowledge. I've built my career on it."

A path led them toward a large field where a crowd milled around an open-sided white marquee tent. A few security guards and several men and women in staff uniforms that marked them as animal keepers mingled with people wearing loose interpretations of fancy dress. At a small booth beside the tent, a middle-aged woman in a black faux-fur capelet examined Uncle Lou's invitation.

"I know who you are," she said, beaming up at him. "I met my husband because of *Athens by Night*. Is this your daughter?"

"My niece." Uncle Lou tucked Nina's arm into his.

The woman checked their names off a list and gestured toward the tent. "Go get some champagne. Enjoy!"

The reception was to raise funds for a new, state-of-the-art Owl House, which would provide habitat for the endangered Eurasian eagle-owl and pygmy owl, along with more common species. Beneath the marquee, tables draped in black and silver held trays of canapés and elaborate hors d'oeuvres made to resemble owls, full moons, and bats. In one corner, a large owl with a slender chain attached to its leg perched upon a leather gauntlet covering the arm of a tall, blond young man in zoo-staff livery. A number of guests had gathered here, and the owl regarded them with baleful hauteur, now and then ruffling its feathers and clicking its beak noisily.

After making a beeline for the bar, Nina and Uncle Lou wandered around the tent, drinking their champagne and admiring a large display with three-dimensional models of the proposed Owl House. A few people walked over to clasp Uncle Lou's hand and greet him by name, including Miranda Eccles, an ancient woman writer of some renown. Nina had often heard the rumor that the two had been lovers. While they spoke, Nina slipped away to get two more glasses of champagne. By the time she returned, the elderly woman was gone.

"Let's go say hello to that owl," said Uncle Lou.

He handed his empty glass to a passing waiter and took a full one from Nina. They edged their way to the front of the group, being careful not to spill their champagne. The owl had turned its back on the onlookers.

"It looks rather like Miranda, doesn't it?" observed Uncle Lou.

The owl's head abruptly swiveled in a disconcerting 260-degree arc. Its yellow eyes fixed on Uncle Lou, the pupils large as pound coins. Without warning it raised its wings and flapped them menac-ingly, beak parting to emit an ear-splitting screech.

Nina gasped. A few people cried out, then laughed nervously as the owl keeper swiftly produced a canvas hood that he quickly dropped over the bird.

"He's getting restless," he explained, adjusting the hood. "Full moon, he wants to hunt. And he's not used to so many people."

"I feel the same way." Uncle Lou took Nina's elbow and steered her toward an exit. "Let's take a walk outside."

They handed off their empty glasses and stepped back into the night. Uncle Lou seemed invigorated by the champagne: He threw his head back, gazing at the moon; laughed, then pointed to a black tracery of trees some distance away.

"There," he said.

He began walking so quickly that Nina had to run to catch up. When she reached his side, he took her hand, slowing his pace.

"You've been a very good niece." He glanced down at her. For the first time Nina noticed he had neglected to shave, perhaps for several days: Gray stubble covered his jaw and chin. "I don't know how my brother and your mother managed to produce such a wonderful daughter, but I'm very glad they did."

"Oh, Uncle Lou." Nina's eyes filled with tears. "I feel the same way about you."

"I know you do. Here." He stopped, and with some effort twisted the heavy silver ring from his hand. He grasped Nina's wrist and slid the ring onto her right pointer finger. "I want you to have this."

She looked at him in surprise. "It fits! It always looked so big."

Moonlight glinted on the silver band as Uncle Lou drew it to his lips and kissed her knuckle, the gray hairs on his chin soft where they brushed her fingertips.

"Of course it fits. You have my hands," he said, and let hers drop. "Come on."

They passed artfully landscaped habitats with placards indicating that antelopes or Bactrian camels lived there, behind hidden moats or fences cunningly designed to resemble vines or reeds or waist-high grass. A gated road permitted cars and zoo buses to drive through a mock savanna where lions and cheetahs prowled.

Nina saw no sign of any animals, though she occasionally caught the ripe scents of dung or musk, the muddy green smell of a man-made pond or marsh. The snorts and hoots had diminished as night deepened and creatures either settled to sleep or, in the case of predators, grew silent and watchful.

But then a single wavering cry rang out from the direction of the trees, ending as abruptly as it began. Nina's entire body flashed cold.

"What was that?" she whispered. But Uncle Lou didn't reply.

They reached the stand of trees, where the gravel walkway forked. Without hesitation Uncle Lou bore to the left.

Here, more trees loomed alongside the path, their branches entwining above unruly thickets of thorny brush. Acorns and beech mast crunched underfoot, so that it seemed as though they had entered a forest. There was a spicy smell of bracken, and another scent, unfamiliar but unmistakably an animal's.

After a few minutes Uncle Lou stopped. He glanced behind them, and for a moment remained still, listening.

"This way," he said, and ducked beneath the trees.

"Are we allowed here?" Nina called after him in a low, urgent voice.

Uncle Lou's words echoed back to her. "At night, everything is allowed. Shhh!"

She hesitated, trying to peer though the heavy greenery; finally ducked and began to push her way through, shielding her face with one hand. Brambles plucked at her dress, and she flinched as a thorn scraped against one leg.

But then the underbrush receded. She stepped into a small clearing thick with dead leaves. Several large trees loomed against the moonlit sky. Uncle Lou stood beneath one of these, breathing heavily as he stared at a small hill several yards away. More trees grew on its slope, between boulders and creeping vines.

"Uncle Lou?"

She took a step toward him, froze as a dark shape flowed between the boulders then disappeared. Before she could cry out she heard Uncle Lou's soft voice.

"There's a fence."

She swallowed, blinking, looked where he pointed, and saw a faint latticework of twisted chain link. She waited for her heart to slow, then darted to his side.

And, yes, now she could discern that behind the chain-link fence was a deep cement moat, maybe twenty feet wide and extending into the darkness in either direction. Vines straggled down its sides, and overhanging mats of moss and dead leaves.

They were at the back of one of the enclosures, a place where visitors were absolutely *not* allowed.

"*Uncle Lou,*" Nina whispered, her voice rising anxiously.

As she spoke, the shadowy form rematerialized, still on the far side of the moat, and directly across from them. It lowered its head between massive shoulders, moonlight flaring in its eyes so that they momentarily glowed red, then stretched out its front legs until its belly grazed the ground. A wolf.

Nina stared at it, torn between amazement and an atavistic fear unassuaged by the presence of the moat. When a second form slipped beside the first, she jumped.

"They won't hurt you," murmured Uncle Lou.

A third wolf trotted from the trees, and another, and another, until at last seven were ranged at the foot of the hill. They gazed at the old man, tongues lolling from their long jaws, and then each lay down in turn upon the grass in a watchful pose.

"What are they doing?" breathed Nina.

"The same thing we are," replied Uncle Lou. "Excuse me for a moment—nature calls. . . ."

He patted her shoulder and walked briskly toward another tree.

Nina politely turned away—he sometimes had to do this when they had embarked upon a long stroll on the Heath, always returning to shake his head and mutter, "Old man's bladder."

She looked back at the wolves, who now appeared somewhat restive. The largest one's head snapped up. It stared at something overhead, then scrambled to its feet. At the same moment, Nina heard a rustling in the treetops, followed by a creaking sound.

"Uncle Lou?" She glanced at the tree where he'd gone to relieve himself. "Everything all right?"

The rustling grew louder. Nina looked up, and saw one of the upper boughs of the tree bending down at an alarming angle, so that its tip hung over the moat. A large whitish animal was clambering down its length, sending dead leaves and bits of debris to the ground beneath. Nina clapped a hand to her mouth as a shaft of moonlight struck the bough, revealing Uncle Lou, naked and slowing to a crawl as the branch bowed under him.

The wolves had all leapt up and stood in a row at the enclosure's edge, eyes fixed on the white figure above them. With a loud *crack*, the bough snapped. At the same instant Uncle Lou sprang from it, his pale form mottled with shadow as he landed upon the grass and rolled between the creatures there.

With a cry, Nina ran forward, stopped, and fought to see her uncle in the blur of dust and leaves and fur on the other side of the hidden moat. The wolves danced around it, tails held low, heads high, then drew back as another wolf struggled to its feet.

It was nearly the same size as the largest wolf, its muzzle white and iron-gray fur tipped with silver. It shook its head, sending off a flurry of leaves and twigs, stood very still as the other big male approached to sniff its hindquarters, then its throat. Finally it touched the newcomer's white muzzle, growling playfully as the two engaged in mock battle and the other wolves darted forward, tails wagging as they joined in.

Nina watched, too stunned to move. Not until the wolves turned and began to stream back into the shadows did she call out.

"Wait!"

The biggest wolf paused to glance back at her, then disappeared into the underbrush with the others. Only the grizzled wolf slowed, and looked over its shoulder at Nina. For a long moment it held her gaze, its tawny eyes and pale muzzle gilded by the moonlight. Then it too turned and trotted into the darkness.

Nina shook her head, trying to catch her breath. Astonishment curdled into terror as she thought of the reception not far away. She raced to the tree Uncle Lou had climbed, and beneath it found the plastic Sainsbury's bag. Stuffed inside were his clothes, velvet jacket and corduroy trousers, socks and underwear, and at the very bottom the worn Moroccan slippers.

At the sight of them she began to cry, but quickly wiped her eyes. Clutching the bag to her chest, she pushed her way through the trees and overgrown brush until she reached the path again.

Somehow she found her way back to the car park where she'd left the Aston Martin. She passed no one, walking as fast as she dared before breaking into a run as she neared the hedge that bounded the lot. The moon had dipped below the trees. The sounds of the reception had long since dwindled to the distant drone of departing cars.

She started the Aston Martin, heart pounding as she eased it onto the access road and headed toward the main highway, sobbing openly now, always careful not to exceed the speed limit.

At last she reached her apartment. She parked the car in the underground garage, leaving a note on the windscreen for the security guard so it would not be towed; retrieved the manila envelope from the glove box, grabbed the bag containing Uncle Lou's clothes, and went upstairs. She poured herself a stiff drink, downed it, and with shaking hands opened the envelope.

Inside was a long, affectionate letter from her uncle, along with the title to the Aston Martin, and precisely detailed instructions as to how to dispose of his clothing and answer the awkward and inevitable questions that would soon arise regarding his disappearance. There was also contact information for his longtime accountant and solicitor—and, of course, a copy of his will.

In addition to the car, he left the Pallas Mews flat and all it contained to Nina, along with his shares in the By Night enterprise. And there was an extremely generous bequest to the Whipsnade Zoo, with a provision that a sizable portion of it be used for the continued upkeep and improvement of the gray wolves' habitat.

Nina sold the Aston Martin. Maintenance was costly, and she worried about its being vandalized or stolen. After six months she moved into the Pallas Mews flat, refurbishing it slightly and donating the unworn clothing to Oxfam, though she kept the Moroccan slippers. She continues to visit Uncle Lou every week, taking the train to Luton and then the bus to the zoo. The gray wolf exhibit is seldom crowded, even on Sundays, and Nina often has it to herself. Sometimes, the grizzled old wolf sits at the edge of the enclosure and gazes at her with his tawny eyes, and occasionally raises his white muzzle in a yodeling cry.

But more often than not, she finds him outstretched on one of the moss-covered boulders, eyes closed, breathing gently: the very picture of lupine bliss as he sleeps in the afternoon sun.

NOTES ON CONTRIBUTORS

RAE ARMANTROUT's most recent book, *Money Shot*, was published by Wesleyan this year. Her book *Versed* (Wesleyan) won the 2010 Pulitzer Prize. She teaches at UC San Diego.

RACHEL TZVIA BACK's books include *Azimuth* (Sheep Meadow), *The Buffalo Poems* (Duration Press), and *On Ruins & Return: Poems 1999–2005* (Shearsman Books). Her poetry translations in *Lea Goldberg: Selected Poetry and Drama* (Toby Press) were awarded a 2005 PEN Translation Grant. She lives in Galilee in northern Israel.

ANN BEATTIE is the 2011 recipient of the Mary McCarthy Award from Bard College. Her book *Mrs. Nixon: A Novelist Imagines a Life* appeared from Scribner in November.

SARAH BLACKMAN is coeditor of fiction for *DIAGRAM* and the director of creative writing at the Fine Arts Center, a public arts high school in Greenville, South Carolina. Her fiction chapbook *Such a Thing as America* is available from the Burnside Review Press.

CAN XUE's most recent books are *Blue Light in the Sky and Other Stories* (New Directions), *Five Spice Street* (Yale University Press), and *Vertical Motion* (Open Letter Books), all translated by Karen Gernant and Chen Zeping. She lives in Beijing, China.

GEORGES-OLIVIER CHÂTEAUREYNAUD has been honored with the Prix Renaudot, the Prix Goncourt de la nouvelle, and the Grand Prix de l'Imaginaire at Utopiales. Edward Gauvin's translation of his volume of selected stories, *A Life on Paper* (Small Beer), won the Science Fiction & Fantasy Translation Award.

CHEN ZEPING is professor of Chinese linguistics at Fujian Normal University, Fuzhou, China. Since 1999, he has collaborated with Karen Gernant in translating contemporary Chinese fiction into English.

ROBERT CLARK is the author of four novels and four works of nonfiction, most recently *Dark Water: Flood and Redemption in the City of Masterpieces* (Doubleday).

Winner of the John Dryden Translation prize, EDWARD GAUVIN is the contributing editor for Francophone comics at *Words Without Borders* and translates comics for Lerner and Archaia.

SCOTT GEIGER's fiction has appeared in the Pushcart Prize anthology and on exhibit at Storefront for Art and Architecture in New York City.

Among KAREN GERNANT and Chen Zeping's translations are *Eleven Contemporary Chinese Writers* (Turnrow Books), Zhang Kangkang's *White Poppies and Other Stories* (Cornell East Asia Series), and Alai's *Tibetan Soul* (forthcoming from MerwinAsia), as well as work by Can Xue.

ELIZABETH HAND is the author of three collections of short fiction and numerous novels, including the forthcoming thriller *Available Dark* (St. Martin's Press) and young-adult novel *Radiant Days* (Viking).

KAREN HAYS's essays have won the Iowa Review Award and the Normal Prize. She lives with her family in Minneapolis.

CHRISTIE HODGEN is the author of the novels *Elegies for the Brokenhearted* and *Hello, I Must Be Going* (both W. W. Norton). Her short-story collection, *A Jeweler's Eye for Flaw* (University of Massachusetts Press), won the 2001 AWP award. She lives in Kansas City.

NOY HOLLAND is the author of two collections of short fiction, *The Spectacle of the Body* (Knopf) and *What Begins with Bird* (Fiction Collective 2). A third collection, *Swim for the Little One First*, is forthcoming from FC2.

A D JAMESON is the author of the prose collection *Amazing Adult Fantasy* (Mutable Sound) and the novel *Giant Slugs* (Lawrence and Gibson). He is the nonfiction/ reviews editor of the online journal *Requited* and a blogger for *Big Other* and *HTMLGIANT*.

DIANE GRECO JOSEFOWICZ coauthored *The Zodiac of Paris* (Princeton University Press) with Jed Z. Buchwald. She teaches in the undergraduate writing program at Boston University.

ROBERT KELLY's most recent books include the novel *The Book from the Sky* (North Atlantic/Random), the fiction collection *The Logic of the World* (McPherson & Co.), and the long poems *Fire Exit* (Black Widow/Commonwealth Books) and *Uncertainties* (Station Hill).

New fiction by CLARK KNOWLES (clarkknowles.com) is forthcoming in *Harpur Palate, Limestone, Nimrod, Eclipse*, and *Glimmer Train*. He teaches writing at the University of New Hampshire.

Poems by GRACIE LEAVITT have recently appeared or are forthcoming in *Sentence, Brooklyn Review, Washington Square, Word For/Word*, and other journals.

MIRANDA MELLIS is the author of *The Revisionist* (Calamari Press), *Materialisms* (Portable Press at Yo-Yo Labs), and *None of This Is Real* (forthcoming from Sidebrow Press). She is an editor at the Encyclopedia Project and teaches at Mills College and the California College of the Arts.

RICK MOODY's forthcoming book is a collection of essays, *On Celestial Music and Other Adventures in Listening* (Little, Brown).

MICAELA MORRISSETTE is managing editor of *Conjunctions*. Her work is anthologized in *The Weird* (Atlantic/Corvus), *Best Horror of the Year* (Night Shade), *Best American Fantasy* (Prime Books), and elsewhere.

ANDREW MOSSIN is the author of two books of poetry, *The Veil* and *The Epochal Body* (both Singing Horse Press).

JOYCE CAROL OATES recently published the memoir *A Widow's Story* (Ecco) and the story collection *Give Me Your Heart* (Otto Penzler/Grove Atlantic).

PETER ORNER is the author of *Esther Stories* (Mariner) and the novels *The Second Coming of Mavala Shikongo* and *Love and Shame and Love* (both Little, Brown).

OCTAVIO PAZ's *Poems 1931–1996* will be published by New Directions in the fall of 2012.

KAREN RUSSELL is the author of the story collection *St. Lucy's Home for Girls Raised by Wolves* and the novel *Swamplandia!* (both Knopf/Vintage).

AURELIE SHEEHAN is the author of *Jack Kerouac Is Pregnant* (Dalkey), *History Lesson for Girls* (Viking), and *The Anxiety of Everyday Objects* (Penguin). She teaches at the University of Arizona in Tucson.

SALLIE TISDALE's most recent book is *Women of the Way* (HarperOne).

Stories by ANDREW R. TOUHY have appeared in *Web Conjunctions, New American Writing, New Orleans Review, Colorado Review, The Collagist*, and elsewhere.

ELIOT WEINBERGER's most recent books of essays are *Oranges & Peanuts for Sale* and *An Elemental Thing*, both published by New Directions.

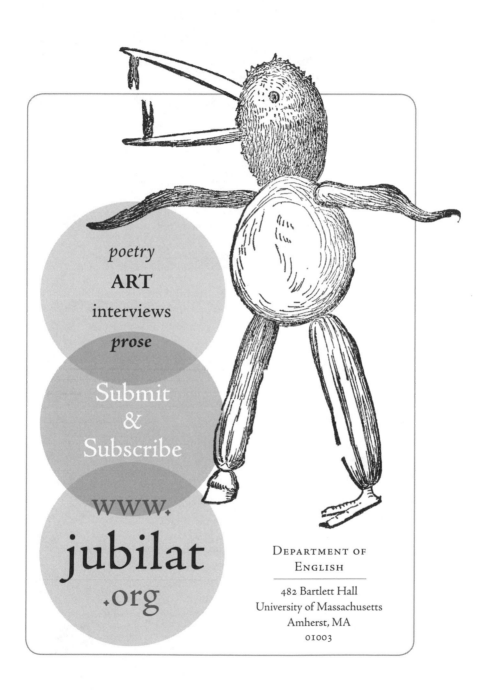

poetry
ART
interviews
prose

Submit
&
Subscribe

www.
jubilat
.org

Department of
English

482 Bartlett Hall
University of Massachusetts
Amherst, MA
01003

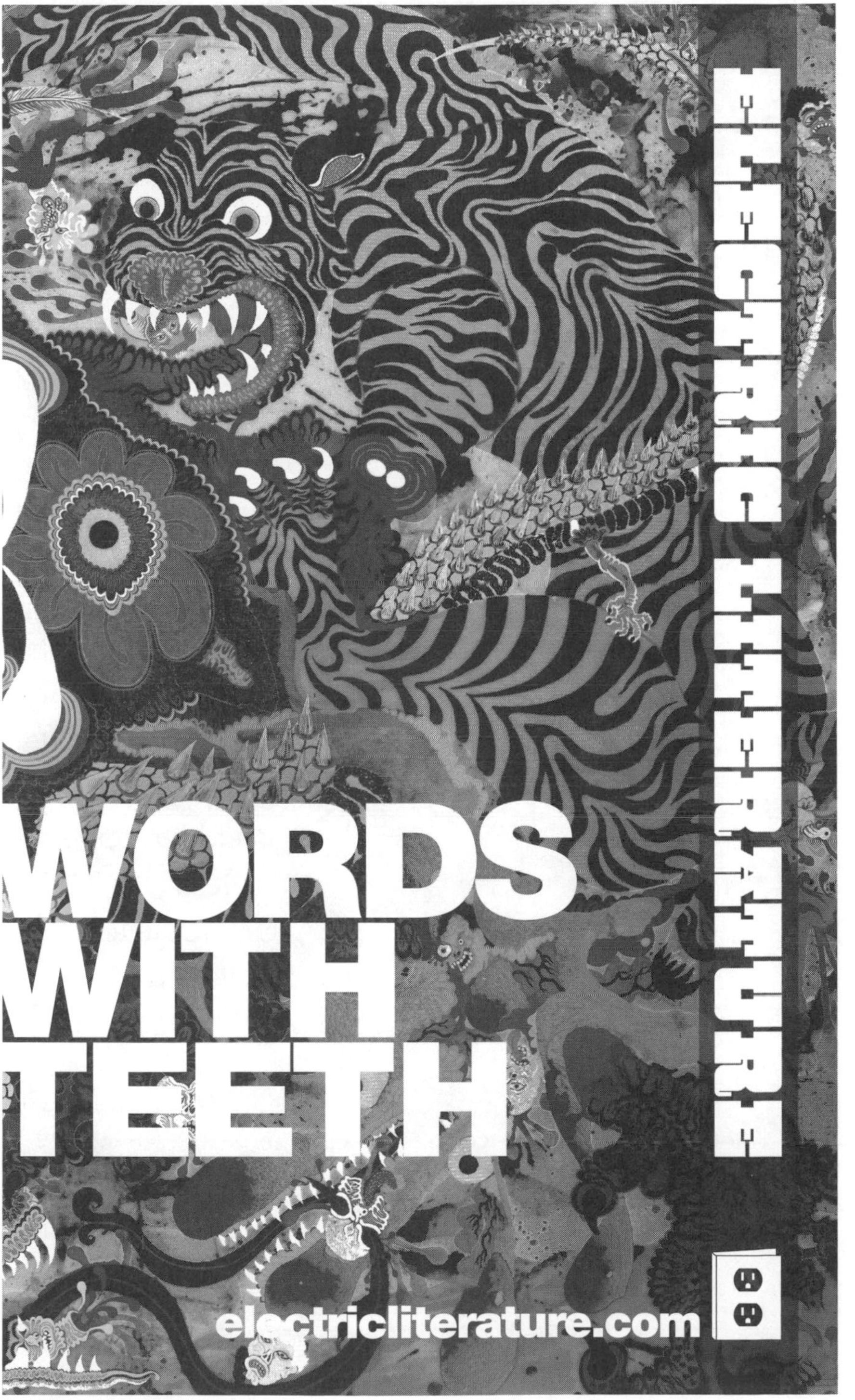
ELECTRIC LITERATURE
WORDS WITH TEETH.
electricliterature.com

BROWN UNIVERSITY LITERARY ARTS

Program faculty

John Cayley
Brian Evenson
Thalia Field
Forrest Gander
Renee Gladman
Michael S. Harper
Carole Maso
Meredith Steinbach
Cole Swensen
CD Wright

Joint-appointment, visiting & other faculty

Robert Coover
Joanna Howard
Ian McDonald
Shahriar Mondanipour
Gale Nelson
John Edgar Wideman

For over 40 years, Literary Arts at Brown University has been a home for innovative writing. To learn about the two-year MFA program and the undergraduate concentration, or to have access to Writers Online, an archive of literary recordings, visit http://www.brown.edu/cw

The online MFA application deadline is 15 December

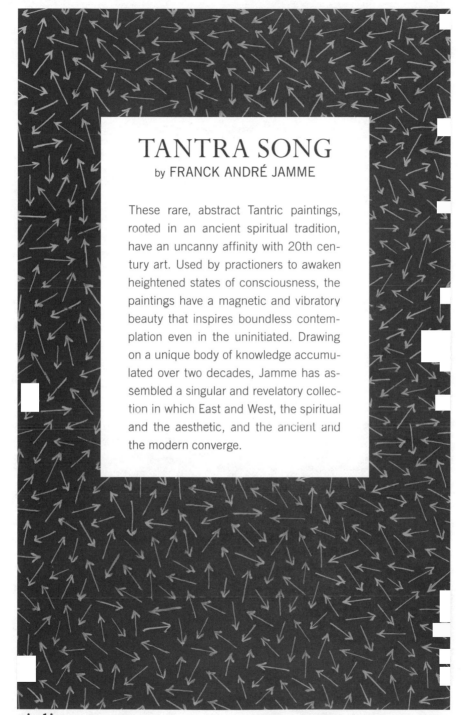

TANTRA SONG
by FRANCK ANDRÉ JAMME

These rare, abstract Tantric paintings, rooted in an ancient spiritual tradition, have an uncanny affinity with 20th century art. Used by practioners to awaken heightened states of consciousness, the paintings have a magnetic and vibratory beauty that inspires boundless contemplation even in the uninitiated. Drawing on a unique body of knowledge accumulated over two decades, Jamme has assembled a singular and revelatory collection in which East and West, the spiritual and the aesthetic, and the ancient and the modern converge.

siglio uncommon books at the intersection of art & literature **www.sigliopress.com**

PUERTO DEL SOL

Volume 46 No. 1 & 2 Available Now
$10 single issue, $20 1-year subscription

Spring 2012
Poetry & Fiction Contests
Deadline March 15

Poetry Judge: Thomas Sayers Ellis
Fiction Judge: Kevin McIlvoy

Prizes for fiction and poetry will be $400 for first
place, $100 for second place, and $50 for third. The
first-place winners will be published in our 2012
spring issue, and the editors will consider all submissions for publication.

Entry Fee: $15, includes 1-year subscription

See www.puertodelsol.org for details
contact@puertodelsol.org

NOON

A LITERARY ANNUAL

1324 LEXINGTON AVENUE PMB 298 NEW YORK NY 10128

EDITION PRICE $12 DOMESTIC $17 FOREIGN

bateau press

Boom Poetry
Chapbook Contest
15 Sept - 31 Dec 2011

Keel Short Short Fiction
Chapbook Contest
15 Feb - 31 May 2012

www.bateaupress.org

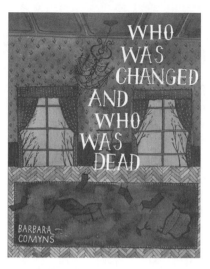

BARBARA COMYNS
Who Was Changed and Who Was Dead

MANUELA DRAEGER
In the Time of the Blue Ball
TRANS. BY BRIAN EVENSON

RENEE GLADMAN
Event Factory

RENEE GLADMAN
The Ravickians

ALL TITLES $16, DISCOUNT PRICING THROUGH OUR WEBSITE:

DOROTHYPROJECT.COM

Gérard Macé: *The Last of the Egyptians*

[translated from the French by Brian Evenson]

Champollion loved the novels of Fenimore Cooper and in particular *The Last of the Mohicans*. Macé explores Champollion's twin interests in Egypt and in "America's savage nations," his deciphering of the Rosetta stone and the Indians' deciphering of the forest. He finally follows Champollion to the Louvre where he set up the Egyptian galleries and saw Indians of the Osage tribe and felt the sadness in their slow song.

Gérard Macé's unclassifiable texts cross the lines between essay, dream, biography, criticism, anthropology, and history. His honors include the Prix France Culture for the present book (1989), and the Grand Prix of the of the Académie française for life achievement (2008).

Novella/Essay, 80 pages, offset, smyth-sewn, original pbk. $14

Monika Rinck:
to refrain from embracing

[translated from the German by Nicholas Grindell]

"As multifaceted and aggressively engaged as any voice in contemporary German poetry, Monika Rinck is a poet of intellect, experimentation and humour. Her work is marked by a singular turn of expression, the profound imbedded in a discourse that disarms the reader."
—S. J. Fowler, *3:AM Magazine*

"A poetry which combines the lyric, the idiosyncratic, the magic and the tragic, the bucolic, the alcoholic, the indisputable and the disreputable, the sonic and the laconic, bits, bobs, flips but not flops, crazy but never lazy, meaning with a flourish, but no finish."
—Alastair Noon

Poetry, 80 pages, offset, smyth-sewn, original pbk. $14

David Lespiau: *Four Cut-ups or The Case of the Restored Volume*

[translated from the French by Keith Waldrop]

Real and fictional characters (Mrs. Lindbergh, Gertrude Stein, William Burroughs, Billy Budd or the Kid) circulate through a kind of mobile whose movement constructs a form out of fragmented perceptions, ideas, stories, quotations, and gives a strangely uncanny sheen to the most realistic details. David Lespiau lives in Marseille. Other recent books are *Ouija Board* and *La poule est un oiseau autodidacte*.

Poetry, 64 pages, offset, smyth-sewn, original pbk. $14

Elizabeth MacKiernan: *Ancestors Maybe*

Three sisters, all named Marie, and their dwarf companion Hugo entertain dead family members in a burlesque of family saga and the Irish-American tall tale.

"MacKiernan is a kind of Connecticut-Yankee version of a magic realist, stylishly anarchical in the James Thurber manner, with wonderful pace and a gift for wry oblique humor. A great read."—Robert Coover

Novella, 160 pages, offset, smyth-sewn, original pbk. $14

Orders: www.spdbooks.org, www.burningdeck.com, www.audiatur.no/bokhandel

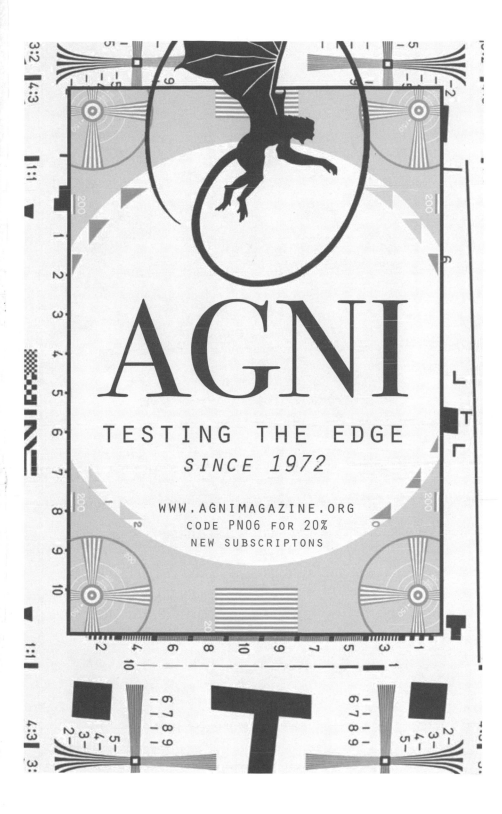

AGNI

TESTING THE EDGE

SINCE 1972

WWW.AGNIMAGAZINE.ORG

CODE PN06 FOR 20%

NEW SUBSCRIPTONS

READ
New Letters Magazine

LISTEN
New Letters on the Air

ENTER
The *New Letters* Literary Awards

ATTEND
The *New Letters* Weekend Writers Conference

JOIN
Our Family of Subscribers

LOOK
Visit www.newletters.org

New Letters

77
YEARS

University House
5101 Rockhill Road
University of Missouri-Kansas City
Kansas City, MO 64110
(816) 235-1168 www.newletters.org

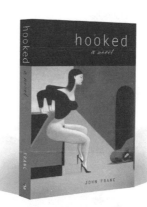

Index